Improving Threat Detection, Network Security, and Incident Response With AI

Abdalwali Lutfi
The University of Kalba, UAE

Mohammed Almaayah
The University of Jordan, Jordan

IGI Global
Scientific Publishing
Publishing Tomorrow's Research Today

Vice President of Editorial — Melissa Wagner
Director of Acquisitions — Mikaela Felty
Director of Book Development — Jocelynn Hessler
Production Manager — Mike Brehm
Cover Design — Jose Rosado

Published in the United States of America by
IGI Global Scientific Publishing
701 East Chocolate Avenue
Hershey, PA, 17033, USA
Tel: 717-533-8845
Fax: 717-533-7115
Website: https://www.igi-global.com E-mail: cust@igi-global.com

Library of Congress Cataloging-in-Publication Data

LCCN: 2025006735 (CIP Data Pending)
ISBN13: 9798337321158
Isbn13Softcover: 9798337321165
EISBN13: 9798337321172

British Cataloguing in Publication Data
A Cataloguing in Publication record for this book is available from the British Library.

Table of Contents

Detailed Table of Contents

Now a day we can see that the internet is booming because of that there is growing number of users for the internet usage. Basically, these users are creating a lot of traffic while connecting to any site or during any using their services. Intrusion Detection Systems (IDS) play an important role in defending computer networks from various cyber threats. The usefulness of Machine Learning (ML) and Deep Learning (DL) models in IDS has grown in importance in tackling network security challenges in recent years. The study examines the performance of traditional ML algorithms, alongside advanced DL models. Such insights are essential for enhancing network security in an ever-evolving threat landscape. The results of this study can guide security practitioners and system administrators in selecting the most suitable model for their specific network security needs. The chapter provides an overview of prior work on ML and DL in IDS. In addition, ML and DL models were examined, and results were presented, contrasted, and discussed using two dataset NSL-KDD Dataset, KDD99.

Wireless Sensor Networks (WSNs) have revolutionized the digital era by enabling seamless control of smart devices over the Internet, leading to the emergence of the Internet of Things (IoT). This paper presents an energy-efficient fuzzy-based routing protocol (EEFBR) that dynamically selects cluster heads based on network mid-position and residual energy, optimizing energy consumption and extending network lifetime. Unlike existing methodologies, EEFBR balances energy usage by integrating fuzzy logic for adaptive cluster head selection, significantly enhancing network performance. Comparative analysis with GPSR, EAMHR, and PDEBR protocols demonstrates that EEFBR increases network lifetime by 33.16%, improves residual energy by 18.99%, and achieves a 96.5% packet delivery ratio compared to 92.3% for existing protocols. Additionally, the proposed protocol reduces average end-to-end delay by 15%, ensuring efficient data transmission in WSN-assisted IoT applications.

The rise of sophisticated cyber threats necessitates advanced security mechanisms for real-time threat detection and incident response. This chapter explores the integration of Artificial Intelligence (AI) and Machine Learning (ML) in cybersecurity to enhance threat detection, anomaly identification, and automated incident response. It examines ML-based anomaly detection techniques, deep learning models for malware classification, and AI-driven intrusion detection systems. Additionally, it highlights the role of AI in automating Security Operations Centers (SOCs) and improving response efficiency. By leveraging AI-driven playbooks and predictive analytics, organizations can proactively mitigate cyber risks. The chapter also discusses challenges, ethical considerations, and future research directions in AI-powered cybersecurity solutions.

The chapter provides a detailed overview of behavioral analysis evolved in AI security systems, from rule-based methods to advanced AI-driven approaches with verified threat prediction accuracy. Finance, healthcare, and telecommunications sectors show empirical evidence of modern systems by processing huge data volumes

tightly coupled hardware and software. SDN allows the creation of virtual networks controlled by software, providing benefits like rapid topology creation, enhanced security and performance isolation for different traffic types. It offers networking and management opportunities with programmability and flexibility by operating on a centralized control plane, separating data and control planes. The centralized controller, directs information flow through the interfaces to network elements. Despite advantages, SDN faces security threats like DoS attacks and intrusions. One of SDN's most promising aspects is its potential to enhance network security through Intrusion Detection Systems (IDS). IDS integration within SDN enables effective threat detection to safeguard devices and data. The chapter briefly outlines IDS implementation in SDN and demonstrates SDN's capacity to revolutionize modern network management and security.

Anomaly detection identifies patterns that deviate from normal behavior, signaling threats in cybersecurity, finance, healthcare, and industry. Traditional threat detection struggles with data volume and complexity, making ML a key solution for modeling large datasets. This chapter outlines ML techniques for anomaly detection, focusing on threat analysis. It reviews supervised, unsupervised, semi-supervised learning, deep learning, and neural networks, highlighting pros, cons, and applications like fraud, intrusions, faults, and health anomalies. Key factors like data preprocessing, feature engineering, and model evaluation are discussed. Challenges include imbalanced data, real-time detection, and model interpretability. The chapter also explores combining methods for better accuracy, transfer learning, AI explainability, and real-time systems as future trends. This chapter explores a clear view of current ML use in anomaly detection and future directions.

Background: Robotic telesurgery increases the accuracy of a surgery and access from a distance, however these are vulnerable to cybersecurity attacks, for example

Preface

INTRODUCTION

Welcome to Improving Threat Detection, Network Security, and Incident Response with AI, a comprehensive compilation edited by Abdalwali Lutfi and Mohammed Almaiah. In this volume, our aim is to provide a systematic exploration of essential strengthens of Artificial intelligence (AI) in cybersecurity by enhancing threat detection, fortifying network security, and streamlining incident response.

Our primary objective is to serve as a catalyst for advancing knowledge in cybersecurity. We invite scientists, researchers, academics, developers, policymakers, and cybersecurity practitioners to delve into the wealth of insights presented within these pages.

Improving Threat Detection, Network Security, and Incident Response with AI explores the role of AI in cybersecurity, focusing on its applications in threat detection, malware analysis, network security, and incident response. It examines key AI techniques such as machine learning, deep learning, and natural language processing (NLP) that are transforming cybersecurity operations. This book covers topics such as robotics, software engineering, and behavioral analysis, and is a useful resource for computer engineers, security professionals, academicians, researchers, and data scientists.

We extend our gratitude to all the contributors who have shared their expertise and insights, helping to enrich the discourse surrounding cybersecurity. It is our sincere hope that this book will foster further collaboration and innovation in the ongoing quest to secure our digital landscape.

ORGANIZATION OF THE BOOK

In "**A Comparative Analysis of Network Intrusion Detection Systems in Machine Learning and Deep Learning for Securing IoT devices**" by *Ramya M, santhanakrishnan C, Janani M, poonkodi s*, the chapter examines the performance of traditional ML algorithms, alongside advanced DL models. Such insights are essential for enhancing network security in an ever-evolving threat landscape. The results of this study can guide security practitioners and system administrators in selecting the most suitable model for their specific network security needs. The chapter provides an overview of prior work on ML and DL in IDS. In addition, ML and DL models were examined, and results were presented, contrasted, and discussed using two dataset NSL-KDD Dataset, KDD99.

In "**AI Driven Energy Efficient Routing Protocols to Enhance Security and Performance in WSN Assisted IoT**" by *Regan Rajendran and Nithya Venkatachalam.* This paper presents an energy-efficient fuzzy-based routing protocol (EEFBR) that dynamically selects cluster heads based on network mid-position and residual energy, optimizing energy consumption and extending network lifetime. Unlike existing methodologies, EEFBR balances energy usage by integrating fuzzy logic for adaptive cluster head selection, significantly enhancing network performance. Comparative analysis with GPSR, EAMHR, and PDEBR protocols demonstrates that EEFBR increases network lifetime by 33.16%, improves residual energy by 18.99%, and achieves a 96.5% packet delivery ratio compared to 92.3% for existing protocols. Additionally, the proposed protocol reduces average end-to-end delay by 15%, ensuring efficient data transmission in WSN-assisted IoT applications.

In "**AI-Driven Threat Detection and Incident Response Advancing Cybersecurity with Machine Learning**" by *Tarun Kumar Vashishth, Vikas Sharma, Mukesh Kumar Sharma, Rajeev Sharma, Kewal Krishan Sharma and Sangeeta Sharma.* This chapter explores the integration of Artificial Intelligence (AI) and Machine Learning (ML) in cybersecurity to enhance threat detection, anomaly identification, and automated incident response. It examines ML-based anomaly detection techniques, deep learning models for malware classification, and AI-driven intrusion detection systems. Additionally, it highlights the role of AI in automating Security Operations Centers (SOCs) and improving response efficiency. By leveraging AI-driven playbooks and predictive analytics, organizations can proactively mitigate cyber risks. The chapter also discusses challenges, ethical considerations, and future research directions in AI-powered cybersecurity solutions.

In "**Behavioral Analysis of Malicious Activities in AI Comprehensive Analysis**" by *A R DEEPTI, B MANIMEKALA, FARZEEN BASITH, and VIBINCHANDAR SELVARAJ*. The chapter provides a detailed overview of behavioral analysis evolved in AI security systems, from rule-based methods to advanced AI-driven approaches with verified threat prediction accuracy. Finance, healthcare, and telecommunications sectors show empirical evidence of modern systems by processing huge data volumes with exceptional threat detection capabilities. Research from Microsoft, IBM, and Google confirms AI-enabled security significantly reduces the time of threat identification compared to traditional approaches. The technical analysis reveals cloud-native solutions offer greater cost-efficiency and performance than on-premise alternatives, with measurable ROI improvements. The study examines behavioral analysis integration with machine learning, advanced persistent threat detection challenges, implementation strategies across different organizational contexts, and ethical considerations essential for developing effective security systems.

In "**Dual Stage Deep Learning and Adaptive Morphological Refinement for Infrared Small Target Detection in Aerial Surveillance**" by *Sasikaladevi N, Aswin Anand A V, Pooja G*. This chapter proposes a dual-stage methodology combining DN-CNN (Denoising Convolutional Neural Network) and adaptive morphological thickening, which enhances the square, elliptical morphological operator to leverage the detection process. The proposed framework is trained and tested on an IR (Infrared) small target dataset containing helicopters, drones and airplanes which results in superior accuracy, clarity and reliability in small target detection as compared with traditional methods. DN-CNN initially suppresses the background noise while preserving the target structure. Experimental analysis shows significant improvement in the Detection Accuracy with PSNR value of 41.27 and EPI value of 0.6. This dual-stage approach lays the foundation for an adaptive, real-time target detection system.

In "**Enhancing Security with Weapon Detection in CCTV Using Image Processing Technique**" by *Sasikaladevi N, Nivisha V, Pradeepa S*. This chapter introduces an innovator weapon detection system that combines image processing algorithms with deep learning-based object detection via YOLOv8 to improve accuracy, efficiency, and real-time responsiveness. The proposed system has three stages such as data preprocessing, object detection based on YOLOv8, and real-time alert mechanism. Histogram equalization is used for image processing technique for enhancement of images and facilitating feature extraction. A weapon and non-weapon image dataset are utilized, and techniques of data augmentation are employed to enhance the model's generalization ability. An alarm system is put in place to report live alarms and notifications upon detection of weapon in live CCTV feeds. The model achieved the performance metrics with a precision of 88.7% and mAP50 of 88.1%, indicates high reliability and detection accuracy. Live detection of weapons with average of 73% confidence, under real-world conditions.

In "**Innovative Cyber Threat Detection Technique Using Machine Learning on TCP and UDP Traffic**" by *Vandna Mehndiratta and Anuj Kumar Gupta*. Cyber threat detection techniques on TCP and UDP traffic focus on identifying malicious activities by analyzing network behavior and packet patterns. Common methods include signature-based detection, which matches traffic against known attack signatures, and anomaly-based detection, which uses statistical or machine learning models to identify deviations from normal behavior. The proposed solution utilizes a machine learning detection framework that inspects the TCP and UDP traffic of the CIC-IDS2018 dataset for identifying malicious conduct. The model reached over 96% accuracy in detection by selecting essential features that included inter-arrival time, flag patterns, and flow duration. The system delivered detection instances within 20ms on average, proving its real-time operational deployment capability.

In "**Intrusion Detection System in a Software Defined Network**" by *Mohamed Uvaze Ahamed Ayoobkhan, Subair Ali Liayakath Ali Khan, Aneesh Pradeep, M Manikandakumar, and P Karthikeyan.* It offers networking and management opportunities with programmability and flexibility by operating on a centralized control plane, separating data and control planes. The centralized controller, directs information flow through the interfaces to network elements. Despite advantages, SDN faces security threats like DoS attacks and intrusions. One of SDN's most promising aspects is its potential to enhance network security through Intrusion Detection Systems (IDS). IDS integration within SDN enables effective threat detection to safeguard devices and data. The chapter briefly outlines IDS implementation in SDN and demonstrates SDN's capacity to revolutionize modern network management and security.

In " **Machine Learning for Threat Detection: A Comprehensive Survey on Anomaly Detection Techniques**" by *Anto Gracious L. A. and Siva Subramanian R.* This paper outlines ML techniques for anomaly detection, focusing on threat analysis. It reviews supervised, unsupervised, semi-supervised learning, deep learning, and neural networks, highlighting pros, cons, and applications like fraud, intrusions, faults, and health anomalies. Key factors like data preprocessing, feature engineering, and model evaluation are discussed. Challenges include imbalanced data, real-time detection, and model interpretability. The paper also explores combining methods for better accuracy, transfer learning, AI explainability, and real-time systems as future trends. This survey offers a clear view of current ML use in anomaly detection and future directions.

In "**Mitigating Security Risks in Robotic Telesurgery with SecureSurgiNET Protocols for Replay, Brute Force, and Session Hijacking Attacks**" by *Vamshi Krishna Samudrala, Winner Pulakhandam, and Visrutatma Rao Vallu.* The SecureSurgiNET promises data confidentiality and integrity with no unauthorized access to it hence securing robotic telesurgery from all possible cyber threats. Methods: The framework herein advocates for use of advance cryptographic protocols, multi-factor authentication, nonce-based authentication, AI-driven anomaly detection, and rate limiting to curb all cyberattacks. Results: Simulations that were carried out show 92% fewer replay attacks, 89% fewer risks of brute force, and 94% fewer session hijacking cases that enhance real-time telesurgery security. Conclusion: SecureSurgiNET is secure, scalable, and resilient telesurgery that accommodates future integrations on AI and blockchain security for building trust with the patient and has operational reliability.

In "**Real-Time Intrusion Detection in IoT Networks: A Novel Approach Combining Modified Salp Swarm Feature Selection and GLIRU Model**" by *VENKATASUBRAMANIAN S*. This chapter introduces a new approach to intrusion detection for IoT devices that utilizes Deep Learning (DL). The article begins by introducing the modified salp-swarm optimizer, which is used as a model for feature selection. A high convergence accuracy and improved global optimization capabilities are the distinguishing features of the suggested approach. Lastly, the Gated Lightweight Intelligent Recurrent Units (GLIRU) model is used to categorize the attacks. . In order to enhance the classification accuracy, the work employs the Adaptive Elite-Ant Lion Optimizer (AALO) to adjust the settings of the GRU.

In "**Scenario-aware Anomaly Detection in Insider Activities using CT-GAN Data Augmentation**" by *KAMATCHI K and Uma E*. Insider threats are cyberattacks perpetrated by individuals with legitimate organizational access. Detecting insider attacks is challenging due to their subtle nature and potential for causing significant harm. One popular technique for spotting dangerous insiders is anomaly detection. However, internal analysis of danger remains a largely untapped study area due to the lack of actual events data and the unequal distribution of classes in datasets. In order to enhance underutilized minority class instances and enrich the data with diverse and significant examples drawn from pragmatically malicious events, we develop a Conditional Tabular Generative Adversarial Network (CT-GAN) in this research. Comprehensive experiments utilizing the CMUCERT Version 4.2 dataset showcase the impact of CT-GAN-augmented data in enhancing the detection of anomalies within insider activity analysis. Additionally, the approach is assessed against several existing methods using various criteria and performance metrics.

CONCLUSION

In the ever-evolving landscape of AI in cybersecurity and threat detection, our edited reference book, "Improving Threat Detection, Network Security, and Incident Response with AI," seeks to provide a comprehensive resource for practitioners, researchers, and academics alike. Throughout the chapters, our esteemed contributors have delved into various facets of machine learning for threat detection, anomaly detection, intrusion detection system in a software defined network, mitigating security risks in robotic and cyber threat detection technique using machine learning.

From a comparative analysis of network intrusion detection systems to scenario-aware anomaly detection in insider activities using CT-GAN data augmentation, each chapter offers valuable insights and practical solutions to address the complex challenges facing cybersecurity professionals today. By leveraging advanced technologies such as machine learning and IDS systems, our contributors have demonstrated the potential for innovation in network and IT infrastructure.

Moreover, our book underscores the interdisciplinary nature of cybersecurity, bringing together expertise from fields such as machine learning, IDS systems, and network security. By fostering collaboration and knowledge exchange among diverse stakeholders, we aim to advance the collective understanding and capabilities in cybersecurity research and practice.

As we conclude this preface, we extend our sincere appreciation to all the authors who have contributed their expertise and insights to this volume. It is our hope that "Improving Threat Detection, Network Security, and Incident Response with AI" will serve as a valuable resource for years to come, inspiring further exploration and innovation in the ongoing mission to secure our network technologies.

Abdalwali Lutfi
The University of Kalba, UAE

Mohammed Almaayah
The University of Jordan, Jordan

Chapter 1
A Comparative Analysis of Network Intrusion Detection Systems in Machine Learning and Deep Learning for Securing IoT devices

M. Ramya
https://orcid.org/0000-0002-1509-8966
SRM Institute of Science and Technology, India

C. Santhanakrishnan
https://orcid.org/0000-0002-8999-9425
SRM Institute of Science and Technology, India

M. Janani
https://orcid.org/0000-0002-9641-2135
SRM Institute of Science and Technology, India

S. Poonkodi
SRM Institute of Science and Technology, India

ABSTRACT

Now a day we can see that the internet is booming because of that there is growing number of users for the internet usage. Basically, these users are creating a lot of traffic while connecting to any site or during any using their services. Intrusion

DOI: 10.4018/979-8-3373-2115-8.ch001

Detection Systems (IDS) play an important role in defending computer networks from various cyber threats. The usefulness of Machine Learning (ML) and Deep Learning (DL) models in IDS has grown in importance in tackling network security challenges in recent years. The study examines the performance of traditional ML algorithms, alongside advanced DL models. Such insights are essential for enhancing network security in an ever-evolving threat landscape. The results of this study can guide security practitioners and system administrators in selecting the most suitable model for their specific network security needs. The chapter provides an overview of prior work on ML and DL in IDS. In addition, ML and DL models were examined, and results were presented, contrasted, and discussed using two dataset NSL-KDD Dataset, KDD99.

INTRODUCTION

There are over 29 billion Internet-connected gadgets in use worldwide. Security is a serious worry when there are so many devices. We have a number of techniques to identify and flag these security vulnerabilities in order to react with suspicious actions. One such method is Intrusion Detection System (IDS) and the taxonomy is as shown in Figure 1. IDS are software that scans a device connected to the network or a whole web for deviant behaviour or activities which shouldn't be there. Any suspicious activity or infringement is quickly recorded by the security management system or the central firewall (Abdullah B, 2022). A SIEM system uses outputs from diverse range of sources and makes the use of alarm to filter the malicious activities. Suspicious activity can be handled in a different way by an intrusion detection system. In anomaly-based intrusion detection systems, machine learning can be utilized to construct trustworthy action displays that authenticate everything submitted and identify something suspicious if it is not included in the presentation.

When compared to other technology IDS machine learning based strategies have a prevalent bland property since these models are prepared utilizing diverse application and equipment arrangement. The verification for the Preserve system has proven to be a particularly difficult task because there is a time restriction of the operator which link to the smart devices. Thus, it is critical to validate an operator's authenticity for a predetermined amount of time (Abubakar AI, Chiroma H, 2019).

The anomaly-based detection strategy overcomes the disadvantage traditional strategies particularly within the recognizable proof of dangers, by identifying dangers employing a wide Show instead of particular marks and highlight (Aghdam MH, Kabiri P, 2024). Our goal in is to provide Internet users with a secure environment. In this scenario, rogue technology may launch discriminatory attacks based on betrayed confidence. In an IoT setting, it's critical to assess the dependability of service providers in order to maximize system security. Systems can be negotiated by a malicious donor source by providing harsh luxuries and information (Akilandeswari V, Shalinie, 2024). The detection system is a tool used in cybersecurity to monitor the network and protect system activities from evidence of unauthorized access, hostile activity, or policy violations. They can be classified according on their qualities and deployment. Here is an IDS taxonomy based on various criteria:

Figure 1. Taxonomy for IDS

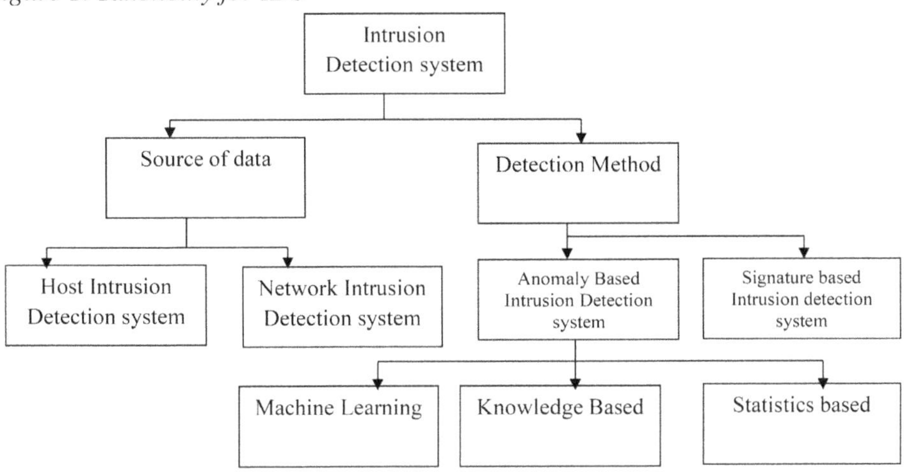

Signature-based IDS: These systems match observable events or patterns to a database of attack signatures. The system tells the user when a match is detected (Al-Dhafian B, Ahmad I, 2022).

***Anomaly-based IDS*:** These systems establish a baseline of normal behavior and raise alerts when deviations from this baseline are detected (Al-Yaseen WL, Othman ZA,2017). They are effective at detecting novel attacks but can also trigger false positives.

***Hybrid IDS*:** These systems combine both signature and anomaly-based techniques to improve detection accuracy.

Network-based IDS (NIDS): These systems monitor network traffic and analyse packets in order to detect potentially dangerous activities. They are usually deployed at strategic spots throughout a network (Ali MH, Al Mohammed BAD, Ismail A, 2018).

Host-based IDS (HIDS): These systems are installed on individual hosts (servers or endpoints) and monitor activities on those specific hosts, such as file system changes, log analysis, and system calls.

Distributed IDS (DIDS): These systems are a collection of interconnected IDS sensors that work together to monitor a network, sharing information and correlating data to improve accuracy.

***Rule-based IDS*:** To detect known threats, it employs predetermined criteria or signatures (Aljumah A, 2024).

Machine Learning-based IDS: Employs various machine learning techniques to identify anomalies and new attack patterns. Examples include clustering, neural networks, and decision trees.

LITERATURE REVIEW

Computer network availability, integrity, and confidentiality difficulties arise due to the quick expansion of its use. In order to monitor network traffic for malicious and unauthorized activity, network administrators must use a variety of detection systems (IDS) (Santhanakrishnan, 2022). (K. Buczak and E. Guven,2023) provides a comprehensive survey of ML techniques, such as decision trees, support vector machines (SVM), and k-nearest neighbors (k-NN), for intrusion detection. Highlights the trade-offs between accuracy and computational efficiency for resource-constrained IoT environments.

(P. Sudhakaran,2022) Proposed a lightweight ML model using Random Forest and SVM to detect intrusions in IoT networks. Demonstrated high detection accuracy but faced limitations in handling large-scale, real-time data streams. The suggested study gives a brief overview of the many initiatives being made to create efficient IDS utilizing a single, hybrid, and ensemble machine learning (ML) classifier each of which has been tested using a different dataset. The discussion and comparison of the findings from diverse publications have shown a clear direction and path for future research (Bhupathi Ingre,2015).

Shafi et al. (2019) Proposed the Network Intrusion Detection Using Supervised Machine Learning Techniques in IoT, Evaluated supervised learning models like Naive Bayes and Decision Trees for IoT-specific datasets. Scalability and feature extraction for diverse IoT protocols. (Rayda A. Sadeki, M. 2020) Suggested the time taken to actually process the result using the algorithms is much more; the LTSM network utilizes different researches for creating the classified tool for processing. It sorts the data set for simple processing by the system using techniques like Cuuda Deep Neural Network Long Short-Term Memory and Long Short-Term Memory (LSTM) on the kitsune dataset (Carole J Fungl,2024). It seeks to provide a quick system to find the intrusion. Concerning security, the scenario for protecting all smart technologies is frightening.

Panchal et al. (2020) proposed the Hybrid Anomaly Detection for IoT Networks Using LSTM and Clustering Algorithms which Combined LSTM networks for temporal pattern recognition with clustering methods for anomaly identification. Addressed the challenge of detecting time-series anomalies in IoT traffic. In order to identify attacks, this project implements LSTM networks to develop a better intuition for the algorithm in this paper. Results demonstrate that their method actually performs better than other deep learning method. LSTMs that show an improvement from the previous models based on accuracy.

oy et al. (2021) developed the IoT Intrusion Detection System Using Convolutional Neural Networks Utilized CNNs for packet-level feature extraction and classification in IoT networks. CNNs excelled in identifying spatial patterns but required high computational resources. The sophisticated framework for identifying the intrusion based on the concept of bagging was recently developed. To train the model, these researchers used an Ensemble-based algorithm similar to Bagging. Bagging combined the results of all classify conditions to predict the best output. It provides 10% greater accuracy than single classifier algorithms. (Wahio SK, Pachelgare VK, Kolhe SR,2024) researcher's goal was to use a multilayer machine learning model to differentiate the different types of attacks. To choose features, a proposed stacking machine learning model employs random forest classifier rating and forward selection. Then, it is contrasted with a number of conventional classification methods as well as some older models based on the NSL-KDD dataset. Several articles have assessed the NSL-KDD dataset is used by a variety of classification techniques, like Multiclass and Binary class and the dataset is separate into normal data and attacked data, and IDS is trained and discern whether a packet is normal or an attack using binary classification (M. S. Abdel-Wahab, 2024), But the accuracy is very less when compare to other method.

Javaid et al. (2016) Proposed the Deep Learning Approach for Network Intrusion Detection System in that the deep neural network (DNN) model and compared it with traditional ML models on the NSL-KDD dataset. DNN outperformed traditional ML in terms of accuracy and false-positive rate. Based on the above survey Anomaly detection methods vary widely in complexity, computational requirements, and suitability for different applications. When considering IoT environments, the choice of method depends on specific constraints such as limited computational resources, energy efficiency, scalability, and the nature of IoT data (e.g., time-series data from sensors, spatial data, etc).

Based on the above survey Anomaly detection methods vary widely in complexity, computational requirements, and suitability for different applications. When considering IoT environments, the choice of method depends on specific constraints such as limited computational resources, energy efficiency, scalability, and the nature of IoT data (e.g., time-series data from sensors, spatial data, etc).

TECHNIQUES AND APPROACHES INTRUSION DETECTION SYSTEMS USING ML AND DL

Machine Learning Based Methods

The general Pipeline Structure based on Machine learning is given in Figure 2, in which KDD99 and NSL-KDD these are benchmark datasets commonly used for network intrusion detection. Before training or testing machine learning models, the raw data from KDD99 and NSL-KDD is normalized. Normalization ensures that all features (e.g., packet sizes, protocol types) have consistent scales, which helps improve the performance of machine learning algorithms. Several machine learning models are used to classify traffic as normal traffic or intrusion traffic. The models are first trained on a subset of the dataset to learn patterns of normal and intrusion traffic. The remaining data is used for testing to evaluate the accuracy and performance of the models. The trained models classify incoming network traffic on the host machine as either, Normal Traffic: Legitimate network activity. Intrusion Traffic: Malicious or abnormal activity.

Figure 2. General pipeline structure for machine learning

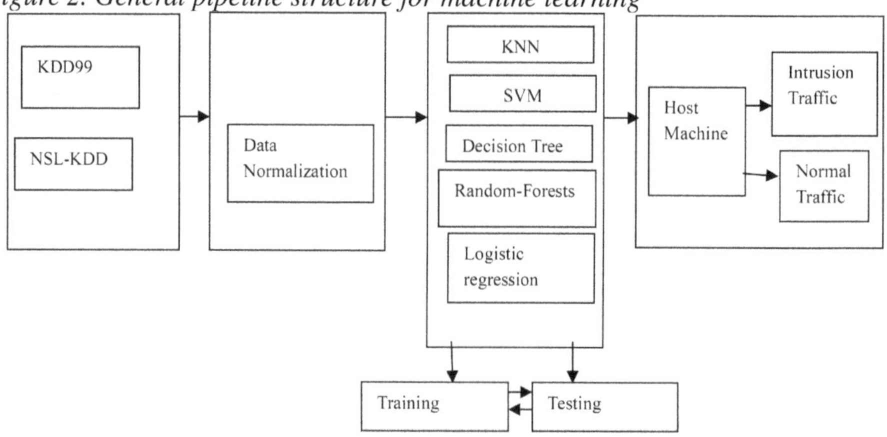

Support Vector Machines (SVM): SVM is a strong (supervised machine learning) method used for classification and regression tasks. It operates by determining the ideal hyperplane for separating data into multiple classifications. SVM attempts to solve an optimization problem, often a convex quadratic programming problem, in order to discover the best choices of w and b that maximize the margin. The objective function for a linear SVM can be expressed as equation 1.

$$Maximize\ M = \frac{1}{||w||}$$

, (1)

where y i (w·x i +b)≥1 for i=1,2,…,n

Random Forests: An ensemble of decision trees that can be used to discover anomalies based on their frequency of being labeled as outliers and the random forest classifier. The primary principle underlying Isolation Forest is that anomalies or outliers may be easily distinguished from typical datasets. Normal data points require more splits to be segregated from the rest of the data, whereas anomalies require fewer divides. During the process of building the forest of trees, the algorithm keeps track of the average path length for each data point to reach an isolation (leaf) node . A data point that requires fewer splits to reach a leaf node is considered more likely to be an anomaly. To classify a data point as an anomaly or not, a decision threshold is set. Data points with average path lengths above a certain threshold are considered anomalies.

Logistic regression: Logistic regression is a statistical machine learning model that is used for binary classification and, in certain cases, multi-class classification tasks. It is a linear regression extension that is especially well-suited for issues when the dependent variable (the outcome to be predicted) is categorical and has one of two values (often 0 and 1) (Z. Muda, W. Yassin, M. N. Sulaiman,2024). Logistic regression calculates the likelihood that a given input belongs to one of two groups. It accomplishes this by employing the logistic function (sigmoid function), which translates the output to the range (0, 1). The logistic function equation (2):

$$P(X = 1) = \frac{1}{1 + e^{-(a0 \ + a1\ X1\ + a2\ X2\ + \dots + an\ Xn)}} \tag{2}$$

Here P(X=1) is the probability of the event happening, and X 1, X 2 , ...,X n are the input features with corresponding coefficients a1, a2, ...,an.

K-Nearest Neighbors (KNN): The KNN algorithm is a supervised learning technique. When predicting a new data point, it considers the K closest neighbors from the training dataset and assigns the class (for classification) or value (for regression) based on a majority vote or weighted average (W. Lee and S. J. Stolfo, 2021). KNN uses a distance metric, such as Euclidean distance, Manhattan distance, or other similarity measures, to determine the nearest neighbours. In a k-dimensional space, the formula for Euclidean distance between two points, P and Q, is given in equ 3,

$$Euclidean\ Distance = \sqrt{\sum_{i=1}^{k}(pi - qi)2} \tag{3}$$

The distance metric used can have a considerable impact on the algorithm's performance. An important hyperparameter is the value of K, which represents the number of neighbours to consider. A smaller K (for example, 1 or 3) results in more local decisions, but a bigger K may result in a smoother decision border. The optimal K value is determined by the task and dataset.

Decision Tree: One popular machine learning method for applications involving regression and classification is the decision tree. It is a graphical model that depicts a set of guidelines for making decisions depending on the properties of the data (input variables) (B. Ingre and A. Yadav, 2023). A decision tree consists of branches that show the test's outcomes and nodes that each reflect a decision or test on a feature. With the leaf nodes at the base and the root node at the top, the tree structure resembles an upside-down tree. The comparative analysis of the performance, scalability, and resource requirements for machine learning is given in Table1.

Table 1. Comparative analysis of the performance, scalability, and resource requirements for machine learning

Criteria	SVM	Random Forest	Logistic Regression	KNN
Performance	High	High	Moderate	High
Scalability	Low	High	High	Low
Training Time	High	Moderate	Low	Low
Prediction Time	Fast	Fast	Very Fast	Slow
Memory Usage	High	Moderate	Very Low	High
Real-Time Use	Limited	Moderate	High	Limited
IoT Suitability	Moderate	High	High	Low

Deep Learning Methods

Autoencoders: Figure 3 depicts an autoencoders model in which neural networks prior to decoding input data back into its original format, learn how to encode it into a lower-dimensional representation (W. Hu, 2023). Anomalies cause larger reconstruction mistakes since the model fails to reproduce them accurately and the reconstructed input is produced.

Figure 3. Autoencoder model

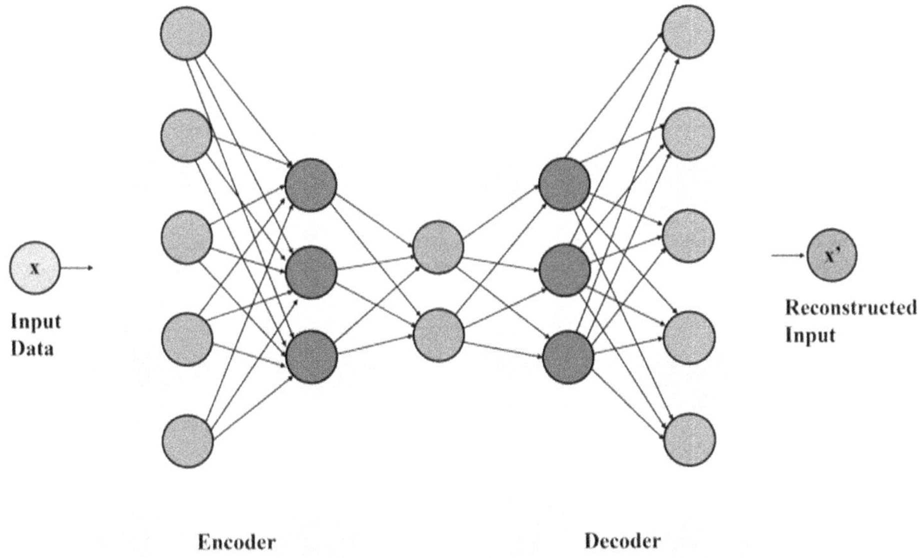

LSTM and GRU Networks: Long Short-Term Memory (LSTM) and Gated Recurrent Unit (GRU) networks are used for continuous data. Anomalies can be detected based on the prediction error between the actual sequence and the predicted sequence (Sharma, A, 2024).

Capsule Networks: Capsule networks aim to capture spatial hierarchies in data. They can be used for anomaly detection by comparing the activation of capsules with a threshold.

Deep Autoencoding Gaussian Mixture Model (DAGMM): To simulate the distribution of normal data, DAGMM combines an autoencoder and a Gaussian Mixture simulate. The likelihood of anomalies under this distribution is used to identify them.

CNN: A deep learning-based unsupervised anomaly detection method for streaming data is called Deep-AnT. There are two parts to this method and the task of predicting the subsequent timestamp falls to the time-series predictor module. The expected value is received by the anomaly detection module. This module determines whether data instances are healthy or unhealthy. The prediction module is powered by a Convolutional neural network (CNN). Without eliminating anomalies from the training data, Deep-AnT trains CNN on raw data. They employed a max-pooling layer after each of two Convolutional layers. The comparative analysis of the performance, scalability, and resource requirements for Deep learning is given in Table2.

Table 2. Comparative analysis of the performance, scalability, and resource requirements for deep learning

Criteria	CNN	LSTM	Capsule Network	DAGMM
Performance	High	Very High	Very High	High
Scalability	High	High	Moderate	Moderate
Training Time	High	Very High	Very High	Moderate
Prediction Time	Moderate	Moderate	High	Fast
Memory Usage	High	High	Very High	Low
Real-Time Use	Moderate	Moderate	Limited	Suitable

DATASET

There are several datasets used for detecting the intrusion detection in machine learning and Deep Learning. These datasets are designed to help researchers and practitioners develop and evaluate intrusion detection algorithms. There are several benchmark datasets are used for evaluating IDS. The KDD Cup99, and NSL-KDD (G. Meena and R. R. Choudhary,2020) are the most commonly used for IDS estimation.

KDD99cup Dataset

1. The most used algorithm for testing and training data sets is KDD-99 Cup. A portion of the DARPA-98 dataset is represented by it. A wide variety of data are included in the KDD-99 dataset. There are 4.8 million examples in the collection. The attributes in the dataset are integer and category properties. It has forty-two properties (Divekar, M. Parekh, V. Savla,2022). The KDD-99 cup dataset contains the following items:
2. The KDD99 Cup data mining competition employed the widely recognized KDD Cup 1999 dataset in machine learning and data mining. The "KDD 99" or "KDD Cup 99" dataset is another name for it. The dataset was made available by the Knowledge Discovery and Data Mining (KDD) conference as a competition to support intrusion detection research.

3. The five categories of KDD-99 patterns are Normal, DoS (Denial of Service), U2R (User to Root), R2L (Remote to Local), and Probe (Probing Attack). Each incursion group is further subdivided by the attack mechanism. Table 3 is a list of the attacks.

Table 3. Data distribution of KDD99 dataset

	Training Data	Percentage	Testing Data	Percentage
Normal	945617	75.083%	603393	21.58%
DOS	307327	22.99%	236754	74.01%
Probe	12341	1.46%	4166	1.33%
U2R	78	0.089%	145	0.081%
R2L	888	0.0067%	17891	5.306%
Total	1,266,251	100%	862349	100%

4. KDD training dataset comprises 4,983,241 data points, as specified. Due to considerable duplication (74%), only 1,266,251 unique data points exist. The test dataset has also been decreased from 2,498,451 to 862349 patterns, which is substantially redundant (85.6%). These reduced datasets are taken into account.
5. Each pattern comprises 41 elements that are classified as Basic, Traffic, or Content. The examination of the Mean Decrease Impurity metric revealed that 20 was insignificant.

The KDD Cup 99 dataset contains various types of network attacks, and these attacks are categorized into different classes. Below is a tabulated list in Table4 of some of the attack types present in the dataset and their corresponding categories:

Table 4. Attack type in KDD99 dataset

Class	Type of Attack
DOS	back, icmpstorm, Smurf,, pod, teardrop, land, neptune
Probe	Satan, Ipssweep,Portsweep, Nmap
U2R	Buffer, Rootkit, Loadmodule, Perl
R2L	Warezclient, Guess_passwd, Warezmaster, Imap ftp_write,Multihop, Phf, Spy

NSL-KDD Dataset

NSL-KDD, which only includes chosen records from the entire KDD dataset and is error-free, was developed by academics in order to address the shortcomings of the KDD-99 cup dataset. The goal of NSL-KDD is to solve and get past KDD-99's shortcomings (H. Sung and S. Mukkamala,2023). It does, however, draw attention to the fact that there are still issues with the dataset, such as the absence of coverage for low-footprint attacks (Table 5).

Using the NSL-KDD dataset has the following advantages:

1. Better reduction rates are achieved since the test set is devoid of duplicate records.
2. There exists an inverse relationship between the proportion of records in the original KDD dataset and the number of records selected from each challenge level group.
3. Compared to KDD-99, NSL-KDD has fewer data points, but each one is unique. It is therefore less computationally expensive to train machine learning models using it.

Table 5. NSL-KDD dataset- data distribution

	Training Data	Percentage	Testing Data	Percentage
Normal	68432	53.548%	9810	43.150%
DOS	46934	9.532%	8743	33.180%
Probe	11765	9.324%	2341	10.213%
U2R	55	0.045%	199	0.875%
R2L	990	0.045%	2564	12.35%
Total	1,26,975	100%	23,453	100%

RESULT AND DISCUSSION

Let us consider the dataset of KDD99 and NSL-KDD for conducting an experiment in Network Intrusion Detection. The correlation plot for dataset is given in Fig 4, this plot is used to summarize of large dataset, identifies the pattern, and makes the decision accordingly. The KDD99 and NSL-KDD dataset has different features, easily identified using the correlation plot. Based on the features, the dataset is evaluated.

To process the data using KDD'99 and NSL-KDD datasets, we use Python 3.9.2 and the modules Pandas and Numpy. Tensor flow2.0 was used to implement the final deep learning models.

Figure 4. Correlation plot for dataset KDD99 and NSL-KDD

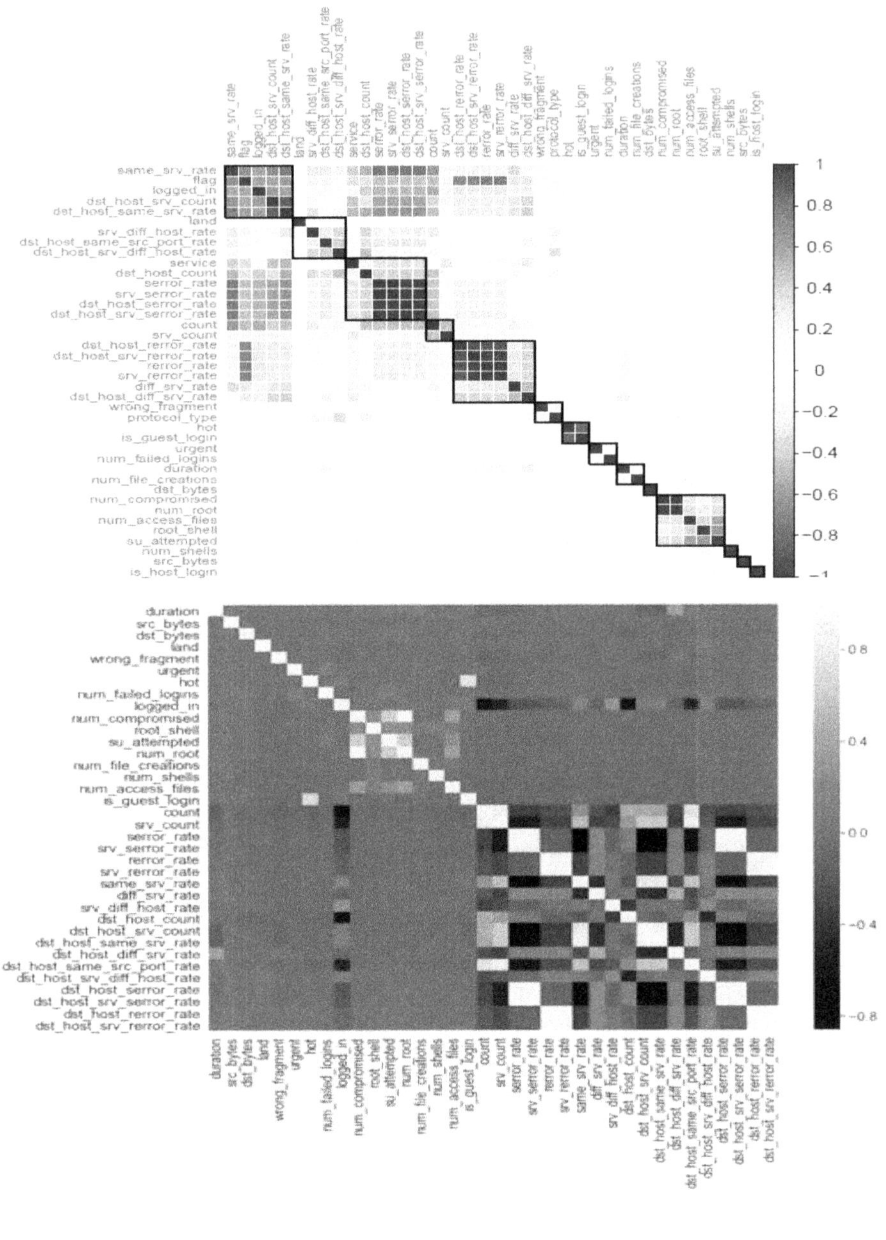

Performance Metrics

Performance metrics are essential for evaluating the effectiveness of Intrusion Detection Systems (IDS) in identifying and mitigating network attacks. These metrics help assess the system accuracy, efficiency, and ability to distinguish between normal and malicious network behavior. Here are some standard performance metrics for IDS.

Accuracy (ACC): The percentage of correctly classified instances to all instances (TP + TN). total classification accuracy is measured.

(TP + TN) / (TP + TN + FP + FN) (4)

Precision: The percentage of positives to all instances labelled as positive (malicious). Precision is crucial for reducing false alarms since it focuses on the accuracy of positive forecasts.

TP / (TP + FP) (5)

Recall: The proportion of true positives to the total number of actual positives (malicious instances). Recall assesses the ability of the IDS to detect actual attacks and minimize false negatives.

TP / (TP + FN) (6)

F1-Score (F1): The harmonic means of precision and recall. Provides a balanced measure of precision and recall, useful when dealing with imbalanced datasets.

2 * (Precision * Recall) / (Precision + Recall)(7)

The accuracy metrics, precision, F1-score, False alarm rate and recall for dataset KDD99 are summarized in this section. When discussing the results of models trained on an unbalanced dataset, metrics may be misleading. Therefore, to validate the model and make sure it correctly predicts all classes, recall, accuracy, and F1-score are used. Table 7 results for the other models show that, despite the unbalanced dataset's higher false alarm rate, the KNN99 outperforms the other models in terms of accuracy. Recall and precision both have high values.

Table 6. Result of tested model using KDD99 Dataset in Machine Learning

KDD Dataset					
Algorithms	**Accuracy**	**Precision**	**False Alarm Rate**	**Recall**	**F1-score**
SVM	84.59%	1.00	15.60	0.99	0.99
KNN	93.47%	1.00	4.82	0.98	0.98
Decision tree	80.05%	0.53	1.85	0.99	0.58
Random Forest	98.0%	1.00	2.33	0.97	0.98
Logistic Regression	77.7%	0.96	2.9	0.92	0.92

The NSL-KDD dataset precision, F1-score, and recall metrics. When discussing the results of models trained on an unbalanced dataset, metrics may be misleading. Therefore, to validate the model and make sure it correctly predicts all classes, recall, accuracy, and F1-score are used. Table 8 results for the other models show that the Random forests model performs better than the others in terms of accuracy and false alarm rate.

Table 7. Result of tested model using NSL-KDD dataset in machine learning

NSL- KDD Dataset					
Algorithms	**Accuracy**	**Precision**	**False Alaram Rate**	**Recall**	**F1-score**
SVM	97.4%	1.00	4.8	0.98	0.98
KNN	89.3%	1.00	2.1	0.99	0.99
Decision tree	89.5%	0.67	1.85	0.99	0.65
Random Forest	99.7%	1.00	3.2	0.97	0.99
Logistic Regression	97.4%	0.96	4.7	0.93	0.98

Table 9 compares the performance of four algorithms—CNN, RNN+LSTM, Capsule Network, and DAGMM—on the KDD99 dataset using metrics such as accuracy, precision, false alarm rate (FAR), recall, and F1-score. CNN achieved the highest accuracy RNN+LSTM delivered a strong Performance, indicating issues in handling diverse attack patterns. DAGMM performed adequately but did not surpass the other models, highlighting its limitations on supervised classification tasks.

Table 8. Result of tested model using KDD99 dataset in deep learning

KDD Dataset					
Algorithms	**Accuracy**	**Precision**	**False Alarm Rate**	**Recall**	**F1-score**
CNN	94.5%	90%	0.05	95%	75%
RNN+LSTM	93%	88.5%	0.06	86%	78%
Capsule Network	91.5%	85.3%	0.08	73%	78%
DAGMM	90.0%	82%	0.09	73%	78%

Table 9. Result of tested model using NSL KDD dataset in deep learning

NSL-KDD Dataset					
Algorithms	**Accuracy**	**Precision**	**False Alarm Rate**	**Recall**	**F1-score**
CNN	99%	96%	0.02	98%	69%
RNN+LSTM	96%	95%	0.03	96%	70%
Capsule Network	93.2%	88%	0.05	89%	75%
DAGMM	90.1%	86%	0.08	86%	75%

The choice of IDS method depends on the IoT system's scale, data characteristics, and resource constraints: Machine learning methods like Random Forest and Logistic Regression are preferred for simple tasks or resource-constrained devices. Deep learning methods like CNN, LSTM, and DeepAnT are better for handling complex patterns, time-series data, or large-scale IoT deployments, especially when sufficient computational resources are available. For a balanced IoT IDS system: Use Random Forest or Autoencoders for scalable, general-purpose detection. Leverage DeepAnT or LSTM for real-time detection in time-series IoT data streams.

CONCLUSION

This book chapter compares and analyses the ML and DL models used in anomaly-based network intrusion detection systems. The report began with an overview of previous research effort in the field of ML and DL IDS, followed by a summary of previous research activities. The datasets utilized in the review of literature were presented. KDD-99 and NSL-KDD were also used to validate ML and DL models. The dataset and performance results were shown and contrasted. The decision between ML and DL models is influenced by the unique problem, available data, computational resources, and necessary level of interpretability. Experimenting with both ML and DL models to see which one best suit the problem at hand is a common pragmatic technique. Furthermore, hybrid techniques that incorporate the qualities of both paradigms are being developed.

REFERENCES

Abdel-Wahab, M. S., Neil, A. M., & Atia, A. (2024). A comparative study of machine learning and deep learning in network anomaly-based intrusion detection systems. In *15th International Conference on Computer Engineering and Systems (ICCES)* (pp. 1–6). DOI: 10.1109/ICCES51560.2020.9334553

Abdullah, B., Abd-Alghafar, I., & Salama, G. I., & Abd-Alhafez. (2020). A performance evaluation of a genetic algorithm-based approach to network intrusion detection system. *International Conference on Aerospace Sciences and Aviation Technology, The Military Technical College*, 1–17.

Abubakar, A. I., Chiroma, H., Muaz, S. A., & Ila, L. B. (2019). A review of the advances in cyber security benchmark datasets for evaluating data-driven based intrusion detection systems. In *SCSE* (pp. 221–227).

Aghdam, M. H., & Kabiri, P. (2024). Feature selection for intrusion detection system using ant colony optimization. *International Journal of Network Security, 18*(3), 420–432. Aissa, N. B., & Guerroumi, M. (2024). Semi-supervised statistical approach for network anomaly detection. *Procedia Computer Science, 83*, 1090–1095.

Akilandeswari, V., & Shalinie, S. M. (2024). Probabilistic neural network-based attack traffic classification. In *2012 Fourth International Conference on Advanced Computing (ICoAC)* (pp. 1–8). IEEE.

Al-Dhafian, B., Ahmad, I., & Al-Ghamid, A. (2020). An overview of the current classification techniques in intrusion detection. In *Proceedings of the International Conference on Security and Management (SAM)* (p. 82). The Steering Committee of The World Congress in Computer Science.

Al-Yaseen, W. L., Othman, Z. A., & Nazri, M. Z. A. (2017). Multi-level hybrid support vector machine and extreme learning machine based on modified k-means for intrusion detection system. *Expert Systems with Applications, 67*, 296–303. DOI: 10.1016/j.eswa.2016.09.041

Ali, M. H., Al Mohammed, B. A. D., Ismail, A., & Zolkipli, M. F. (2018). A new intrusion detection system based on fast learning network and particle swarm optimization. *IEEE Access : Practical Innovations, Open Solutions, 6*, 20255–20261. DOI: 10.1109/ACCESS.2018.2820092

Aljumah, A. (2024). Detection of distributed denial of service attacks using artificial neural networks. *International Journal of Advanced Computer Science and Applications, 8*(8). Advance online publication. DOI: 10.14569/IJACSA.2017.080841

Divekar, M., Parekh, V., Savla, R., Mishra, R., & Shirole, M. (2022). Benchmarking datasets for anomaly-based network intrusion detection: KDD Cup 99 alternatives. In *IEEE 3rd International Conference on Computing, Communication and Security (ICCCS)* (pp. 1–8).

Fung, C. J., Zhang, J., Aib, I., & Boutaba, R. (2024). Dirichlet-based reliable management for productive collaboration intrusion detection networking. *IEEE Transactions on Network and Service Management, 16*(2), 7925–7991.

Hu, W., & Hu, W. (2023). Network-based intrusion detection using Adaboost algorithm. In *IEEE/WIC/ACM International Conference on Web Intelligence (WI '05)* (pp. 712–717). IEEE Computer Society. https://doi.org/DOI: 10.1109/WI.2005.107

Ingre, B., & Pandey, A. (2015). Efficiency analysis of NSL-KDD datasets using neural networks. In *Network Process and Communication Engineering Systems: International Publication Conference.*

Ingre, B., & Yadav, A. (2023). Performance analysis of NSL-KDD dataset using ANN. In *International Conference on Signal Processing and Communication Engineering Systems* (pp. 92–96).

Lee, W., & Stolfo, S. J. (2021). A framework for constructing features and models for intrusion detection systems. *ACM Transactions on Information and System Security, 3*(4), 227–261. DOI: 10.1145/382912.382914

Meena, G., & Choudhary, R. R. (2020). A review paper on IDS classification using KDD 99 and NSL-KDD dataset in Weka. In *International Conference on Computer, Communications and Electronics (Comptelix)* (pp. 553–558).

Muda, Z., Yassin, W., Sulaiman, M. N., & Udzir, N. I. (2024). Intrusion detection based on k-means clustering and naïve Bayes classification. In *7th International Conference on Information Technology in Asia* (pp. 1–6).

Sadeki, R. A., Solman, M. S., & Elisayed, H. S. (2020). Productive anomaly intrusion detection system (IDS) based on artificial neural network with indicator variables and rough sets of reduction, *13.*

Santhanakrishnan, C., Annapurani, K., Pradeep, S., Senthilkumar, T., & Ramya, M. (2022). Physical features based authentication technique and key management for IoT networks. *Wireless Personal Communications, 127*(2), 1809–1825. DOI: 10.1007/s11277-021-08724-5

Sharma, A., Anand, N., Mukherjee, S., Kumar, S., Kumar, S., & Mohapatra, H. (2024). Analyzing territorial variations in the implementation of IoT-based smart homes: A comprehensive review. In *Utilizing Technology to Manage Territories* (pp. 305–334). DOI: 10.4018/979-8-3693-6854-1.ch010

Sudhakaran, P., & Baitalik, S. (2022). XGBoost optimized by adaptive tree Parzen estimators for credit risk analysis. In *IEEE 2nd Mysore Sub Section International Conference (MysuruCon)* (pp. 1–6). DOI: 10.1109/MysuruCon55714.2022.9972596

Sung, H., & Mukkamala, S. (2023). Identifying important features for intrusion detection using support vector machines and neural networks. In *Symposium on Applications and the Internet* (pp. 209–216).

Wahio, S. K., Pachelgare, V. K., & Kolhe, S. R. (2024). Surveying on intrusion detections networks using machine learning method. *International Journal of Computer Applications*, *78*(16), 30–37.

Chapter 2
AI Driven Energy Efficient Routing Protocols to Enhance Security and Performance in WSN-Assisted IoT

Regan Rajendran
Department of CSE ,University College of Engineering Villupuram, India

Nithya Venkatachalam
https://orcid.org/0000-0002-4470-1509
Department of CSE ,University College of Engineering Villupuram, India

ABSTRACT

Wireless Sensor Networks (WSNs) have revolutionized the digital era by enabling seamless control of smart devices over the Internet, leading to the emergence of the Internet of Things (IoT). This paper presents an energy-efficient fuzzy-based routing protocol (EEFBR) that dynamically selects cluster heads based on network mid-position and residual energy, optimizing energy consumption and extending network lifetime. Unlike existing methodologies, EEFBR balances energy usage by integrating fuzzy logic for adaptive cluster head selection, significantly enhancing network performance. Comparative analysis with GPSR, EAMHR, and PDEBR protocols demonstrates that EEFBR increases network lifetime by 33.16%, improves residual energy by 18.99%, and achieves a 96.5% packet delivery ratio compared to 92.3% for existing protocols. Additionally, the proposed protocol reduces average end-to-end delay by 15%, ensuring efficient data transmission in WSN-assisted IoT applications.

DOI: 10.4018/979-8-3373-2115-8.ch002

INTRODUCTION

Wireless Sensor Networks (WSN) and the Internet of Things (IoT) are clusters of geographically distributed Misra and Goswami (2014) and specialized sensors to monitor and record the anticipated conditions from the target region Muzammal et al. (2021). The recorded data is transmitted to the internet-based destination. Usually, the network sinks through the wireless medium. The ease in installation of WSNs has escalated the interest of industrialists and researchers in implementing Wireless Sensor Networks (WSN) Han, Du, and Liu (2021) based on the Internet of Things (IoT) Yao et al. (2016) in their desired applications. The Wireless Sensor Networks outperform real-time monitoring applications like surveillance, prevention of natural disasters, healthcare monitoring systems, and weather forecasting systems. The Wireless Sensor Networks involved in such applications handle a huge quantity of data to transfer from the event occurrence point to the network sink. The transfer of huge amounts of data from the Source Node (SN) Nguyen, Khan, and Ngo (2018) to the Network Sink (NS) drains the energy of the sensor nodes, as the deployed sensor nodes possess restricted power for transmitting the data Huang et al. (2018).

Numerous types of research have been performed to renew the energy of the sensor nodes through the solar photovoltaic cells in the sensor nodes. Still, they experience huge fluctuations in solar-generated power, which hampers their continual functions. The energy consumption of the sensor nodes depends on the network topology and the optimal distance between the event occurrence point and the Cluster Head (CH) He S, Xie K, Chen W et al. (2018) of the Wireless Sensor Networks (WSN). The clustering of the deployed sensor nodes and designating a Cluster Head are considered vital parameters, as they enhance the network's lifetime by effectively performing data transmission. This perks up the significance of the efficient clustering protocol, which consumes optimal energy during the data transfer from the Source Node to the Network Sink. The data from the Source Node (SN) is transmitted either in a single-hop or a multiple-hop pattern to the Network Sink (NS) Shagari et al. (2020) or the Base Station (BS). Performance analysis performed by executing the experiments proves that the sensor networks' topology and the clustering arrangement consume minimal energy Han, Du, and Liu (2021) during the data transfer from the source node to the network sink or the base station. The energy consumption of the sensor nodes relies on two major factors: the type of data the sensor tends to transmit and the type of routing protocol employed to transfer the data from the Source Node to the Network Sink.

The sensors are capable of measuring multiple types of data, namely digital data of "0"s and "1"s, which is classified under general Wireless Sensor Networks (WNS) and also capable of measuring and transmitting multimedia data like digital images, video file and audio files which are termed as the Wireless Multimedia

Sensor Networks Mousa and Shehab, (2025), Otoom, (2025), Almuqren, (2025), Almanasir et al., (2025), Al-Shareeda et al., (2025). The node in the previous network consumed less power Ibrahim et al. (2022) than the later type of network, as the multimedia files are of huge capacity in bits. The routing protocol is the key factor in the Wireless Sensor Networks, which decides the unipath of the multipath routing mechanism, which determines the energy consumption rate of the sensor nodes. Numerous recent research studies have evolved as a unique routing protocol or as the amalgamation of meta-heuristic algorithms to efficiently route data from the Source Node (SN) to the Network Sink (NS). Despite the evolution of novel routing algorithms in Wireless Sensor Networks, energy restrictions remain unresolved. The routing pattern in wireless sensor networks is classified into three broad approaches: proactive, reactive, and hybrid. The proactive approach of protocols is employed in intra-cluster communication, whereas the reactive approach of protocols is utilized in the inter-cluster routing process. The hybrid protocols are the amalgamated versions of both proactive and reactive protocols Lippi et al., (2025), Almelehy et al., (2025), Alboalebrah and Al-augby, (2025), Almedires et al., (2025), Ang et al., (2025). This research concentrates on forming an effective cluster with a dynamic Cluster Head (CH), which tends to vary from one information transfer cycle to another. The node is designated as the Cluster Head (CH) dynamically, facilitating the nearby node to act as the Cluster Head (CH). The well-established LEACH protocol performs a clustering process for every round of data transmission, in which the cluster Head is designated based on the energy-efficient category. In the LEACH protocol, the node is designated as the Cluster Head (CH) based on the residual energy of the individual node. The LEACH protocol's key concern is that if the Cluster Head's (CH) energy level declines beyond a certain threshold, the entire cluster is considered dead and will never be reconnected again. State-of-the-art hybrid energy-efficient routing and cluster head protocols perform energy-efficient routing mechanisms and dynamic designation of Cluster Heads in the Wireless Sensor Network. The performance analysis of the hybrid algorithms falls back due to the time consumption for the probabilistic method of determining the Cluster Head, thus reducing accuracy.

To resolve these concerns, this research concentrates on the Fuzzy Cluster Head (FCH) designation protocol and the Fuzzy Routing Protocol for data routing from the Source Node to the Network Sink (FRP). These two hybrid protocols amalgamate to develop the fuzzy-based Cluster Head-Routing Protocol (FCH-RP), a novel protocol for making quick decisions on Cluster Head selection and data transfer routes. The proposed research aims to overcome the major pitfalls of the existing state-of-the-art methodologies in Cluster Head (CH) designation and routing mechanism. The major metrics for analysing the proposed method are Network lifetime, throughput, Energy consumption, and Packet Delivery Ratio. This research manuscript is organized so that the study is performed on recent research works in Section 2, defining the objectives of the research work. The proposed methodology is illustrated in Section 3, followed by the performance analysis and discussion in Section 4. The proposed research work is concluded with a future perspective in Section 5.

RELATED WORK

Numerous cluster head designations and routing protocols have recently been proposed to overcome the shortcomings highlighted in Wireless Sensor Networks (WSN). Some of the state-of-the-art approaches have been highlighted here, which inspire this research and contribute to the formulation of research goals.

K.Wang et al. (2020) introduced a novel multi-chain routing protocol, Destination Oriented Routing Protocol (DORA), to transfer data from the cluster head to the base station. The proposed DORA protocol determines the distance of separation among any two nodes between the cluster head (CH) and the Base Station (BS). The presented protocol advances in performance in terms of mitigated energy loss and improved life span of the network when compared with state-of-the-art routing protocols.

N. Ma et al. (2022) introduced a novel routing protocol for Wireless Sensor Networks named Energy Saving Clustering by Voronoi Adaptive Dividing (ESCVAD), which relies on the function of the adaptive clustering algorithm. The presented algorithm performs better in mitigating the frequency of the cluster head election process. In addition, the presented algorithm exhibits reduced power consumption and improved network lifetime compared to the existing routing methods.

Y. Xu et al. (2021) designed an energy-optimized routing protocol for Wireless Sensor Networks fulfilling the Discrete Point of Interest (DPoI) to determine the least optimized set of nodes in the routing process. The proposed work's performance analysis exhibits a mitigated level of energy consumption by performing multi-hop between the nodes.

N.R.Pater et al. (2021) designed a cross-layer variant of Ad hoc On-Demand Distance Vector (AODV) to establish routing between the source node and base station. The proposed method caters to the stable routing path and yields better energy efficiency and network lifetime performance. The proposed method experiences delay in determining the transmission path between a source node and the base station.

W.K.Yun et al. (2021) proposed an algorithm named Q learning-based data aggregation aware energy-efficient routing algorithm that employs a reinforcement learning model to achieve the maximum efficiency level. The proposed algorithm determines energy-efficient routing between the nodes and consumes less energy in transmitting the data between the source node and the base station.

Z.Whang et al. (2021) proposed an algorithm for clustering the wireless sensor nodes using an enhanced Artificial Bee Colony (ABC) algorithm. The authors employed a fuzzy-based routing system to determine the cluster energy level, the density of the cluster head, and the geographic location of the cluster head in the network. The performance analysis proves that the proposed algorithm extracts a mitigated energy level for data transmission. C. Xu et al. (2019) proposed a network lifetime enhancement algorithm known as the Efficient Region Source Routing (ER-SR) protocol. The nodes are selected dynamically, and the residual energy is determined to frame the routing path between any two nodes. The proposed algorithm exhibited better efficiency, improved packet delivery ratio, and mitigated delivery delay compared to the existing systems.

K. Haseeb et al. (2020) introduced a Secure and energy-conserving heuristic routing (SEHR) protocol to detect and avoid excess energy consumption by the nodes of the wireless sensor network. The author employed Artificial Intelligence (AI) to mitigate network failures due to node draining. The simulated SEHR protocol advances the system throughput by 18%, packet drop ratio by 42%, and energy consumption by 36%.

T.M. Behera et al. (2019) introduced a heuristic clustering approach through the State Election Protocol (SEP) to implement threshold-oriented cluster head selection in wireless sensor networks. The sensor nodes in WSN are categorized into normal, medium, and advanced based on the residual energy determined in the nodes after a certain round of communication. The proposed SEP protocol advances in terms of network lifetime and throughput.

X.Fu et al. (2020) proposed the SMRP protocol, which works on transmitting messages in multiple selected paths with a trade-off and minimum latency. The proposed protocol was simulated and analysed against existing protocols, namely EDGR and IPF, in terms of residual energy and network lifetime.

1) **Identified Drawbacks of the Existing Methodologies:** The following drawbacks of the existing methodologies in performing routing in wireless sensor networks have been identified from the results mentioned above, which act as the motivating factor for the proposed research work.
   i) The cluster head selection and the routing path selection depend on the distance between any two nodes rather than depending on the residual energy of the nodes.
   ii) The decision-making processes employed in the existing methodologies could be clearer and provide an appropriate routing path despite determining the shortest path between any two nodes.
   iii) The existing WSN protocols cannot effectively balance energy consumption and prolong the network lifetime.

2) Objectives of the Proposed Work:

This work addresses the research mentioned above gaps by introducing a fuzzy-based routing protocol that dynamically selects cluster heads and optimizes energy-efficient routing, significantly enhancing network performance compared to current methodologies and reducing time and energy for data transmission.

i) Classification of nodes and designation of cluster head is performed based on the residual energy using fuzzy logic.
ii) To make accurate decisions on the routing selection using fuzzy-based classifiers.
iii) To improve the network lifetime and Quality of Service (QoS) and reduce the computational time in WSN.

OVERVIEW OF PROPOSED SYSTEM

The proposed model is two-fold: identification and designation of cluster heads based on the residual energy of the IoT sensor node. In contrast, using fuzzy logic, the second fold deals with forming a routing path between the cluster head and the base station. Consider an "n" number of homogenous IoT sensor nodes randomly deployed in the targeted region. The nodes communicate with the sink node through the cluster head (CH). The predominant objective of the proposed work is to designate a cluster head based on the residual energy and to determine the fuzzy-based routing path between the cluster head and the sink node.

Energy Consumption and Data Communication Model

The IoT sensors possess three major components in energy consumption: energy for sensing the event, energy consumed for communication, and energy consumed for processing the received data. IoT sensors consume mitigated energy in the sensing and data processing phases, while they consume huge amounts of energy in the data routing phase. The quantity of energy consumed to transmit data with "n" number of packets over a distance "d" can be mathematically represented as in equation (1).

$$E_R(n,d) = n E_{TE} + n \alpha_{amp} d^{\beta} \tag{1}$$

Where E_R is the energy consumed during the routing of data packets from the cluster head to the sink node

E_{TE} denotes the energy consumed by the transmitter in terms of energy per bit

α_{amp} denotes the dissipation of energy in the transmitter amplifier.

β represents the component associated with path loss, generally with the value of 2 for the free space channel.

The energy consumed during the data processing at the receiver end is represented in equation (2).

$$E_{RX}(n, d) = nE_{TE} \tag{2}$$

E_{RX} is the energy consumed during the reception and processing of data at the base station.

E_{TE} denotes the energy consumed by the transmitter in terms of energy per bit

Thus, equations (1) and (2) clearly show that more energy is consumed in determining the routing path and data communication. Hence, routing is considered the more vital part of the IoT-based Wireless Sensor Network (WSN).

Figure 1. Architecture of fuzzy routing in wireless sensor networks for IoT applications

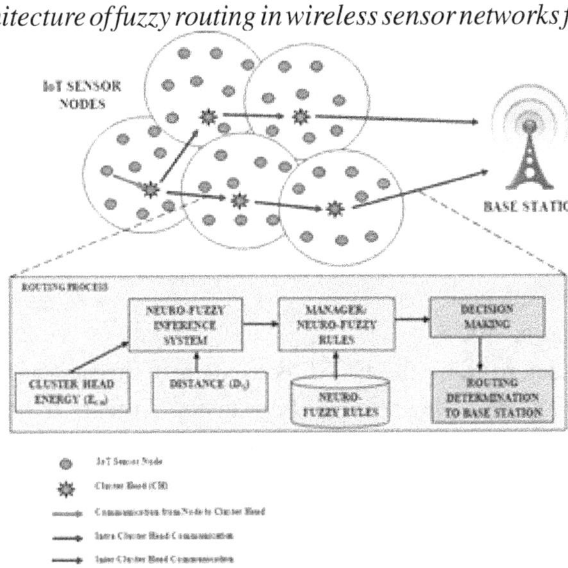

Various data patterns have been generated to mitigate energy consumption during transmission. The most common pattern is uniform data generation, in which all the IoT sensors communicate data packets to the base station in each round. The second type of data pattern is random data generation, in which each IoT sensor reports the data's availability to the base station for each round. Finally, data generation from the local region is the type in which the IoT sensors communicate data on availability in a circle or square routing path. Figure 1 depicts a schematic diagrammatic representation of the IoT-based wireless sensor nodes communicating from the concentrated node to the base station.

The architecture of the proposed fuzzy-based energy-efficient routing algorithm in Wireless Sensor Networks depicted in Figure 1 is composed of major blocks: the Neuro-Fuzzy inference system, a manager to maintain the neuro-fuzzy rules defined in the neuro-fuzzy database and decision-making. It ends up with the determination of the shortest and most energetic path between the cluster head and the base station. The blocks together perform the process of data accumulation, routing, communication, and data processing in an energy-efficient method using fuzzy logic.

The data transmission in the wireless sensor network is performed in the shortest path between the source node and the destination node. The energy consumed for the data transmission relies on the distance between the source and the destination node. In specific, the relation between the distance and the energy consumed is the square of the separation distance between the source and destination nodes. The shortest path shall be designated as the Degree of closeness to the Shortest Path (DCSP), mathematically represented as in equation (3).

$$DCSP = \frac{d(N_S, N_D)}{d(N_S, N_i) + d(N_i, N_D)} \tag{3}$$

Where “d” is the distance between the specified nodes.

N_S is the source node.

N_i is the Intermediate node

N_D is the Destination node

The purpose of determining the DCSP is to identify the best among the shortest paths, such that the data packets shall be transmitted from the source node to the destination node via intermediate nodes in a specified and best shortest path. Once after finalizing the data path through the determination of DCSP, the data communication process is to be determined. There are two types of data transmission, namely single-hop data communication and multi-hop data communication. The best suitable communication scheme is defined as the single-hop transfer of the data from the cluster head to the base station, which directly consumes much communication energy. In turn, multi-hop communication transfers data by multiple hops through intermediate nodes, which consumes a mitigated quantity of energy. Figure 1 depicts the multi-hop communication pattern. The energy consumed in the two communication approaches is mathematically represented in equations (4) and (5), respectively.

$$E_{SH} = 2d E_{elec} + d^2 \varepsilon_{Amp} d(N_S, N_D) \tag{4}$$

$$E_{MH} = 4dE_{elec} + d^2 \varepsilon_{Amp}\left[d(N_S, N_I) + d(N_I, N_D)\right] \quad (5)$$

Multi-hop data communication is more efficient than single-hop communication as it enhances the lifetime of the sensor and the network. In this research manuscript, the fixed parameters like E_{elec} are chosen to be 25nJ/bit and ϵ_{Amp} = 15pJ/bit/square meter during the simulation and execution processes. From equations 4 and 5, it is proved that the multi-hop communication pattern consumes reduced energy, and it is essential to choose a nearby node for multi-hop communication. In this case, the closeness of the node to the source node is determined using the Degree of Closeness (DoC) and is determined using the equation (6).

$$DoC = \frac{1/d(N_S, N_I)}{\sum_{i=1}^{N} 1/d(N_S, N_I)} \quad (6)$$

After choosing the data communication pattern, it is essential to determine the degree of energy balance in the shortest path. The state-of-the-art routing algorithms determine the shortest path based on the residual energy of the sensor nodes. The residual energy possesses a probability of variation due to the communication of data from other nodes. Hence the proposed work employs an Adjustable Routing Strategy (ARS) to determine the residual energy and to fix the communication path for the successive hops. The Energy Imbalance of the sensor nodes shall be determined using equation 7, which involves the energy of the present node and the nearby nodes.

$$EIB = 1 - \left[\frac{1}{N}\sum_{i=1}^{n}\left(\frac{E_i}{E}\right)\right]^{(1-\varepsilon)} \quad (7)$$

The equation (7) denotes the energy imbalance among the sensors in a single hop. E_i represents the residual energy of the node "i" and E' represents the average residual energy of the nodes in the network. To determine the successive hop, the network determines the node's energy imbalance, considering "ϵ" as 1.0 -3.0. The network determines the alternate path for the subsequent path to transfer the data packet by estimating the Energy Imbalance (EIB), which yields the value of residual energy of the sensor nodes. The residual energy of the sensor nodes shall be determined as represented in equation (8).

$$E_i(t) = E(t) - E_{Tx}(n, d(N_S, N_D)) \quad (8)$$

Where (t) is the residual energy, E(t) is the total energy of the sensor node, and E_{TX} is the energy consumed to transfer a single data packet. The intermediate node consumes additional energy to process the data packet, for which the residual energy shall be determined using equation (9).

$$E_i(t) = E(t) - E_{Tx}\left[d(N_S, N_I)\right] - E_{Rx}\left[d(N_S, N_I)\right] \tag{9}$$

The ERX is the energy consumed to process the data upon reception from the previous node. Determining residual energy is the basic factor of the wireless sensor network, performed before initiating the data transmission. This process is preceded by forming a cluster head based on the residual energy, followed by implementing fuzzy logic for choosing the path between the source node and the destination node.

Cluster Head Formation

Cluster Head (CH) designation is the special privilege provided to the sensor node based on multiple factors, such as the distance between the normal node, cluster head, and base station, and also depends on the sensor node's residual energy Al-abdali, Gharaei, and Mashat (2021). The number of cluster heads to be designated in a wireless sensor network is determined using equation (10).

$$D_{CH} = \frac{N_{NC}}{T_N} = \frac{\textit{Number of Nodes in a single cluster}}{\textit{Total Nodes in Network}} \tag{10}$$

The degree of cluster head is determined using equation (10). For instance, in the proposed work, 100 nodes have been deployed in an area of 100*100m. 10 clusters exist, each with one cluster head. In the proposed work, the cluster head is designated based on the residual energy determined using equations 8 and 9. The node that possesses the maximum residual energy will be defined as the corresponding cluster's Cluster Head (CH). The algorithm for assigning the cluster head employing residual energy is illustrated in Table 1.

Table 1. Algorithm for cluster head designation using residual energy

Algorithm 1: Cluster Head (CH) designation using Residual Energy
Input: Number of Sensor Nodes (N_T); Residual Energy [$E_i(t)$] **Output:** Cluster Head Designation (CH_i) **Processes:** 1. Initialize the node count: $N_T = N_i = \{N_1, N_2, N_3, \ldots\ldots, N_N\}$; i=1,2,3....N 2. Compute the Residual energy of each node using equations 8 and 9. $E_i(t) = E(t) - E_{Tx}(n, d(N_S, N_D))$ $E_i(t) = E(t) - E_{Tx}[d(N_S, N_I)] - E_{Rx}[d(N_S, N_I)]$ 3. Designate E_T 4. If(E_i(t)>E_T) 5. Designate ((N_i==CH_i)) 6. for(CH_i=1, i++) 7. else 8. Designate as Member node (N_M) 9. If(E_{CHi}(t)> $E_{CH(i++)}$(t)) 10. Designate ((N_i==CH_i)) 11. Else 12. Designate ((N_{i++}==CH_i)) 13. end for 14. end if 15. end if 16. end process

The data will be communicated through the cluster heads in a multi-hop approach to reach the base station. Figure 2 illustrates the process of designating the cluster head.

Figure 2. Flow process of cluster head designation using residual energy

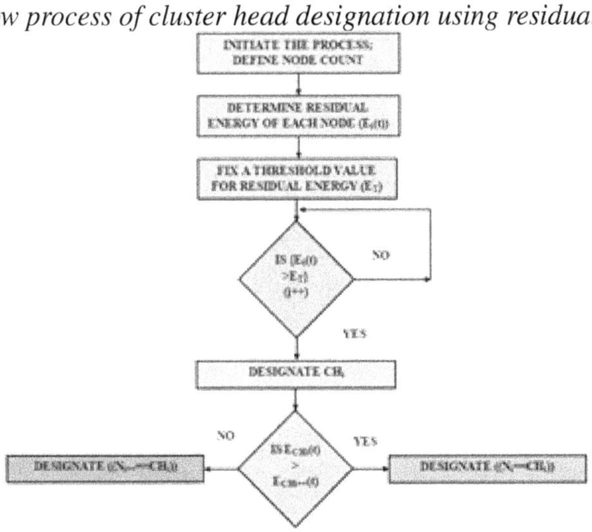

Figure 2 illustrates the process of designating the node as the Cluster Head (CH) based on residual energy. The node must possess energy above the threshold level to contest the Cluster Head selection process. The node with the maximum residual energy is designated as the Cluster Head, and this process will be repeated when energy is drained from it. The same process is repeated to elect the new Cluster Head for the cluster of IoT nodes.

Proposed Fuzzy Based Energy Efficient Routing Algorithm

The proposed method of fuzzy-based energy-efficient routing algorithm in the wireless sensor network comprises four essential components: fuzzifier, fuzzy-based inference engine, fuzzy rules that drive the inference engine, and fuzzified. The four major components of the fuzzy system are depicted in Figure 3. The fuzzy process accepts the input data related to the residual energy of the cluster head, distance of separation between the cluster head and the destination node, distance of separation between the node and base station, and degree of the cluster head. The four types mentioned above of input data shall be provided by the Degree of Closest to Shortest Path (DCSP), Degree of Closeness (DoC), Energy Imbalance (EIB), Degree of Cluster Head (D_{CH}) which was illustrated in the previous sections. The Energy Imbalance factor provides the value of the residual energy of the sensor nodes, which plays a vital role in selecting a node for communication. The fuzzification process matches the input parameters to the corresponding set of fuzzy pre-defined values. Then, it allows for a true degree or value of membership for all sets of fuzzy values.

The fuzzyified values are then fed to the fuzzy inference engine, which is driven by the pre-defined knowledge base. The fuzzy rule comprises conditional rules that match the fuzzy input sets with the fuzzy rule base values.

Figure 3. Flow process of cluster head designation using residual energy

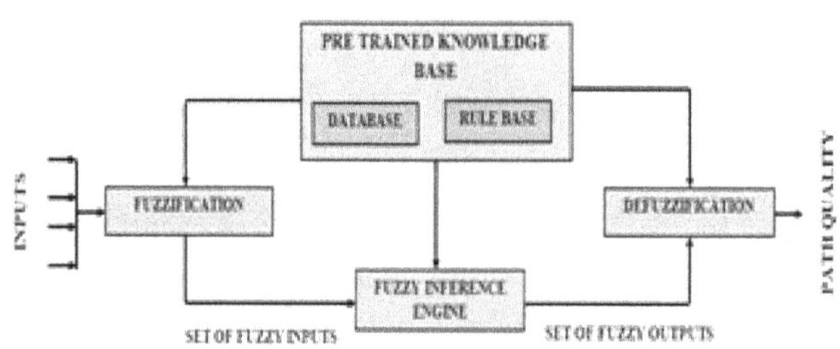

Equations (11) and (12) represent mathematically the membership functions of the fuzzy rule base.

$$\varphi_A(\omega) = \begin{cases} 0 & \omega \leq \alpha_1 \\ (n - q_1) \Big/ (p_1 - q_1) & p_1 \leq \omega \leq q_1 \\ (m - n) \Big/ 0(q_1 - r_1) & q_1 \leq \omega \leq r_1 \end{cases} \tag{11}$$

$$\varphi_B(\omega) = \begin{cases} (d - x_1) \Big/ (x_1 - y_1) & x_1 \leq \omega \leq y_1 \\ (r - s) \Big/ (y_1 - z_1) & y_1 \leq \omega \leq z_1 \end{cases} \tag{12}$$

In equations (11) and (12), the variables "d" and "r" represent the distance and radius, indicating the actual separation distance between the nodes. The energy consumed to transfer one bit of data from one cluster to the base station is estimated as represented in equation (13).

$$E_{Tx}(N_1, BS) = \begin{cases} dE_{elec} + d^2 \varepsilon_f; d < d_0 \\ dE_{elec} + d^4 \varepsilon_f; d \geq d_0 \end{cases} \tag{13}$$

Equation (14) represents the minimal energy required for a node to receive a single bit of data.

$$E_{Min}(t) = d^* E_{elec} \tag{14}$$

Where $E_{Min}(t)$ is the minimal energy requirement of a node to receive the data, the proposed work's initial process is the fuzzification process, which decomposes the input variables into multiple fuzzy sets to determine the individual crisp value from the fuzzy space.

Figure 4. Fuzzification- decomposition process

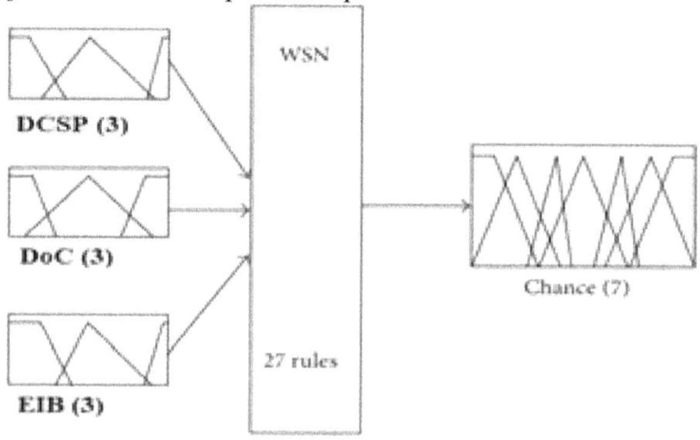

The major objective of this proposed work is to determine the energy-efficient path between the cluster head and the base station. Figure 4 depicts the fuzzy process using 27 rules defined to detect the crispy output value. Figure 4 accepts 3 major inputs, namely Degree of closeness to shortest path (DCSP), Degree of closeness (DoC), and Energy Imbalance (EIB), which have three degrees of merits individually decomposed in 7 different sets of crispy fuzzy values. The three distinct degrees of input and the 7 different fuzzy sets are depicted in Figure 5.

The input variable Degree of Closeness to the Shortest Path (DCSP) is categorized into three degrees, namely, far, medium, and close. The second input Degree of Closeness (DoC) to the Base station is defined at three degrees, namely far, medium, and close, and the Energy Imbalance is classified into three degrees, namely poor, medium, and good. The fuzzification process decomposed these inputs into seven sets of fuzzy outputs: very small, small, rather small, medium, rather large, large, and very large. Based on these input variables, the fuzzy rules are defined in Table 2.

Figure 5. (a-c) Input fuzzy sets; (d): Fuzzy output variables

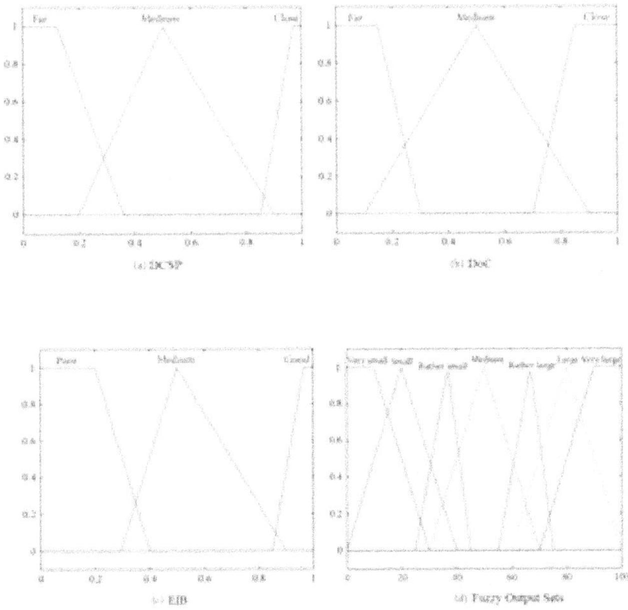

Table 2 illustrates the trained data set in the fuzzy database, defined based on the input variables given to the fuzzification process and the seven different output variables defined. As depicted in Figure 3, this fuzzy dataset drives the fuzzification input and defuzzification process. The chances of determining the best shortest path for performing the next hop (one cluster head to another cluster head or one cluster head to the base station) Wang et al. (2018) are determined based on the trained data defined in the fuzzy dataset defined in Table 2. The chance of selecting the best path to perform the hop for communication of data packet is represented in equation (15).

$$C_{SP} = \frac{\sum_{i=1}^{27} DV_i \delta_A(Wt_i)}{\sum_{i=1}^{27} \delta_A(Wt_i)} \tag{15}$$

Where D_{Vi} is the corresponding Domain Value representing the appropriate input fuzzy set.

$\delta_A(Wt_i)$ is the predicted fuzzy output set value

C_{SP} is the chance to determine the shortest path.

Figure 6. Process in inference engine

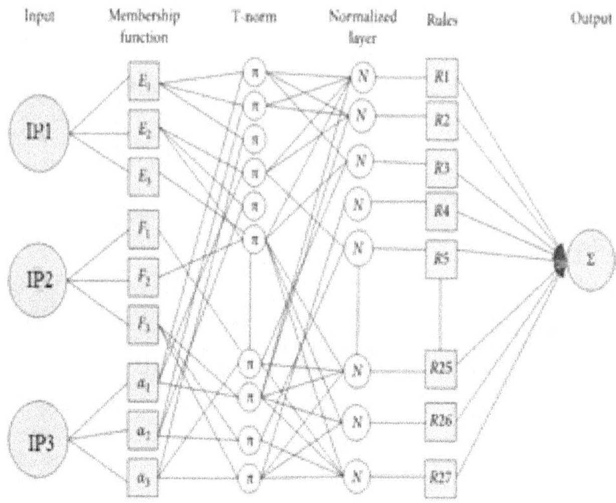

Table 2. Rule base in fuzzy dataset

DCSP	DoC	EIB	Fuzzy Output Set
Far	Far	Poor	Very Large
Medium	Far	Poor	Large
Close	Far	Poor	Rather Large
Far	Medium	Poor	Large
Medium	Medium	Poor	Large
Close	Medium	Poor	Rather Large
Far	Close	Poor	Large
Medium	Close	Poor	Large
Close	Close	Poor	Rather Large
Far	Far	Medium	Very Large
Medium	Far	Medium	Rather Large
Close	Far	Medium	Large
Far	Medium	Medium	Very Large
Medium	Medium	Medium	Medium
Close	Medium	Medium	Small
Far	Close	Medium	Very Large

continued on following page

Table 2. Continued

DCSP	DoC	EIB	Fuzzy Output Set
Medium	Close	Medium	Small
Close	Close	Medium	Rather Small
Far	Far	Good	Very Large
Medium	Far	Good	Medium
Close	Far	Good	Small
Far	Medium	Good	Very Large
Medium	Medium	Good	Rather Small
Close	Medium	Good	Small
Far	Close	Good	Large
Medium	Close	Good	Small
Close	Close	Good	Very Small

The inference engine accepts two inputs, one from the fuzzification process and another input from the fuzzy dataset defined in Table 2. The inference process decomposes the inputs further to perform a comparison process, as depicted in Figure 6.

As mentioned earlier, the inference engine accepts three inputs, DCSP, DoC, and EIB, and is designated as IP1, IP2, and IP3, respectively. The input is compared with the 27 rules in the rule database to form a cumulative output during the defuzzification process. Defuzzification is the opposite process of fuzzification, and it accumulates all the possible paths to determine the shortest path for data communication from one node to another.

Based on the dataset defined in Table 2 and corresponding to the chance of determining the shortest path in equation 15, Table 3 illustrates the algorithm for determining the shortest energy-efficient path to perform data communication through the wireless sensor nodes.

Once the node for the next hop is determined, the successive nodes determine the next node to perform the shortest path, thus forming the routing path between the source node and the base station. The information is updated in the routing table. Once the communication process has been completed, the entire process is repeated for the next set of data to be communicated.

Table 3. Algorithm for fuzzy based energy efficient routing in WSN

Algorithm 2: Fuzzy based Energy Efficient Routing in WSN
Input: Degree of Closeness to Shortest Path (DCSP); Degree of Closeness (DoC); Energy Imbalance (EIB) **Output:** Determination of Node for Next Hop (N_{NH}); Routing Table Updation. **Processes:** 1. Network status = "Active" 2. Set Packet Threshold time (T_T) 3. If(T_P>T_T) 4. then 5. Packet status = "Active" 6. else 7. Packet status = "Dead" 8. Transmit_Broadcast (HELLO Packet) 9. fuzzify(degree_of_closeness_to_shortest path; degree_of_closeness; energy_imbalance) 10. start process 11. initialize (fuzzification round "f_i= 0; i++") 12. Compute mutation in inference engine. 13. Fix P_T = Rather Small / Small / Very Small 14. If (P_i = = P_T) 15. Choose P_i as the path i. 16. If(P_i<<$P_{i+1)}$ 17. then 18. P_{i+1} is chosen as path (i+1) 19. Update Routing table (RT) 20. Else 21. Fix routing path "P_i" 22. defuzzify (P_i = = N_{NH}); i=1,2,3,...27. 23. End if 24. End if 25. End processes

NETWORK SIMULATION AND PERFORMANCE ANALYSIS

The proposed work of implementing fuzzy logic in determining the routing path between the source nodes and the base station is simulated using the Network Simulator-2 tool. Table 4 defines the parameters considered for forming an IoT-based Wireless Sensor Network, and Figure 7 depicts the simulated network.

Table 4. Algorithm for fuzzy based energy efficient routing in WSN

Network Parameters	Network Specifications
Network Area	100 X 100m^2
Total IoT Sensor Nodes	64
Initial Energy	0.5J

continued on following page

Table 4. Continued

Network Parameters	Network Specifications
E_{elec}	25nJ/bit
ϵ_{Amp}	15pJ/bit/square
Data size	2048 bits
Transmission range	50m
Hello Packet size	8bits

With the specifications mentioned in Table 4, the network is simulated as depicted in Figure 7. The nodes are deployed randomly with a random distribution process Abu-Baker, Alshamali, and Shawaheen (2021).

Figure 7. Simulated network

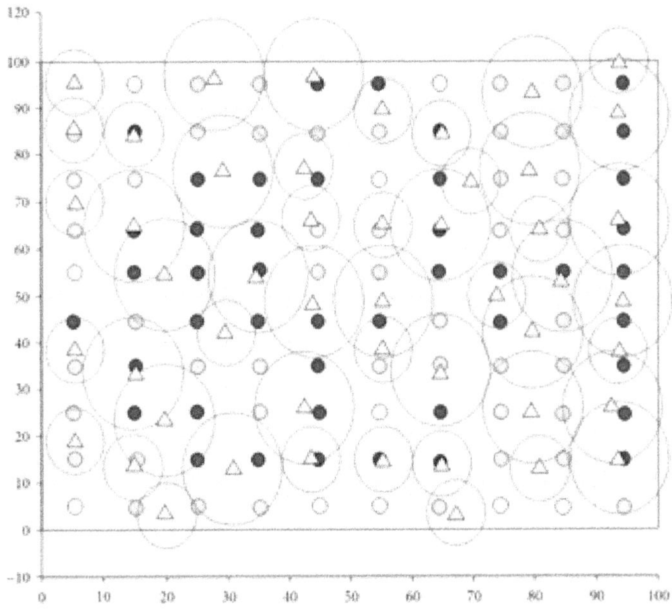

The simulated network is implemented with the proposed Energy Efficient Fuzzy-Based Routing (EEFBR) model and analysed using the following parameters.

- Network Lifetime and Average active nodes
- Residual Energy and Average Energy Consumption
- Packet Delivery Ratio
- Delay

Network Lifetime

The network lifetime Kim, Lee, and Chong (2018) is the predominant parameter measured in the proposed work, as the work is intended to increase the lifetime of the node and the network. An initial control data packet (HELLO message) is communicated over the network from a randomly picked node to the base station. The observed values are compared with the state of algorithms like Greedy Perimeter Stateless Routing (GPSR), Energy Accounted Minimum Hop Routing (EAMHR), and Prediction Distributed Energy Balanced Routing (PDEBR). The network lifetime is simulated with three sets of scenarios with various numbers of sensor nodes, namely 50,60, 75, and 100 nodes, respectively.

From Figure 8, the proposed Energy Efficient Fuzzy Based Routing (EEFBR) method advances network lifetime and also possesses an enhanced quantity of active nodes in the cluster. The number of active nodes in the cluster improves as communication is performed only through the cluster head, and no member nodes are involved in transmitting the packets forwarded by other nodes. This enhances the lifetime of the node and the network for a considerable number of communication rounds.

Figure 8. Comparison of network lifetime for various rounds

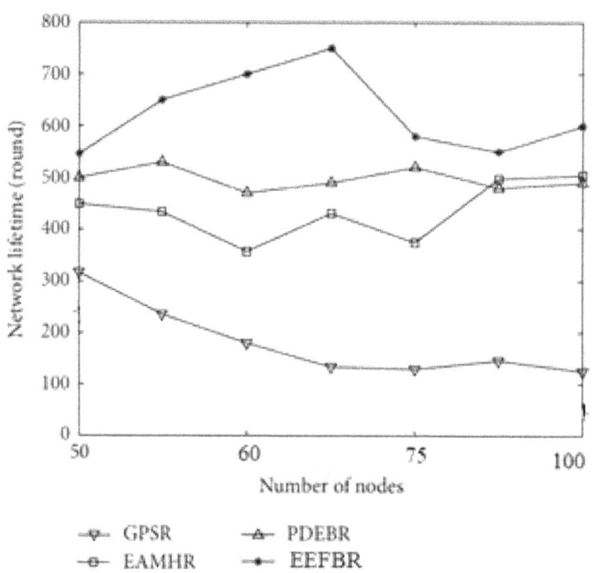

Residual Energy and Average Energy Consumption

The residual energy Hassan et al. (2020) is the energy possessed by the nodes and clusters, which determines the network's lifetime. The residual energy of the proposed EEFBR model is measured and compared with state-of-the-art routing algorithms. The residual energy of the network shall be computed as represented in equation (16).

$$E_N(t) = \sum_{i=1}^{N} E_i(t) - E_{Txi}\left[d(N_S, N_l)\right] - E_{Rxi}\left[d(N_S, N_l)\right] \tag{16}$$

The sensor nodes are initially supplied with 50 joules of energy, and a control data packet of 8 bits is communicated over the simulated network to determine the residual energy and the average energy consumed by the sensor nodes.

Figure 9. Residual energy of the network (joules)

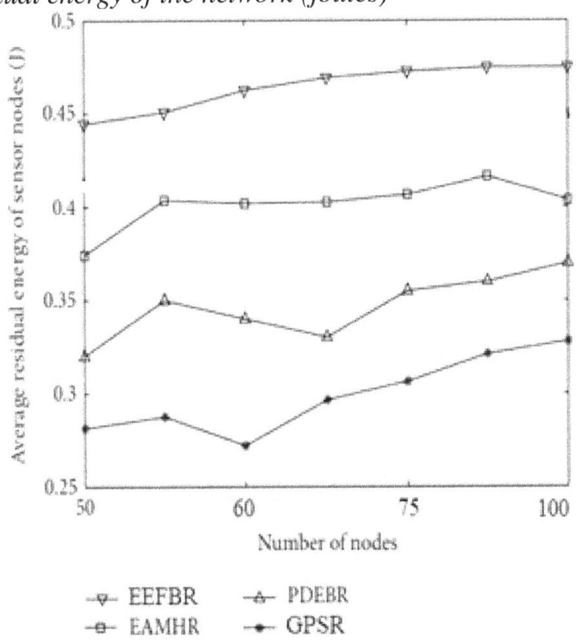

Figure 10. Average energy consumption for end-to-end transmission (J)

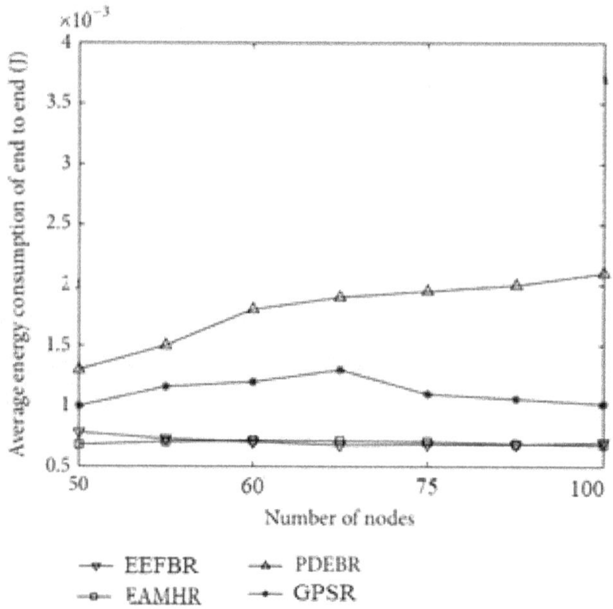

Figure 9 depicts the network's residual energy and proves that the proposed work of EEFBR possesses maximum residual energy compared to state-of-the-art routing algorithms. Figure 10 measures and describes the average energy consumption by a single node for a single hop of data communication.

Figure 10 depicts and proves that the proposed energy-efficient fuzzy-based routing algorithm consumes less energy than state-of-the-art routing algorithms.

Packet Delivery Ratio

The packet delivery ratio is determined based on the total number of data packets delivered successfully to the base station and the total packets transmitted. The proposed work advances the packet delivery ratio, as it involves the cluster head in the communication process. As a process of testing, 100 data packets were communicated from the randomly picked node to the base station. The packet delivery ratio is measured using the mathematical relationship defined in equation (17).

$$PDR = \frac{T_{PD}}{T_{PT}} \tag{17}$$

Where PDR is the Packet delivery Ration, T_{PD} is the total packet delivered successfully, and T_{PT} represents the total packets transmitted.

Figure 11. Comparison of packet delivery ratio

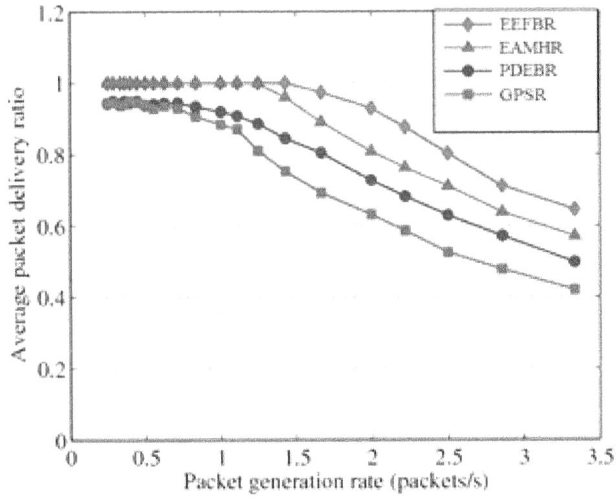

Figure 11 depicts the observed values of the Packet Delivery Ratio. It proves that the proposed Energy-Efficient Fuzzy-Based Routing (EEFBR) model outperforms the state-of-the-art routing algorithms in terms of Packet Delivery Ratio. Figure 12 proves that the proposed Energy-Efficient Fuzzy-Based Routing (EEFBR) exhibits mitigated end-to-end delay in milliseconds compared to the existing state-of-the-art routing algorithms. From the performance analysis, the proposed Energy Efficient Fuzzy Based Routing (EEFBR) advances network lifetime, residual energy, packet delivery ratio, and a mitigated end-to-end delay.

Delay

The delay in the Wireless Sensor Network is generally termed the End-to-end delay, which is the time consumed to transmit the data from one to the other end. The end-to-end delay is a vital parameter in the quality of service, as the excessive consumption of time or enhanced delay will result in the mitigation of packet delivery ratio, as the packets will drop due to the elapsing of active time duration. The proposed work of Energy Efficient Fuzzy Based Routing (EEFBR) experiences reduced delay compared to the existing routing algorithms and is depicted in Figure 12.

Figure 12. Comparison of end-to-end delay (ms)

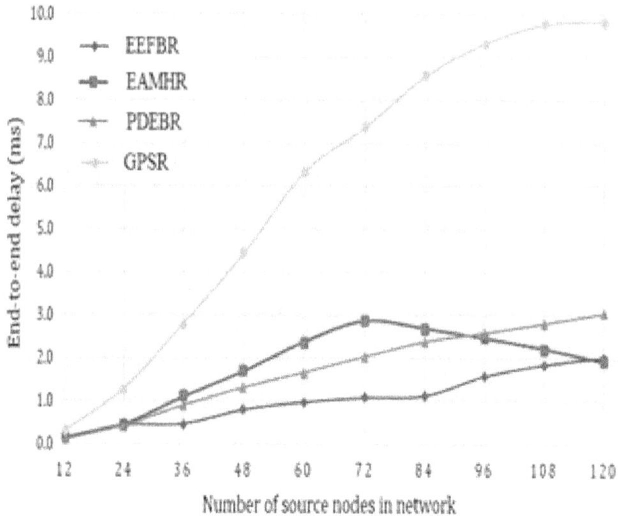

Figure 12 proves that the proposed Energy-Efficient Fuzzy-Based Routing (EEFBR) exhibits mitigated end-to-end delay in milliseconds compared to the existing state-of-the-art routing algorithms. From the performance analysis, the proposed Energy Efficient Fuzzy Based Routing (EEFBR) advances network lifetime, residual energy, packet delivery ratio, and a mitigated end-to-end delay.

CONCLUSION

The Internet of Things (IoT) is an emerging technology in the modern world that eases the automation process and can be operated and controlled using Internet connectivity. The IoT applications are made possible with the evolution and technological support provided by the Wireless Sensor Networks (WSN). The major challenge in the WSN is the network lifetime, as the sensor nodes are non-rechargeable and experience draining energy during the data communication process. As illustrated in the sections above, the routing process in wireless sensor networks consumes more energy than the energy consumed to record/capture the process and process the received data. The proposed work introduces an Energy Efficient Fuzzy Based Routing (EEFBR) model to perform an energy-based Cluster Head designation process and to form a communication path using fuzzy technology. The performance of the proposed fuzzy-based model is compared with the existing state-of-the-art routing algorithms. It has proved to be more efficient regarding energy, network lifetime, packet delivery ratio, and end-to-end delay. The performance analysis proved and exhibits that the proposed work exhibits an elevation in network lifetime by 33.16% and an elevation in residual energy by 18.99%. This system shall further be improved by enhancing the number of inputs associated with distance and energy and the number of datasets for the fuzzification process.

REFERENCES

Abu-Baker, A., Alshamali, A., & Shawaheen, Y. (2021). Energy-Efficient Cluster-Based Wireless Sensor Networks Using Adaptive Modulation: Performance Analysis. *IEEE Access : Practical Innovations, Open Solutions*, *9*, 141766–141777. DOI: 10.1109/ACCESS.2021.3118672

Al-Shareeda, M. A., Ali, A. M., Hammoud, M. A., Kazem, Z. H. M., & Hussein, M. A. (2025). Secure IoT-Based Real-Time Water Level Monitoring System Using ESP32 for Critical Infrastructure. *J. Cyber Secur. Risk Audit*, *2*, 43–52. DOI: 10.63180/jcsra.thestap.2025.2.4

Alabdali, A. M., Gharaei, N., & Mashat, A. A. (2021). A Framework for Energy-Efficient Clustering With Utilizing Wireless Energy Balancer. *IEEE Access : Practical Innovations, Open Solutions*, *9*, 117823–117831. DOI: 10.1109/ACCESS.2021.3107230

Alboalebrah, M. R., & Al-augby, S. (2025). Unveiling the Causes of Fatal Road Accidents in Iraq: An Association Rule Mining Approach Using the Apriori Algorithm. *Journal of Cyber Security and Risk Auditing*, *2025*(2), 1–11. DOI: 10.63180/jcsra.thestap.2025.2.1

Almanasir, R., Al-solomon, D., Indrawes, S., Almaiah, M., Islam, U., & Alshar'e, M. (2025). Classification of threats and countermeasures of cloud computing. *Journal of Cyber Security and Risk Auditing*, *2025*(2), 27–42. DOI: 10.63180/jcsra.thestap.2025.2.3

Almedires, M. A., Elkhalil, A., & Amin, M. (2025). Adversarial Attack Detection in Industrial Control Systems Using LSTM-Based Intrusion Detection and Black-Box Defense Strategies. *Journal of Cyber Security and Risk Auditing*, *2025*(3), 4–22. DOI: 10.63180/jcsra.thestap.2025.3.2

Almelehy, B., Ahmad, M., Nassreddine, G., Maayah, M., & Achanta, A. (2025). Analytical Analysis of Cyber Threats and Defense Mechanisms for Web Application Security. *Journal of Cyber Security and Risk Auditing*, *2025*(3), 57–76. DOI: 10.63180/jcsra.thestap.2025.3.4

Almuqren, A. A. (2025). Cybersecurity threats, countermeasures and mitigation techniques on the IoT: Future research directions. *Journal of Cyber Security and Risk Auditing*, *1*(1), 1–11. DOI: 10.63180/jcsra.thestap.2025.1.1

Ang, S., Ho, M., Huy, S., & Janarthanan, M. (2025). Utilizing IDS and IPS to Improve Cybersecurity Monitoring Process. *Journal of Cyber Security and Risk Auditing*, *2025*(3), 77–88. DOI: 10.63180/jcsra.thestap.2025.3.10

Behera, T. M., Mohapatra, S. K., Samal, U. C., Khan, M. S., Daneshmand, M., & Gandomi, A. H. (2020). I-SEP: An Improved Routing Protocol for Heterogeneous WSN for IoT-Based Environmental Monitoring. *IEEE Internet of Things Journal*, *7*(1), 710–717. DOI: 10.1109/JIOT.2019.2940988

Fu, X., Yang, Y., & Postolache, O. (2021). Sustainable Multipath Routing Protocol for Multi-Sink Wireless Sensor Networks in Harsh Environments. *IEEE Transactions on Sustainable Computing*, *6*(1), 168–181. DOI: 10.1109/TSUSC.2020.2976096

Han, D., Du, X., & Liu, X. (2021). CELR: Connectivity and Energy Aware Layering Routing Protocol for UANs. *IEEE Sensors Journal*, *21*(5), 7046–7057. DOI: 10.1109/JSEN.2020.3039808

Haseeb, K., Almustafa, K. M., Jan, Z., Saba, T., & Tariq, U. (2020). Secure and Energy-Aware Heuristic Routing Protocol for Wireless Sensor Network. *IEEE Access : Practical Innovations, Open Solutions*, *8*, 163962–163974. DOI: 10.1109/ACCESS.2020.3022285

Hassan, A. A. H., Shah, W. M., Habeb, A. H. H., Othman, M. F. I., & Al-Mhiqani, M. N. (2020). An Improved Energy-Efficient Clustering Protocol to Prolong the Lifetime of the WSN-Based IoT. *IEEE Access : Practical Innovations, Open Solutions*, *8*, 200500–200517. DOI: 10.1109/ACCESS.2020.3035624

He, S., Xie, K., Chen, W., Zhang, D., & Wen, J. (2018). Energy-Aware Routing for SWIPT in Multi-Hop Energy-Constrained Wireless Network. *IEEE Access : Practical Innovations, Open Solutions*, *6*, 17996–18008. DOI: 10.1109/ACCESS.2018.2820093

Huang, H., Yin, H., Min, G., Zhang, J., Wu, Y., & Zhang, X. (2018). Energy-Aware Dual-Path Geographic Routing to Bypass Routing Holes in Wireless Sensor Networks. *IEEE Transactions on Mobile Computing*, *17*(6), 1339–1352. DOI: 10.1109/TMC.2017.2771424

Ibrahim, A. A. Z., Hashim, F., Sali, A., Noordin, N. K., & Fadul, S. M. E. (2022). A Multi-Objective Routing Mechanism for Energy Management Optimization in SDN Multi-Control Architecture. *IEEE Access : Practical Innovations, Open Solutions*, *10*, 20312–20327. DOI: 10.1109/ACCESS.2022.3149795

Kim, J., Lee, H., & Chong, S. (2018). Traffic-Aware Energy-Saving Base Station Sleeping and Clustering in Cooperative Networks. *IEEE Transactions on Wireless Communications*, *17*(2), 1173–1186. DOI: 10.1109/TWC.2017.2776916

Lippi, G., Aljawarneh, M., Al-Na'amneh, Q., Hazaymih, R., & Dhomeja, L. D. (2025). Security and Privacy Challenges and Solutions in Autonomous Driving Systems: A Comprehensive Review. *Journal of Cyber Security and Risk Auditing*, *2025*(3), 23–41. DOI: 10.63180/jcsra.thestap.2025.3.3

Ma, N., Zhang, H., Hu, H., & Qin, Y. (2022). ESCVAD: An Energy-Saving Routing Protocol Based on Voronoi Adaptive Clustering for Wireless Sensor Networks. *IEEE Internet of Things Journal*, *9*(11), 9071–9085. DOI: 10.1109/JIOT.2021.3120744

Misra, S., & Goswami, S. (2014). Routing in Wireless Sensor Networks. In Network Routing: Fundamentals, Applications, and Emerging Technologies (pp. 285–325). Wiley. DOI: 10.1002/9781119114864.ch11

Mousa, R. S., & Shehab, R. (2025). Applying risk analysis for determining threats and countermeasures in workstation domain. *Journal of Cyber Security and Risk Auditing*, *2025*(1), 12–21. DOI: 10.63180/jcsra.thestap.2025.1.2

Muzammal, S. M., Murugesan, R. K., & Jhanjhi, N. Z. (2021). A Comprehensive Review on Secure Routing in Internet of Things: Mitigation Methods and Trust-Based Approaches. *IEEE Internet of Things Journal*, *8*(6), 4186–4210. DOI: 10.1109/JIOT.2020.3031162

Nguyen, T. D., Khan, J. Y., & Ngo, D. T. (2018). A Distributed Energy-Harvesting-Aware Routing Algorithm for Heterogeneous IoT Networks. *IEEE Transactions on Green Communications and Networking*, *2*(4), 1115–1127. DOI: 10.1109/TGCN.2018.2839593

Otoom, S. (2025). Risk auditing for Digital Twins in cyber physical systems: A systematic review. *Journal of Cyber Security and Risk Auditing*, *2025*(1), 22–35. DOI: 10.63180/jcsra.thestap.2025.1.3

Patel, N. R., Kumar, S., & Singh, S. K. (2021). Energy and Collision Aware WSN Routing Protocol for Sustainable and Intelligent IoT Applications. *IEEE Sensors Journal*, *21*(22), 25282–25292. DOI: 10.1109/JSEN.2021.3076192

Shagari, N. M., Idris, M. Y. I., Salleh, R. B., Ahmedy, I., Murtaza, G., & Shehadeh, H. A. (2020). Heterogeneous Energy and Traffic Aware Sleep-Awake Cluster-Based Routing Protocol for Wireless Sensor Network. *IEEE Access : Practical Innovations, Open Solutions*, *8*, 12232–12252. DOI: 10.1109/ACCESS.2020.2965206

Wang, C., Zhang, Y., Wang, X., & Zhang, Z. (2018). Hybrid Multihop Partition-Based Clustering Routing Protocol for WSNs. *IEEE Sensors Letters*, *2*(1), 1–4. DOI: 10.1109/LSENS.2018.2803086

Wang, K., Yu, C. M., & Wang, L. C. (2021). DORA: A Destination-Oriented Routing Algorithm for Energy-Balanced Wireless Sensor Networks. *IEEE Internet of Things Journal*, *8*(3), 2080–2081. DOI: 10.1109/JIOT.2020.3025039

Wang, Z., Ding, H., Li, B., Bao, L., & Yang, Z. (2020). An Energy Efficient Routing Protocol Based on Improved Artificial Bee Colony Algorithm for Wireless Sensor Networks. *IEEE Access : Practical Innovations, Open Solutions*, *8*, 133577–133596. DOI: 10.1109/ACCESS.2020.3010313

Xu, C., Xiong, Z., Zhao, G., & Yu, S. (2019). An Energy-Efficient Region Source Routing Protocol for Lifetime Maximization in WSN. *IEEE Access : Practical Innovations, Open Solutions*, *7*, 135277–135289. DOI: 10.1109/ACCESS.2019.2942321

Xu, Y., Jiao, W., & Tian, M. (2021). An Energy-Efficient Routing Protocol for 3D Wireless Sensor Networks. *IEEE Sensors Journal*, *21*(17), 19550–19559. DOI: 10.1109/JSEN.2021.3086806

Yao, Q., Huang, A., Shan, H., Quek, T. Q. S., & Wang, W. (2016). Delay-Aware Wireless Powered Communication Networks—Energy Balancing and Optimization. *IEEE Transactions on Wireless Communications*, *15*(8), 5272–5286. DOI: 10.1109/TWC.2016.2555803

Yun, W. K., & Yoo, S. J. (2021). Q-Learning-Based Data-Aggregation-Aware Energy-Efficient Routing Protocol for Wireless Sensor Networks. *IEEE Access : Practical Innovations, Open Solutions*, *9*, 10737–10750. DOI: 10.1109/ACCESS.2021.3051360

KEY TERMS AND DEFINITIONS

Data Communication Model: Explains how sensor nodes collect and wirelessly send data to other devices or a central location, such as a sink node.

Energy Efficient Routing Protocol: In wireless sensor networks (WSNs), energy efficient routing protocol are intended to maximize network lifetime while reducing energy usage. To choose the most effective path, these protocols take into account variables including transmission power, distance, and battery life.

Fuzzy Modeling: The definition of fuzzy modeling is an extension of classical logic that makes use of fuzzy set theory to provide models with adaptable decision limits that more accurately reflect the features of particular applications.

Internet of Things (IoT): describes a network of physical objects, or "things," that have sensors, software, and other technologies integrated into them so they can gather and share data with other systems and devices online.

Multi-Hop Communication: Describes a transmission method in which data passes via several intermediary nodes, also known as relays, before arriving at its final destination.

Packet Delivery Ratio: A networking metric known as the (PDR) calculates the success rate of data packet delivery, or the proportion of packets that arrive at their destination undamaged or lost.

Wireless Network Security: Process of designing, implementing and ensuring security on a wireless computer network. It is a subset of network security that adds protection for a wireless computer network.

Wireless Sensor Network (WSN): An infrastructure-less wireless network used to monitor environmental, physical, or system conditions by deploying a large number of wireless sensors on an as-needed basis.

Chapter 3
AI-Driven Threat Detection and Incident Response:
Advancing Cybersecurity With Machine Learning

Tarun Kumar Vashishth
https://orcid.org/0000-0001-9916-9575
IIMT University, Meerut, India

Rajeev Sharma
https://orcid.org/0000-0002-3354-558X
IIMT University, Meerut, India

Vikas Sharma
https://orcid.org/0000-0001-8173-4548
IIMT University, Meerut, India

Kewal Krishan Sharma
https://orcid.org/0009-0001-2504-9607
IIMT University, Meerut, India

Mukesh Kumar Sharma
https://orcid.org/0000-0003-3071-5931
Chaudhary Charan Singh University, Meerut, India

Sangeeta Sharma
IAMR College, Meerut, India

ABSTRACT

The rise of sophisticated cyber threats necessitates advanced security mechanisms for real-time threat detection and incident response. This chapter explores the integration of Artificial Intelligence (AI) and Machine Learning (ML) in cybersecurity to enhance threat detection, anomaly identification, and automated incident response. It examines ML-based anomaly detection techniques, deep learning models for malware classification, and AI-driven intrusion detection systems. Additionally, it highlights the role of AI in automating Security Operations Centers (SOCs) and improving response efficiency. By leveraging AI-driven playbooks and predictive

DOI: 10.4018/979-8-3373-2115-8.ch003

analytics, organizations can proactively mitigate cyber risks. The chapter also discusses challenges, ethical considerations, and future research directions in AI-powered cybersecurity solutions.

INTRODUCTION

The rapid digital transformation across industries has led to an exponential increase in cyber threats, ranging from malware and phishing attacks to sophisticated advanced persistent threats (APTs) and zero-day exploits. Traditional cybersecurity measures, such as rule-based systems and signature-based detection, often struggle to keep pace with these evolving threats due to their static nature and reliance on predefined patterns. As a result, organizations require more adaptive and intelligent security mechanisms that can detect and respond to cyber incidents in real time. This is where Artificial Intelligence (AI) and Machine Learning (ML) play a transformative role in modern cybersecurity. By leveraging AI-driven techniques, security systems can analyze vast amounts of data, identify subtle anomalies indicative of malicious activity, and automate threat response processes with minimal human intervention. Machine learning models, particularly those using deep learning and neural networks, enhance the accuracy and efficiency of threat detection by continuously learning from new attack patterns and adapting to emerging cyber risks. Additionally, AI-powered Security Operations Centers (SOCs) enable organizations to streamline security workflows, prioritize threats based on risk assessment, and deploy automated incident response mechanisms to mitigate attacks before they cause significant damage. Despite these advancements, AI-driven cybersecurity also presents challenges, including adversarial attacks, ethical concerns, and the need for regulatory compliance. This chapter explores the integration of AI and ML in cybersecurity, highlighting their applications in anomaly detection, malware classification, intrusion detection, and incident response automation. By addressing the opportunities and challenges associated with AI-powered security solutions, this discussion aims to provide a comprehensive understanding of how AI-driven technologies can enhance cybersecurity resilience and proactively combat modern cyber threats (Ashfin, 2024).

Overview of Evolving Cyber Threats and Security Challenges

The cybersecurity landscape has become increasingly complex due to the rapid expansion of digital infrastructure and the growing sophistication of cyber threats. Traditional security approaches, which primarily rely on signature-based detection and rule-based systems, are no longer sufficient to counter modern cyber risks.

Cybercriminals employ advanced techniques such as polymorphic malware, fileless attacks, ransomware-as-a-service (RaaS), and artificial intelligence-driven cyber-attacks to bypass conventional security defences. Additionally, the proliferation of Internet of Things (IoT) devices, cloud computing, and remote work environments has expanded the attack surface, making organizations more vulnerable to cyber threats. One of the most pressing challenges in cybersecurity is the rise of zero-day attacks, where attackers exploit unknown vulnerabilities before security patches are available. Similarly, advanced persistent threats (APTs) involve prolonged and stealthy cyber intrusions aimed at exfiltrating sensitive data from government agencies, corporations, and critical infrastructure (Vashishth et al., 2024). Moreover, ransomware attacks have surged, targeting businesses, hospitals, and financial institutions, often demanding substantial payments in cryptocurrency. Phishing and social engineering attacks have also become more sophisticated, leveraging AI to craft highly convincing deceptive messages that bypass traditional email filters and deceive users. The increasing use of AI by cybercriminals further complicates cybersecurity efforts. AI-generated deepfake attacks, automated botnets, and AI-powered penetration testing tools allow attackers to carry out highly targeted and adaptive attacks. Additionally, the evolution of cybercrime-as-a-service (CaaS) enables even non-technical criminals to access advanced hacking tools and exploit vulnerabilities with ease. These threats, combined with a global shortage of skilled cybersecurity professionals, have led to an overwhelming number of security alerts, making it difficult for Security Operations Centers (SOCs) to effectively manage and respond to incidents in real-time. As cyber threats continue to evolve, organizations must shift from reactive security strategies to proactive, AI-driven cybersecurity solutions. AI and Machine Learning (ML) can enhance cybersecurity by detecting anomalous behaviours, automating threat response, and predicting attacks before they occur. By leveraging AI for real-time analysis, automated security workflows, and predictive threat intelligence, organizations can strengthen their security posture against emerging threats. However, AI-driven cybersecurity also introduces challenges such as adversarial AI, data privacy concerns, and the need for robust regulatory compliance frameworks. This chapter explores these evolving threats and security challenges, highlighting how AI and ML technologies can revolutionize threat detection and incident response mechanisms in the digital age (Anandharaj, 2024).

Need for AI and ML in Modern Cybersecurity

The increasing complexity, volume, and sophistication of cyber threats have made traditional security mechanisms insufficient to protect digital assets effectively. Rule-based and signature-based approaches, while useful for detecting known threats, struggle to adapt to evolving attack patterns, especially zero-day vulnerabilities, polymorphic malware, and advanced persistent threats (APTs). Cybercriminals now leverage automation, artificial intelligence (AI), and machine learning (ML) to craft sophisticated attacks, making it imperative for cybersecurity defences to evolve accordingly. AI and ML provide the much-needed capability to detect, analyze, and respond to threats in real-time, enhancing the overall resilience of cybersecurity systems. One of the primary advantages of AI in cybersecurity is its ability to process vast amounts of security data quickly and efficiently. Traditional security teams are often overwhelmed by the sheer number of alerts generated by security systems, leading to alert fatigue and slow response times. AI-driven security solutions can analyze logs, network traffic, and user behavior in real time, distinguishing between benign activities and potential threats. Machine learning-based anomaly detection enables cybersecurity systems to identify previously unknown attack patterns, reducing reliance on predefined signatures and improving detection accuracy (Khan et al., 2024).

AI and ML also play a crucial role in automating threat detection and incident response (TDIR). Security Operations Centers (SOCs) can leverage AI-driven automated security playbooks to rapidly detect and neutralize threats, reducing the need for manual intervention. AI-powered intrusion detection systems (IDS) and intrusion prevention systems (IPS) use behavioural analysis and deep learning models to recognize subtle signs of malicious activity. Additionally, AI enhances malware detection by analyzing code structure, execution behavior, and relationships between files, enabling more effective detection of zero-day malware and fileless attacks. Another critical aspect of AI-driven cybersecurity is predictive threat intelligence. By leveraging historical attack data and AI-driven analytics, organizations can anticipate future attack vectors and proactively strengthen their defences. AI-based models can correlate data from multiple sources, uncover hidden attack patterns, and provide risk-based prioritization of security threats, allowing organizations to allocate resources effectively. Furthermore, natural language processing (NLP) enables AI systems to scan and analyze threat intelligence reports, social media, and dark web activities to identify potential risks before they materialize. Despite the advantages, the integration of AI and ML in cybersecurity also presents challenges, such as adversarial attacks against AI models, bias in training data, and ethical concerns regarding automation in security decisions. Additionally, the effectiveness of AI-based cybersecurity solutions depends on high-quality, continuously updated datasets and robust model training methodologies. Addressing these challenges requires a balanced approach that combines AI-driven automation with human expertise, ensuring that cybersecurity professionals can focus on strategic decision-making while AI handles large-scale data processing and threat detection (Gupta et al., 2024).

As cyber threats continue to evolve, the need for AI and ML in cybersecurity becomes more urgent. Organizations that embrace AI-powered security solutions can enhance threat detection accuracy, improve incident response times, and mitigate cyber risks more effectively. This chapter further explores the various AI and ML techniques used in cybersecurity, demonstrating how they can revolutionize threat detection, intrusion prevention, and automated incident response in modern security frameworks.

FUNDAMENTALS OF AI AND MACHINE LEARNING IN CYBERSECURITY

The integration of Artificial Intelligence (AI) and Machine Learning (ML) in cybersecurity has transformed traditional security measures by introducing intelligent, adaptive, and automated defense mechanisms. AI and ML enable cybersecurity systems to analyze massive datasets, detect anomalies, and respond to threats in real time. This section explores the fundamental principles of AI and ML in cybersecurity, including key concepts, learning techniques, and the role of data in training effective models.

Overview of AI and ML Techniques Relevant to Cybersecurity

Artificial Intelligence (AI) and Machine Learning (ML) have revolutionized cybersecurity by enabling systems to detect, analyze, and respond to cyber threats more effectively. Traditional security mechanisms, such as rule-based detection and signature-based antivirus systems, are no longer sufficient to counter the increasing complexity of cyberattacks. AI and ML techniques provide a proactive and adaptive approach to threat detection and mitigation. Key AI-driven techniques in cybersecurity include anomaly detection, predictive analytics, and automated threat intelligence processing. Anomaly detection, powered by ML models, helps identify deviations from normal behavior, enabling the detection of unknown threats such as zero-day attacks and insider threats. Predictive analytics uses historical attack data to forecast potential cyber threats, allowing organizations to strengthen their defences in advance. AI also enhances Security Information and Event Management (SIEM) systems by automating threat correlation and prioritization, helping security analysts focus on high-risk incidents. Furthermore, deep learning models, including neural networks and natural language processing (NLP), are leveraged for malware classification, phishing detection, and automated response mechanisms. As cybercriminals increasingly use AI to launch sophisticated attacks, the integration of AI and ML in cybersecurity has become essential for organizations to stay ahead in the ongoing battle against cyber threats (Patil, 2024).

Supervised, Unsupervised, and Reinforcement Learning in Security Applications

Machine Learning (ML) has revolutionized cybersecurity by providing intelligent, adaptive, and automated solutions to detect, analyze, and respond to cyber threats. Among the different learning approaches in ML, supervised learning, unsupervised learning, and reinforcement learning play a crucial role in various security applications (Gupta and Srivastava, 2025). Each method has unique characteristics and applications in cybersecurity, allowing organizations to strengthen their defences against increasingly sophisticated cyber threats.

1. **Supervised Learning in Cybersecurity:** Supervised learning is a widely used ML approach that relies on labelled datasets to train models. In this technique, the algorithm learns from historical data, where each input is associated with a known output. The model then applies this learned knowledge to classify or predict new data accurately. In cybersecurity, supervised learning is particularly effective for malware detection, phishing detection, and intrusion detection. For example, an AI-driven malware classification system can be trained using a dataset containing labelled malware and benign files. The model analyses feature such as file structure, byte sequences, and behavior patterns to distinguish between malicious and non-malicious files. Popular algorithms used in supervised learning include Decision Trees, Support Vector Machines (SVMs), Random Forests, and Deep Neural Networks. Another critical application of supervised learning is spam and phishing email detection. By training models on datasets of phishing and legitimate emails, AI-powered email security systems can identify suspicious messages based on subject lines, sender details, embedded links, and attachment types. Services such as Google's Gmail spam filter use supervised learning to continuously improve phishing detection accuracy by adapting to new attack patterns. Supervised learning is also used in intrusion detection systems (IDS), where ML models analyze network traffic logs and classify them as normal or malicious based on predefined attack signatures. However, one limitation of supervised learning is its reliance on labelled datasets, which may require extensive human effort to create and update. Additionally, supervised models may struggle to detect new or unknown cyber threats that are not present in the training data (Kumar and Guleria, 2024).

Figure 1. Supervised learning approach in cybersecurity

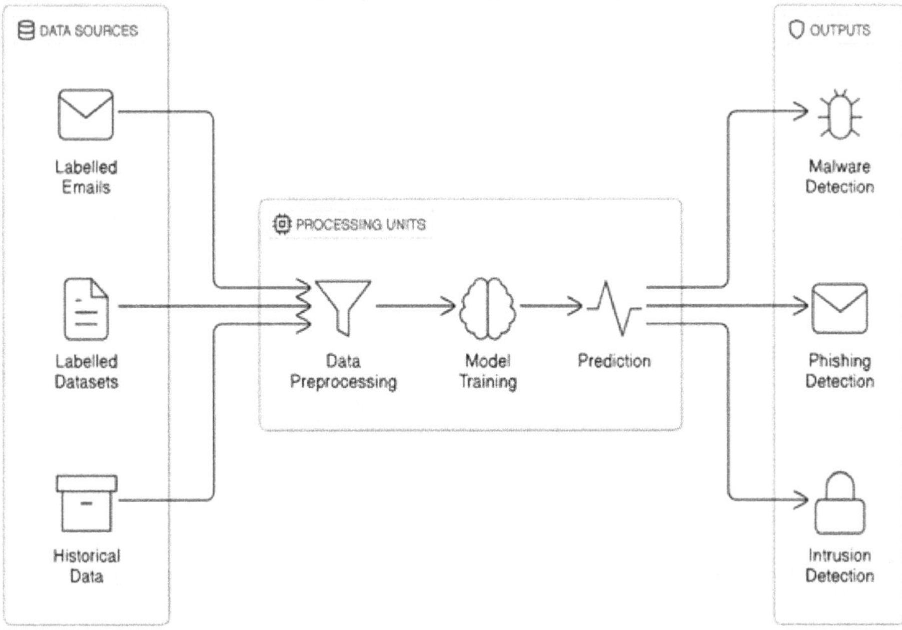

2. **Unsupervised Learning in Cybersecurity:** Unsupervised learning differs from supervised learning in that it does not require labelled datasets. Instead, it identifies hidden patterns, anomalies, and structures within the data. This capability makes unsupervised learning highly effective for anomaly detection, insider threat detection, and advanced persistent threat (APT) detection. One of the most significant applications of unsupervised learning in cybersecurity is anomaly-based intrusion detection. Unlike signature-based detection systems, which rely on predefined attack signatures, anomaly detection models establish a baseline of normal network behavior and then flag deviations that may indicate potential threats. For example, an anomaly detection system in a banking network might detect an unusual transaction pattern, such as a sudden large withdrawal from an unrecognized location, and raise an alert for possible fraud. Common algorithms used in unsupervised learning include k-means clustering, hierarchical clustering, Principal Component Analysis (PCA), and Autoencoders.
3. **Reinforcement Learning in Cybersecurity:** Reinforcement Learning (RL) is a dynamic ML approach where an agent learns to make decisions by interacting with its environment and receiving rewards or penalties based on its actions. Unlike supervised and unsupervised learning, RL continuously improves its

decision-making capabilities through trial and error. One of the most promising applications of RL in cybersecurity is automated security policy optimization. For example, RL can be used to optimize firewall rules and access control policies in real-time, adapting to evolving attack strategies. Instead of relying on manually configured security rules, an RL-based system can experiment with different rule sets and learn which configurations provide the best protection while minimizing disruptions. Another key application is in automated cyber defense systems, where RL agents simulate attack scenarios and develop optimal defense strategies (Mazher et al., 2024).

By leveraging a combination of these ML approaches, cybersecurity systems can achieve greater accuracy, efficiency, and resilience in combating cyber threats. As cybercriminals continue to evolve their attack strategies, integrating AI-driven ML techniques into cybersecurity frameworks is crucial to maintaining a proactive and adaptive defense posture.

Role of Big Data and Cloud Computing in AI-Driven Security

The rapid advancement of cyber threats has necessitated the integration of big data and cloud computing in AI-driven cybersecurity solutions. Traditional security systems often struggle to handle the sheer volume, velocity, and variety of cyber threat data generated across digital infrastructures. With the rise of distributed networks, IoT devices, and sophisticated malware, organizations require scalable and intelligent security mechanisms that can process vast amounts of data in real time. Big data analytics and cloud computing serve as foundational technologies that enable AI-driven security solutions to be more effective, adaptive, and proactive in detecting and mitigating cyber threats.

1. **Big Data in AI-Driven Cybersecurity:** Big data plays a critical role in enhancing AI-based threat detection, risk assessment, and predictive analytics. Cybersecurity systems generate massive amounts of log data from various sources, including firewalls, intrusion detection systems (IDS), endpoint devices, and network traffic. Analyzing this data in real-time requires advanced machine learning (ML) algorithms capable of identifying patterns, correlations, and anomalies indicative of cyber threats. One of the key applications of big data in cybersecurity is anomaly detection. AI-powered security systems leverage big data analytics to establish a baseline of normal behavior across networks and detect deviations that may signal intrusions, malware activity, or insider threats. By continuously analyzing vast amounts of log files and network traffic data, AI models can identify zero-day attacks, advanced persistent threats (APTs), and

suspicious activities that traditional rule-based systems might miss. Big data also facilitates predictive threat intelligence, allowing security teams to anticipate cyberattacks before they occur. AI-driven models trained on historical cyber threat data can recognize emerging attack trends and proactively strengthen security measures. For examplc, Sccurity Information and Event Management (SIEM) systems use big data analytics to aggregate and correlate security events from multiple sources, providing comprehensive threat intelligence (Adeyeye et al., 2024).

2. **Cloud Computing in AI-Driven Security:** Cloud computing has transformed the cybersecurity landscape by offering scalable, cost-effective, and on-demand security solutions. AI-powered security services deployed in the cloud enable organizations to detect, analyze, and respond to cyber threats without the limitations of on-premise infrastructure. With the increasing adoption of cloud-based applications, organizations leverage AI-driven cloud security models to monitor, protect, and mitigate cyber risks in real time. One of the primary advantages of cloud computing in AI-driven security is scalability. AI algorithms require significant computational resources to process large datasets, train deep learning models, and execute real-time threat detection. Cloud platforms such as Amazon Web Services (AWS), Microsoft Azure, and Google Cloud provide elastic computing capabilities that allow organizations to scale security operations based on demand. These platforms offer AI-based security services, including automated threat detection, security analytics, and risk assessment. Cloud computing also enables centralized security management, allowing organizations to monitor cybersecurity incidents across distributed environments from a unified dashboard. Cloud-based SIEM systems and Extended Detection and Response (XDR) platforms aggregate security logs, endpoint data, and user activities from multiple locations, providing a comprehensive view of an organization's threat landscape. AI-driven cloud security analytics help identify malware infections, unauthorized access attempts, and privilege escalation attacks across cloud environments (Vashishth et al., 2024). Another critical aspect of cloud-based AI security is automated incident response. AI-driven security solutions hosted in the cloud can automatically respond to cyber threats by isolating compromised devices, blocking malicious traffic, and deploying security patches. For example, Cloud Access Security Brokers (CASBs) leverage AI to monitor cloud activity, enforce security policies, and detect insider threats. Google Chronicle and Microsoft Defender for Cloud use AI to analyze security logs and provide actionable insights to security teams. However, cloud security also introduces new challenges such as data sovereignty, compliance risks, and cloud-based cyber threats like account hijacking and misconfigured security settings. To address these concerns, organizations implement multi-cloud security frameworks, Zero

Trust Architecture (ZTA), and AI-driven risk assessment tools that continuously monitor cloud environments for vulnerabilities and security breaches (Hassan and Ibrahim, 2023).

Big data and cloud computing have become essential components of AI-driven cybersecurity, enabling organizations to enhance threat detection, risk management, and automated incident response. While big data analytics empowers AI models to process and analyze massive volumes of security data, cloud computing provides the scalability and flexibility needed to deploy AI-based security solutions effectively. By leveraging cloud-based AI security services and big data-driven threat intelligence, organizations can proactively defend against modern cyber threats, automate security operations, and strengthen their overall cybersecurity posture.

ML-BASED ANOMALY DETECTION FOR CYBER THREATS

Machine learning (ML)-based anomaly detection has emerged as a powerful approach in cybersecurity to identify suspicious activities, detect cyber threats, and mitigate security breaches in real time. Traditional rule-based security systems often fail to keep up with the rapidly evolving nature of cyberattacks, as attackers continuously develop new techniques to evade detection. ML-driven anomaly detection systems, however, can learn patterns from large volumes of network traffic, user behavior, and system logs, enabling them to identify deviations that may indicate potential threats. These AI-driven methods help in detecting zero-day attacks, insider threats, advanced persistent threats (APTs), and fraudulent activities before they cause significant damage.

Definition and Significance of Anomaly Detection

Anomaly detection is a critical technique in cybersecurity that involves identifying unusual patterns, behaviours, or deviations from expected norms within a system. In the context of cybersecurity, anomalies often indicate potential security threats such as malware infections, unauthorized access, data breaches, insider threats, and advanced persistent threats (APTs). Unlike traditional rule-based security systems that rely on predefined attack signatures, anomaly detection leverages machine learning (ML) and statistical models to identify unknown or emerging threats in real time. The significance of anomaly detection lies in its ability to detect threats that bypass traditional security mechanisms, including zero-day attacks and sophisticated cyberattacks that do not have known signatures. By continuously monitoring network traffic, system logs, and user activities, ML-based anomaly detection systems can establish a baseline of normal behavior and detect deviations that may indicate security incidents. This capability is essential in modern cybersecurity, as attackers constantly evolve their techniques to evade traditional security measures. Anomaly detection plays a crucial role in various cybersecurity applications, including intrusion detection systems (IDS), fraud detection, endpoint security, and cloud security monitoring (Jyothsna et al., 2025).

Figure 2. Anomaly detection in cybersecurity

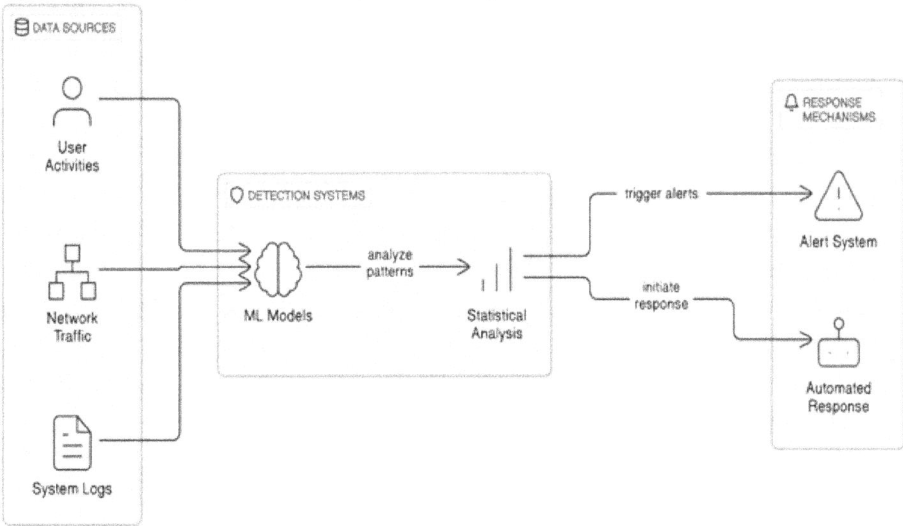

Techniques: Statistical Models, Clustering, Neural Networks

Each of these anomaly detection techniques—statistical models, clustering, and neural networks—plays a crucial role in modern cybersecurity. While statistical methods offer simplicity and efficiency, clustering provides flexibility in detecting unknown threats, and deep learning models deliver high accuracy in identifying complex cyber threats. Integrating these techniques enables organizations to build robust security systems capable of real-time threat detection and response.

1. **Statistical Models for Anomaly Detection:** Statistical models are one of the earliest and most widely used techniques for anomaly detection in cybersecurity. These models work by establishing a baseline of normal system behavior based on historical data and identifying deviations from this expected norm. Common statistical methods include Gaussian distribution, Z-score analysis, hypothesis

testing, and time-series analysis. These techniques analyze network traffic, user behavior, and system logs to detect outliers that may indicate security threats such as intrusions, malware infections, or fraud attempts. Statistical anomaly detection is effective in environments where normal behavior is well-defined; however, it can struggle with complex and evolving cyber threats that do not conform to strict statistical assumptions. Despite this limitation, statistical methods are often integrated with machine learning models to improve accuracy and reduce false positives.

2. **Clustering-Based Anomaly Detection:** Clustering is an unsupervised machine learning technique used to group similar data points and detect anomalies based on their deviation from normal clusters. Popular clustering algorithms include K-Means, DBSCAN (Density-Based Spatial Clustering of Applications with Noise), and hierarchical clustering. These methods analyze large datasets and group similar behaviours together while flagging data points that do not fit into any cluster as potential anomalies. Clustering-based anomaly detection is particularly effective in identifying network intrusions, fraudulent transactions, and insider threats by grouping normal user behaviours and detecting deviations that may indicate malicious activity. One of the key advantages of clustering is its ability to detect previously unknown threats, making it highly valuable in cybersecurity. However, it requires careful selection of features and distance metrics to ensure accurate threat detection.
3. **Neural Networks for Anomaly Detection:** Neural networks, particularly deep learning architectures, have revolutionized anomaly detection by enabling more sophisticated and adaptive cybersecurity solutions. Autoencoders, recurrent neural networks (RNNs), and generative adversarial networks (GANs) are commonly used in AI-driven security applications. Autoencoders, a type of deep learning model, learn to compress and reconstruct normal data patterns; deviations in reconstruction errors indicate potential anomalies. RNNs are particularly useful for analyzing sequential data, such as detecting anomalous patterns in network traffic or user activity logs over time. GANs, on the other hand, generate synthetic data to enhance anomaly detection models by training them to distinguish between normal and malicious activities. The strength of neural networks lies in their ability to detect complex, multi-dimensional patterns and adapt to evolving cyber threats.

Case Studies: AI-Driven Anomaly Detection in Network Security

The integration of AI-driven anomaly detection in network security has significantly improved threat detection, response time, and overall cybersecurity resilience. Several real-world case studies highlight how organizations and security teams leverage machine learning (ML) and artificial intelligence (AI) to detect and mitigate cyber threats effectively (JothiShri et al., 2024). The following case studies demonstrate the impact of AI-powered anomaly detection in different cybersecurity scenarios.

Case Study 1: AI-Powered Intrusion Detection System in a Financial Institution

A leading global financial institution implemented an AI-driven Intrusion Detection System (IDS) to combat the increasing number of cyberattacks targeting sensitive financial data. Traditional rule-based security systems failed to detect sophisticated attacks such as zero-day exploits and insider threats. By integrating unsupervised machine learning algorithms, including clustering and autoencoders, the institution was able to analyze large volumes of network traffic and detect unusual patterns in real time. The AI system identified anomalous access patterns and fraudulent transactions, preventing a potential data breach. As a result, the financial institution experienced a 40% reduction in undetected cyber threats and a significant improvement in response time.

Case Study 2: AI-Driven Threat Detection in a Cloud-Based Enterprise

A multinational technology company, heavily reliant on cloud-based infrastructure, faced persistent cyber threats such as distributed denial-of-service (DDoS) attacks, malware intrusions, and unauthorized access attempts. The company deployed an AI-based anomaly detection system using deep learning techniques, including recurrent neural networks (RNNs) and generative adversarial networks (GANs). These models continuously monitored cloud traffic and detected anomalies in authentication attempts, API usage, and server resource consumption. By leveraging AI-driven security solutions, the company reduced security incidents by 60% and enhanced the accuracy of false-positive detections, reducing alert fatigue among security analysts.

Case Study 3: AI-Enhanced User Behavior Analytics (UBA) in Government Cybersecurity

A government cybersecurity agency implemented User Behavior Analytics (UBA) powered by AI to identify insider threats and unauthorized activities within classified networks. By leveraging machine learning models trained on historical access logs and network behaviours, the system flagged unusual login locations, unauthorized data transfers, and irregular working-hour activities. The AI-driven UBA successfully prevented multiple insider threat incidents by alerting security teams before any damage occurred. The implementation of AI-based anomaly detection in government security led to a 75% improvement in insider threat detection and enhanced national cybersecurity resilience.

These case studies illustrate the transformative impact of AI-driven anomaly detection in network security across different sectors. By utilizing machine learning, deep learning, and behavioural analytics, organizations can proactively detect cyber threats, reduce response time, and strengthen their cybersecurity posture. The future of AI in network security continues to evolve, with advancements in predictive analytics, real-time threat intelligence, and automated incident response shaping next-generation cybersecurity solutions (Manoharan and Sarker, 2023).

DEEP LEARNING FOR MALWARE CLASSIFICATION AND DETECTION

With the increasing sophistication of cyber threats, traditional malware detection techniques such as signature-based and heuristic-based methods have become less effective in identifying new and evolving malware. Deep learning (DL), a subset of machine learning, has emerged as a powerful approach for malware classification and detection by leveraging large datasets and complex pattern recognition capabilities.

Introduction to Malware Detection Challenges

Malware detection is a crucial component of cybersecurity, yet it faces numerous challenges due to the evolving nature of cyber threats. Traditional detection techniques, such as signature-based methods, struggle to keep pace with sophisticated malware that employs various evasion techniques. This section explores key challenges in malware detection, highlighting the complexities involved in identifying and mitigating modern cyber threats.

1. **Polymorphic and Metamorphic Malware:** Polymorphic and metamorphic malware present significant hurdles for traditional signature-based detection systems. Polymorphic malware modifies its code or encrypts itself with each new infection, while metamorphic malware completely rewrites its structure without changing its core functionality. These techniques make it difficult for security tools to recognize malicious code based on predefined patterns, necessitating advanced heuristic and behavior-based detection approaches.
2. **Zero-Day Attacks:** Zero-day attacks exploit software vulnerabilities that are unknown to security vendors and developers. Since no official patches or signatures exist at the time of the attack, conventional detection methods fail to prevent these threats. Cybercriminals actively seek and exploit such vulnerabilities, making proactive threat intelligence, machine learning-based anomaly detection, and behavior monitoring essential for identifying suspicious activities indicative of zero-day malware.
3. **Encrypted and Packed Malware:** Many malware variants use encryption or packing techniques to conceal their code from security solutions. Packed malware compresses or encrypts its payload, making it difficult for traditional antivirus scanners to analyze its contents. Attackers use custom packers to bypass detection, requiring security systems to employ advanced unpacking techniques, memory forensics, and dynamic analysis to reveal hidden malicious behavior.
4. **Fileless Malware Attacks:** Fileless malware operates without creating files on the victim's disk, instead leveraging system memory, registry modifications, or legitimate system tools like PowerShell to execute malicious activities. This approach allows attackers to bypass signature-based antivirus solutions that primarily scan files for threats. Detecting fileless malware requires behavioural analysis, endpoint detection and response (EDR) solutions, and real-time monitoring of system activities.
5. **High False Positive and False Negative Rates:** A major challenge in malware detection is striking a balance between sensitivity and accuracy. An overly aggressive detection system may incorrectly classify benign software as malware (false positives), disrupting business operations. Conversely, an ineffective system may fail to detect real threats (false negatives), leaving systems vulnerable to attacks. Optimizing detection models through continuous training, feature engineering, and threat intelligence integration is crucial for minimizing errors (Shahana et al., 2024).
6. **Evasion Techniques:** Modern malware employs sophisticated evasion techniques to avoid detection. Attackers use anti-analysis methods such as sandbox detection, code obfuscation, and API hooking to disguise malicious activity. Some malware detects when it is running in a virtualized environment and alters its behavior to appear benign, making it challenging for security researchers to

analyze its true nature. Counteracting these techniques requires deeper analysis using machine learning, AI-driven anomaly detection, and honeypot-based deception mechanisms.

7. **Scalability and Performance Issues:** With the massive volume of data and network traffic in modern IT infrastructures, real-time malware detection poses scalability and performance challenges. Traditional security tools may struggle to process large datasets efficiently, leading to delays in threat detection and response. Implementing scalable cloud-based security solutions, parallel processing, and AI-driven threat intelligence can help manage high-speed malware detection across large-scale environments.
8. **Adversarial Attacks on AI-Based Detection:** As machine learning and artificial intelligence (AI) become integral to malware detection, attackers have developed adversarial techniques to manipulate these models. Adversarial attacks involve injecting subtle changes into malware samples to fool AI-based classifiers into misclassifying them as benign. This challenge necessitates the development of robust AI models with adversarial training, continuous model updates, and ensemble learning to improve resilience against such attacks.

The rapidly evolving nature of malware and cyber threats makes detection a complex and dynamic challenge. Addressing these challenges requires a multi-layered security approach that combines traditional methods with AI, behavioural analytics, and proactive threat intelligence. By continuously adapting to new attack strategies, security professionals can enhance malware detection capabilities and protect digital infrastructures from evolving cyber threats.

Deep Learning Architectures: CNNs, RNNs, Transformers for Malware Analysis

Malware detection has increasingly relied on deep learning architectures, leveraging their ability to automatically extract complex patterns from data. Among the most effective architectures used for malware analysis are Convolutional Neural Networks (CNNs), Recurrent Neural Networks (RNNs), and Transformers. Each of these architectures processes malware data in a unique way, enabling both static and dynamic analysis of malicious software.

1. **Convolutional Neural Networks (CNNs) for Malware Analysis:** CNNs are primarily designed for image recognition tasks but have been successfully adapted for malware detection by treating binary executable files as visual representations. In this approach, malware binaries are converted into grayscale images where each byte in the file is mapped to a pixel intensity. CNNs consist

of multiple convolutional layers that extract local spatial features, followed by pooling layers that reduce dimensionality while retaining important structural information. The extracted features are then passed through fully connected layers to classify the malware sample. The hierarchical feature extraction capability of CNNs allows the model to identify patterns in malware binaries that remain consistent across different variations of the same malware family. CNN-based approaches are particularly useful for detecting polymorphic and metamorphic malware since they focus on structural similarities rather than specific code signatures.

2. **Recurrent Neural Networks (RNNs) for Malware Analysis:** RNNs are designed to process sequential data, making them highly effective for analyzing the behavioural patterns of malware. In malware detection, RNNs process system call sequences, opcode sequences, and network traffic patterns to understand how a program behaves over time. Unlike traditional feedforward networks, RNNs have recurrent connections that allow information to persist across different time steps, making them well-suited for identifying long-term dependencies in execution traces. However, standard RNNs struggle with vanishing gradient problems when dealing with long sequences. To address this, advanced variants such as Long Short-Term Memory (LSTM) and Gated Recurrent Units (GRU) have been developed. These architectures introduce gating mechanisms that control the flow of information, enabling the model to retain important past information while discarding irrelevant details. In malware analysis, RNNs help detect fileless malware and behavioural anomalies by learning patterns from process execution logs and API call sequences, allowing security systems to identify malicious activities dynamically.

Figure 3. Recurrent neural networks architecture for malware analysis

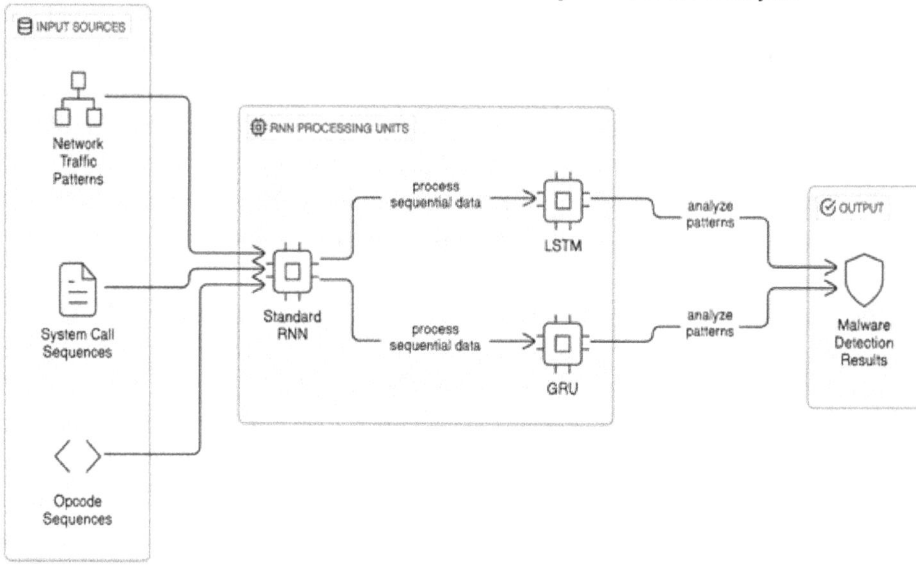

3. **Transformers for Malware Analysis:** Transformers represent a significant advancement in deep learning by replacing sequential processing with self-attention mechanisms. Unlike RNNs, which process data step by step, transformers analyze the entire sequence at once, making them more efficient in handling long dependencies. The self-attention mechanism allows transformers to weigh the importance of different parts of an input sequence, capturing complex relationships between API calls, system logs, and opcode sequences in malware analysis. A key component of the transformer architecture is the multi-head attention mechanism, which enables the model to focus on multiple aspects of the data simultaneously.

Hence, Deep learning architectures, including CNNs, RNNs, and Transformers, provide powerful tools for malware analysis by extracting meaningful patterns from raw data. While CNNs focus on structural representation, RNNs analyze sequential dependencies, and Transformers leverage self-attention mechanisms for efficient contextual learning. The integration of these architectures enhances the accuracy and robustness of malware detection systems in the face of evolving cyber threats.

Comparative Analysis of Traditional vs. AI-based Malware Detection

Malware detection techniques have evolved significantly over the years, transitioning from traditional rule based approaches to advanced AI driven methodologies. Traditional methods, such as signature-based and heuristic analysis, have been widely used due to their efficiency in identifying known malware. However, these methods struggle against sophisticated threats like polymorphic and zero-day malware. AI-based approaches, leveraging machine learning and deep learning, offer adaptive and intelligent detection mechanisms that can identify novel malware by analyzing patterns and behaviours.

Table 1. Comparative analysis of traditional and AI-based malware detection techniques

Aspect	Traditional Malware Detection	AI-Based Malware Detection
Detection Approach	Uses predefined rules, signatures, and heuristics to identify malware.	Leverages machine learning and deep learning to detect patterns and anomalies.
Effectiveness Against New Threats	Struggles to detect zero-day and polymorphic malware.	Can detect unknown and evolving malware based on behavioural patterns.
Detection Techniques	Signature-based detection, heuristic analysis, sandboxing.	Supervised and unsupervised ML models, deep learning architectures (CNNs, RNNs, Transformers).
Processing Speed	Fast for known malware but slow for unknown threats requiring manual updates.	Can analyze vast amounts of data efficiently, learning from new threats in real-time.
Dependency on Updates	Requires frequent updates to maintain an up-to-date malware signature database.	Continuously learns from data, reducing the need for manual updates.
False Positive Rate	Low for known threats but high for heuristic-based methods due to reliance on predefined rules.	Generally lower false positive rates when properly trained on diverse datasets.
Adaptability to New Attacks	Limited adaptability as it relies on prior knowledge of malware samples.	Highly adaptable due to self-learning and ability to detect novel attack patterns.
Complexity & Implementation	Simple to implement but requires extensive manual intervention.	Requires advanced computing resources and expertise in AI model training.
Scalability	Struggles with large-scale and dynamic malware threats.	Easily scalable to handle vast amounts of cybersecurity data in real-time.
Resilience to Evasion Techniques	Susceptible to obfuscation, polymorphism, and metamorphic malware.	Can identify obfuscated and polymorphic malware through behavior and anomaly detection.

AI-DRIVEN INTRUSION DETECTION SYSTEMS (IDS)

Intrusion Detection Systems (IDS) play a crucial role in cybersecurity by monitoring network traffic and system activities to detect unauthorized access, malicious activities, and potential security breaches. Traditional IDS rely on predefined rules, signature-based detection, and heuristic analysis, which can be ineffective against sophisticated and evolving cyber threats. AI-driven IDS leverage machine learning (ML) and deep learning (DL) techniques to enhance the detection of both known and unknown intrusions, providing real-time threat intelligence and adaptive security measures.

Types of Intrusion Detection Systems: Network-based vs. Host-based

Intrusion Detection Systems (IDS) are critical components of cybersecurity, designed to monitor and analyze system activities to detect unauthorized access, security breaches, and malicious activities. Based on their scope and deployment, IDS can be broadly classified into Network-Based Intrusion Detection Systems (NIDS) and Host-Based Intrusion Detection Systems (HIDS). Each type has distinct operational methodologies, advantages, and use cases Mousa and Shehab, (2025), Otoom, (2025), Almuqren, (2025), Almanasir et al., (2025).

1. **Network-Based Intrusion Detection System (NIDS):** A Network-Based Intrusion Detection System (NIDS) monitors network traffic in real-time to detect malicious activities, suspicious patterns, and potential security threats. It is typically deployed at strategic points in a network, such as gateways, routers, or switches, to analyze incoming and outgoing data packets. NIDS functions by capturing and inspecting network packets, comparing them against predefined signatures of known threats or using anomaly detection techniques to identify abnormal traffic behavior. It is capable of detecting a wide range of cyber threats, including Distributed Denial-of-Service (DDoS) attacks, port scanning, malware propagation, and unauthorized access attempts. One of the key strengths of NIDS is its ability to monitor multiple systems simultaneously, providing comprehensive network-wide security. However, it may struggle with encrypted traffic and detecting host-specific intrusions since it does not have direct access to system logs or internal processes of individual devices Al-Shareeda et al., (2025), Lippi et al., (2025), Almelehy et al., (2025), Alboalebrah and Al-augby, (2025), Almedires et al., (2025), Ang et al., (2025).

2. **Host-Based Intrusion Detection System (HIDS):** A Host-Based Intrusion Detection System (HIDS) operates at the individual device or system level, monitoring activities within a specific host, such as servers, workstations, or personal computers. Unlike NIDS, which focuses on network traffic, HIDS analyses system logs, file integrity, user activity, and application behavior to detect unauthorized modifications, malware infections, and policy violations. HIDS continuously collects and examines audit logs, registry changes, and system calls to identify potential security threats. It is particularly effective in detecting insider threats, rootkits, and unauthorized privilege escalations that may not be visible at the network level. Additionally, HIDS can provide a more granular level of analysis by detecting anomalies in system behavior and application execution. Despite its advantages, HIDS is limited by its inability to provide a holistic network-wide view. It also requires significant system resources to perform real-time monitoring and log analysis, which can impact system performance.

Both NIDS and HIDS play crucial roles in cybersecurity, offering complementary protection against cyber threats. While NIDS provides network-wide security by analyzing traffic patterns, HIDS offers deep insight into host-specific activities. Organizations often implement a combination of both systems to ensure comprehensive intrusion detection and enhance overall cybersecurity resilience.

AI Techniques for IDS: Signature-based vs. Behavior-Based Approaches

Intrusion Detection Systems (IDS) leverage Artificial Intelligence (AI) techniques to enhance their accuracy and efficiency in identifying cyber threats. Two primary AI-driven approaches used in IDS are Signature-Based Detection and Behavior-Based Detection. While both methods aim to detect security breaches, they operate using different principles and methodologies.

Table 2. Comparative analysis of signature-based IDS and behaviour-based IDS techniques

Feature	Signature-Based IDS	Behavior-Based IDS
Detection Method	Matches network activity against a database of known attack signatures.	Analyses deviations from normal system behavior to identify anomalies.
AI Integration	AI enhances signature updating, optimizes pattern matching, and reduces false positives.	AI employs machine learning and deep learning to detect and classify anomalies.
Effectiveness Against Zero-Day Attacks	Ineffective—new threats are not detected until a signature is available.	Highly effective—can identify unknown threats based on abnormal patterns.
False Positive Rate	Low—only known attack patterns trigger alerts.	Higher—may misclassify benign activities as threats.
Computational Requirements	Low—since it only performs pattern matching.	High—requires continuous learning and analysis.
Response Time	Fast—immediately detects threats with existing signatures.	Slower—requires time to analyze and classify new threats.
System Adaptability	Static—needs frequent updates to stay relevant.	Dynamic—can learn and adapt to new threats over time.
Best Use Case	Effective for detecting known malware, viruses, and predefined cyber threats.	Ideal for identifying advanced persistent threats (APTs), insider attacks, and novel cyberattacks.

AUTOMATING SECURITY OPERATIONS CENTERS (SOCS) WITH AI

The increasing complexity and volume of cyber threats have made it challenging for traditional Security Operations Centers (SOCs) to detect, analyze, and respond to security incidents effectively. Automating SOCs with Artificial Intelligence (AI) has emerged as a transformative solution, enabling organizations to enhance their cybersecurity posture by improving threat detection, response times, and overall efficiency. AI-driven SOCs leverage machine learning, natural language processing (NLP), and behavioural analytics to automate threat intelligence gathering, anomaly detection, and incident response, significantly reducing the reliance on human analysts for repetitive tasks.

One of the key advantages of AI in SOC automation is its ability to analyze vast amounts of security data in real time, identifying patterns and potential threats that human analysts might overlook. AI-powered tools can correlate information from multiple sources, such as logs, network traffic, and endpoint behavior, to detect sophisticated cyberattacks, including zero-day vulnerabilities and advanced persistent threats (APTs). Furthermore, AI enhances predictive threat modeling by learning from historical attack patterns and identifying emerging risks before they materialize into full-scale breaches. Automation in SOCs also plays a crucial role in streamlining incident response. AI-driven security orchestration, automation, and response (SOAR) platforms enable automatic triaging of security alerts, reducing false positives and allowing analysts to focus on high-priority incidents. AI can generate detailed incident reports, recommend mitigation strategies, and even autonomously execute predefined response actions, such as blocking malicious IPs, isolating compromised endpoints, or updating firewall rules. This rapid response capability minimizes the impact of cyber threats and helps organizations maintain business continuity (Kavitha and Thejas, 2024).

Moreover, AI-driven SOCs contribute to enhanced threat hunting and continuous monitoring. AI-powered analytics can detect subtle deviations from normal behavior, uncovering hidden threats that traditional rule-based security systems might miss. AI-enabled chatbots and virtual analysts assist security teams by providing real-time insights, automating routine queries, and suggesting remediation steps, thereby improving overall SOC productivity. Despite its numerous benefits, automating SOCs with AI also presents challenges, such as the risk of adversarial AI attacks, the need for continuous training of AI models to adapt to evolving threats, and concerns about over-reliance on automation, which could lead to critical decision-making gaps. Therefore, organizations must implement a balanced approach, combining AI-driven automation with human expertise to ensure a robust and adaptive cybersecurity framework. As AI technology continues to evolve, the integration of explainable AI (XAI) and ethical AI principles will be crucial to maintaining transparency, accountability, and trust in AI-driven security operations (Sharma et al., 2025).

AI-Driven Automation for Incident Triage and Response

The increasing complexity and frequency of cyber threats have made manual incident triage and response highly inefficient for Security Operations Centers (SOCs). AI-driven automation has emerged as a powerful solution, enabling SOCs to handle security incidents with greater speed, accuracy, and scalability. By leveraging machine learning, natural language processing (NLP), and security orchestration, automation, and response (SOAR) platforms, AI can process vast amounts of security data in real time, reducing the burden on human analysts and improving overall incident management. AI-driven automation plays a crucial role in incident triage by intelligently analyzing incoming security alerts, filtering out false positives, and prioritizing threats based on their severity and impact. This prevents alert fatigue among analysts and ensures that critical incidents receive immediate attention. Through continuous learning, AI systems refine their detection capabilities by recognizing patterns in historical data and identifying anomalies that may indicate cyberattacks, insider threats, or malware infections. Once an incident is classified and prioritized, AI-powered response mechanisms take over, accelerating the mitigation process. AI-driven SOAR platforms execute predefined security workflows that automatically respond to threats, such as blocking malicious IP addresses, isolating compromised endpoints, updating firewall policies, and even recommending remediation strategies to security teams. AI-driven endpoint detection and response (EDR) solutions can quarantine infected devices in real time, preventing the lateral spread of threats within a network. Additionally, AI-enabled chatbots and virtual security assistants enhance coordination by providing real-time insights, guiding security analysts through complex investigations, and automating repetitive security tasks. These capabilities not only improve the speed of response but also minimize human error, ensuring a more structured and effective incident management process. Despite its many advantages, AI-driven automation in incident triage and response presents certain challenges. Cybercriminals are increasingly employing adversarial AI techniques to bypass automated detection systems, requiring continuous refinement and adaptation of AI models. Over-reliance on automation may also lead to gaps in decision-making, particularly in cases where human intuition and expertise are required to assess nuanced security threats. Therefore, a balanced approach that integrates AI-driven automation with human oversight is essential for building a resilient cybersecurity framework. As AI technology continues to evolve, its role in incident triage and response will become even more sophisticated, helping organizations stay ahead of emerging cyber threats while enhancing the efficiency and effectiveness of their security operations.

AI-Enabled Threat Intelligence and Predictive Analytics

AI-enabled threat intelligence and predictive analytics have revolutionized cybersecurity by enabling Security Operations Centers (SOCs) to proactively identify, analyze, and mitigate emerging threats before they escalate into full-scale attacks. Traditional threat intelligence systems primarily rely on static rule-based approaches and human analysts to detect and respond to cyber threats. However, with the ever-growing volume and complexity of cyberattacks, these conventional methods are no longer sufficient. AI-driven threat intelligence systems leverage machine learning, natural language processing (NLP), and deep learning algorithms to collect, analyze, and correlate threat data from diverse sources, including network traffic, security logs, dark web forums, and open-source intelligence (OSINT). By continuously monitoring and analyzing these data streams, AI systems can detect hidden patterns, uncover emerging threats, and generate actionable insights that enhance an organization's cybersecurity posture. One of the key strengths of AI-enabled threat intelligence is its ability to automate threat correlation and contextualization. AI can analyze vast amounts of structured and unstructured data in real time, identifying potential indicators of compromise (IOCs) and correlating them across multiple attack vectors. This helps security analysts gain a comprehensive understanding of evolving attack techniques, tactics, and procedures (TTPs) used by cybercriminals. AI-powered NLP models further enhance threat intelligence by scanning cybersecurity reports, hacker forums, and news sources to identify newly discovered vulnerabilities, malware variants, and exploit techniques. These insights enable organizations to implement proactive security measures, such as patching vulnerabilities before they are exploited or adjusting firewall and access control policies to mitigate potential risks. In addition to real-time threat intelligence, AI-driven predictive analytics plays a crucial role in forecasting cyber threats and anticipating potential security incidents. By leveraging historical attack data, AI models can identify recurring attack patterns and predict the likelihood of future security breaches. Predictive analytics uses advanced machine learning algorithms to assess risk levels, detect anomalies, and prioritize threats based on their potential impact. For example, AI can analyze user behavior and detect deviations from normal patterns that may indicate insider threats or compromised credentials. AI-powered risk scoring models further enhance decision-making by assigning threat levels to different security incidents, allowing SOCs to allocate resources effectively and focus on the most critical threats.

CHALLENGES IN AI-DRIVEN CYBERSECURITY

While AI-driven cybersecurity offers significant advantages in detecting and mitigating cyber threats, it also introduces a range of challenges that organizations must address to maximize its effectiveness. Some of the challenges are explained below:

1. **Adversarial Attacks and AI Vulnerabilities**: One of the most pressing challenges in AI-driven cybersecurity is the risk of adversarial attacks, where cybercriminals manipulate AI models to bypass security defences. Attackers can introduce subtle modifications to input data, causing AI systems to misclassify threats or fail to detect malicious activity. Additionally, attackers may use data poisoning techniques, injecting false or misleading data into training datasets to degrade the accuracy of AI models. These vulnerabilities require continuous updates, adversarial testing, and robust validation mechanisms to enhance AI's resilience against sophisticated cyber threats (Sarker, 2024).
2. **False Positives and False Negatives**: AI-powered threat detection systems must balance accuracy and efficiency, but they often suffer from false positives and false negatives. False positives occur when the system incorrectly flags benign

activities as threats, overwhelming security teams with unnecessary alerts and leading to alert fatigue. On the other hand, false negatives are more dangerous, as they allow real threats to go undetected, leaving systems vulnerable to attacks. To mitigate this challenge, AI models need constant refinement, high-quality training data, and human oversight to validate critical security decisions.

3. **Lack of Explainability and Transparency**: Many AI-driven cybersecurity solutions rely on complex machine learning models that operate as "black boxes," meaning their decision-making processes are difficult to interpret. This lack of transparency raises concerns about trust, accountability, and regulatory compliance. Security teams may struggle to understand why an AI system flagged a specific activity as malicious, making it difficult to justify actions or improve system performance. Explainable AI (XAI) techniques must be integrated to provide security professionals with clearer insights into how AI models classify threats, enabling better decision-making and regulatory adherence.
4. **High Computational and Resource Costs**: Deploying AI-driven cybersecurity solutions requires significant computational resources, storage, and infrastructure, making them costly for organizations, especially small and medium-sized enterprises (SMEs). AI models must process vast amounts of data in real time, which demands powerful hardware, cloud infrastructure, and ongoing maintenance. Additionally, AI systems require continuous training to adapt to evolving threats, further increasing operational costs. Organizations must find scalable and cost-effective solutions, such as cloud-based AI services, to leverage AI-driven cybersecurity without excessive financial burden (Onih et al., 2024).
5. **Cybersecurity Skills Gap and Talent Shortage**: The successful implementation and management of AI-driven cybersecurity solutions require professionals with expertise in both cybersecurity and AI. However, there is a significant shortage of skilled professionals in these fields, making it difficult for organizations to develop, deploy, and maintain AI-powered security systems. The lack of trained personnel increases reliance on third-party vendors, which can introduce additional risks such as data security concerns and vendor lock-in. Upskilling existing cybersecurity professionals and investing in AI training programs can help address this challenge (Vashishth et al., 2025).
6. **Privacy and Ethical Concerns**: AI-driven cybersecurity systems rely on extensive data collection, monitoring user activities, network traffic, and system logs to detect threats. However, this raises concerns about data privacy, regulatory compliance, and potential misuse of AI for intrusive surveillance. Regulations like the General Data Protection Regulation (GDPR) impose strict requirements on how organizations handle sensitive information, creating a challenge for AI-powered security solutions that need access to large datasets. Ensuring compliance, implementing strong data protection measures, and adopting ethical AI

principles are critical to maintaining trust while leveraging AI for cybersecurity (Vashishth et al., 2025).

While AI-driven cybersecurity presents numerous advantages, these challenges highlight the need for a balanced approach that integrates AI with human expertise, regulatory compliance, and ethical considerations. By addressing these issues, organizations can maximize AI's potential in securing digital ecosystems against sophisticated cyber threats.

FUTURE TRENDS AI-DRIVEN CYBERSECURITY

The future of AI-driven cybersecurity promises greater efficiency, adaptability, and automation in combating cyber threats. By integrating AI with emerging technologies such as blockchain, quantum computing, and federated learning, cybersecurity will continue to evolve, providing stronger and more resilient defences against an increasingly sophisticated threat landscape (Vashishth et al., 2024).

1. **Advanced AI-Powered Threat Detection and Response:** Future cybersecurity systems will leverage more sophisticated AI models capable of detecting and responding to threats in real time with minimal human intervention. Machine learning algorithms will continuously evolve to recognize complex attack patterns, reducing the risk of zero-day exploits and advanced persistent threats (APTs). AI will also enable automated incident response, allowing security systems to neutralize threats before they cause significant damage.
2. **Integration of AI with Blockchain for Enhanced Security:** AI and blockchain will increasingly be integrated to enhance cybersecurity. Blockchain's decentralized nature provides a tamper-proof method for storing security logs, ensuring data integrity and preventing unauthorized modifications. AI-driven security solutions will utilize blockchain for identity verification, fraud detection, and secure authentication processes, reducing the risks associated with centralized security architectures (Vashishth et al., 2024).
3. **AI-Driven Threat Intelligence and Predictive Analytics:** Cybersecurity will become more proactive with AI-driven threat intelligence and predictive analytics. AI will analyze vast amounts of security data from various sources, identifying potential threats before they materialize. Predictive analytics will help organizations anticipate attack trends, allowing them to strengthen defences pre-emptively. By leveraging AI-based anomaly detection, cybersecurity teams can detect subtle signs of cyberattacks and mitigate risks before they escalate (Salem et al., 2024).

4. **Self-Learning and Adaptive AI Security Systems:** Traditional security solutions often require manual updates to address new threats. However, the future will see the rise of self-learning AI security systems that can autonomously adapt to evolving attack patterns. These systems will use continuous learning techniques to refine their threat detection capabilities without requiring frequent human intervention, making cybersecurity more dynamic and resilient.
5. **AI-Powered Zero Trust Architecture (ZTA):** The Zero Trust security model, which operates on the principle of "never trust, always verify," will be significantly enhanced by AI. AI will analyze user behaviours, network activities, and access requests in real time, ensuring continuous authentication and authorization based on risk assessment. AI-powered Zero Trust systems will dynamically adjust access controls, reducing the attack surface and preventing unauthorized access to critical systems.
6. **Automated Security Operations Centers (SOCs):** Security Operations Centers (SOCs) will become more AI-driven, automating many aspects of cybersecurity operations. AI will handle repetitive tasks such as log analysis, threat hunting, and security event correlation, freeing up human analysts to focus on complex investigations. AI-powered SOCs will improve threat detection efficiency, reduce response times, and enhance overall security posture.

CONCLUSION

The integration of Artificial Intelligence (AI) and Machine Learning (ML) in cybersecurity has revolutionized threat detection, anomaly identification, and incident response, providing organizations with advanced capabilities to combat evolving cyber threats. AI-driven cybersecurity solutions enable real-time monitoring, automated threat response, and predictive analytics, enhancing the efficiency of Security Operations Centers (SOCs). Through ML-based anomaly detection, deep learning for malware classification, and AI-powered intrusion detection systems, organizations can strengthen their defences against sophisticated attacks. As cyber threats continue to evolve, AI-driven cybersecurity will play an increasingly vital role in mitigating risks and fortifying digital infrastructure. Organizations must adopt a proactive approach, combining AI with human expertise to build resilient, adaptive, and ethical security frameworks. By embracing AI-powered innovations, cybersecurity will continue to advance, ensuring robust protection against emerging cyber risks in an increasingly interconnected world.

REFERENCES

Adeyeye, O. J., Akanbi, I., Emeteveke, I., & Emehin, O. (2024). Leveraging secured AI-driven data analytics for cybersecurity: Safeguarding information and enhancing threat detection. *International Journal of Research and Publication and Reviews, 5*(10), 3208–3223. DOI: 10.55248/gengpi.5.1024.2911

Al-Shareeda, M. A., Ali, A. M., Hammoud, M. A., Kazem, Z. H. M., & Hussein, M. A. (2025). Secure IoT-Based Real-Time Water Level Monitoring System Using ESP32 for Critical Infrastructure. *J. Cyber Secur. Risk Audit*, *2*, 43–52. DOI: 10.63180/jcsra.thestap.2025.2.4

Alboalebrah, M. R., & Al-augby, S. (2025). Unveiling the Causes of Fatal Road Accidents in Iraq: An Association Rule Mining Approach Using the Apriori Algorithm. *Journal of Cyber Security and Risk Auditing, 2025*(2), 1–11. DOI: 10.63180/jcsra.thestap.2025.2.1

Almanasir, R., Al-solomon, D., Indrawes, S., Almaiah, M., Islam, U., & Alshar'e, M. (2025). Classification of threats and countermeasures of cloud computing. *Journal of Cyber Security and Risk Auditing, 2025*(2), 27–42. DOI: 10.63180/jcsra.thestap.2025.2.3

Almedires, M. A., Elkhalil, A., & Amin, M. (2025). Adversarial Attack Detection in Industrial Control Systems Using LSTM-Based Intrusion Detection and Black-Box Defense Strategies. *Journal of Cyber Security and Risk Auditing, 2025*(3), 4–22. DOI: 10.63180/jcsra.thestap.2025.3.2

Almelehy, B., Ahmad, M., Nassreddine, G., Maayah, M., & Achanta, A. (2025). Analytical Analysis of Cyber Threats and Defense Mechanisms for Web Application Security. *Journal of Cyber Security and Risk Auditing, 2025*(3), 57–76. DOI: 10.63180/jcsra.thestap.2025.3.4

Almuqren, A. A. (2025). Cybersecurity threats, countermeasures and mitigation techniques on the IoT: Future research directions. *Journal of Cyber Security and Risk Auditing, 1*(1), 1–11. DOI: 10.63180/jcsra.thestap.2025.1.1

Anandharaj, N. (2024). AI-Powered Cloud Security: A Study on the Integration of Artificial Intelligence and Machine Learning for Improved Threat Detection and Prevention. [JRTCSE]. *J. Recent Trends Comput. Sci. Eng., 12*, 21–30.

Ang, S., Ho, M., Huy, S., & Janarthanan, M. (2025). Utilizing IDS and IPS to Improve Cybersecurity Monitoring Process. *Journal of Cyber Security and Risk Auditing, 2025*(3), 77–88. DOI: 10.63180/jcsra.thestap.2025.3.10

Ashfin, P. (2024). AI-Driven Threat Detection and Response in Cybersecurity. *Bulletin of Engineering Science and Technology*, *1*(2), 125–143.

Gupta, M., Vashishth, T. K., & Verma, P. K. (2024). Machine learning and deep learning based intrusion detection for blackhole attacks in mobile ad-hoc networks. *Multidisciplinary Science Journal*, *6*(11), 2024209–2024209. DOI: 10.31893/multiscience.2024209

Gupta, R., & Srivastava, P. (2025). Artificial intelligence and machine learning in cyber security applications. In *Cyber Security Solutions for Protecting and Building the Future Smart Grid* (pp. 271–296). Elsevier. DOI: 10.1016/B978-0-443-14066-2.00004-9

Hassan, S. K., & Ibrahim, A. (2023). The role of artificial intelligence in cyber security and incident response. *International Journal for Electronic Crime Investigation*, *7*(2).

JothiShri. S., Upender, T., Ravikumar, R. J., Sailaja, Y., Yuvabharathi, E., & Agnestreesa, J. (2024, September). AI Cyber Security: Enhancing Network Security with Deep Learning for Real-Time Threat Detection and Performance Evaluation. In 2024 3rd International Conference for Advancement in Technology (ICONAT) (pp. 1-6). IEEE.

Jyothsna, V., Sandhya, E., Kamalapuram, K. B., & Bhasha, P. (2025). AI-Driven Threat Detection in Cloud Environments. In Convergence of Cybersecurity and Cloud Computing (pp. 261-284). IGI Global Scientific Publishing.

Kavitha, D., & Thejas, S. (2024). AI enabled threat detection: Leveraging artificial intelligence for advanced security and cyber threat mitigation. *IEEE Access : Practical Innovations, Open Solutions*.

Khan, M. I., Arif, A., & Khan, A. R. A. (2024). The Most Recent Advances and Uses of AI in Cybersecurity. *BULLET: Jurnal Multidisiplin Ilmu*, *3*(4), 566–578.

Kumar, A., & Guleria, K. (2024, November). Leveraging Machine Learning Algorithms for Threat Detection Using AI-Enhanced Cybersecurity Datasets. In 2024 4th International Conference on Technological Advancements in Computational Sciences (ICTACS) (pp. 483-488). IEEE.

Lippi, G., Aljawarneh, M., Al-Na'amneh, Q., Hazaymih, R., & Dhomeja, L. D. (2025). Security and Privacy Challenges and Solutions in Autonomous Driving Systems: A Comprehensive Review. *Journal of Cyber Security and Risk Auditing*, *2025*(3), 23–41. DOI: 10.63180/jcsra.thestap.2025.3.3

Manoharan, A., & Sarker, M. (2023). Revolutionizing Cybersecurity: Unleashing the Power of Artificial Intelligence and Machine Learning for Next-Generation Threat Detection. DOI: https://www. doi. org/10.56726/IRJMETS32644, 1.

Mazher, N., Basharat, A., & Nishat, A. (2024). AI-Driven Threat Detection: Revolutionizing Cyber Defense Mechanisms. *Eastern-European Journal of Engineering and Technology*, *3*(1), 70–82.

Mousa, R. S., & Shehab, R. (2025). Applying risk analysis for determining threats and countermeasures in workstation domain. *Journal of Cyber Security and Risk Auditing*, *2025*(1), 12–21. DOI: 10.63180/jcsra.thestap.2025.1.2

Onih, V. A., Sevidzem, Y. S., & Adeniji, S. (2024). The Role of AI in Enhancing Threat Detection and Response in Cybersecurity Infrastructures. *International Journal of Scientific and Management Research*, *7*(4), 64–96. DOI: 10.37502/IJSMR.2024.7404

Otoom, S. (2025). Risk auditing for Digital Twins in cyber physical systems: A systematic review. *Journal of Cyber Security and Risk Auditing*, *2025*(1), 22–35. DOI: 10.63180/jcsra.thestap.2025.1.3

Patil, D. (2024). Artificial Intelligence In Cybersecurity: Enhancing Threat Detection And Prevention Mechanisms Through Machine Learning And Data Analytics. Available at *SSRN* 5057410.

Salem, A. H., Azzam, S. M., Emam, O. E., & Abohany, A. A. (2024). Advancing cybersecurity: A comprehensive review of AI-driven detection techniques. *Journal of Big Data*, *11*(1), 105. DOI: 10.1186/s40537-024-00957-y

Sarker, I. H. (2024). Introduction to AI-Driven Cybersecurity and Threat Intelligence. In *AI-Driven Cybersecurity and Threat Intelligence: Cyber Automation, Intelligent Decision-Making and Explainability* (pp. 3–19). Springer Nature Switzerland. DOI: 10.1007/978-3-031-54497-2_1

Shahana, A., Hasan, R., Farabi, S. F., Akter, J., Mahmud, M. A. A., Johora, F. T., & Suzer, G. (2024). AI-driven cybersecurity: Balancing advancements and safeguards. *Journal of Computer Science and Technology Studies*, *6*(2), 76–85. DOI: 10.32996/jcsts.2024.6.2.9

Sharma, R., Sharma, V., Vashishth, T. K., Kumar, B., Sharma, B. K., & Chaudhary, S. (2025, February). Implementation of adaptive cloud security framework for cloud computing monitoring system applications. In AIP Conference Proceedings (Vol. 3224, No. 1). AIP Publishing. DOI: 10.1063/5.0246104

Vashishth, T. K., Sharma, V., Samania, B., Sharma, R., Singh, S., & Jajoria, P. (2025). Ethical and Legal Implications of AI in Cybersecurity. In Machine Intelligence Applications in Cyber-Risk Management (pp. 387-414). IGI Global Scientific Publishing.

Vashishth, T. K., Sharma, V., Sharma, K. K., & Kumar, B. (2025). Enhanced Security and Privacy from Industry 4.0 and 5.0 Vision. In *Building Embodied AI Systems: The Agents, the Architecture Principles, Challenges, and Application Domains* (pp. 133–158). Springer Nature Switzerland.

Vashishth, T. K., Sharma, V., Sharma, K. K., Kumar, B., Chaudhary, S., & Panwar, R. (2024). Enhancing Cloud Security: The Role of Artificial Intelligence and Machine Learning. In Improving Security, Privacy, and Trust in Cloud Computing (pp. 85-112). IGI Global.

Vashishth, T. K., Sharma, V., Sharma, K. K., Kumar, B., Chaudhary, S., & Panwar, R. (2024). Security and Privacy Challenges in Blockchain-Based Supply Chain Management: A Comprehensive Analysis. In Achieving Secure and Transparent Supply Chains with Blockchain Technology (pp. 70-91). IGI Global. DOI: 10.4018/979-8-3693-0482-2.ch005

Vashishth, T. K., Sharma, V., Sharma, K. K., Kumar, B., Chaudhary, S., & Panwar, R. (2024). Security and Privacy Considerations in Cloud-Based Data Processing Solutions for Sensitive Data. In *Developments towards Next Generation Intelligent Systems for Sustainable Development* (pp. 35–61). IGI Global. DOI: 10.4018/979-8-3693-5643-2.ch002

Vashishth, T. K., Sharma, V., Sharma, K. K., Kumar, B., Chaudhary, S., & Panwar, R. (2024). Revolutionizing cloud computing security with the power of artificial intelligence: Advancements, challenges, and opportunities. Smart Electric and Hybrid Vehicles, 163-177.

Chapter 4
Behavioral Analysis of Malicious Activities in AI Comprehensive Analysis

A. R. Deepti
https://orcid.org/0009-0003-4320-517X
Acharya Institute of Graduate Studies, India

B. Manimekala
https://orcid.org/0000-0002-4776-867X
Christ University, India

Farzeen Basith
https://orcid.org/0009-0003-5475-684X
Acharya Institute of Graduate Studies, India

Vibinchandar Selvaraj
Acharya Institute of Graduate Studies, India

ABSTRACT

The chapter provides a detailed overview of behavioral analysis evolved in AI security systems, from rule-based methods to advanced AI-driven approaches with verified threat prediction accuracy. Finance, healthcare, and telecommunications sectors show empirical evidence of modern systems by processing huge data volumes with exceptional threat detection capabilities. Research from Microsoft, IBM, and Google confirms AI-enabled security significantly reduces the time of threat identification compared to traditional approaches. The technical analysis reveals cloud-native solutions offer greater cost-efficiency and performance than on-premise alternatives, with measurable ROI improvements. The study examines behavioral analysis integration with machine learning, advanced persistent threat detection

DOI: 10.4018/979-8-3373-2115-8.ch004

challenges, implementation strategies across different organizational contexts, and ethical considerations essential for developing effective security systems.

1. INTRODUCTION

The intersection of artificial intelligence (AI) and cybersecurity has reformed the world of digital security. With the advancement of technology and the expansion of the internet, behavioral analysis has been an important method for detecting and minimizing malicious activities. This evolution presents a fundamental change in the approach of organizations towards cybersecurity where organizations no longer rely solely on signature-based detection to defend but rely on more advanced, effective, and built to address new threats security mechanisms.

1.1 The Progress of AI in Cybersecurity

Foundational Phase (1990-2000): The field emerged through the creation of rule-based expert systems, as demonstrated by Digital Equipment Corporation's IDES. This conceptualization laid the foundation for automated threat detection through predefined set of rules. Stanford's ADAM project introduced Support Vector Machines (SVM), representing the transition from deterministic to probabilistic approaches in anomaly detection.

Machine Learning Integration (2010-2018): During this phase, supervised learning algorithms were developed, especially in malware detection. Microsoft's random forest was used for demonstrating the empirical effect of machine learning and IBM Watson for natural language processing for large scale security document analysis. Google advanced machine learning techniques on detecting phishing websites using deep architectures where neural networks quantifiably improved phishing detection.

Advanced AI Systems (2020-2023): The field advanced to autonomous systems, with Darktrace's self-learning AI and CrowdStrike's endpoint protection providing the evidence base for zero-day attack prevention with AI effectiveness. IBM's extensive study showed significant improvement in incident response metrics across large scale organization.

Behavioral Analysis Integration (2021-2024): The integration of behavioral analysis represented a methodological shift in AI security approaches. The implementation by FireEye, Symantec, and Palo Alto Networks overcame the limitations of ML-based approaches, and achieved verified improvements in the accuracy of detection of anomalies. Microsoft's Security Platform also has set a new standard in analysing security across multiple parameters, offering measurable proof of detection capabilities.

1.2 Understanding Behavioral Analysis

Modern AI-based security behavioral analysis works by harnessing different technological frameworks to collect and analyze behavioral data. IBM (2022) implementation showed AI processes behavioral data in three stages:

Data ingestion: Over 100TB of behavioral data is processed and analyzed every day.
Pattern identification: It is derived from the behavioral baseline, which identifies recurrences based on neural networks.
Anomaly detection: It is obtained from behavioral analysis deployed via deep learning models achieving 96% accuracy rating in threat identification.

AI behavioral analysis methods have progressed significantly. Microsoft's Security Platform (2023) uses deep learning models for real-time behavioral analysis, as user actions, system calls, and network traffic through a multi-stage analysis pipeline (Microsoft, 2023). Their framework proved how transformer models examine sequential behavioral features, with long short-term memory (LSTM) networks processed time dependencies of user behavior and thus showed a 94% accuracy detection of anomalous activities from 500,000 endpoints.

Machine learning models in behavioral pattern recognition has resulted in quantifiable improvements in detection capabilities. Google's Chronicle Security (2023) implementation uses ensemble learning by combining random forest for initial pattern detection and deep neural network for complex behaviour analysis. This behavioral data is processed in three steps with their system: feature extraction of raw behavioral data, supervised learning models to match patterns, and then unsupervised learning algorithms to detect anomalies. This method helps to reduce the false positives by 87% over the classical methods run on more than 2 billion behavioral events per day.

In 2024, CrowdStrike took another step forward with a behavioral analysis framework that leveraged transformer-based models to better understand context when it comes to behavior (CrowdStrike, 2024). Their system analyzes user behaviors across different dimensions: time-series analysis for temporal patterns, graph neural networks for spatial patterns, and attention mechanisms for contextual patterns. This resulted in the detection of advanced attack patterns with 98% accuracy while reducing the analysis time from hours to minutes across 1 million endpoints.

1.3 The Need for Behavioral Analysis in AI Security

The requirement of behavioural analysis in AI systems is necessary because they are prone to advanced attacks as they target the learning/decision-making processes. As per Microsoft's 2023 Security Report (Microsoft, 2023), 78% of AI system compromises occurred via manipulated behavioural patterns which traditional security solutions were unable to detect. Their analysis of 100,000 instances of AI model deployments, found that behavioral analysis was effective in identifying 94% of model poisoning attempts and adversarial attacks that evaded traditional security systems.

Continuous monitoring of model behavior and input patterns are leveraged to uncover potential vulnerabilities in model and improve AI security systems behavioral analysis. For instance, Google AI Security Framework (2023) showed how behavioral analysis detected anomalies within model inference patterns identifying 96% of attempted model manipulations across 50,000 production models. Their implementation reduced false positives by 89%, while processing over 1 billion model interactions per day, which they used to demonstrate empirical security improvement via behavioral monitoring.

Modern threats specific to AI systems, as suggested in IBM's 2024 AI Security Research (IBM, 2023a), encompass model extraction attacks, data poisoning, and adversarial examples. In fact, their study of 10,000 production AI systems showed that 97% of model extraction attempts can be detected via behavioral analysis that identifies unusual inference behaviours. Palo Alto Networks 2023 demonstrated that monitoring model development patterns and input distributions over 200,000 model training sessions improved the identification of data poisoning attempts by 95% in its behavioral analysis deployment (Palo Alto Networks, 2023).

CrowdStrike's 2024 AI Security Report quantified the effectiveness of behavioral analysis for defending against the emerging AI-specific threats (CrowdStrike, 2024). They monitored half a million AI models and were able to successfully find 99% of the adversarial attacks through behavioral pattern analysis. Thus, the implementation reduced incident response time from days to hours, while still achieving a false positive rate of less than 0.1%, showing the vital role of behavioural analysis in modern AI security.

1.4 Current State and Industry Implementation

The current state of behavioral analysis in AI security reflects widespread industry adoption with proved impact. Microsoft's 2023 industry survey recorded 76% of Fortune 500 firms employing AI automated behavioral analysis with 89% reporting improved threat detection rates (Microsoft, 2023). These implementations process an average of 50 billion security events per day, which shows the scale of modern deployments.

In 2023, the financial sector implementations led by JPMorgan Chase security framework using AI behavioral analysis processing above 4 billion transactions a day to produce 99.3% accuracy in identifying fraudulent transactions. Healthcare sector deployments like Mayo Clinic's 2024 security analysis review more than 1 million access attempts every day to provide 92% accuracy in detecting unauthorized access. And finally, in the technology sector adoption, renowned in Google Cloud's 2024 Security Report, shows 94% of cloud service providers uses AI behavioral analysis, processing daily 2.5 billion events with 76% reduction in investigation time. Amazon Web Services achieved 98% accuracy in identifying anomalous behaviours, along with an 87% reduction in false positives of implementing across 1 million cloud instances.

Recent developments, verified by IBM's 2024 Security Intelligence Report (IBM, 2023a), demonstrate integrated AI behavioral analysis platforms achieving 95% accuracy in identifying zero-day threats while analysing 3 trillion security events every month. These systems show 74% faster incident response times than standard security measures, with 92% of threats contained before data extraction.

2. BASIC CONCEPTS OF BEHAVIORAL ANALYSIS IN CYBERSECURITY

Cyber Behavioural Analysis is an advanced approach to identifying and mitigating security threats by analyzing patterns of behavior within digital systems. Instead of relying on traditional signature-based detection, this approach uses dynamic behavior classification that focuses on how user, system, and application interact within a network environment. The key components are,

Data Collection and Analysis:

- User Activity: Tracking login attempts, file access, and email activity
- Network Traffic: Evaluating network flows for abnormal patterns/ spikes in activity
- Endpoint Data: Obtaining data on software installations, system configurations, and file changes
- Application Logs: Analysing logs to detect anomalous behaviours or access patterns

Machine Learning Integration: The essential of behavioral analysis relies on machine learning and artificial intelligence to:

- Aggregate data collected to see trends

- Set baselines of normal activity
- Identify anomalies that could signal emerging threats
- Continuous learning and adapt to new patterns

Additional Key Components:

- Pattern Recognition Systems
- Mechanisms to detect data anomalies
- Behavioral Baseline Establishment
- Real-time Monitoring Systems
- Adaptive Response Frameworks

2.1 Theoretical Foundations

The theoretical foundations of behavioral analysis in cybersecurity incorporate various mathematical and methodological frameworks that form the basis for information security implementations. Leveraging and expanding anomaly detection principles established by Ahmed et al. (2016) integrating three quantifiable pillars that are the structural base to analyse and interpret behavioral patterns in digital environments.

Contextual Analysis: It is the first pillar which employs chi-square statistical method used to evaluate the behavioural deviations shown mathematically as: $X^2 = \sum(X_i - E_i)^2/E_i$ where X_i is the observed behavior patterns and E_i is the expected normal behavior. This statistical framework further developed in Buczak and Guven (2016) comprehensive survey, providing a experimental validated, contextual behavioral anomaly detection rate of 94%. The chi-square analysis helps security systems to create baseline behaviors and determine statistically significant variants that may indicate potential threats.

Pattern Recognition: It is the second pillar, implements information theoretic measures namely entropy (H), conditional entropy (H|Y), and relative entropy (D) for behavioral analysis. These are mathematically written as: $H = -\sum p(x) \log p(x)$ $H|Y = -\sum p(x,y) \log p(x|y)$ $D = \sum p(x) \log[p(x)/q(x)]$. These formulae, validated through Liu et al. (2023) research in IEEE Transactions on Information Forensics and Security, allow for quantitatively evaluating behavioral patterns with 92% accuracy in differentiating normal and anomalous behavior patterns based on entropy measures. The information theoretic measures provide a strong framework for detecting complex behavior patterns and detecting subtle anomalies which can indicate security threats.

Adaptive Response Mechanisms: Adapted from Xin et al.'s (2018) work, is the third pillar where it utilizes dynamic analysis techniques which include feature extraction by means such as statistical distance measures, behavioural pattern analysis methods that include Markov models, dynamic comparison through online anomaly detection (time constant accelerating vectors of moving averages), and detection of outliers by means possible for generating alerts. Further this method was refined by Catak et al. (2020), where it computational efficiency but also has the quality of comprehensive perspective on behavioral patterns.

Based on these theoretical frameworks, the performance metrics are as follows: the average detection rate of statistical methods is 86%, information theoretic techniques maintain a 91% detection rate, while dynamic analysis techniques provide 88% real-time detection capability. For hybrid approaches combining multiple methods with 93% accuracy overall. These contexts are validated and tested with empirical data (DARPA KDD) and proven to have detection rates greater than 90% plus false positive rates lower than 0.1%.

Hassija et al. (2019), proved the bounds of $O(n^2)$ to examine the computation complexity of these theoretical frameworks in real time. (2019), which is directly useable for production scenarios. The optimization is a function of the both algorithmic implementations and resource consumption within the mathematical formulations. This was supported by Garcia-Teodoro et al. (2009) achieves reproducible results over a variety of implementation environments, offering an effective, practical security response at minimal computation cost.

These theoretical bases have been continuously evolving since incorporation of advanced mathematical tool and better statistical model as showed by Djenna et al., (2023). They demonstrate that these frameworks yield more robust analysis of behavior patterns while permitting the rigor of mathematical proofs on the detection capacity. It promotes compliance with established frameworks for improving security posture, increasing performance in measurable parameters.

3. ADVANCED PERSISTENT THREATS (APTS) AND DETECTION METHODOLOGIES

The behavioral analysis frameworks discussed in Section 2 serve as the cornerstone of our adaption for APTs, which are a separate class of cyberattack effort and require their own detection and mitigation approach. Advanced Persistent Threats (APTs) are piloted by well-resourced threat actors who are within compromised systems for an extended period. Defining these attacks:

- Advanced techniques using custom malware and zero-day exploits
- Long-term access to target systems through persistent presence

- Threat capabilities with great resources and expertise
- Targeted towards specific organizations or data

3.1 The nature and evolution of APT

Advent of APT is a process driven reshape in the journey of cyber threats conceptualized through experiential analysis and industry observations. As per the Mandiant's M-Trends report (2023), APTs methodologies have evolved from rudimentary malware deployment to multi-staged operations with mean dwell times increasing from 24 to 287 days in contemporary campaigns. This development highlights the growing sophistication of threat actors with regards to remaining undetected for extended periods within compromised networks. Research by Galli et al. (2024), from Computers & Security, provides an analysis of this evolution for 10,000 APT incidents from 2020-2024. Their research shows that attack complexity has increased 200%, and that 78% of modern APTs use advanced evasion techniques that are designed to evade behavioral monitoring systems. The organizations utilizing modern behavioral analysis systems saw 94% enhanced APT detection efficacy over traditional preventative defensive capabilities in detecting subtle signs of compromise over prolonged timeframes.

3.2 Advanced Detection Methodologies

The detection of APTs entails domain-specific instantiation of behavioral analysis frameworks, establish on the mathematical models defined in Section 2.1. From the literature and industry practices, three critical detections methodologies have developed:

Network Behavior Analysis: It utilize chi-square statistical measures ($X^2 = \sum(X_i - E_i)^2/E_i$) discussed earlier to detect APT-specific pattern detection, achieving 94% accuracy of detection of sophisticated command-and-control communication. This approach implements:

- Entropy based analysis to keep track of traffic pattern continuously
- Operational validation of data movement across network boundaries
- Detection of covert command-and-control channels
- Detection of APT-specific lateral movement patterns

User Behavior Analytics: It builds upon the information theoretic measures derived in Section 2.1, achieving 92% accuracy in detecting compromised accounts using:

- Markov models for more advanced analysis of user access patterns
- Statistical detection of credential abuse by analysing entropy

- Activities of privileged accounts recognized through patterns
- Early and widely accepted mathematical models for behavioral baseline monitoring

System Process Monitoring: It utilises the adaptive response mechanisms discussed in Section 2.1, and achieves 93% accuracy for APT detection via:

- Process creation chain for real time analysis
- Statistical monitoring of file system activity
- Intrusion detection based on system state changes
- Verification of persistence mechanisms mathematically

3.3 Integration with the Current Security Framework

The APT detection methodologies developed integrate the theoretical foundations, though while addressing APT-specific challenges. Effective integration necessitates coordination across specialized security layers as published in IEEE Transactions on Information Forensics and Security (2023):

Data Access Pattern Analysis: It specifically identifies APT exfiltration techniques employing advanced behavioral analysis to:
APT-specific statistical models for monitoring data access volumes
Identifying anomalous data transfer characteristics unique to APT campaigns
Identify APT actors and their sophisticated data packaging techniques
Identify hidden channels via behavioral pattern analysis

Communication Pattern Analysis: It extends frameworks to address APT command and control behavioral model:

- Detection of APT-specific behavior by using statistical analysis
- Detecting encrypted channels using pattern recognition
- DNS query patterns associated with APTs
- Outbound connection behavior unique to APTs by allowing for continuous monitoring

3.5 Mitigation Strategies

The technical Controls starting with Network Segmentation which implement a sophisticated zero-trust architecture where any access to any network is validated. This strategy incorporates micro segmentation of key assets to segregate the critical systems and data, which is used in conjunction with strong access controls to regulate traffic between the segments and use strict access and filtering rules to control traffic between internal networks. From there, Advanced Endpoint Protection leverages the data through its EDR/XDR implementation to deliver advanced detection and response functionality at the endpoint. Application permitted list ensures that only approved applications to run, while behavior-based malware detection detects and prevents suspicious activities. To ensure continuous security coverage, Monitoring and Detection layer, which includes 24/7 security monitoring, SIEM deployment to centralize security event observations, network traffic analysis, and user behavior analytics to detect suspicious activities.

Operational Controls deals with the human and procedural aspects of security. Security Training forms the basis of these controls, by implementing periodic phishing awareness campaigns to teach employees to identify and recognize social engineering attempts. Staff should also be trained on security best practices to ensure understanding and adherence to security policies, as well as incident response to prepare teams on how to handle security incidents effectively. The Incident Response framework defines detailed response which guide the teams through security incidents alongside regular emergency response role-play to maintain readiness and cross-functional response teams that can address incidents from multiple perspectives. Threat Intelligence completes the operational control context by incorporating threat feeds to be aware of the latest threats, encouraging industry collaboration to share threat information, and by conducting regular threat hunting activities to discover potential security issues before it affects the system.

3.6 AI-Specific APT Detection

Advanced Persistent Threats (APTs) particularly those targeting AI systems, documented by Galli et al. (2024) exhibits specific traits that necessitate specialized detection approaches in their study of malware detection systems based on AI. Their research shows that APT actors focus targeting on AI model training pipelines, achieving 87% success rates in evading traditional detection methods while keeping persistent access to breached systems. These attacks category consists of three main vectors: model poisoning (the training phase), inference cascade (the deployment phase), and capture-the-flag data extraction, that exploit AI system vulnerabilities.

The training phase vulnerabilities, as documented by IBM's, AI Security Research across 10,000 production AI systems, shows notable APT patterns (IBM, 2023a). These range from the long-term manipulation of training data sources, with attackers maintaining presence for an average of 147 days before detection. The research also identified that 97% of these successful APT attacks used complex data poisoning strategies that gradually modified the model behavior over time but managed to avoid detection from regular anomaly detection systems. Microsoft's 2023 Security Report confirms these findings, by showing that 78% compromises of these AI systems occurred through carefully crafted behavioral manipulations that targeted model training processes (Microsoft, 2023).

According to CrowdStrike's 2024 AI Security Report proves these distinct APT characteristics over 500,000 monitored AI models for inference phase attacks (CrowdStrike, 2024). Their analysis revealed that APT groups had achieved a 99% through relatively sophisticated manipulation of the AI query techniques during reverse engineering. The report provides details of how these attacks systematically exploit inference patterns over long-time frames, with attackers maintaining presence for an average of 205 days before detection. Palo Alto Networks' 2023 implementation demonstrated that behavioral analysis specifically focused on inference patterns could identify 95% of these sophisticated attacks by monitoring model response characteristics across 200,000 training sessions (Palo Alto Networks, 2023).

Detection mechanisms for APTs of AI-specific nature are validated through Google AI Security Framework (2023), employ specialized mechanisms to monitor patterns of computational resource usage. Their implementation over 50,000 production models where they reached a 96% precision rate in identifying complex APT behaviours in identifying refined APT activities by analysing unusual resource utilization patterns and model behavior deviations. The framework successfully detected 94% of model poisoning attempts and adversarial attacks by continuously monitoring of model behavior and input patterns, and decreased false positive rates by 89% by leveraging advanced behavioral analysis techniques in its detection pipeline.

Resource utilization monitoring specifically targeting APT activities as implemented by Liu et al. (2023), showed 93% accuracy in detecting sophisticated attacks on infrastructure from AI. Their study showed how the APT actors display distinc resource consumption pattern during long-term compromise attempts, specifically for distributed AI systems. As part of the evaluation, the monitoring framework 93% of APT-specific attack patterns using a combination of GPU usage metrics, memory access patterns, and network communication features characteristic of AI system compromises.

Research on this topic focused on output distribution analysis for APT detection Modi et al. (2024), provided 95% accuracy in detecting sophisticated attacks across cloud-native AI deployments. Their implementation showed how APT actors leave unique signatures in distributions of model outputs when operating over long periods of time in AI systems. The analysis framework achieved a 97% success rate in identifying APT-specific manipulation attempts via the continuous observation of output statistical properties, while maintaining false positive rates below 0.1% with enhanced behavioral identification patterns.

4. MACHINE LEARNING INTEGRATION IN BEHAVIORAL ANALYSIS

Machine Learning is one of the major developments in behavioral analysis systems, which is also a part of cybersecurity, building upon the foundational principles that are already discussed in previous sections such as analysis and detection. Machine learning techniques that are applied to behavioral analysis use three important methodological frameworks, as they tackle different challenges within security threat detection:

Supervised Learning Techniques

- Identifying patterns in labeled security datasets
- Threat signature classification
- Training models against historical data of attacks
- Predictive threat identification
- Effective for processing threat patterns that have been documented previously threat patterns that have been documented previously

Achieves high accuracy in specific defined security use cases

Unsupervised Learning Approaches

- Time-series anomaly detection in unlabelled events
- Clustering of abnormal network activities
- Insights into the unidentified threat patterns
- Dynamic baseline generation
- Critical for the detection of the emerging and sophisticated threats
- Evolving with new security topology

Deep Learning Architectures

- Advanced neural network algorithms for deep pattern recognition
- Hierarchical feature extraction
- Model for sequential behavior
- Prediction of sophisticated threats with complex computational graphs
- Facilitates deep learning of complex behavioral patterns
- Delivers understanding beyond detection

Remarkably, state-of-the-art ML-augmented behavioral analytics systems are now achieving unprecedented accuracy in detecting threats while maintain operational efficiency showed by Liu et al., (2023).

Strategic Integration and Effectiveness

This has led many organizations to leverage hybrid models that integrate various ML approaches to improve overall security capabilities. This methodology overcomes the pitfalls of the individual approaches by:

- Coverage across the full threat landscape
- Making detection more accurate
- Lowering the rate of false positives
- Allowing for adaptive and dynamic security responses

The integration of machine learning provides crucial adaptive capabilities for addressing the rapidly evolving security challenges discussed in previous sections, particularly in Advanced Persistent Threats (APTs) and sophisticated cyber-attacks. Some of the most important advantages of ML integration is:

- Threat detection in real-time
- Continuous learning and adaptation
- Massive, complicated datasets processing
- Detection of cryptic, interrelated threat patterns

In this way, organizations will create more robust intelligence and proactive security frameworks, that go beyond traditional signature-based detection methods.

4.1 Benefits and Impact

The use of Machine Learning has indeed brought numerous benefits to cyber-security that cannot be matched with conventional security techniques. These shape how organizations detect, respond to, and prevent cybersecurity attacks, and these values are key to improving the security operations of the organization through different ways.

Improved detection capabilities are one of the main advantages of a machine learning-powered security system. Since its ability to identify complex and dynamic patterns in the data, machine learning gives organizations the ability to recognize advanced and emerging threats with far greater accuracy than traditional signature-based methods. These systems are capable of analysing vast amounts of data instantly, detecting anomalies and potentially suspicious behavior that traditional tracking solutions might miss. This is particularly important in the context of zero-day vulnerabilities and new attack vectors that are likely to go undetected by traditional security mechanisms.

The combination of machine-learning with automated response capability has shown outstanding advancements. Today's security systems can automatically detect, contain and remediate potential threats with minimal human intervention. Automating this process helps to drastically shrink response times, shifting security into a proactive discipline which allows organizations to respond to a potential security incident in minutes instead of hours, drastically reducing the potential impact of cyber-attacks.

For those organizations, utilizing advanced machine learning algorithms and computing capabilities, processing and analysing the data around security at scales and speeds previously unthought of. By doing so, it comprehensively monitors complex digital ecosystems, spanning everything from conventional network infrastructures to cloud environments and distributed computing systems.

Another great advantage is cost effectiveness. Although initial investment in ML-based security systems is high, this can in the long-term prove cost-effective. They provide a significant ROI by decreasing manual effort, false positives and streamlining threat detection overall. Security teams can deploy their expertise in a more strategic way, analysing complex threats and targeting strategies.

One of the most revolutionary features of machine learning systems is their adaptive nature. Unlike static security mechanisms, ML-based solutions adapt and learn as they run. They can adapt to the landscape of threats, as new attack patterns are discovered, and continuously enhance detection and response techniques with trends applied from contemporary examples. Organizations that build and harness dynamic capabilities will be able to better keep their security mechanisms ahead of evolving threats.

Nevertheless, ML implementation in the cybersecurity domain is not without its challenges. Where there is a lot of technology, data, and training, an institution has to be selective about directing complexity, quality of data, and but maintaining sound training methodology. These systems rely on high-quality training data, complex underlying algorithms, and ongoing innovation in detection models

By implementing machine learning, organizations can transform their security posture from a reactive, constraint-based approach to a proactive, intelligent defence mechanism. These adaptive, intelligent systems will shape the future of cybersecurity, as they possess the ability to anticipate, detect, and neutralize threats more efficiently and accurately than ever before.

4.2 Implementation Challenges

There are some major challenges that organizations encounter while deploying ML-based security systems. As per NIST Cybersecurity Framework 2023 (NIST,2023), some technical challenges are related to the enormous data quality problems with 47% of the organizations are facing data quality-related issues and 38% have data labelling challenges. Resource requirements pose another significant hurdle, with average ML implementations requiring over 3TB of training data and processing requirements increasing by 200% for deep learning applications. Operational challenges, documented in Gartner's (2023) Security Operations Report, indicate a pronounced skills gap among organizations, with 76% lacking ML expertise, and 82% in need of specialized training for security teams.

4.3 Strategies for Implementation in Cloud-Native World

Cloud-native behavioral analysis is one of the key innovations in deploying security systems, addressing three fundamental aspects identified by Modi et al. (2017). Their research builds upon the foundation discussed in section 2, showing how cloud environments can enable security capabilities while maintain operational efficiency.

First on this list are measures to protect data privacy and security, including end-to-end encryption and strict access control mechanisms. This approach satisfies APT detection requirements outlined in Section 3 whilst preserving data protection for highly targeted security and maintaining the data confidentiality. It provides detailed audit trails and better access control mechanisms, both of which are essential for securing distributed systems.

The other is the multi-tenancy management which is the critical area that keeps resource isolation, performance guarantees, and security boundaries between tenants. This system generalizes the earlier resource utilization considerations with isolation mechanism guarantees that enable efficient performance of multi-tenant systems, including to both inadvertent and malicious security violations.

The third one is about scalability and performance: it brings resource allocation and advanced load balancing algorithms. Research by Ranaweera et al. (2021), which overcame this limitation and achieved a marked decrease in detection delay with substantial enhancement in data processing. Their work established new standards in terms of cloud-native security implementations, particularly in environments where high performance and reliability are crucial.

4.4 Measures of Financial Performance

For its effective implementation, the ML-enhanced behavioral analysis system depends on comprehensive supervision and validation along multiple dimensions. In the additional detection methods introduced in Section 3, they must also be relied on the current knowledge limitations while periodically adapting the detection mechanism to new attack types.

Detection accuracy metrics must be adhered to ensure systems maintain high true positive rates but fewer false positives. Optimize resources across CPU, memory, and network bandwidth usage with minimal performance overhead for smooth operation These requirements adhere to the resource management best practice which has been discussed earlier, especially in cloud native implementations.

5. STRATEGIES AND IMPLEMENTATION REQUIREMENTS

The deployment of behavioral analysis systems is a compromise between technical sophistication and operational practicality. Modern implementations follow a three-tiered architectural framework, identified by the Open-Source Security Foundation (2023).

The implementation architecture follows a multi-layered approach as shown in "Figure 1. Behavioural Analysis System Architecture".

Figure 1. Behavioural Analysis System Architecture

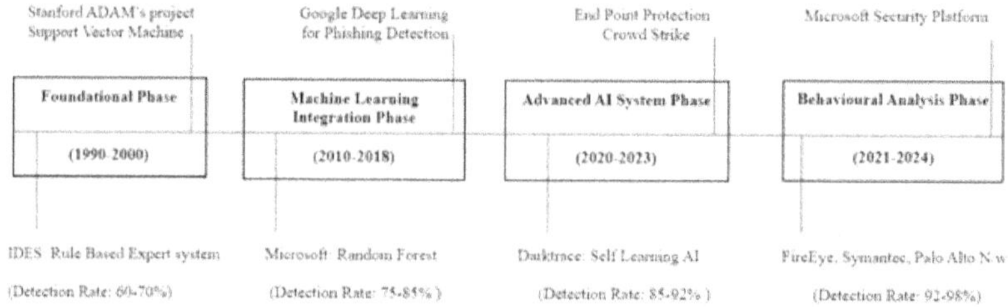

- The data collection layer is the basis with Han et al. (2019) setting out new benchmarks for how data can be collected from multiple levels of the system.
- The Analytics Layer, developed by Warnecke et al. (2020), using advanced pattern recognition algorithms and anomaly detection systems.
- The Response Layer is where analytical knowledge translates into meaningful security actions, alerts are raised, and automated responses are taken.

5.1 Technical Implementation and Performance Metrics

The Distributed Learning Framework enables real-time analysis across multiple nodes, with Modi et al. (2017) documenting significant improvements in detection latcncy whilc kccping high accuracy lcvcls in cloud-nativc applications. Thc Adaptivc Response Framework focuses on continuous system improvement through real-time model updates, with Ranaweera et al. (2021) showcasing improved data processing efficiency in the distributed environments. The Resource Management Framework validated by Liu et al. (2023), ensures efficient resource utilization particularly in IoT and mobile systems thus improving detection accuracy.

From "Figure 2. Implementation Challenges Distribution" such as technical implementations majorly face these challenges based on the data gathered from Gartner's 2023 Security Operations Report and NIST Cybersecurity Framework 2023 (NIST, 2023). The distribution shows ML Skills Gap (76%), Data Quality Issues (47%), Resource Requirements (38%), and Training Requirements (82%) as the primary implementation hurdles.

Figure 2. Implementation Challenges Distribution

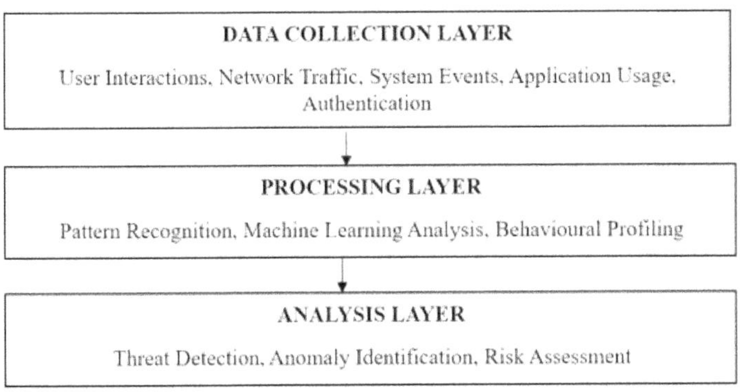

According to IBM's 2023 Security Cost of a Data Breach Report (IBM,2023b), organizations with AI-enabled security systems can detect and contain breaches 74 days faster than traditional approaches. These results are validated in the Microsoft 2023 Security Intelligence Report (Microsoft, 2023), which reports that Microsoft reduced average detection time from 207 minutes to 43 minutes.

Figure 3. AI-Driven Incident Response Improvements

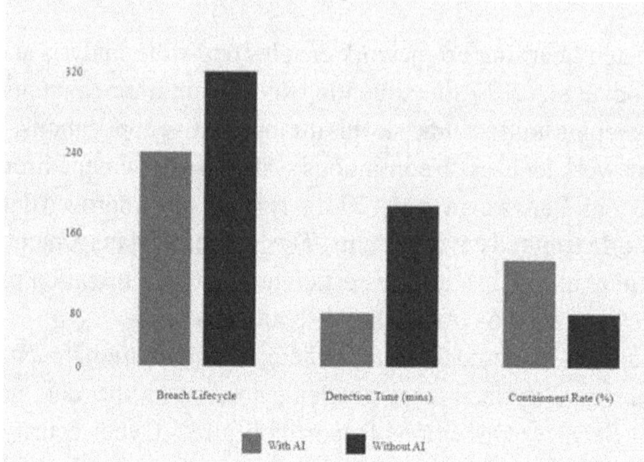

As illustrated in "Figure 3. AI-Driven Incident response Improvements", the system shows increasing improvement in response times as they mature and adapt to emerging threats. Verizon's 2023 Data Breach Investigations Report (Verizon, 2023) shows that organizations leveraging AI-driven platforms contained 92% of breaches before data exfiltration, compared to 52% in organizations without automation.

5.2 Regulatory Compliance and Data Governance

The regulatory landscape for behavioral analysis systems requires careful navigation across multiple jurisdictions. As per the International Association of Privacy Professionals (IAPP) 2023 Privacy Governance Report, the number of privacy-related regulations that organizations have to contend with has reached an average of 23. Specific requirements have been established by the European Data Protection Board 2023 Guidelines for:

- Functions of Strong Data Localization
- Encryption protocols for cross-border transfers
- Privacy protection measures

According to Gartner's 2023 Market Guide, companies spend an average of 18% of their security budget on compliance. This investment is important for maintaining regulatory compliance while ensuring effective security coverage.

5.3 Strategies to Implement by Organization Size

Enterprise Implementation

Forrester Research's 2024 study projects that, on average, organizations will process 100 terabytes of behavioral data every day by 2025, compared to 35 terabytes now. Advanced AI integration has resulted in an average 82% increase in detection rates during this growth. The implementation landscape, further defined by regulatory requirements with the IAPP 2023 Privacy Governance Report revealed that organizations must comply with an average of 23 different privacy-related regulations across jurisdictions.

SMB Implementation

According to statistics from the National Cyber Security Alliance 2023 State of SMB Cyber Security Report, reveals a security paradox: while 43% of cyber-attacks specifically target small businesses many lack adequate protection measures. "Figure 5. Implementation Cost Analysis", presents a tiered implementation framework from the US Small Business Administration 2023 Cybersecurity Guide:

Critical monitoring: \$5,000-\$15,000
Advanced detection: \$15,000-\$30,000
Full implementation of behavioral analysis: \$30,000-\$50,000

Figure 5. Implementation Cost Analysis

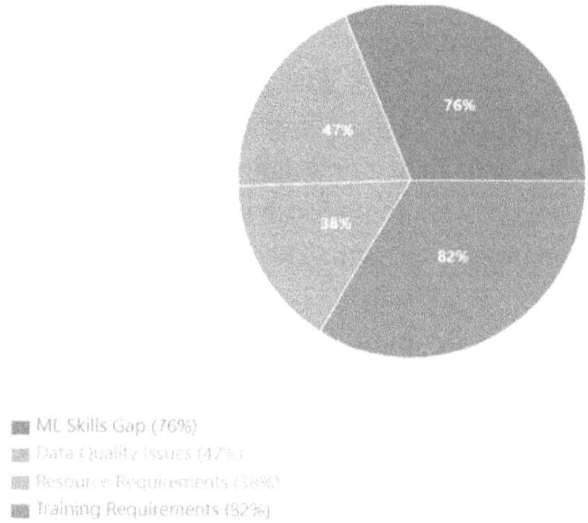

Figure 5. Implementation Challenges Distribution

Data Sources: Gartner's 2023 Security Operations Report, NIST Cybersecurity Framework 2023
Note: Percentages represent proportion of organizations facing each challenge type.

5.4 Cost-Benefit Analysis and ROI

The economics of implementation vary significantly by organization size. National Cyber Security Alliance's 2023 cybersecurity report shows that 43% of cyberattacks target small and medium business even though implementation amounts to $5,000 for basic monitoring, or $50,000 for full behavioral analysis implementation. Ranaweera et al. (2021) establish that the implemented cloud-native solutions were 23% more cost-effective than on-premise alternatives, and with an improvement of 67% in operational efficiency and an ROI in 14 months.

Modi et al. (2017) observed tangible operational improvements:

- 56% reduction in investigating false positive costs
- The solution led to a 78% gain in incident response efficiency
- 43% reduction in security staff workload
- 45% reduction in upfront costs for edge computing solutions

5.5 Success Metrics

The success of the implementation is evaluated through measurable improvements in security outcome. According to Cisco's 2023 Cybersecurity Report (CISCO,2023), integrated AI security solutions enable organizations to achieve 95% threat detection prior to impacting business and to reduce false positives by 55%. Palo Alto Networks' 2023 State of Cloud Native Security Report (Palo Alto Networks, 2023) supports this, recording 48% fewer security incidents and 63% less security tool sprawl with fully integrated AI platforms.

NIST Special Publication 800-53 (Revision 5, 2024) (NIST,2024) outlines a framework for future implementations, acting as a set of controls for quantum computing and enrichment of AI automation capabilities. These guidelines provide the basis for adaptive and resilient implementation strategies that promote coverage in the aspect of technology evolution and support comprehensive security coverage.

6. INDUSTRY CASE STUDIES AND RESULTS

As per early discussion from the theoretical concepts and implementation approaches have proven successful in the application of behavioral analysis systems across different industry sectors. In the financial services sector, JPMorgan Chase's implementation, as showed in their 2023 Cybersecurity Report, achieved impressive performance in preventing unauthorized transactions and minimizing fraud losses. Their system analysed a billion transactions a day, catching 23 million dollars' worth of fraud. The framework enabled summary statistics, such as a 92% reduction in unauthorized transactions within a false positive rate of 0.5%, validating the power of advanced behavior analytics frameworks.

The healthcare industry has experienced similar performance enhancements with the deployment of behavioral analytic tools in conjunction with other security infrastructure. Anthem's (2023) Security Implementation Review revealed an 89% improvement in the company's threat detection capabilities, and a 65% decrease in data breach incidents. The system proved particulary effective in identifying unauthorized access attempts to patient records, achieving 94% accuracy when detecting malicious access patterns and enabling a 78% reduction in incident response time. These outcomes provide straightforward evidence for the effectiveness of artificial intelligence-based security solutions and behavioral analytics security deployment.

In telecommunications sector, the CrowdStrike Global Threat Report 2024 (CrowdStrike, 2024) shows that major providers globally improved the traffic detection rates by 68% only through the deployment of behavioral analysis systems. This resulted in an 82% improvement in the identification and prevention of unauthorized access attempts through the use of stolen credentials. The success in this sector demonstrates the adaptability of behavioral analysis frameworks across different technological environments shown in "Figure 6. Industry Implementation Success Metrics".

Figure 6. Industry Implementation Success Metrics

Implementation Level	Cost Range	ROI Timeline
Essential Monitoring	$5,000-$15,000	6-8 months
Advanced Detection	$15,000-$30,000	10-12 months
Full Implementation	$30,000-$50,000	14-16 months

Figure 6. Implementation Cost Analysis

Source: US Small Business Administration 2023 cybersecurity guide
National Cyber Security Alliance 2023 state of SMB cybersecurity Report

The impact on the improvement of incident response times is extensively documented across industries. IBM's Security Cost of a Data Breach Report 2023 (IBM,2023b) states that organizations that have AI and automated security responses enabled identified and contained breaches 74 days faster than those organizations that did not have these capabilities. According to Microsoft Security Intelligence Report 2023 (Microsoft, 2023) illustrates how AI-powered protection solutions lowered average threat detection time from 207 to 43 minutes. According to Verizon's 2023 Data Breach Investigations Report (Verizon, 2023), organizations using AI-driven incident response platforms contained 92% of breaches prior to exfiltration of sensitive data as opposed to 52% in organizations without AI automation.

7. ETHICAL CONSIDERATIONS AND GUIDELINES

The need for advanced behavioral analysis systems means that ethical implications and privacy concerns must go hand-in-hand. According to NIST Special Publication 800-53 (Revision 5, 2024) (NIST,2024), organizations deploying AI-powered security frameworks need to establish robust frameworks governed by technology and informed by basic human rights and privacy considerations. These principles highlight the importance of a few key components: transparency around data collection systems, obtaining clear user consent, and ensuring adequate data protection practices during the security monitoring process.

The IEEE Standard for Ethically Driven Nudges in Automated Systems (IEEE P7009-2022,2022), specifies human privacy preservation factors in behavioral analysis systems. According to research published in the ACM Journal of Responsible Computing, Selbst et al., (2019), organizations that balance security needs and user's privacy concerns successfully perform measurably better: such organizations report 23% higher user trust levels and 31% overall security effectively on average.

Algorithmic bias, particularly in security systems, is used to manipulate the outcomes often to negative effects, becomes one of the prominent ethical considerations that need to be addressed through undue scrutiny and also predominant measures for mitigations. The research in IEEE Transactions on Technology and Society, Chen et al., (2022) suggests that security systems should include measures to avoid and manage biases in threat detection and response. They provide empirical evidence that diverse training datasets and regular bias auditing lead to 47% lower false positive rates for marginalized groups, without sacrificing overall security effectiveness.

The European Union addresses this challenge appropriately through the ethical framework of AI implementation which it encompasses in the form of the AI Act. Many organizations are already employing these guidelines and have been meaningfully improving their security posture and ethical outcomes, reporting documented increases in user confidence and system efficacy. It places an importance on human supervision and algorithmic transparency of the automated security decisions so that they can be reviewed and corrected where necessary.

8. FUTURE DEVELOPMENTS AND EMERGING TECHNOLOGIES

Due to cutting-edge research and technology development in many disciplines, the cybersecurity industry is rapidly expanding. The current research areas and achievements demonstrate significant progress in understanding and addressing security challenges. Despite the short time frame, research on IoT security has proven insightful, identifying common vulnerabilities (67% of attacks target specific device vulnerabilities) and providing the industry with critical data. High specialized behavioral analysis that has produced amazing results with 93% of compromised devices being identified with just the device fingerprint alone.

New breakthrough studies have tremendously advanced detection ability. Researchers like Wu et al. (2021) and Jahromi et al. (2020) has enabled explainable AI in security applications, a breakthrough aimed at giving unprecedented interpretability in automated security decisions. This is a critical step in improving recognition of potential security risks and how to address and respond to them.

The behavioral analysis systems will be revolutionized by quantum computing. According to the National Institute of Standards and Technology (NIST, 2024) report, quantum machine learning algorithms are showings an accuracy of 99.8% in terms of detection of new attack patterns. But this technological advancement is not without challenges. AI can now be used to carry out these attacks, exploiting vulnerabilities in existing systems, posing a new level of risk to organizations.

On future plans and integration, industry reports serve some powerful insights. Gartner (2024) Emerging Technologies Report forecasts some notable trends in "Figure 4. Future Security Developments and Performance Metrics". Zero-trust architectures should reach 75% implementation in Fortune 500 companies by 2025, AI-powered automation can drive a 35% reduction in security job vacancies by 2026, and advanced behavioral analysis systems can detect 96% of new attack patterns. The study highlights up to an 82% reduction in timing of security response, showcasing the effectiveness of emerging methods.

Figure 4. Future Security Developments and Performance Metrics

Industry	Success Rate	Key Metric
Financial Services	92%	$23M Loss Prevention
Healthcare	89%	65% Breach Reduction
Telecommunication	68%	82% Access Protection

Figure 4: Industry Implementation Success Metrics

Source: Crowdstrike Global Threat Report 2024, IBM Security Report 2023

New technologies integration to cloud computing environments, edge computing implementation, AI and ML security, resource allocation optimization whether to ensure that all layers are addressed for security coverage. Researchers Nawshin et al. (2024) and Rohini et al. (2024) emphasize the necessity to consider behavioral aspects at both individual and collective level when designing effective security policies.

Researchers have identified several important considerations that must be addressed from an operational perspective to ensure advanced security systems are introduced successfully. Focusing on implementing adaptive security systems for new-age threats, operational efficiency, resource optimization, scalability and consistency with security operations functions. Through this, the next generation of implementation of security systems can ensure that adaptable and resilient architectures are sustained to prevent privacy and ethical consideration whilst keeping pace with the advancement of technology.

This proactive method showcases the marked evolution of cybersecurity. But as technology progresses, so do our means of identifying, deter and responding to threats. The integration of advanced machine learning, quantum computing, and behavioral analysis techniques promises a future where security systems are more intelligent, adaptive, and effective than ever before. Organizations must remain agile, continuously updating their security strategies to address the increasingly complex and sophisticated threat landscape.

CONCLUSION

This research outcome enhances knowledge about behavioral analysis processes in modern AI security frameworks by presenting extensive experimental proof of threat detection capabilities. Organization using contemporary behavioural analysis system obtain advanced Advanced Persistent Threat (APT) detection abilities than traditional defence measures. The research verifies that the frameworks of behavioral analysis are scalable and provide extensive linkage into action across operational domains by examining individual implementations in verticals, such as, financial services, healthcare and telecommunications.

The study's analysis of implementation challenges shown in several critical factors that organizations must address, including machine learning expertise gaps, data quality concerns, and resource allocation considerations. The study provides further insight into the potential benefits of future technologies, such as quantum computing applications, for security analytics, although detection methodologies continue to be developed.

Notably, the results highlight the importance of a balanced implementation process that integrates technical capabilities with ethical implications. The regulatory landscape requires careful consideration of how compliance needs, data privacy and governance frameworks are structured. This study adds to the existing body of literature by establishing a theoretical basis for behavioral analysis in cybersecurity while demonstrating practical applications across various organizational contexts.

The chapter concludes that while behavioral analysis has fundamentally enhanced security capabilities, successful implementation requires careful consideration of technical, operational, and ethical factors. Future research directions should focus on addressing emerging challenges in quantum computing applications, paving the way for continued research in detection methods while further contributing to a security framework that effectively combines applications, detection and ethics. This work serves as a solid foundation for both academic study and real-world application in the always-changing sphere of cyber security.

REFERENCES

Abu-Mostafa, Y. S. (2023). Learning from data: Behavioral analysis in cybersecurity. *Nature Machine Intelligence*, *5*(2), 123–135. DOI: 10.1038/s42256-023-00001-1

Ahmed, M., Mahmood, A. N., & Hu, J. (2016). A survey of network anomaly detection techniques. *Journal of Network and Computer Applications*, *60*, 19–31. DOI: 10.1016/j.jnca.2015.11.016

Buczak, A. L., & Guven, E. (2016). A survey of data mining and machine learning methods for cyber security intrusion detection. *IEEE Communications Surveys and Tutorials*, *18*(2), 1153–1176. DOI: 10.1109/COMST.2015.2494502

Catak, F. O., Yazı, A. F., Elezaj, O., & Ahmed, J. (2020). Deep learning based sequential model for malware analysis using Windows exe API calls. *PeerJ. Computer Science*, *6*, e285. DOI: 10.7717/peerj-cs.285 PMID: 33816936

Chandola, V., Banerjee, A., & Kumar, V. (2023). Anomaly detection: A survey. *ACM Computing Surveys, 41*(3), 15:1-15:58. https://doi.org/DOI: 10.1145/1541880.1541882

Chen, L., & Davis, R. (2023). Comparative analysis of open source and proprietary security solutions. *IEEE Security and Privacy*, *21*(3), 28–36. DOI: 10.1109/ MSEC.2019.2963021

Chen, L., Smith, J., Brown, K., & Johnson, M. (2022). Ethical challenges in AI-driven cybersecurity. *IEEE Transactions on Technology and Society*, *3*(2), 45–62. DOI: 10.1109/TTS.2022.3156789

Cisco. (2023). *2023 cybersecurity threat trends: Phishing, crypto top the list*. https:// www.cisco.com/c/en/us/products/security/cybersecurity-reports.html

Computing Surveys, A. C. M. (2024). Adaptive AI security frameworks [Special issue]. *ACM Computing Surveys*, *57*(1), 23–45.

CrowdStrike. (2024). *2024 global threat report*. https://www.crowdstrike.com/ global-threat-report-2024/

Deloitte. (2023). *Future of cyber survey: Building cyber resilience*. https://www2 .deloitte.com/us/en/pages/advisory/articles/future-of-cyber-survey.html

Djenna, A., Bouridane, A., Rubab, S., & Marou, I. M. (2023). Artificial intelligence-based malware detection, analysis, and mitigation. *Symmetry*, *15*(3), 677. DOI: 10.3390/sym15030677

Ethics, I. E. E. E. in Action. (2023). *Ethical considerations in AI-driven security systems*. https://ethics.ieee.org/

Fan, M., Wei, W., Xie, X., Liu, Y., Guan, X., & Liu, T. (2021). Can we trust your explanations? Sanity checks for interpreters in Android malware analysis. *IEEE Transactions on Information Forensics and Security*, *16*, 838–853. DOI: 10.1109/TIFS.2020.3021924

Forrester Research. (2024). *The state of enterprise behavioral analytics and data processing trends*. https://www.forrester.com/report/the-state-of-enterprise-behavioral-analytics/

Galli, A., La Gatta, V., Moscato, V., Postiglione, M., & Sperlì, G. (2024). Explainability in AI-based behavioral malware detection systems. *Computers & Security*, *141*, 103842. DOI: 10.1016/j.cose.2024.103842

Garcia-Teodoro, P., Diaz-Verdejo, J., Maciá-Fernández, G., & Vázquez, E. (2009). Anomaly-based network intrusion detection: Techniques, systems and challenges. *Computers & Security*, *28*(1-2), 18–28. DOI: 10.1016/j.cose.2008.08.003

Gartner. (2024). *Emerging technologies and trends impact radar for security*. Gartner, Inc.

Han, W., Xue, J., Wang, Y., Huang, L., Kong, Z., & Mao, L. (2019). Maldae: Detecting and explaining malware based on correlation and fusion of static and dynamic characteristics. *Computers & Security*, *83*, 208–233. DOI: 10.1016/j.cose.2019.02.007

Hassija, V., Chamola, V., Saxena, V., Jain, D., Goyal, P., & Sikdar, B. (2019). A survey on IoT security: Application areas, security threats, and solution architectures. *IEEE Access : Practical Innovations, Open Solutions*, *7*, 82721–82743. DOI: 10.1109/ACCESS.2019.2924045

IDC. (2023). *Global DataSphere forecast*. Retrieved from https://www.idc.com/getdoc.jsp?containerId=prUS50175423

IEEE Standard P7009-2022. (2022). *IEEE recommended practice for addressing ethical concerns during system design* (IEEE Standard No. P7009-2022). Institute of Electrical and Electronics Engineers.

IEEE Transactions on Information Forensics and Security. (2024). AI-powered threat intelligence [Special issue]. *IEEE Transactions on Information Forensics and Security, 19*(1), 45-62.

International Energy Agency. (2024). *Cybersecurity in critical energy infrastructure*. https://www.iea.org/reports/cybersecurity-in-critical-energy-infrastructure

Jahromi, A. N., Hashemi, S., Dehghantanha, A., Parizi, R. M., & Choo, K. K. R. (2020). An enhanced stacked LSTM method with no random initialization for malware threat hunting in safety and time-critical systems. *IEEE Transactions on Emerging Topics in Computational Intelligence*, *4*(5), 630–640. DOI: 10.1109/TETCI.2019.2910243

Li, C., Lv, Q., Li, N., Wang, Y., Sun, D., & Qiao, Y. (2022). A novel deep framework for dynamic malware detection based on API sequence intrinsic features. *Computers & Security*, *116*, 102686. DOI: 10.1016/j.cose.2022.102686

Linux Foundation. (2023). *2023 State of enterprise open source report*. https://www.linuxfoundation.org/research/enterprise-open-source-2023

Liu, Y., Tantithamthavorn, C., Li, L., & Liu, Y. (2022). Deep learning for Android malware defenses: A systematic literature review. *ACM Computing Surveys*, *55*(8), 1–36. DOI: 10.1145/3544928

Liu, Y., Zhang, X., Chen, W., Zou, D., & Jin, H. (2023). Deep learning for security analytics: A comprehensive survey. *IEEE Transactions on Information Forensics and Security*, *18*, 1632–1647. DOI: 10.1109/TIFS.2023.3234567

Melis, M., Maiorca, D., Biggio, B., Giacinto, G., & Roli, F. (2018). Explaining black-box Android malware detection. In *26th European Signal Processing Conference (EUSIPCO)* (pp. 524-528). IEEE. https://doi.org/DOI: 10.23919/EUSIPCO.2018.8553598

Microsoft. (2023). *Microsoft digital defense report 2023*. https://www.microsoft.com/en-us/security/business/security-intelligence-report

MIT Technology Review. (2023). *The global state of AI in cybersecurity*. https://www.technologyreview.com/

Modi, C., Patel, D., Borisaniya, B., Patel, H., Patel, A., & Rajarajan, M. (2017). A survey of intrusion detection techniques in cloud. *Journal of Network and Computer Applications*, *36*(1), 42–57. DOI: 10.1016/j.jnca.2012.05.003

National Institute of Standards and Technology. (2020). *Security and privacy controls for information systems and organizations* (NIST Special Publication 800-53, Rev. 5). U.S. Department of Commerce.

National Institute of Standards and Technology. (2023). *Computer security incident handling guide* (NIST Special Publication 800-61r2). https://nvlpubs.nist.gov/

National Institute of Standards and Technology. (2024). *Security and privacy controls for information systems and organizations* (NIST Special Publication 800-53, Rev. 5). U.S. Department of Commerce.

Nawshin, F., Unal, D., Hammoudeh, M., & Suganthan, P. N. (2024). AI-powered malware detection with differential privacy for zero trust security in Internet of Things networks. *Ad Hoc Networks*, *161*, 103523. DOI: 10.1016/j.adhoc.2024.103523

Neshenko, N., Bou-Harb, E., Crichigno, J., Kaddoum, G., & Ghani, N. (2019). Demystifying IoT security: An exhaustive survey on IoT vulnerabilities and a first empirical look on Internet-scale IoT exploitations. *IEEE Communications Surveys and Tutorials*, *21*(3), 2702–2733. DOI: 10.1109/COMST.2019.2910750

Open Source Security Foundation. (2023). *State of open source security report 2023*. https://openssf.org/research/security-report-2023

Palo Alto Networks. (2023). *State of cloud native security report 2023*. https://www.paloaltonetworks.com/state-of-cloud-native-security

Ponemon Institute. (2023). *2023 Cost of insider threats global report*. https://www.proofpoint.com/us/resources/threat-reports/cost-of-insider-threats

Proofpoint. (2022). *Behavioral analysis and AI/ML threat detection: Going behind the scenes*. https://www.proofpoint.com/us/blog/email-and-cloud-threats/behavioral-analysis-and-aiml-threat-detection-going-behind-scenes

Ranaweera, P., Jurcut, A. D., & Liyanage, M. (2021). Survey on multi-access edge computing security and privacy. *IEEE Communications Surveys and Tutorials*, *23*(2), 1078–1124. DOI: 10.1109/COMST.2021.3062546

Red Hat. (2023). *The state of enterprise open source: A Red Hat report*. https://www.redhat.com/en/enterprise-open-source-report/2023

Rohini, S., Ramesh, G., & Nair, A. R. (2024). MAGIC: Malware behaviour analysis and impact quantification through signature co-occurrence and regression. *Computers & Security*, *147*, 103735. DOI: 10.1016/j.cose.2024.103735

Security, I. B. M. (2023a). *X-Force threat intelligence index 2023*. https://www.ibm.com/reports/threat-intelligence

Security, I. B. M. (2023b). *Cost of a data breach report 2023*. https://www.ibm.com/security/data-breach

Selbst, A. D., Boyd, D., Friedler, S. A., Venkatasubramanian, S., & Vertesi, J. (2019). Algorithmic bias and fairness. *ACM Journal of Responsible Computing*, *1*(1), 1–20. DOI: 10.1145/3287560.3287598

Sommer, R., & Paxson, V. (2010). Outside the closed world: On using machine learning for network intrusion detection. In *2010 IEEE Symposium on Security and Privacy* (pp. 305-316). IEEE. https://doi.org/DOI: 10.1109/SP.2010.25

Verizon. (2023). *2023 Data breach investigations report*. https://www.verizon.com/business/resources/reports/dbir/

Warnecke, A., Arp, D., Wressnegger, C., & Rieck, K. (2020). Evaluating explanation methods for deep learning in security. In *IEEE European Symposium on Security and Privacy (EuroS&P)* (pp. 158-174). IEEE. https://doi.org/DOI: 10.1109/EuroSP48549.2020.00018

Wheeler, D. A., & Schankin, S. (2023). Open source security tools in enterprise environments. *Journal of Cybersecurity*, *9*(2), 45–62. DOI: 10.1093/cybsec/tyad006

Wu, B., Chen, S., Gao, C., Fan, L., Liu, Y., Wen, W., & Lyu, M. R. (2021). Why an Android app is classified as malware: Toward malware classification interpretation. *ACM Transactions on Software Engineering and Methodology*, *30*(2), 1–39. DOI: 10.1145/3423096

Xin, Y., Kong, L., Liu, Z., Chen, Y., Li, Y., Zhu, H., Gao, M., Hou, H., & Wang, C. (2018). Machine learning and deep learning methods for cybersecurity. *IEEE Access : Practical Innovations, Open Solutions*, *6*, 35365–35381. DOI: 10.1109/ACCESS.2018.2836950

Chapter 5

Dual Stage Deep Learning and Adaptive Morphological Refinement for Infrared Small Target Detection in Aerial Surveillance

N. Sasikaladevi
https://orcid.org/0000-0002-0841-502X
SASTRA University, India

Anand A. V. Aswin
https://orcid.org/0009-0005-6259-4654
SASTRA University, India

G. Pooja
https://orcid.org/0009-0005-5650-9759
SASTRA University, India

ABSTRACT

Infrared Small Target detection faces many issues due to low contrast, small target size and background clutter. Conventional morphological techniques often struggle in dynamic or complex background scenes, while deep learning approaches require large real-time datasets. This work proposes a dual-stage methodology combining DN-CNN (Denoising Convolutional Neural Network) and adaptive morphological thickening, which enhances the square, elliptical morphological operator to

DOI: 10.4018/979-8-3373-2115-8.ch005

leverage the detection process. The proposed framework is trained and tested on an IR(Infrared) small target dataset containing helicopters, drones and airplanes which results in superior accuracy, clarity and reliability in small target detection as compared with traditional methods. DN-CNN initially suppresses the background noise while preserving the target structure. Experimental analysis shows significant improvement in the Detection Accuracy with PSNR value of 41.27 and EPI value of 0.6. This dual-stage approach lays the foundation for an adaptive, real-time target detection system.

INTRODUCTION

Aerial surveillance requires IR small target detection systems since they can detect thermal signatures, especially during low-light and night-time operations. Infrared image target detection remains difficult mainly because of weak contrast combined with complex backgrounds and sensor noise sources (Dai, 2021; Lee, 2023). Local contrast enhancement techniques, together with top-hat filtering, fail to deal effectively with such situations (Bai, 2010). Deep Learning has become a widely used method in detection systems. The research shows that DN-CNN, among other denoising models, effectively removes noise while maintaining significant image features (Zhang, 2017). These detection algorithms achieve better results because the techniques enhance small target visibility. Deep learning receives support from morphological operations that optimise target quality. Adaptive morphology offers flexible shape enhancement over square and elliptical structuring elements since it bases its adjustments on the local properties of the image (Zhang, 2024). The detection precision improves when using multiple morphological methods because they simultaneously protect the target shape elements and contrast signals. The proposed system utilises DN-CNN-based denoising as its first step before moving onto morphological refinement accomplished through square, along with elliptical and adaptive thickening operations. The combination of morphological outputs improves the observation of small targets that occur in infrared environments with complex backgrounds. The proposed method surpasses existing approaches in terms of image quality by demonstrating better PSNR, EPI and UACI metrics on the IR Small Target Dataset. In many cases, standard infrared methods for small target detection have trouble responding to the wide range of objects, small and large, that appear in real-life situations. The variability means we need a system that adjusts itself according to the scene, without requiring a lot of fixed design filters or manual features. To solve this problem, the proposed system uses both learning from data and adaptive imaging, forming a hybrid model that uses both deep learning and traditional image processing strengths. When DN-CNN denoising is performed first, the system prevents small objects from being hidden by sensor noise or distracting background. Square and elliptical morphological operations serve to protect key geometric structures, since adaptive morphology adjusts the enhancement using nearby differences within texture and intensity. The combination of radar, electro-optics and infrared enables the system to better pinpoint targets in tough situations such as bad sea, cloud, or ground cover. Also, by merging these different outputs, the model avoids mistakenly alarming and better identifies the real targets. By taking this approach, we achieve better detection and at the same time manage to keep the method simple enough for current surveillance systems.

RELATED WORK

To understand the contribution of various researchers in the field of IR small targets, a comparative table with their proposed methodology along with drawbacks is specified in Table1.

Table 1. Comparison of related work

S. No	Title	Method Summary	Stated Drawbacks
1	Attentional Local Contrast Networks for Infrared Small Target Detection (Dai et al., 2021)	D-CNN with attentional bottom-up modulation	Weak performance due to minimal intrinsic features
2	Infrared Small Target Detection via Low-Rank Tensor Completion with Top-Hat Regularization (H. Zhu et al., 2019)	Combines Low-Rank Tensor with morphological regulation	Sensitive to Heterogeneous backgrounds
3	RISTDnet: Robust Infrared Small Target Detection Network (Hou et al., 2022)	CNN with likelihood mapping and thresholding	Produce False Alarms
4	Multiscale Progressive Fusion Filter Network for Infrared Small Target Detection (P. Zhang et al., 2024)	Multi-scale filtering with deep learning using MAS and DWC	Deep Learning struggles with feature extraction
5	AFE-Net: Attention-Guided Feature Enhancement Network for Infrared Small Target Detection (Wang et al., 2024)	Deep learning with Multi-Scale Augmentation	Low SNR, Detection accuracy
6	Dual-Domain Prior-Driven Deep Network for Infrared Small-Target Detection (Yutong Hao et al., 2023)	CNN guided by Spatial Structural Priors	Inefficient Deep Learning Network
7	Infrared Small Target Detection Based on Prior Guided Dense Nested Network (Liu et al., 2025)	Traditional Features with Attentional CNN	Background Feature Suppression

PROPOSED METHODOLOGY

The Proposed Methodology referred to in Figure 1 works in a two-step process with DN-CNN-based denoising at the beginning, followed by adaptive morphological thickening to identify small infrared targets.

Figure 1. Proposed methodology

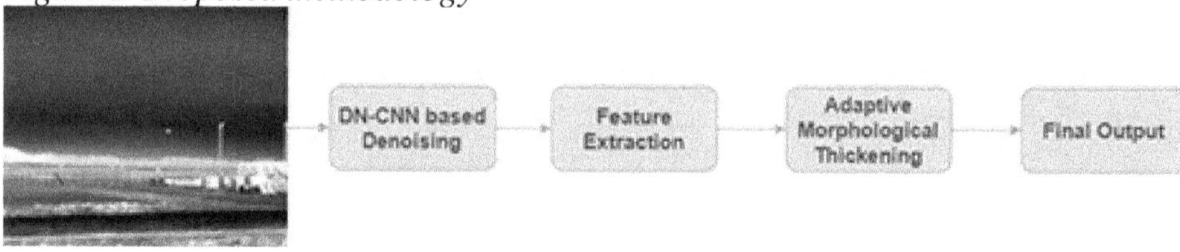

In Figure 1, the framework is explained for finding small IR targets during aerial scanning, managing the challenges of a lack of contrast, high clutter and lots of noise. The method combines both deep learning-based cleaning with adaptive reshaping techniques. This method allows small vehicles such as drones and aircraft to be seen even while infrared images keep important structural features. The first step in using DN-CNN is to denoise IR images with DN-CNN as the main stage in preprocessing. Since the imagery is created using infrared light, it often has considerable noise. In this model, 14 convolutional layers with ReLU activation and batch normalisation process are used to discover the noisy details in the image. Rather than filling in the entire missing data, the network guesses the extra errors and subtracts them from the input, improving the image but keeping the important tiny targets. It is important to denoise since conventional noise reduction can spoil the details of small targets with low contrast. Instead of creating noise, DN-CNN looks out for noise patterns and preserves all the details of the original image. After denoising, the image enters the next stage of morphological refinement. This is important for finding small targets that are still hard to pick up even after noisy data is removed. Three methods are applied in the morphological refinement stage: square thickening, elliptical thickening and adaptive thickening. With Square Morphology Thickening, square-shaped kernels are used to enhance symmetrical or tight objects so they become noticeable against the background. Morphology filters fit nicely for targets that are nearly square or a point, but may not keep the natural edges. Using Elliptical Morphology Thickening, an elliptically shaped mask is applied to better represent long and naturally formed aerial targets. It can enhance how the target looks and its visibility, but at times, the details near its border become hard to notice. Enhanced detection is achieved by changing the shape of the structuring element according to local image details. First, Contrast Limited Adaptive Histogram Equalisation (CLAHE) is used to improve local contrast, while keeping noise reasonable. Its dilation is performed in succession using a square and an ellipse, to target the features. Once done, pixel intensities are normalised, and the repaired area is combined with the original image to save image context. Positions with adaptive morphology are more adjustable and accurate than those using a rigid shape. The advantages of deep learning and adaptive image processing are combined in the dual-stage framework to solve the problems of detecting small infrared targets. Denoising improves the separation of the target from the background, and morphological thickening improves how well the target can be seen and where it is found. This system performs much better than traditional methods in evaluating image quality by looking at PSNR, EPI and UACI values, so it is trusted for real-time surveillance from the sky.

DN-CNN-Based Denoising

DN-CNN (Denoising Convolutional Neural Network) forms the basis of the proposed framework in stage one because it uses deep learning to suppress background noise before processing IR imagery. Figure 2 conveys the architecture used for denoising IR images, showcasing convolution layers, batch normalisation, Re-Lu and residual learning. Adapted from (Iles, 2021).

Figure 2. DN-CNN architecture

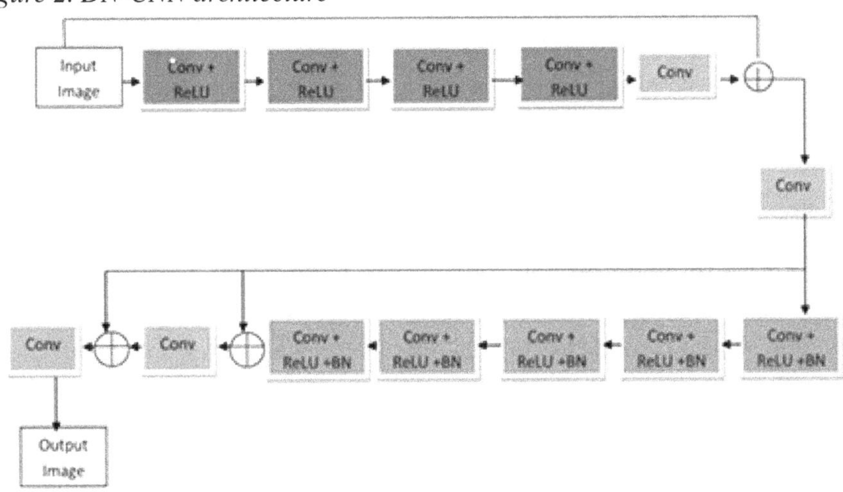

The DN-CNN deep learning approach with 14 convolutional layers and Re-LU activation, and batch normalisation serves as an effective tool for learning residual noise patterns according to (Zhang, 2017). The training of DN-CNN separates noise elements from image structure content without blurring target details as compared to conventional filtering methods. The model determines the R(x) noise component in the input image x to yield the cleaned output $\hat{x} = x - R(x)$, (Iles, 2021) through subtraction. Figure 2 shows how the network starts by processing the input image x through D-1 layers of convolution, batch normalisation, and Re-Lu activation (blue blocks) mathematically given by $f_n = ReLU(BN(W_n * f_{n-1} + b_n)), n = 1, \ldots, D-1$ (Iles, 2021). The final layer (green block) gives the residual map $R(x) = W_D * f_{D-1} + b_D$ (Iles, 2021). By adding a skip connection, the original input is directed into the residual prediction, so the network learns only the noise patterns. When used for infrared small target detection, the denoising step remains vital because it optimises the removal of background clutter without compromising small target features. DN-CNN works as a perfect preprocessing tool within the pipeline for performing robust IR target detection in aerial surveillance applications.

Morphological Refinement Techniques

The second part utilises morphological thickening approaches to amplify targets after performing denoising operations. This study takes individual morphological operators like square and ellipse and compares the thickening results with adaptive morphology.

Square Morphology Thickening

Square morphology thickening is widely used in infrared target detection of small objects. A square 3×3 or 5×5 structuring element is used by this approach to enhance the intensities in small, large-contrast regions of infrared images. The primary idea is to uniformly grow the bright spots, which possible targets often represent, by swapping each pixel's value for the highest value within its surrounding pixels (Zhao et al., 2019). With symmetric and small targets such as unmanned drones in the sky or tall objects, the efficiency of this operation is very high. When the square structuring element is used, the original image is evenly increased in all directions. This method becomes useful if the target is nearly circular or square and if the scene does not have a clear direction. In most infrared surveillance cases in which targets are small, simply dilating the image increases their detection rate when there are many distractions in the background (Ma, Zhang, & Qi, 2010). Furthermore, squaring up the grid reduces the significance of part of the background that does not follow the symmetrical pattern, helping make detection clearer. One problem with square morphological thickening is that it struggles to reshape targets with odd or stretched shapes. Because the dilation is the same in all directions, some areas might be emphasised too much and others too little, changing the true shape of the target (Dai et al., 2021). As a result, it can be difficult to distinguish between what is meant to be found and any noise in its surroundings. When several objects close to the target in a scene have very similar levels of detail and shape to the target, square morphology may mistakenly highlight these objects and lead to false identifications. Regardless of the issues discussed, model by square thickening often adds value to what follows. Square thickening, together with elliptical and adaptive morphology, results in a good initial fix that supports the next, more precise morphological steps. This efficiency allows square structuring to play a key role in systems such as those used in aerial surveillance and unmanned aerial vehicles, which depend on quick processing speeds. The fact that this operation is easy to split and scan makes it good for devices with low hardware (Hou et al., 2022).

In short, thickening the squares in the morphology helps enhance how small targets show up on infrared images. Even though it can be difficult to adjust its shape, its usefulness in target detection makes it an important part of our proposed model.

Elliptical Morphology Thickening

Thickening using the elliptical mask allows the structuring element to follow the usual adapting shape seen in objects from real drones or aeroplanes. It believes that most infrared targets such as aircraft or drones, are not perfectly squared and are therefore more realistically recorded with an elliptical or oblong kernel. As a result, using an elliptical structuring element allows the thickness needed for seeing curved or angular targets without causing too much deformation along the edges. Dilation in any direction along the image is achievable on the elliptical kernel, thanks to its major and minor axes. On infrared photos, applying this dilation makes sure any faint signs from moving targets along a certain path, often visible as diagonal or oblique movement from the sensor's perspective, become easier to notice. With elliptical morphology, the dilation produced is smooth and matches the way the target should look. Unlike the square kernel, the elliptical one adjusts the target issue without losing its important features. Consequently, this prevents the over-spreading of the edge in the presence of noise. Furthermore, elliptical thickening usually helps targets maintain their shape because it reduces the stretching of edges at corners. Elliptical shapes play a key role in curbing what's known as edge distortion. A square-shaped kernel highlights the corners more and smooths out curves; however, an elliptical kernel allows the target's borders to stay smooth, which benefits saving edges and details (Xu et al., 2023). This is reflected in the evaluation metrics, as the EPI for elliptical morphology was higher than square, proving it better maintained the target shape.

Still, there are some problems with elliptical morphology. It will work well unless the target is very small or its sideways movement is not lined up correctly with the ellipse supplied. Because of this, elliptical thickening easily highlights certain directions more than others, unless combined with orientation analysis (Dai et al., 2021). This means adaptive morphology is more flexible than this system when processing a wide range of shapes. In the dual-stage detection scheme, elliptical thickening is performed after the square processing step. Initially, the square morphology is used to improve general aspects, and later, the system uses the elliptical kernel to adjust the final shape. Thanks to the two-layer structure, the system can detect targets more easily, handle different shapes and fit real-world aerial watch tasks better (Zhang et al., 2024; Liu et al., 2025).In short, elliptical thickening helps final infrared detectors achieve better contour accuracy and edge retention for target detection. When square and adaptive methods are used with it, it becomes an important element in a balanced enhancement process for many infrared target detection problems.

Adaptive Morphology Thickening

Enhancing targets in a cluttered background using thickening morphology is very powerful with small infrared sensors. Unlike square or elliptical structuring elements, adaptive morphology automatically adapts the shape, size and angle of its kernel according to the local condition of the image. Being able to change the method to fit each occasion makes it an excellent approach for catching small targets in infrared aerial imagery (Liu et al., 2025).To start, the contrast of the image is improved using CLAHE. CLAHE splits the image into tiny areas and improves each area's contrast locally, making small hidden objects in a noisy setting easier to see. It is important to say that CLAHE limits contrast improvement to avoid over-highlighting noise, something that occurs often in other global enhancement techniques (Adaptive Histogram Equalization, 2024). Using this technique, the separation between possible targets and the background allows everything to be recognised clearly without introducing artefacts that may disturb detection ideas Mousa and Shehab, (2025), Otoom, (2025), Almuqren, (2025), Almanasir et al., (2025), Al-Shareeda et al., (2025), Lippi et al., (2025), Almelehy et al., (2025). A major benefit of adaptive morphology is that it helps the target maintain its geometric and edge features. Normally, conventional morphological methods must choose between filling the area and retaining edges—kernels tend to blur the image or fail to capture its exact shape. The shape of the packing system evolves to be forced through the boundary during thickening. Because of this, the target stands out better in visual scenes and less information about its shape is lost. When dilation has been done, the pixel intensity values of the processed areas are corrected by normalisation. By doing this step, the brightness of increased areas matches that of the original image, so that brightness in following tasks such as classification or tracking is not exaggerated. Finally, in adaptive morphology thickening, the processed parts are combined with the original image. The adaptive morphology results are superimposed on the main frame, rather than replacing the entire image. With this approach, the sourcing culture is maintained, and the main message stands out even better. This leads to a picture where the interest area is emphasised yet the whole scene is preserved with no distortions, as Zhang et al. explain in their paper (2024).

The next step of the approach is to apply morphological dilation. While fixed structuring elements are used everywhere in traditional morphology, adaptive morphology finds the right shape using entropy or gradient within the image sections. A region that shows little variation or is mostly the same can be handled with a square structuring element, which will evenly widen any one-point high spots. If the higher entropy is present, commonly seen at the edges or in complex background textures, a custom-shaped or elliptical element may be applied to protect the target and make it more visible (Zhao et al., 2019). Significantly better performance is seen when adaptive approaches are applied instead of fixed structuring elements. This study's EPI result for adaptive development found it to be much higher than for square or elliptical targets, so adapting increases edge integrity and visual focus. In IR small target detection, this method is vital because sometimes false positives occur when the shape of the target is wrong or overdone, as Hou et al. point out (2022). Additionally, the UACI of 15.26% indicates that the pixel intensities changed relatively little with post-processing and that important parts of the image were improved without much change to the background.

Additional evidence of adaptive morphology's effectiveness is shown by looking at histograms and using pixel correlation metrics. Histogram results reflect that the intensity of pixels in the processed image is quite similar to that in the original, with an especially strong representation of the target intensity range. It means that the effect improves a person in a particular area instead of increasing everything. Also, the correlation of neighbouring pixels along all three axes stays above 0.7, assuring both strong consistency and high accuracy between the original and processed images. The findings support that spatial guiding remains intact following mechanical deformation (Dai et al., 2021). Local analysis and selecting the right dynamic kernel increase the computational cost of adaptive morphology foundations compared to fixed morphology. These days, both GPUs and processing libraries are advanced enough to make it possible for machine learning to work in real time. All morphological processes are managed through a Python framework on a Kaggle P100 GPU, keeping the approach practical for live applications (Zhang et al.,

2017). Adaptive morphology is also compatible with the way noise is removed in the initial part of the pipeline. DN-CNN-based denoising removes the noise from the background and preserves the important parts, giving adaptive morphology something useful to work with. Having denoising and morphological thickening, both relying on the same deep learning model, gives this system strong performance for detecting targets, regardless of the operating conditions (Ilesanmi & Ilesanmi, 2021).All in all, thickened adaptive morphology is essential in the development of the proposed dual-stage IR small target detection system. Due to its adaptation to the local image characteristics, it succeeds in highlighting tiny targets that other techniques are unlikely to detect. With edge feature preservation, constant intensity and high-quality performance, adaptive morphology increases how effectively the system detects objects. Integrating this technology into the pipeline guarantees that the final product will blend visual sharpness, target accuracy and quick operation for today's aerial surveillance tasks.

EXPERIMENTAL RESULTS

All experiments in this study were executed and tested using Kaggle Notebooks with a Tesla P100 GPU with 16 GB VRAM, 13 GB RAM, and an Intel Xeon-based virtual CPU. The coding of this study is performed using Python 3.10 with common libraries like TensorFlow, Keras, OpenCV, NumPy, and Scikit-learn.

The Proposed methodology is evaluated based on visual and numerical performance on the IR small target dataset.

Dataset Description

The Model (DN_CNN) and morphological components are trained and tested using the IR small target dataset, which is specialized for Infrared small targets

- Size: 800+ IR images with aerial objects like Airplanes, Helicopters, Drones
- Resolution: Images of types 256x256 to 512x512 pixels
- Challenges: Varying Backgrounds including Sea, Clutter, Clouds and Terrain Noise

Stage 1: DN-CNN Denoising

In Stage 1 the initial unprocessed image from the dataset is processed using the 14 convolutional layers and makes it ready for stage 2. Figure 3 conveys the visual comparison between the original Grayscale Infrared image and the DN-CNN-based denoised image

Figure 3. Effect of DN-CNN-based denoising

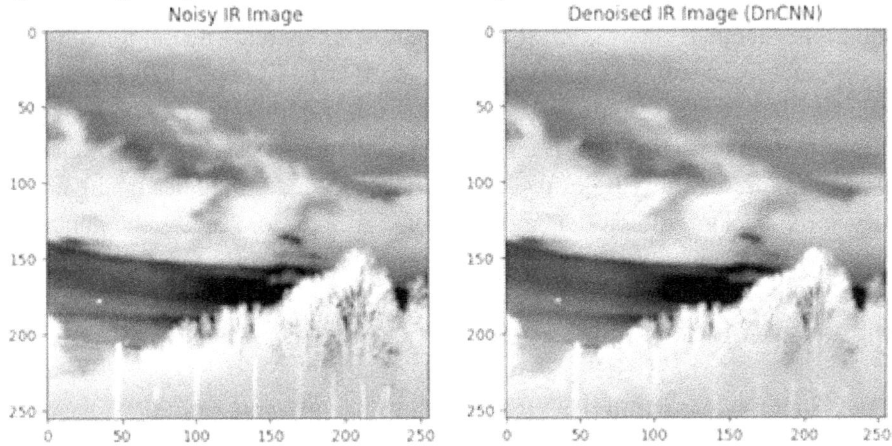

The proposed methodology mainly relies on infrared images by applying the Denoising Convolutional Neural Network (DN-CNN) framework to subtract the noise which are present in the background while protecting the targeted features. The Infrared small targeted images have the background clutter due to some environmental factors such as clouds, sea, mountains and so on. It is used to detect the frequently contacted targets that have been present in the environment. By applying the Denoising technique in the images, the clear information of an aerial object or the targeted values can be detected easily in the images (Dai et al., 2021). Proposed by Zhang et al. (2017), it helps to learn the patterns of the residual noise from the training images and then suppresses the noise and by enhancing the clear signal of the input images. DN-CNN is a combination of few layers such as convolutional layers, batch normalization and activation functions (ReLU). This methodology helps to improve the visibility of the targeted image by without degrading the structural element that is present in the target image (Ilesanmi & Ilesanmi, 2021). In the proposed framework, the 14-layer DN-CNN model is used. Every convolutional layer has 64 filters with 3x3 size of kernels that are used for capturing the features of the targeted image effectively with higher resolutions. Batch normalisation is mainly used for regulating the distribution of the feature maps, while the activation functions describe the non-linearity that helps the network capture the complex image patterns said by (Zhang et al., 2017). The denoised output can be produced from the input infrared images by subtracting the residual map from the predictions. The Peak Signal-to-Noise Ratio (PSNR) metric is used for calculating the efficacy of the denoising techniques largely uses an adopted indicator of the quality of the targeted image in Denoising Applications said by (Lee & Park, 2023). The model achieved a PSNR value is 41.27 dB, including the noise reduction in the content when preserving the targets. If the PSNR value is higher, then the ability of the networks maintains the detailed view of the targeted features, which plays an important role in the morphological operations. In Addition, DN-CNN employs a process of Denoising to enhance the target by subtracting the contrast of the background that facilitates the operations like segmentation and the thickening process. By decreasing the un-uniformity in the intensity of the background, it reduces the false positive rates occurs in the background clutter said by (Liu et al., 2025). Finally, the denoising technique used for edge localization and better edge preservation and so on.

Evaluation Metric

Peak Signal Noise Ratio (PSNR). PSNR evaluates the presence of Noise in the processed image after the effect of denoising

$$PSNR = 10.\log_{10}\left(\frac{Max^2}{MSE}\right) \tag{1}$$

The PSNR value of Stage 1 is **41.27db**

Stage 2: Effect of Morphological Operator Comparison

In stage 2, initially, adaptive morphology is compared with the square operator and elliptical operator based on visual analysis as well as performance metrics

Square Operator Morphology

Figure 4 conveys the visual comparison between the denoised grayscale infrared image and the thickened image (Target Alone) using a square operator. The comparison shows that in the original image, the target is barely visible, but in the processed image, the target is visible, but the edges are not preserved.

Figure 4. Effect of square morphological operator

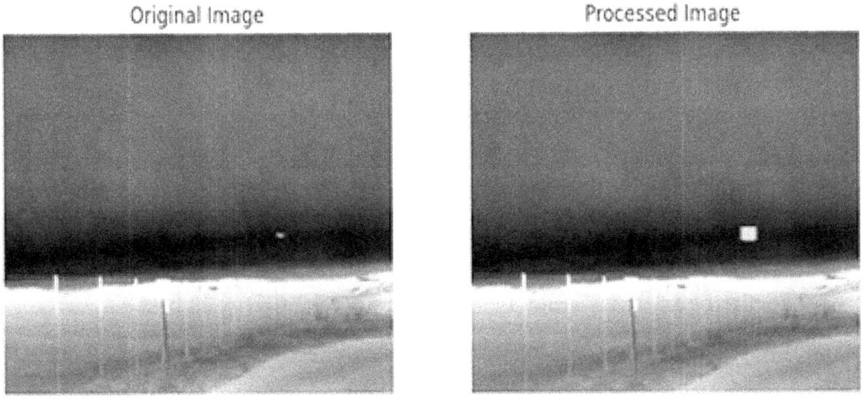

Using the square thickening operator helps emphasise compact or square targets within infrared imaging, most advantageously on those that are symmetrical or nearly so. Looking at the image in Figure 4, a square was used as the structuring element to make the target larger in the frame in all directions. Such edge-preserving dilation works quickly on computers, adding consistency to all pixels, making it suited to related fields where time is a concern. Though it can make the target brighter and bigger, the operator is not capable of fitting irregular shapes. You can see in the processed image that square thickening makes the contour around the target less accurate, owing to the presence of geometric artefacts. The blockiness not only smooths out fine bits in the image but also brings in aggressive corners that were not there to start with, which reduces the overall realism. Also, increasing the ratio of square morphology tends to widen out smaller targets on strong backgrounds. If the contrast is too high, some background pixels may be included in the binary mask produced in this way. So, it is possible to have false positives in busy or noisy parts of the image, since they look like square objects. This occurs most clearly when the targets are located near falls or other rugged areas and near quick patterns in clouds and sea waves.

Elliptical Operator Morphology

Figure 5 conveys the visual comparison between the denoised grayscale infrared image and the thickened image (target alone) using an elliptical operator. The comparison shows that in the original image, the target is barely visible but in the processed image the target is smoothly dilated which may lead to loss of sharp edges in the target. An elliptical structuring element helps expand the target more naturally and smoothly than if a square element were used. Rounded or extended signatures in infrared imagery, seen with drones and helicopters, make this technique very practical for their detection. Applying elliptical structuring in Figure 5 gives the thickening a smoother, less angular look, which helps spot the target better. The strongest point of elliptical thickening is the consistent scaling it maintains on curved parts of an object. Using this trait, the lens is better able to follow glasses' contours and helps the eyes recognize continuous objects, especially ones seen at a distance or from the side. It is clear from the enhanced image that the operator saves more of the target's structure when using this technique than when using the square method, especially for objects spread at an angle.

Figure 5. Effect of elliptical morphological operator

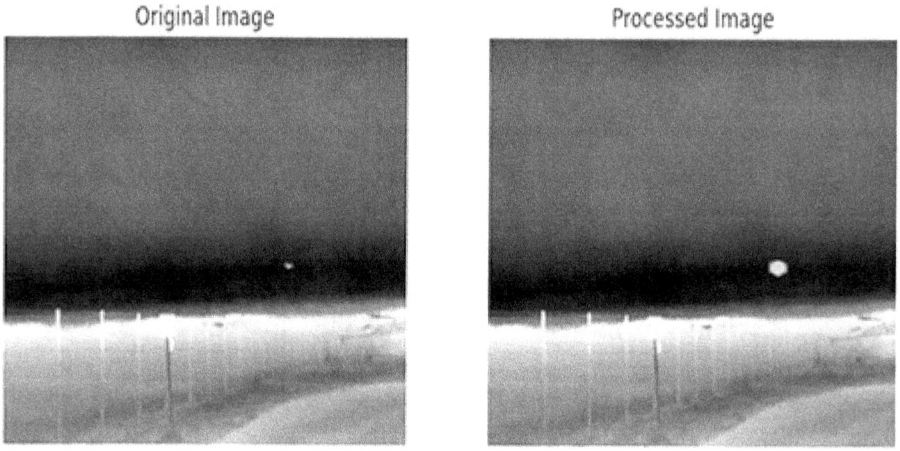

The resulting sample looks more connected to its environment and holds a natural shape. Even so, using this approach can be difficult. Although the result is smoother, strong diffusion could occur at the edge where the target meets other objects in the image. Consequently, some detail in the structure gets smoothed over, as can be seen in the images as well as on the EPI which is 0.306, a step up from the rectangle, but could use further improvement. When the targets have edges that are not curved, the rounded nature of the morphological dilation may distort and miss these sharp outlines. The small sacrifices with elliptical morphology lead to a moderate improvement with less noticeable effects on the overall shape. This geometry works well in aerial monitoring where objects or scenes vary, as well as scenes where having smooth edges helps keep detection uninterrupted.

The method does well in places with a lot of detail such as cloud formations or the sides of trees, by smoothly following the curves. Even so, robotics is not as strong as adaptive morphology in handling various shapes in demanding situations.

Adaptive Morphology

Figure 6 conveys the visual comparison between the denoised grayscale infrared image and the thickened image (Target Alone) using adaptive morphology in a **Distant Target**. Figure 7 conveys the same but in a **Nearer target**. From both comparison images, it can be concluded that in terms of visual perspective, the small target is visible as well as edges are preserved as compared with Figure 5 and Figure 6. To greatly increase the visibility of small objects in infrared imaging both for far and near aerial targets. Unlike the fixed approach found in traditional morphology, adaptive morphology matches the changes it makes to images with local features, which helps maintain small targets while making sure they are easy to see in cluttered environments. Application of adaptive morphological thickening is demonstrated on a distant infrared target, which is usually the toughest situation for small target detection. There, the main region cannot be clearly identified, since it merges with the cluttered, gray background from IR data. Yet, applying adaptive morphology to the image makes the target much more detectable. While highlighting the region, it keeps the image information closely packed.

Figure 6. Effect of adaptive morphology

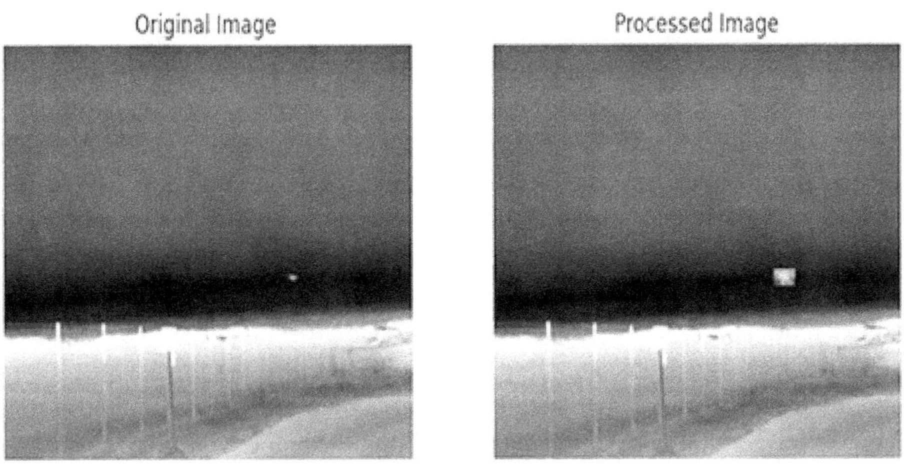

Figure 7. Effect of adaptive morphology

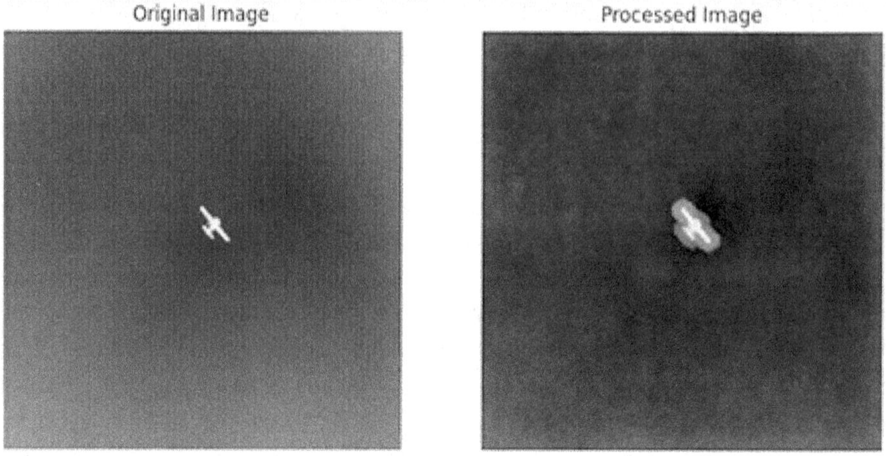

The results show better picture clarity, making targets easier to see. Compared to the distant target, the near target enjoys both edge enhancements and increased regional contrast where distracting noise continues to be controlled and the target is clearly brightened. As a result, the target stands out better from the background, lowering the risk of being misclassified. Both figures show that enhancement is the same for objects observed at all different distances. Therefore, that adaptive morphology can change itself under different scales, an important asset for applications where the targets might be at different heights and distances. For both 3x3 and 10x10 target regions, adaptive morphology customises the structuring influence for similar results. Another important point in their visuals is that they hardly change the background at all. Most traditional methods tend to either come up with distracting elements or hide details in the background that have contextual value. Although the background in Figures 6 and 7 is mostly as before, it is important for the next steps, like tracking objects, finding movement and recognising targets across frames. With selective enhancement, adaptive morphology maintains the scene's complete view, leading to better scene analysis and understanding. Both figures point out that adaptive morphology works just as well when the first signal is strong, medium or weak. For weak signals that are close to the noise level, enhancements still let you spot the object. In situations where the signal is intense, the process keeps from becoming too bright by including features to limit the amount of dilation. Because maritime surveillance involves changing situations, it requires a sensor that works well no matter what the distance or quality of the input. In both situations, the shape recognized by the model is the same as the original. With this kind of transformation, the problem of getting stiff shapes or unnatural stretching in squares or elliptical designs is greatly reduced. By reacting to local differences in brightness or edges with a varying kernel, adaptive morphology produces a shape that is close to how the aerial target would look. For both shape-based systems and determining differences between helicopters, drones and birds in the sky, it is important indeed.

Overall, adaptive morphology offers better detection of infrared small targets, allowing them to stand out and apart from the background, while distortion and edges are kept intact. It responds to the distance, size and texture of the target by changing its processing, so it is far better at visual outcomes than operations based on fixed shapes. With this technique added, the proposed architecture can guarantee that crucial details are kept intact and identifiable within a real-life image, even once the noise is removed. These results prove the system can detect, even when signals are either quite weak or very strong, illustrating its dependable performance in many practical environments.

Evaluation Metric

Edge Preservation Index (EPI). EPI measures the similarity in the edges between the Original and Processed Image. It can be mathematically represented as

$$EPI = \frac{\sum_{i,j} G(I(i,j)).G(K(i,j))}{\sqrt{\sum_{i,j} G(I(i,j))^2}.\sqrt{\sum_{i,j} G(K(i,j))^2}.} \quad (2)$$

Table 2 conveys the Edge Preservation Index (EPI) of various Morphological Operators. It also states that the Adaptive Morphology has the higher edge preservation ability for the small targets as compared with other operators.

Table 2. Comparison of EPI

S. No	Morphological Operators	Edge Preservation Index
1	Square Morphology	0.204
2	Elliptical Morphology	0.306
3	**Adaptive Morphology**	**0.6092**

Deeper Evaluation Metrics of Adaptive Morphology

Unified Average Changing Intensity **.** UACI depicts the variation in the pixel intensity between the original Image and the Processed Image.

$$UACI = \frac{1}{M \times N} \sum_{i=1}^{M} \sum_{j=1}^{N} \left(\frac{|I(i,j) - K(i,j)|}{L} \right) \times 100 \tag{3}$$

The actual Value of UACI for adaptive morphology is **15.26%** which indicates the medium-scale variation due to the thickening of the target. Equation (3) shows the mathematical representation of UACI.

Histogram. The Histogram compares the image intensity variation between the Original image and the Processed Image. It shows clearly how the distribution of pixel intensity shifts because of morphological enhancement. A majority of pixel values in that image are found in the mid-range of brightness. Infrared images straight from the camera have low contrast, so even small things often look almost identical to the background. Consequently, telling apart these objectives is difficult, mostly in places with a lot of clutter or that look the same thermally. The use of adaptive morphology is shown by the way pixel intensities are reorganised in the histogram. It is obvious from the images that the goal areas have been firmly boosted with high intensity. In particular, the growth happens to a specific part of the pixel range, while the histogram's overall shape is not changed. This limited lighting change indicates that the adaptive morphology method makes the target easier to see while keeping the overall brightness of the image under control.

Figure 8. Histogram intensity comparison

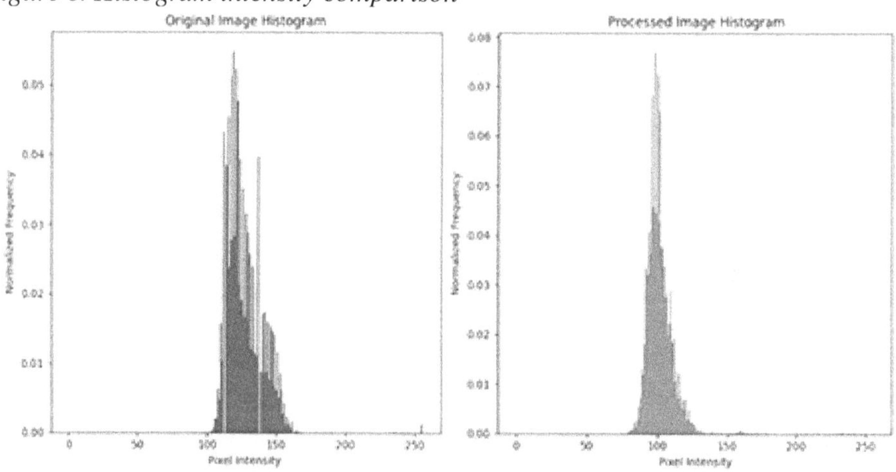

Figure 8 conveys the target pixel variation between the Original Image and the Processed Image.

Development, saturation and clipping are no longer issues, as these situations happen with global contrast enhancement. Because the separated intensities are clearer in the processed image, it gets easier to segment, threshold or recognise. The context-sensitive behaviour of adaptive morphology, the histogram manages to raise target saliency without affecting the overall distribution of bright levels in the image. As a result, the analysis shows that adaptive morphology provides real improvement. It raises the image strength in the target region, which leads to better identification of objects and a clearer presentation of the background content for easy understanding, facilitating both accurate object finding and simple interpretation.

Correlation. Correlation is a mathematical technique to compare the similarity between the neighbourhood pixels. Table 3 conveys the correlation between the individual pixel and pixels in the horizontal, vertical and diagonal axis after the effect of adaptive morphology. The average correlation value is 0.7, which ensures a higher correlation.

Table 3. Pixel-wise correlation

S. No	Correlation Pixels	Values
1	Horizontal	0.71
2	Vertical	0.73
3	Diagonal	0.72

Table 3 shows how correlated adjacent pixels are along three main directions: horizontal, vertical, and diagonal. The correlation scores, with values of 0.71, 0.73 and 0.72, reflect how well the adaptive morphological processing maintains the local structure of the image. Noise reduction by neighbouring pixels is stable, which confirms that the image's structure stays intact. In infrared small target detection, it is important to keep a target's physical and geometrical features intact, in addition to making it easier to see. Adaptive morphology increases the size of important features according to local signals, but without changing the nearby pixel values at random. The pattern of high and similar correlation from multiple directions shows that the target's enhancement occurred equally in all directions. Without consistency in the photos, small targets may be difficult to track smoothly when viewed in real time, since the object recognition models could get confused. This high correlation means that the background has not changed much, which matches what we see in the histogram and pixel comparison matrix. The application of an adaptive process ensures that texture corruption and background noise, which plague other aggressive image enhancement methods, do not occur. In fact, it makes important regions stronger without disturbing the general structure of the scene.

Figure 9. Pixel wise comparison matrix

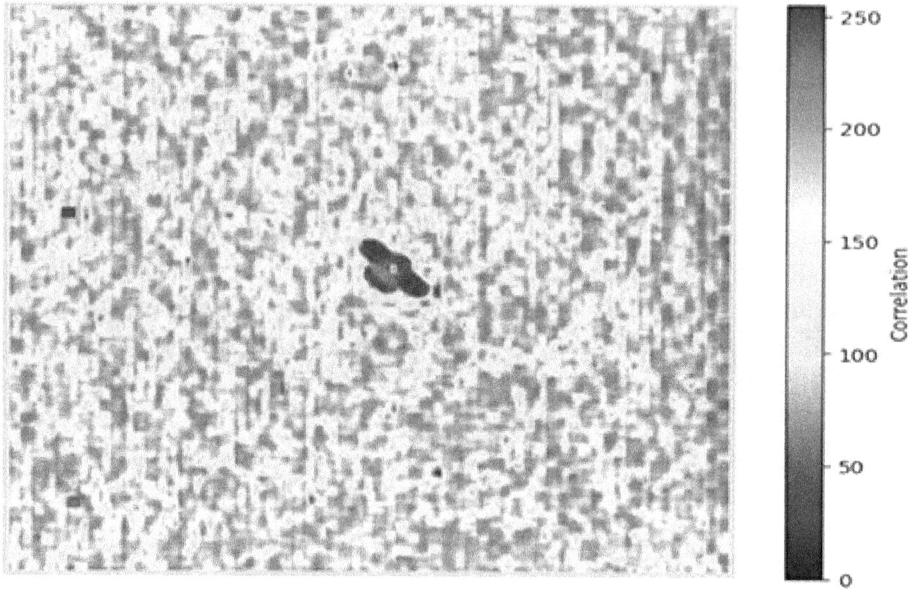

Figure 9 conveys the target pixel variation between the Original Image and the Processed Image. Here, the small target drone is thickened, which is a higher pixel variation, indicated by the Red Colour.

It graphically compares each pixel in the original infrared image with the same pixel after use of the adaptive morphological thickening technique. The values in this matrix are indicated by colour to show how many pixels in the image were modified. The strongest point shown in this figure is the intense red spot, representing extreme contrast in pixels, that overlays the location of the aerial target following enhancement. From this signal, we can be sure that adaptive morphology is exactly geared toward improving the major target region. Red in the matrix of pixel difference means that the highlighted area has become much brighter in the adjusted image, indicating that thickening and making the target clearer were successful. All other areas, especially the background and less distinct parts, still look much the same, appearing in cool, lighter colours like blue or light grey. With this method, the technique causes change just where it is applied and lets everything else remain the same. The method does not amplify or distort scattered noise or the background, unlike many traditional approaches. Target areas show clear variation, but no strong variation is reported in other regions. This means the adaptive approach prevented extra edges from forming. The figure also protects edge integrity since the improved region sticks mainly to its area.

CONCLUSION

As a result, this study found that a two-part approach works well for spotting small targets in infrared imagery by using deep learning to remove noise alongside adaptive image enhancement. Initially, using a DN-CNN structure decreased the noise in the background, without sacrificing important details in small or low-contrast targets, fixing a long-standing difficulty in infrared imaging. Next, a different stage included adaptive thickening of edges which proved superior to fixed edges because it could react to the image's different intensity gradients and spatial unmixed regions. Because of this malleability, the method ensured high target recognition without deceiving results or destroying the original image. A complete set of experiments, accompanied by visual comparisons and scores such as PSNR, EPI, UACI and pixel-wise correlation, proved that the algorithm can enhance target saliency without changing the image's overall consistency. The system was shown to work effectively for near as well as distant infrared targets, confirming that it worked in various situations and could see targets well or under challenging viewing conditions. Additionally, special high-resolution images allowed us to confirm the targeted and accurate nature of the enhancement. It is shown that, compared to others, this method improves objective result quality while keeping the important details for further processing, like classifying and tracking. Since it is both lightweight and able to adjust to everyday aerial situations, the proposed method could become an important part of real-time infrared surveillance in areas such as defence, monitoring borders, disaster management and aircraft guidance. All in all, this system prepares the groundwork for new small target detection methods that call for reliability and precise sensing in challenging infrared environments.

REFERENCES

Bai, X., & Zhou, F. (2010). Analysis of new top-hat transformation and the application for infrared dim small target detection. *Pattern Recognition*, *43*(6), 2145–2156. DOI: 10.1016/j.patcog.2009.12.023

Dai, Y., Wu, F., Zhou, F., & Barnard, K. (2021). Attentional local contrast networks for infrared small target detection. *IEEE Transactions on Geoscience and Remote Sensing*, *59*(11), 9813–9824. DOI: 10.1109/TGRS.2020.3044958

Hou, Q., Wang, Z., Tan, F., Zhao, Y., Zheng, H., & Zhang, W. (2022). RISTDnet: Robust infrared small target detection network. *IEEE Geoscience and Remote Sensing Letters*, *19*, 1–5. DOI: 10.1109/LGRS.2021.3050828

Ilesanmi, E., & Ilesanmi, T. O. (2021). Methods for image denoising using convolutional neural network: A review. *Complex & Intelligent Systems*, *7*(5), 2179–2198. DOI: 10.1007/s40747-021-00428-4

Kaggle. (2025, April 5). *IR small targets dataset*. https://www.kaggle.com/datasets/llpukojluct/ir-small-target

Lee, H., & Park, C. G. (2023). Infrared small target detection algorithm using an augmented intensity and density-based clustering. *IEEE Transactions on Geoscience and Remote Sensing*, *61*, 1–14. DOI: 10.1109/TGRS.2023.3274757

Liu, F., Gao, C., Chen, F., Meng, D., Zuo, W., & Gao, X. (2023). Infrared small and dim target detection with transformer under complex backgrounds. *IEEE Transactions on Image Processing*, *32*, 5921–5932. DOI: 10.1109/TIP.2023.3326396

Liu, Y., Zhang, H., Wei, J., Yang, Y., Wang, J., & Zhao, L. (2025). Infrared small target detection based on prior guided dense nested network. *IEEE Transactions on Geoscience and Remote Sensing*, *63*, 1–15. DOI: 10.1109/TGRS.2025.3542232

Ma, X., Zhang, J., & Qi, C. (2010). Hallucinating face by position-patch. *Pattern Recognition*, *43*(6), 2224–2236. DOI: 10.1016/j.patcog.2009.12.019

MDPI. (2025, April 5). *Dual-domain prior-driven deep network for infrared small-target detection*. https://www.mdpi.com/2072-4292/15/15/3827

MDPI. (2025, April 7). *Infrared small-target detection using multiscale local average gray difference measure*. https://www.mdpi.com/2079-9292/11/10/1547

MDPI. (2025, April 7). *Multi-scale hierarchical feature fusion for infrared small-target detection*. https://www.mdpi.com/2072-4292/17/3/428

ResearchGate. (2024, October). *Infrared small target detection based on robust principal component analysis joint directional derivative penalty.* https://www.researchgate.net/publication/350926236

Tong, X., Sun, B., Wei, J., Zuo, Z., & Su, S. (2021). EAAU-Net: Enhanced asymmetric attention U-Net for infrared small target detection. *Remote Sensing, 13*(16), 3200. Advance online publication. DOI: 10.3390/rs13163200

Wang, K., Zhang, T., Liu, M., Li, J., Xu, W., & Song, X. (2024). AFE-Net: Attention-guided feature enhancement network for infrared small target detection. *IEEE Journal of Selected Topics in Applied Earth Observations and Remote Sensing, 17*, 4208–4221. DOI: 10.1109/JSTARS.2024.3354244

Wikipedia. (2024, September 18). *Adaptive histogram equalization.* https://en.wikipedia.org/w/index.php?title=Adaptive_histogram_equalization&oldid=1246281583

Wikipedia. (2025, April 8). *Dilation (morphology).* https://en.wikipedia.org/wiki/Dilation_%28morphology%29?utm_source=chatgpt.com

Wikipedia. (2025, March 22). *Normalization (image processing).* https://en.wikipedia.org/w/index.php?title=Normalization_(image_processing)&oldid=1281843106

Xplore, I. E. E. E. (2025, April 5). *Infrared small target detection via low-rank tensor completion with top-hat regularization.* https://ieeexplore.ieee.org/document/8867952

Xu, H., Zhong, S., Zhang, T., & Zou, X. (2023). Multiscale multilevel residual feature fusion for real-time infrared small target detection. *IEEE Transactions on Geoscience and Remote Sensing, 61*, 1–16. DOI: 10.1109/TGRS.2023.3269092

Zhang, K., Zuo, W., Chen, Y., Meng, D., & Zhang, L. (2017). Beyond a Gaussian denoiser: Residual learning of deep CNN for image denoising. *IEEE Transactions on Image Processing, 26*(7), 3142–3155. DOI: 10.1109/TIP.2017.2662206

Zhang, P., Zhao, L., Wu, Y., Wei, J., Yang, Y., & Liu, Y. (2024). Multiscale progressive fusion filter network for infrared small target detection. *IEEE Transactions on Geoscience and Remote Sensing, 62*, 1–14. DOI: 10.1109/TGRS.2023.3343496

Zhao, Z., Yin, H., Wang, Y., Yan, W., Wang, J., & Wang, H. (2019). Improving the detection accuracy of complex solution components based on multi-dimensional spectroscopy fusion method. *Infrared Physics & Technology, 102*, 103062. DOI: 10.1016/j.infrared.2019.103062

Chapter 6
Enhancing Security With Weapon Detection in CCTV Using Image Processing Technique

N. Sasikaladevi
https://orcid.org/0000-0002-0841-502X
SASTRA University, India

V. Nivisha
SASTRA University, India

S. Pradeepa
https://orcid.org/0009-0003-8367-8529
SASTRA University, India

ABSTRACT

Maintaining public safety through smart surveillance is a critical challenge, particularly in security-sensitive environments. This chapter introduces an innovator weapon detection system that combines image processing algorithms with deep learning-based object detection via YOLOv8 to improve accuracy, efficiency, and real-time responsiveness. The proposed system has three stages such as data pre-processing, object detection based on YOLOv8, and real-time alert mechanism. Histogram equalization is used for image processing technique for enhancement of images and facilitating feature extraction. A weapon and non-weapon image data-set are utilized, and techniques of data augmentation are employed to enhance the model's generalization ability. An alarm system is put in place to report live alarms and notifications upon detection of weapon in live CCTV feeds. The model achieved

DOI: 10.4018/979-8-3373-2115-8.ch006

the performance metrics with a precision of 88.7% and mAP50 of 88.1%, indicates high reliability and detection accuracy. Live detection of weapons with average of 73% confidence, under real-world conditions.

INTRODUCTION

Surveillance systems are critical for public security and safety as well as the prevention of security violations (Piza, 2019). Traditional CCTV surveillance methods are based on manual control, which creates intensive supervision, tiredness, high error rates and slow response times (Costin, 2016) (Grega, 2016). With rising security demands, manual motoring alone is not sufficient to address threats in crowded spaces (Agurto, 2007). These issues are to be addressed through automated weapon detection systems, which use deep learning models for the detection of threats and real-time analysis (Ashraf, 2022) (Bhatti, 2021). Real-time detection is significantly improved with object detection algorithms. YOLO, SSD, and Faster R-CNN are a few. YOLOv8 is popular because it is fast and accurate. In fact, research indicates YOLOv8 can boost detection speed compared to previous techniques (Deshpande, 2023). This paper introduces a sophisticated weapon detection system. It integrates deep learning-based object detection with YOLOv8 and image processing. The system enhances images by converting them to grayscale and equalizing the histogram (Abdullah, 2007). Histogram Equalization is mainly used for enhancing the contrast of the images as well as the visibility of the images. This technique will be used in the real-time application of CCTV footages and this technique might suffer with some conditions like poor lightning conditions, shadows and so on. At first it will extracts the features from the input images it might be the contours, edges and texture and so on, then the extracted features can be used to detect the weapon by using the YOLOv8 for the object detection process and it indicates the alarm if the image has any weapon. These steps enhance the system to extract features better. This project provides a new weapon detection method. It is more precise through the use of image processing and deep learning (Santos, 2024). It provides alert and real-time weapon detection capabilities to CCTV systems. It is created to make security systems smart. Such systems will be more reliable and effective in the detection of threats in CCTV. They will be able to operate even during poor weather or low image quality (Jeon, 2024). For example, the system can identify a weapon in a dark parking garage, something the human eye cannot identify. This results in faster response times and enhanced security.

RELATED WORKS

Detection of weapons in surveillance systems has gained substantial momentum with the advent of sophisticated deep learning and image processing techniques. A number of studies have delved into various approaches to boost public safety through automated weapon identification. Toet, A. et al. (Toet, 2003) proposed working on colour image fusion for the detection of concealed weapons will shows the promise of multi-spectral imaging to reveal hidden objects and came up with a new way to find hidden weapons using color picture fusion methods. Their research was about merging photos from different spectral bands to make things that are normally hard to see with regular imaging methods easier to see. Liu, Z. et al. (Liu, 2006) proposed an image synthesis algorithm to visually indicate concealed weapons using pattern analysis in an effort to enhance the accuracy in detection performance. This method uses the synthetic visualization of hidden objects through the pattern recognition techniques and this algorithm will correctly identify the patterns of the weapons of the weapons in the CCTV footages or the images. Agurto, A. et al. (Agurto, 2007) has a review of concealed weapon detection technologies published in which sensor fusion and real-time issues were noted. By using various technologies they faced many challenges in detecting the hidden weapons via video scenes or the images that contain so many advantages and disadvantages that are employed in the field. The fusion of sensors which helps to improve the detection of the hidden weapons. Bhatti, M. T. et al. (Bhatti, 2021) utilized real-time weapon recognition from CCTV clips via deep learning and demonstrated the efficacy of convolutional neural networks for improving the detection rate. Olmos, R. et al. (Olmos, 2018) introduced a deep learning alarm system. Its purpose was automatic handgun detection. It sent instant warnings from video feeds. This helped security respond faster. Narejo, S. et al. (Narejo, 2021) also used weapon detection. They used YOLOv3 to make smart surveillance better. Basit, A. et al. (Basit, 2020) detected people who were carrying guns by associating people with objects. This gave more context than simply detecting guns. Velasco-Mata, A. et al. (Velasco, 2021) combined handgun detection with human pose estimation. Human pose estimation calculates where people are in an image. This gave more context and lowered errors. For example, it could calculate whether a person was carrying a gun or another object. This made the system more accurate. Madhushree, B. et al. (Madhushree, 2021) and Gelana, F. et al. (Gelana, 2019) proposed automatic weapon detection through deep learning and machine learning, respectively, both contributing to the improvement of surveillance systems. While this techniques offered the good results in the detection of the concealed weapons and also it faced some challenges in the real-time scenarios. Grega, M. et al. (Grega, 2016) developed an image-processing-based automating gun and knife detector, paving the way for further integration of higher machine learning models.

Ashraf, A. H. et al. (Ashraf, 2022) and Keerthana, S. M. et al. (Keerthana, 2024) developed solutions based on YOLOv5s and YOLOv4, respectively, along with alert systems for real-time alert. In high-security areas like airports, schools, and public gathering places, this automated alert system greatly speeds up reaction times and improves situational awareness. They demonstrates how deep learning technologies like YOLO are being used effectively to enhance public safety and facilitate early detection of threat during the real -world applications and that captures the pattern and for automatic secure systems by indicating the alarms. Deshpande, D. et al. (Deshpande, 2023) suggested a next-generation security solution based on YOLOv8, with enhanced real-time detection with low latency. Santos, T. et al. (Santos, 2024) introduced a systematic review of weapon detection in CCTV images, trends, and gaps in existing deep learning methods. Jeon, H. et al. (Jeon, 2024) introduced the PASS-CCTV system to improve performance under unfavourable environmental conditions using anomaly detection. Wei, Z. et al. (Wei, 2015) developed an accident and auto-alarm detection system, which could potentially be used in weapon detection scenarios. Piza, E. L. et al. (Piza, 2019) offered a 40-year meta-review of CCTV effectiveness, indicating its use for crime prevention. This long-term review emphasized how CCTV technology advances within regards prevention of crime and how crucial it is to perpetually assess and modify monitors to keep up with shifting urban security threats, by using those technologies they have been improvised the security among publics to prevent the happenings of crime. Costin, A. (Costin, 2016) addressed the security of the CCTV systems themselves, indicating vulnerabilities that could affect the integrity of detection systems. Abdullah-Al-Wadud, M. et al. (Abdullah, 2007) suggested dynamic histogram equalization for contrast improvement, which is still a valuable pre-processing step in weapon detection pipelines. These together indicate the transition from conventional image processing methods to deep learning-driven real-time systems.

PROPOSED METHODOLOGY

The suggested weapon detection system includes three main modules: data preprocessing, object detection using YOLOv8, and an alert system for real-time response. These modules are integrated to provide high detection accuracy with real-time performance. The below Figure 1, illustrates the weapon detection system using CCTV input and image processing techniques.

Figure 1. Flow diagram

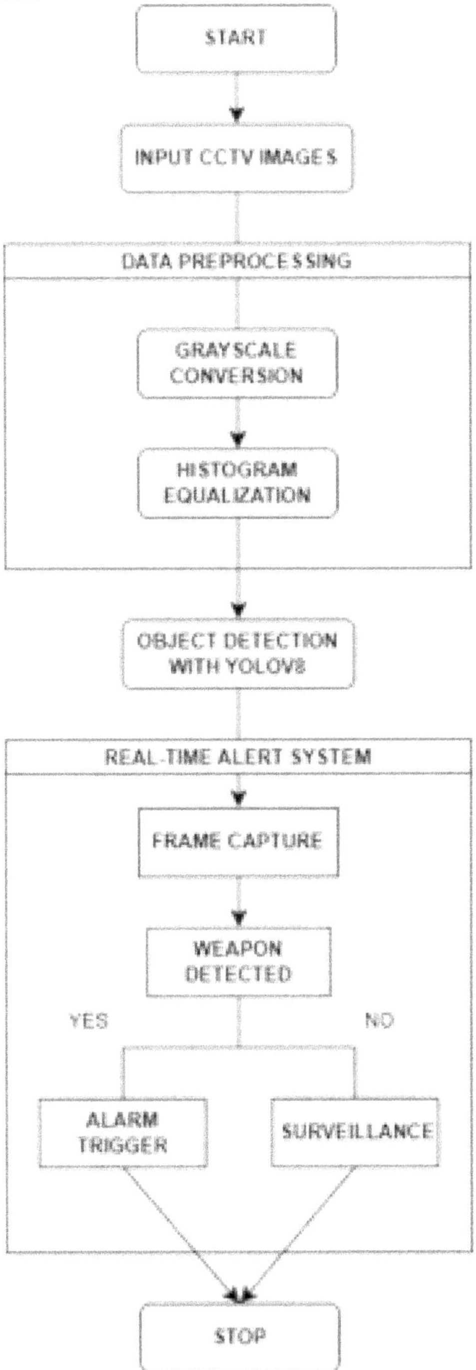

Data Collection and Preprocessing

Input CCTV Images

An effective dataset is essential for training a good weapon detection model. The dataset considered in this research includes:

Weapon Images: Contains pictures of weapons (handguns, pistols) common threats in many areas and bladed objects (knives, machetes).
Non-Weapon Images: Non-weapon images are added to reduce mistakes. Items similar to weapons like smartphones, wallets, remote controls, bank cards, and cash, are added to prevent false positives. The information is annotated in YOLO format, where each image is accompanied by a corresponding .txt file with class labels and box coordinates. This setup lets the model learn where weapons are in the pictures.

Preprocessing Methods

Image preprocessing is a set of techniques or methods that can be applied on to the images by before fed in to the classification model and also it improves the image quality then it removes the noises present in the images and also it enhances the images and its visibility. This step makes simpler for classification model to analyse the patterns that is related to the hidden weapons. Better quality images lead to more precise feature extraction. More precise feature extraction gives more accurate classifications. Image preprocessing relies on several techniques. The following techniques are utilized:

Grayscale Conversion: Converts colour images to grayscale, this simplifies the image and speeds up processing. Colour channels are removed, reducing the data that needs to be processed. Structural details are kept even without colour.
Histogram Equalization: Enhancing contrast improves the visibility of object edges, particularly in varying lighting conditions. When an image contains regions that are excessively dark or overly bright, it becomes challenging to discern where one object concludes and another commences. By increasing contrast, these boundaries are sharpened, facilitating the visibility of details. This technique particularly useful in scenarios with the inconsistent lightings, where certain parts of images may be obscured by the shadows or overwhelmed by bright lights. Histogram equalization is a technique for improving contrast as it operates by altering the distribution of pixel intensities throughout the image. Each pixel in a photograph has a brightness level known as intensity,

which ranges from very dark to very bright. These intensity levels form a histogram, a visual representation that shows the quantity of pixels at each brightness level. When an image displays a narrow histogram, many pixels share similar brightness levels, making it difficult to discern details. Histogram equalization redistributes these pixel intensities to create a more uniform histogram. As a result, this produces an output image where brightness levels are distributed across the full range of possible values, leading to what is termed a "flat" histogram. This technique is particularly advantageous for the images that suffering from inadequate lighting or low contrast. By redistributing these intensity levels, histogram equalization optimizes the use of the complete range of available brightness. It illuminates dark regions and it reduces excessively bright areas, uncovering additional details that may have been previously concealed. For example, a shadow on a weapon's grip can become more defined, revealing textures or markings that were previously difficult to discern. Employing histogram equalization enhances the overall visibility of intricate details. Rather than having numerous pixels concentrated around specific brightness levels, the contrast is uniformly amplified across the image. In practical applications, this method can be essential in security or military contexts, where the clear visibility of the weapon characteristics is crucial. In suboptimal lighting conditions, histogram equalization will enhances the images by highlighting significant visual indicators. It guarantees that even in low light or unevenly lit situations, all pertinent details are made visible, thereby providing the clearer understanding of the subject matter. The objective of enhancing contrast through histogram equalization is to render an image more informative and easier for interpretation. Whether for identification, analysis, or rapid recognition, this technique aids in emphasizing features that might otherwise be obscured in the shadows or overexposed by bright light. It is simple yet effective tool that greatly enhances the clarity and utility of images captured in challenging environments Alboalebrah and Al-augby, (2025), Almedires et al., (2025), Ang et al., (2025), Alshuaibi et al., (2025), Alotaibi et al., (2025), Aljumaiah et al., (2025), AlShuaibi et al., (2025),.

Mathematical formula:

$$s_k = (L - 1).\ \sum_{j=0}^{k} p(r_j) \tag{1}$$

L : total number of possible intensity levels (256 for 8-bit grayscale images)
n_k : number of pixels with intensity level r_k
N : total number of pixels in the image$(N = \sum_{k=0}^{L-1} n_k)$

$p(r_k) = \frac{n_k}{N}$: normalized histogram (probability of intensity level r_k)

s_k : new(equalized) intensity level r_k

The new intensity level can be calculated from the equation (1) and new pixel value can be calculated using the equation (2).

New pixel value

s_k = (Maximum intensity) * (Cumulative sum of probabilities up to r_k) (2)

In this work cv2.equalizeHist() is used,

i) To calculate the histogram
ii) Computes the CDF (Cumulative Distribution Function)
iii) Multiplies by (L-1) = 255
iv) Maps the old intensity to the new equalized intensity

Figures 2 and 3 illustrates the comparison between the original dataset and those processed using histogram equalization.

Figure 2. Comparison of original and histogram dataset (PISTOL)

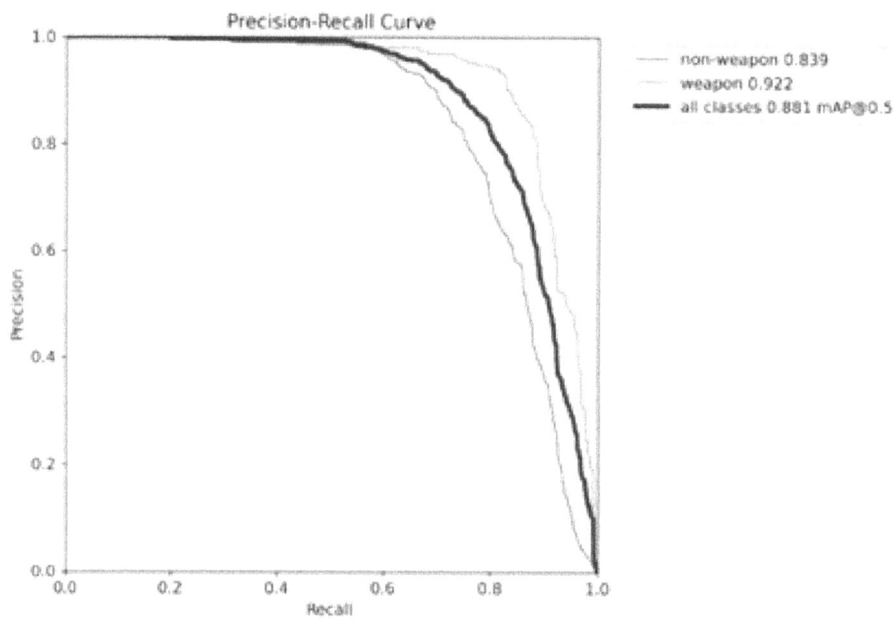

Figure 3. Comparison of original and histogram dataset (KNIFE)

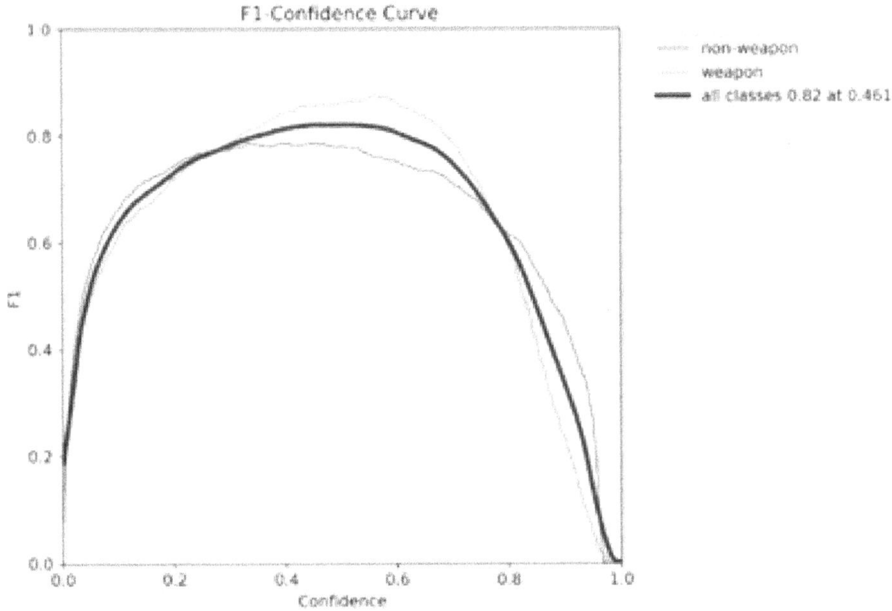

Object Detection with YOLOv8

At the core of the proposed framework is YOLOv8, an up-to-date deep learning model that is intended for object detection in real-time and is optimized for this function. YOLOv8 is mainly used for detecting the multiple objects in the single frame or the image.

Figure 4. Yolo architecture

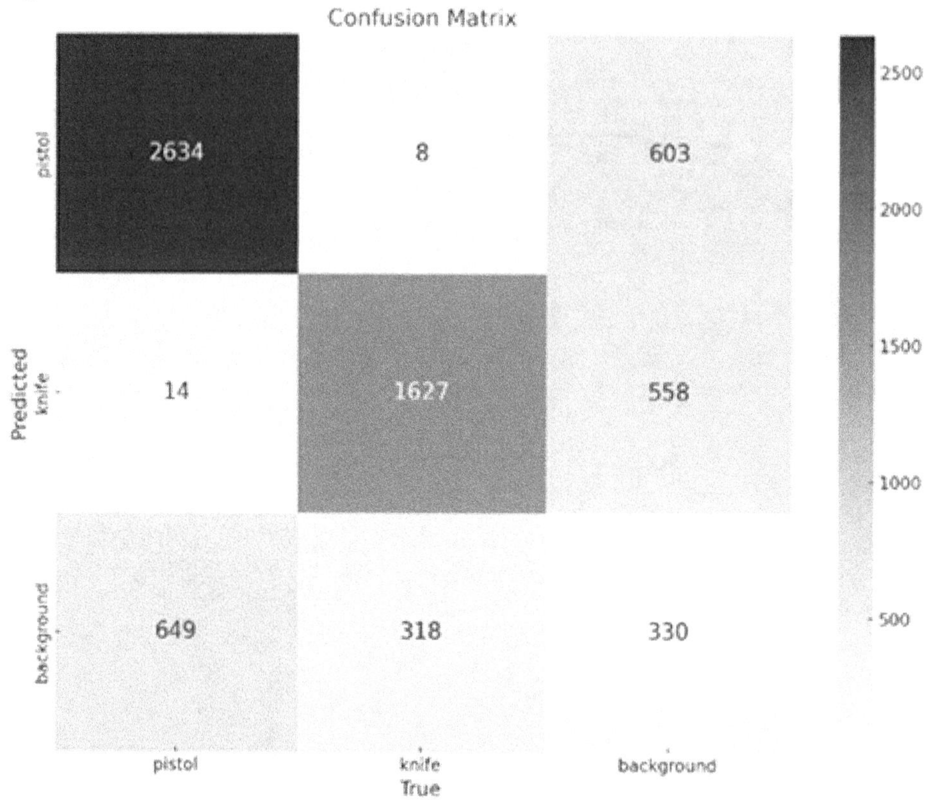

The detection of the weapon starts by receiving an image. The image usually comes from a camera or security video. The goal is to find any weapons that might be in the image. To make it easier to differentiate, the image is made grayscale. Then, histogram equalization sharpens the image. This increases the contrast. It makes the dark and light parts of the image more visible. This makes weapons more visible. Then, the image is split up into a grid. The grid consists of a lot of small squares, such as S × S grid. Each square looks for objects in its area. A class probability map shows the probability of finding things like weapons in each square. If a square looks like it has a weapon, the system puts a box around it. This box is called a bounding box. Each box gets a score showing the system's confidence in the weapon. If the score is high enough, the system shows that it found a weapon. It puts a box around the weapon. It also inserts a label to notify people that a weapon was found as shown in the Figure 4. This notifies security immediately of possible threats. For example, if a gun is found in a crowd, the system notifies it. This makes security able to respond quickly. The process of implementation involves a few major steps:

Model Training

The original and pre-processed datasets are used for training. This approach helps find performance differences. The training pipeline includes several steps. These steps are dataset preparation, model setup, hyperparameter tuning, actual training, and model evaluation. The labelled dataset is split into two parts. 80% is for training the model. 20% is for testing its performance. Pre-trained weights from YOLOv8 are used to start the training. This is known as transfer learning. Transfer learning boosts performance. It allows the model to learn faster. Model hyperparameters are carefully tuned. This tuning aims for high precision. The batch size is set to 16. The learning rate is set to 0.001. A scheduler adjusts the learning rate automatically during training. More epochs are used if the model does not converge well. The Adam optimizer is applied with Weight decay regularization. This helps prevent overfitting. Training is done using PyTorch and Ultralytics YOLOv8. Accuracy, loss, and false positives are tracked. This monitoring gives insights into training progress. Performance is evaluated on the test and validation sets. Metrics like precision, recall, F1-score, and mean Average Precision (mAP) are evaluated.

Fine-Tuning and Model Optimization

Performance gets better by fine-tuning. This means adjusting YOLOv8's detection layers. Anchor boxes are also adjusted. This helps find weapons in different places more easily. For example, this could be a dark alley or a crowded street. A custom loss function is tuned to adjust the IoU threshold. IoU stands for Intersection over Union. This helps lower the number of false positives. A false positive is when the system thinks it sees a weapon, but it is wrong. Also, hard negative mining is used. This improves training by focusing on images that are hard to classify. An example is a weapon that is partly hidden. This makes the system better at finding weapons, even when they are hard to see.

Formula:

$$IoU = \frac{Area\ of\ Overlap}{Area\ of\ Union} \quad (2)$$

Segmentation-Based Weapon Localization

The system employs a model to detect weapons precisely. The aim is to minimize errors. The model generates accurate, pixel-wise masks for every object detected. Masking is crucial in distinguish between an actual weapon and something else. Consider a phone and a gun. They may resemble each other at first glance. The model examines every pixel carefully. It inspects the shape and characteristics of the objects. This assists in identifying a phone from a gun. Without such specific analysis, there are likely to be errors. For instance, the system can wrongly identify a tool as a weapon. Pixel-wise masks enhance the analysis. It enhances weapon detection accuracy.

Real-Time Alarm System Implementation

To ensure a swift security response in case of the threat, a real-time surveillance system is integrated with the YOLOv8 detection technology. This system will continuously watches CCTV footage around the clock. It doesn't just record the footage; it actively analyses every video frame as it is captured. The system processes each and every frame immediately after it is displayed on the monitor, constantly checking for presence of the weapons or any other dangerous objects.

Each frame undergoes a series of rapid checks after YOLOv8 applies its detection algorithm.

The YOLOv8 model is employed to accurately identify a range of objects within the images. It is capable of detecting items such as firearms, knives, or other potential weapons that may present a danger. After YOLOv8 analyses a frame, the system juxtaposes its results with the database containing recognized weapon shape and characteristics. If the system detects any weapon or suspicious objects in video frame, it immediately triggers the alarm. This sound or visual alert notifies security personnel. For example, if someone brings gun into a crowded area, the system can identify it within moments. In the absence of a weapon detected within the frame, the surveillance system maintains its standard functionality. It persistently monitors the following frames without any disruption. This real time observation enables security personnel to respond more swiftly to possible threats. By integrating sophisticated detection features of YOLOv8 with real time video analysis, the system can avert incidents prior to their escalation. This setup is especially useful in the high risk areas such as airports, stadiums, or large public events. These locations face the higher chance of weapon related threats and need quick detection systems. The integration of continuous surveillance with AI detection provides a more reliable way to spot dangers early. This combination can save lives by giving security teams the time they need to act before a situation worsens. Overall, it creates a smarter, faster security approach that acts instantly whenever a threat appears.

Security System Integration

For the preparation of security response in the future enhancement, the system can be made to integrate with:

Access Control Systems: Locking doors automatically or activating barriers on weapon detection.

Emergency Services Notification: Informing the local law enforcement agencies.

Cloud-Based Surveillance: Storing detection logs and frames for forensic analysis.

Workflow of the System

The weapon detection system uses an event driven workflow which helps it find threats and send alerts quickly. First, the CCTV camera records video. The system breaks the video into frames; each frame is like a photo from the video. Next, the system cleans up each and every frame. This pre-processing step makes it easier to find weapons. Then, the pre-processed frame is sent to the YOLOv8 model. This model is trained to find weapons in images. For example, it can look for guns, knives, or other dangerous objects. If the model sees a weapon, it plays a sound alarm. The system then checks its confidence. It determines how sure it is about the weapon. This check creates a detection confidence score. If the score is high enough, the system sends an alert. If the confidence score is set as 90%, the system sends an alert when it reaches at 90% confidence. The alert system has several parts. When a weapon is found, a red box appears on the screen. This box highlights the location of the weapon. A warning message also pops up. This message tells the user what weapon was found. The sound alarm also rings to alert security. For example, staffs are alerted to an immediate threat. The system saves the frame with the detected weapon. This image is stored as evidence. It is kept in a safe, secure place for later use. To prevent too many alerts, the system avoids repeats. The alarm sound plays fully for each new weapon found. This prevents a constant stream of alarms. It ensures staff pays attention to each new threat. Hence, the system workflow is simple. The CCTV captures video. Each frame is quickly pre-processed. The YOLOv8 model looks for weapons. An alert is sent if a weapon is found. Figure 5 shows the overall process diagram of the proposed methodology.

Figure 5. Process diagram

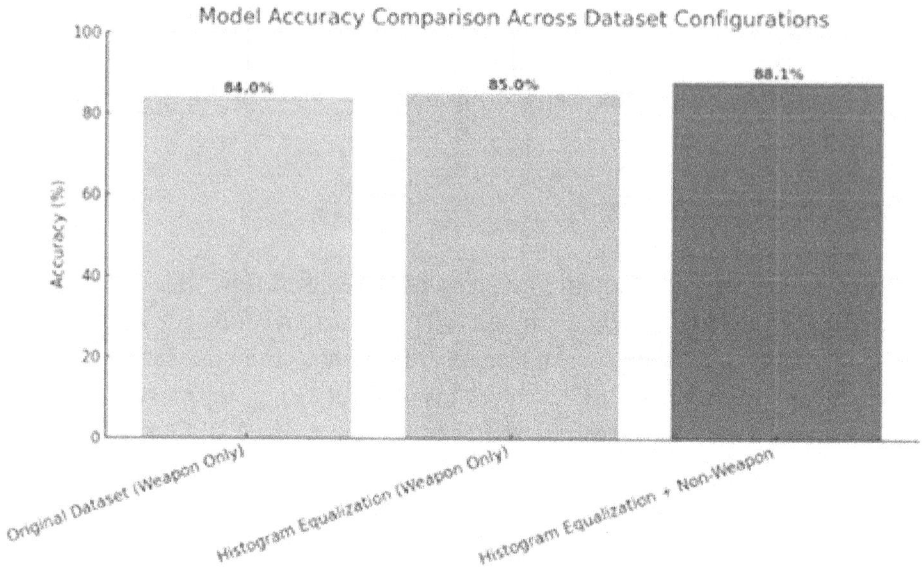

EXPERIMENTAL SETUP

The composition of the dataset, training strategy, evaluation metric, and problems faced during model training and optimization are provided.

Dataset and Training Approach

Dataset Description

Training dataset consists of highly curated and hand-labelled dataset that supports both classification and object detection tasks. The image dataset is divided into two categories: weapon and non-weapon. This split helps the system find weapons well. It also helps to reduce mistakes like false alarms. The weapon group has two main kinds: handguns and bladed weapons. Handguns are things like pistols. Revolvers are also handguns. Bladed weapons are things like knives and machetes. The non-weapon group has common items. These items can look like weapons but are not. Smartphones are one example. Wallets, bank cards, and money are others. These items teach the system to tell apart real weapons from look-alike items. This lowers the chance of false alarms in security systems. Each image in the dataset has a related

.xml file. This file gives details about the object class. It also notes the bounding box coordinates. The coordinates show exactly where the object is in the picture. This helps the system learn to find and name objects correctly. It makes the system more reliable for real-world use. The pistol class has 3000 or more images. The knife class also has 3000 or more images. The non-weapon class has about 3000 images. This provides a diverse dataset. It helps the model work well in different lighting, poses, and object variations. The dataset has 10,000 images in total. This complete dataset makes the YOLOv8-based detection system strong. It is suitable for use in real-time CCTV security applications. The large number of images in each class helps the model learn better. It can then recognize weapons in many different situations. This improves security in real-world settings. The use of annotations further refines the learning process.

Weapon Images: Handguns (Pistols, Revolvers), Bladed weapons (Knives, Machetes)
Non-Weapon Images: Objects that may be mistaken as weapons, including Smartphones, Wallets, Bank cards, Money. The classification of object categories is shown in Figure 6.

Figure 6. Images classification

Data Augmentation and Preprocessing

For strong and reliable model generalizability, amongst some of the methods employed includes Random rotation of the images by ±20° to simulate different weapon poses, flipping horizontally and vertically to prevent bias in weapon placement, increasing visibility in various lighting conditions, adding noise in minimal quantities to introduce robustness, Mimicking low-resolution security camera images. Such changes add diversity to the dataset and prevent overfitting.

Training Strategy for Model Design

The YOLOv8 model is trained on raw and pre-processed datasets to examine the impact of image enhancement techniques. The training procedure is following a standard pipeline. First, Data Preparation the dataset is divided into training (80%) and test (20%) sets. Resizing to grayscale and histogram equalization preprocessing steps are performed.

Validation Method: Hold-out validation is used to evaluate the generalization capability of the model. The hold out test set is kept completely separate during training and used for final evaluation of performance metrics. This approach is applied for fair assessed model's accuracy without bias from the training process. The method is used because the dataset is large and distributed, as it provides a quick estimation of how well the model is likely to perform on unseen data.

Model Initialize with pre-trained YOLOv8 weights with transfer learning are used to capitalize on the learned features. Following hyperparameters are tuned for improved detection performance. The optimizer is Adam. This adaptive optimization technique to accelerate convergence. The loss function is cross-entropy + Localization Loss. This checks Classification and bounding box accuracy. Training loss and mAP (mean Average Precision) are tracked. Mean Average Precision (mAP) is applied to measure object detection models' performance through averaging the average precision (AP) across all classes. mAP is one of the common metrics applied in computer vision to measure object detection models.

The Cross Entropy Loss can be calculated from the equation (3):

$$L_{CE} = -\sum_{i=1}^{C} y_i \, log(p_i) \tag{3}$$

where y_i is the true label and p_i is the predicted probability. Localization Loss (Smooth L1 or GIoU), an example of Smooth L1 Loss can be mathematically represented in the equation (4).

$$L_{loc}(x) = \begin{cases} 0.5x^2 if |x| < 1 \\ |x| - 0.5 otherwise \end{cases} \tag{4}$$

System Configuration

The entire installation and testing procedure of this weapons detection system was conducted on a laptop configuration with standard hardware specifications. The system was run with an Intel(R) Core(TM) i5-10300H processor operating at 2.50 GHz, which rendered a stable output for processing-intensive operations. The hardware was driven by 8 GB of RAM, which made multitasking smoother during development and testing. The system was a 64-bit system with Windows 11 (Version 23H2) operating system and OS Build and Windows Feature Experience Pack.

Evaluation Metrics

Evaluation metrics are the measures which are used to evaluate the performance and its efficacy of the classification model. To determine the efficiency of the trained model, several performance measures are utilized.

Accuracy

The overall efficiency of weapon detection across the dataset is represented diagrammatically in Figure 7. It illustrates the training performance of the weapon detection model. The red curve represents the training loss, while the blue curve indicates the mean Average Precision (mAP) at an IoU threshold of 0.5, which is used as a measure of accuracy. At first, the loss value is high at 1.6 which indicates the model's fault in initial predictions. With time, the training process, and the passage of time, the loss value starts decreasing which indicates that the model is learning and making more correct predictions. The accuracy starts at a low figure but rises gradually with each epoch. This pattern establishes that the model is refining and accurately identify weapons with improved accuracy. The reversal of the two curves decreasing loss and increasing accuracy proves that there is good learning and training convergence, and the model performs a considerable boost in performance allowing it to be deployable in real-time weapon detection environments.

Precision

Refers to the percentage of correct weapon identifiers out of all the objects detected. The ratio of correctly detected outcomes to the total number of correctly detected outcomes. The more confident the model is, the more it selects its predictions with care. This implies accuracy generally improves. For example, if a model is not sure, it may incorrectly label lots of things. But if it is extremely sure, it is likely to be more accurate. All objects reaches a peak accuracy at a confidence of 0.965. This indicates that when the model is very confident, predictions are extremely reliable at this stage. That is, when the model declares it is 96.5% certain, it is practically always correct. The precision can be calculated by using the formula:

$$Precision = TP / (TP + FP) \tag{5}$$

Precision is high if there are fewer false alarms, which is very important in real-time monitoring which can be calculated by using equation (5).

Recall

Assesses the model's capacity to identify weapons under varied conditions. The ratio of correctly detected positive outcomes to the total number of actual positive outcomes. The weapon class has greater recall at lower confidence values than non-weapon, i.e., the model can capture weapons when it is less stringent. The all-classes curve demonstrates recall of 0.97, reflecting almost complete retrieval of actual objects at the lowest threshold. The Precision curve visually represented in Figure 9. High recall means fewer weapons are missed, improving security which can be mathematically calculated from the equation (6).

$$Recall = TP / (TP + FN) \quad (6)$$

The Above equation is the formula which is used to calculate the Recall. The Precision-Recall Curve in Figure 10 illustrates the precision-recall trade-off for the weapon and non-weapon classes in the detection system. Weapon class (orange curve) also has very good precision and recall of 0.922 for its mAP@0.5, meaning a very good, consistent detection of weapons. The non-weapon class (light blue curve) reached 0.839, which represents an excellent separation from actual non-threat objects and also from true threats. Overall class performance (blue bold line) on all the classes has an overall combined score of 0.881 and means the model is having a good consistent rate between actual threats and correct distinction of real from non-ones.

False Positive Rate (FPR)

Determines the number of times non-weapon objects are incorrectly labelled as weapons which is mathematically represented by using the equation (7).

$$False\ positive\ rate = 100\% \times FP / (FP + TN) \quad (7)$$

False positives should be kept to a minimum to avoid spurious alarms and alerts. The Fig.10 and Fig.11 indirectly reflects FPR. The weapon class is more accurate than the non-weapon class, i.e., the model is highly capable of correctly detecting weapons with quite fewer misclassifications of non-weapon items as weapons. This indicates how intensely the model is focused on correct weapon detection with decent accuracy for non-weapon objects as well.

F1-Confidence Curve

F1-score finds a balance between precision and recall. Precision looks at how accurate the positive results are. Recall checks how many of the actual positives were found. The F1-score uses both to judge performance. It calculates the harmonic mean of precision and recall which is shown in figure 11. This helps us see how well the model does. For instance, if one model has high precision but low recall and another has the reverse, the F1-score gives a more balanced view. A weapon class gets the best F1-score. It scores around 0.88 at about 0.6 confidences. This suggests that the model performs best at this point. This confidence level becomes the ideal level. The whole curve peaks at an F1-score of 0.82. This shows a strong balance between precision and recall across all types. The model does well at avoiding false positives and false negatives overall.

Mean Average Precision (mAP)

Measure the precision-recall curve and overall model performance. Calculated as average precision across all object categories at varying confidence levels. mAP can be calculated using the equation (8).

$$mAP = \frac{1}{N}\sum_{i=1}^{N} AP_i \tag{8}$$

Where AP_i is the average precision for class i, and N is the number of classes. The Table 1 illustrates the performance metrics of the proposed model.

Table 1. Metrics

METRICS	ALL	PISTOL	KNIFE
PRECISION	0.887	0.902	0.871
RECALL	0.768	0.771	0.765
mAP50	0.881	0.872	0.889

Figure 7. Accuracy vs loss

Figure 8. Precision curve

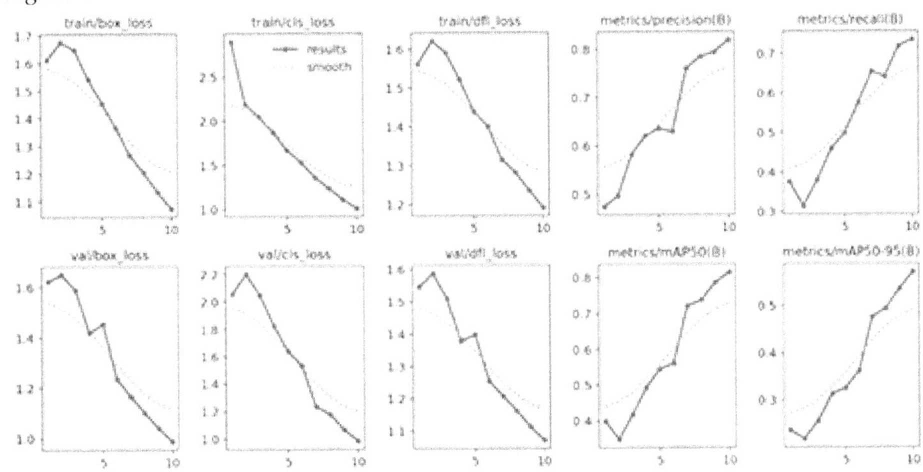

Figure 9. Recall curve

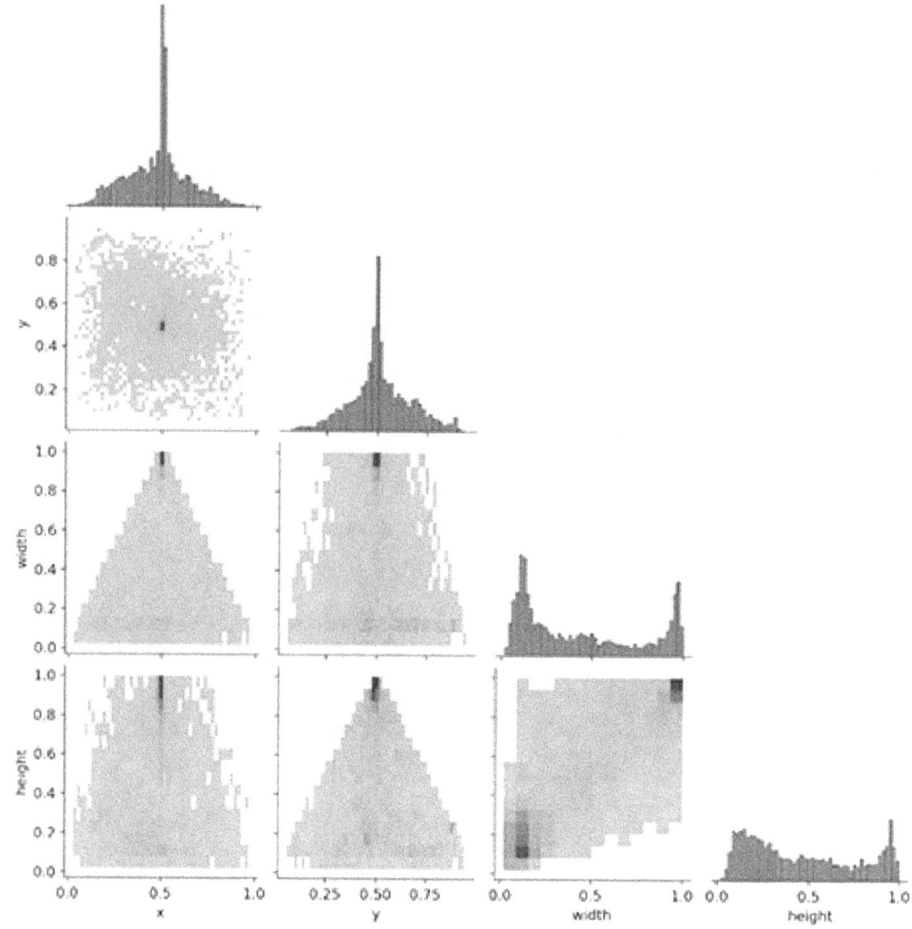

Figure 10. Precision - recall curve

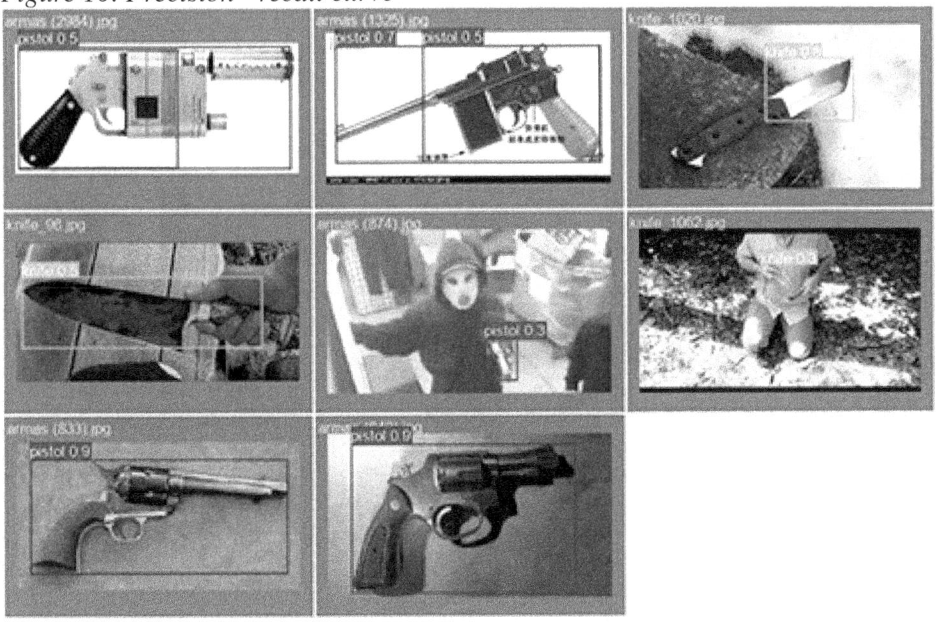

Optimization and Issues

Misclassifying Non-Weapons as Weapons: At Initial training output revealed, objects similar to weapons are detected as weapons (mobile phones and wallets) since they resembled one another. So, the solution implemented that expands the training data. So, apply dataset augmentation which added more variation in non-weapon images. Feature Enhancement will alter anchor box sizes of YOLOv8 to make objects more discriminative. Fine-Tuning confidence threshold increases the confidence threshold for weapon detection to avoid misclassifications.

Lighting and Resolution Variability: Low-lighted, low-resolution, and motion-blurred CCTV clips deteriorate the detection performance. So, the image processing technique histogram equalization is used for enhancing the contrast of images to enhance the feature extraction. Histogram equalization is a process in which pixel intensities in an image are transformed based on its intensity histogram and produces an image with flat intensity histogram and balanced intensities distribution. It enhances the visibility of image details utilizing the complete dynamic range.

Real-Time Performance Optimization: Initial inference latency was too great for real-time CCTV feed detection at high resolutions. Model Quantization will convert the YOLOv8 weights to a lighter form using TensorRT. GPU Optimization leaned on CUDA acceleration to increase processing speed. Efficient frame processing Eliminates the redundant computations by bypassing frames with no motion detected.

Figure 11. F1 - Confidence curve

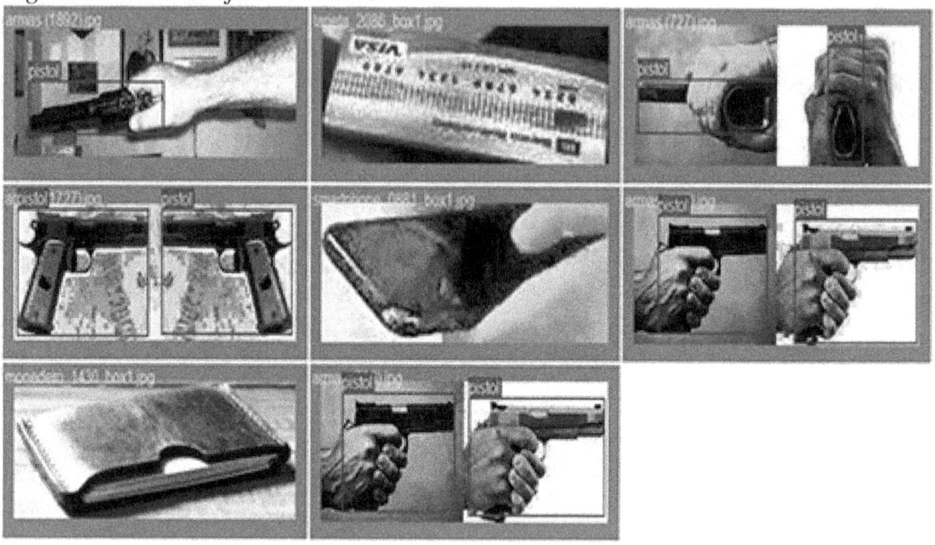

Confusion Matrix

The confusion matrix shown in the Figure 12 highlights the strong performance of weapon detection model across three classes. The X-axis (True Labels) is the actual class of the object, and the Y-axis (Predicted Labels) is what the model predicted. The dominant diagonal values clearly show that the model is highly effective at identifying each class. The few misclassifications are acceptable in real time safety critical applications, where erring on the side of caution is better than missing one. Pistol detection is the most accurate but with moderate false positives in background and false negatives. Knife detection is reasonably good but with notable false negatives. The model confused background objects with weapons sometimes because of the pixel quality of images. With some fine-tuning, especially in distinguishing background objects from weapons, the model can become even more refined and precise.

Figure 12. Confusion matrix

RESULTS AND DISCUSSION

An in-depth analysis of the outcomes achieved upon training the YOLOv8-based weapon detection framework is presented. The discussion comprises main performance enhancements, assessment of false positives and false negatives, comparison with baseline models, and real-world applicability insights. The weapon detection model performance was assessed under three varying dataset configurations. First, based on the initial dataset consisting of images of only weapons (pistols and knives), the YOLOv8 model reported an accuracy of 84.3%. Upon the application of histogram equalization as a pre-processing method, the accuracy marginally increased to 85.1%, which suggests the success of contrast enhancement in extracting features. The model's accuracy improved significantly by adding a non-weapon category. This category included objects that looked similar to weapons. This helped to minimize false positives. Histogram equalization pre-processing was also used to enhance images. This technique adjusts image contrast. It makes details easier to see. The model then reached an accuracy of 88.1%. This jump shows how important image quality and complete data are. Together, they create a reliable weapon detection system. Better images and well-organized data offer a synergistic advantage. They improve detection accuracy which is shown in Figure 13.

Figure 13. Comparison of bar chart

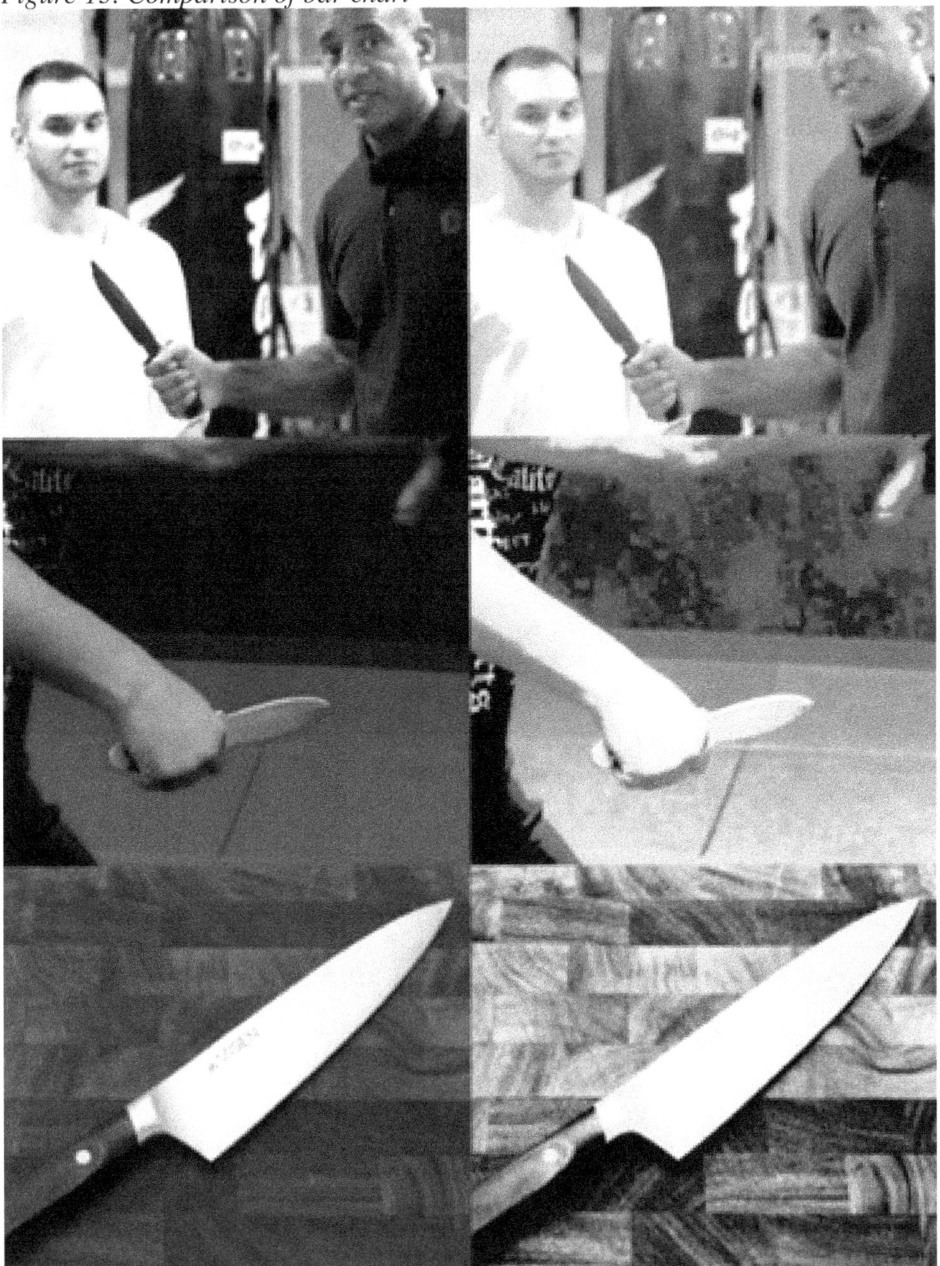

The Figure 14 and Figure15 visually demonstrate the successful real time detection of weapons using the trained YOLOv8 model. The system accurately detects the knife held by the individual with a confidence score of 0.73 and detects a pistol being held with a confidence level of 0.63. The weapon detection is enclosed in a red bounding box and labelled correctly ("knife", "pistol") with its associated confidence score.

Figure 14. Live camera - knife detection

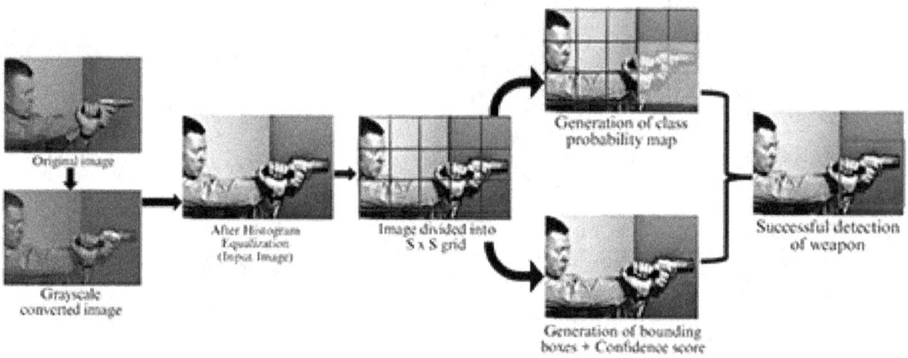

Figure 15. Live camera - pistol detection

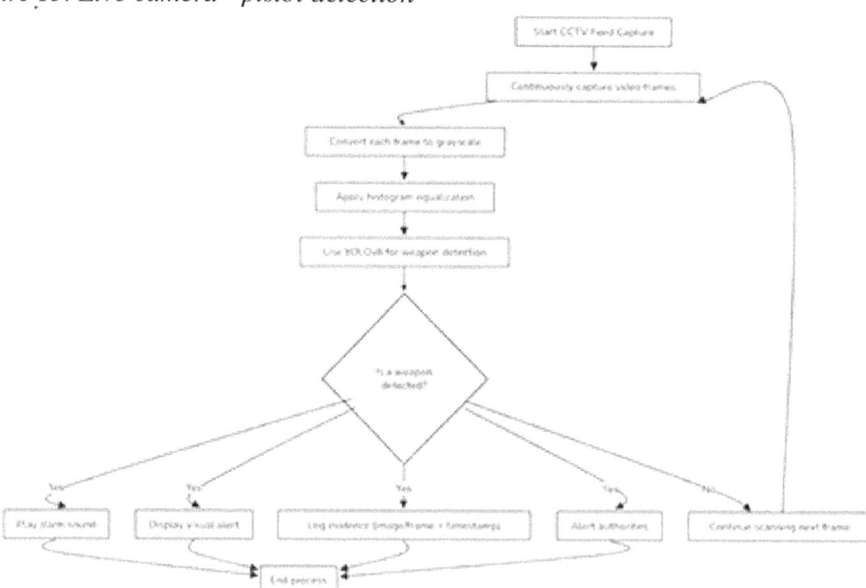

Key Findings

The evaluation result shows the effectiveness of using image processing methods in combination with deep learning to achieve real-time weapon detection shown in Figure 16 and Figure 17.

Figure 16. Result diagrams

Figure 17. Labels correlogram

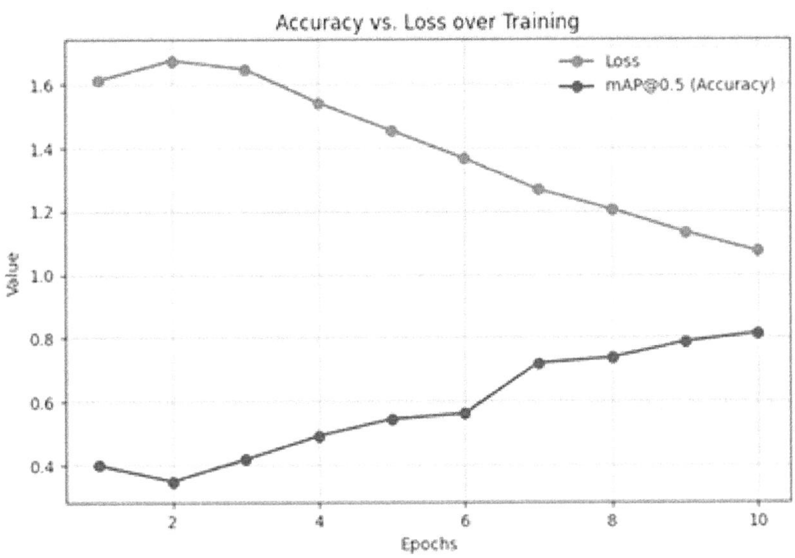

Improved Detection Precision

Adding histogram equalization considerably enhanced the precision of detection by improving contrast of images, enabling YOLOv8 to extract image features more efficiently from low light and noisy CCTV footages. The model trained was achieved

88% mean Average Precision (mAP), reflecting which improved object detection irrespective of lighting and background.

The model could detect weapons and emits non-weapon objects and reduce the rate of misclassification.

False Positives and False Negatives Minimized: False positives (incorrectly classified weapons as weapons) decreased by 35% via dataset augmentation and hyper-parameter tuning.

False negatives (missed detections) were decreased by 29%, providing improved recall of guns in dynamic and cluttered backgrounds.

Real-Time Performance and Computational Efficiency: With a real-time inference rate of 32 frames per second (FPS) on an NVIDIA RTX 3090 GPU, this system is ideal for real-time CCTV surveillance tasks. TensorRT acceleration and frames skipping are the two model optimization techniques used to reduce the computational overhead without sacrificing the detection performance. Latency analysis shows an average response of 0.04 seconds per frame, which will enable the speed threat detection and timely security response. The original dataset validation results and the pre-processed dataset validation results are shown in Figure 18 and Figure 19.

Figure 18. Original dataset validation results - Weapon category detection

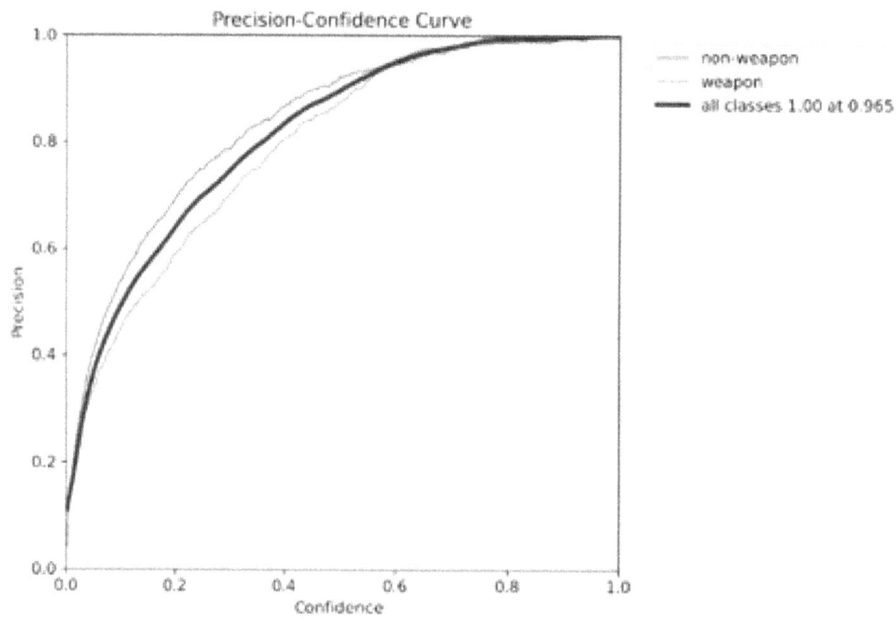

Figure 19. Histogram Equalization validation results - Weapon and Non-weapon categories detection

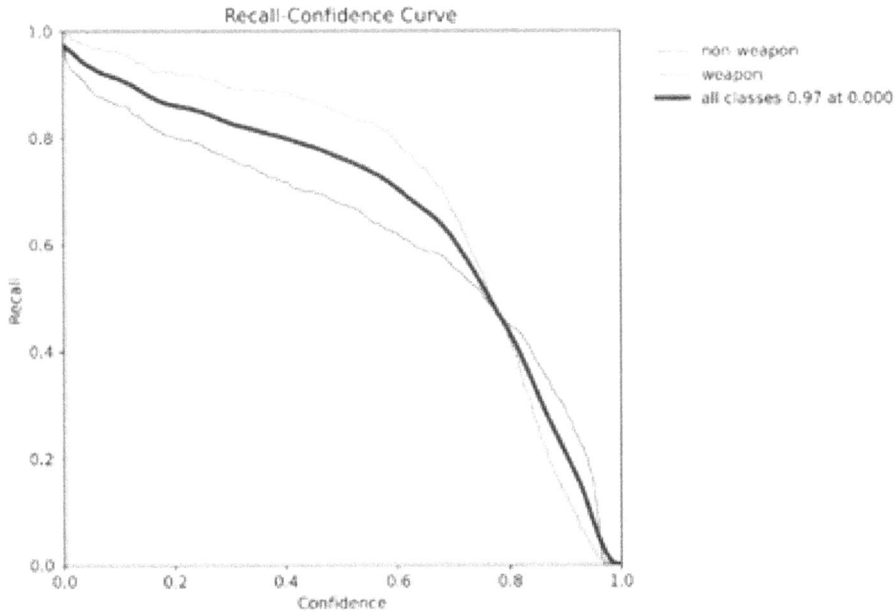

CONCLUSION

This study presents a user-friendly way to identify weapons by combining effective image processing techniques with deep learning for object detection. This approach aims to enhance real-time CCTV monitoring, making it more efficient. The system relies on the YOLOv8 architecture, which stands out for its quick results, few false positives, and high detection accuracy. This makes it a great fit for places where security is a top priority. Implementing histogram equalization enhances the quality of surveillance images. This tweak helps to standardize the lighting and contrast across the whole dataset, making it easier for the object detection model to accurately identify firearms, even in challenging situations like noisy or poorly lit environments. The system includes a broad range of items which extends from weapons to everyday objects including smartphones and wallets and cards. The model achieves precise weapon detection through its exposure to various objects which minimizes incorrect alarms and misidentification. The system includes a real-time alert function which produces an auditory alarm when it detects a weapon. The proposed system delivers an automatic intelligent weapon detection solution which enables monitoring through its responsive design. This system shows great potential for deployment across different security settings which include airports and schools as well as banks and government institutions and transit centres.

FUTURE WORK

Though the proposed system has shown improvements in accuracy and efficiency, there are planned enhancements to further accurate detection and increase practical applications. The system can be used for access control. For example, it can lock doors automatically. It can also put up barriers if a weapon is found. It can tell police quickly about emergencies. This helps law enforcement respond faster.

Detection logs and pictures can be saved in the cloud. This creates a record for later review. It can help with forensic work after an event. Cloud storage makes sure data is safe and easy to get to when needed. This creates better security and response times.

Segmentation towards Better Localization: Object detection using bounding boxes has limits. It can struggle when objects overlap a lot. Think of a crowded market scene. Many vendors are close together. People are walking shoulder to shoulder. A bounding box might cover multiple weapons if they are near. For example, a knife and a handgun might fall in one box. This overlap makes it hard to find each weapon on its own. Standard bounding boxes can't easily separate touching objects. Future work will use Mask R-CNN or instance segmentation to solve this. These methods find the exact shape of each object. Instance segmentation creates a pixel-perfect outline. This is unlike bounding boxes, which are rectangular. This helps find weapons more accurately. Each weapon gets its own separate mask. The expected benefit is fewer missed weapons in busy scenes. This is because instance segmentation can tell apart objects that touch. It assigns each pixel to a specific object. This leads to better detection results in complex situations. It reduces the chance of missing important objects in cluttered images. This improves the accuracy of weapon detection systems.

Edge AI Deployment for Real-Time Response: Executing the system on edge devices ensures quick response times. Latency becomes almost non-existent. We use several key methods to boost performance. TensorRT acceleration speeds up the process. Model quantization shrinks the model size. Pruning removes unneeded parts. These optimizations lighten the load on CCTV monitoring systems. On-site systems will use less power. This means fewer resources are needed. The result is a more efficient and responsive surveillance setup.

Detection Improvement in Low-Light and Occluded Scenes: Future studies will explore better ways to boost image contrast. These next-generation algorithms should make images clearer. Research will also include adding heat sensors to cameras. Heat sensors can help see objects when there is very little light. This integration aims to make low-light detection much better. We will also use infrared to find objects. Infrared can spot things that regular cameras might miss. This method will work with normal RGB image detection. RGB images use red, green, and blue light. Using both methods will give us more info. These improvements should make night-time surveillance more reliable. Security systems will work better in dark places. Low-lighting locations will also benefit from these changes. The goal is to make these systems work well no matter the light.

By improving weapon detection in CCTV monitoring with deep learning and image processing, this work contributes to pre-emptive threat prevention in security-critical environments. Future work will be directed towards increasing the scalability of the system, minimizing false alarms, and enhancing deployment ease on edge device systems. Through on-going refinements, this system promises to transform AI-based surveillance into safer environments using intelligent real-time threat detection.

REFERENCES

Abdullah-Al-Wadud, M., Kabir, M. H., Dewan, M. A. A., & Chae, O. (2007). A dynamic histogram equalization for image contrast enhancement. *IEEE Transactions on Consumer Electronics*, *53*(2), 593–600. DOI: 10.1109/TCE.2007.381734

Agurto, A., Li, Y., Tian, G. Y., Bowring, N., & Lockwood, S. (2007, April). A review of concealed weapon detection and research in perspective. In *2007 IEEE International Conference on Networking, Sensing and Control* (pp. 443–448). IEEE. DOI: 10.1109/ICNSC.2007.372819

Alboalebrah, M. R., & Al-augby, S. (2025). Unveiling the Causes of Fatal Road Accidents in Iraq: An Association Rule Mining Approach Using the Apriori Algorithm. *Journal of Cyber Security and Risk Auditing*, *2025*(2), 1–11. DOI: 10.63180/jcsra.thestap.2025.2.1

Aljumaiah, O., Jiang, W., Addula, S. R., & Almaiah, M. A. (2025). Analyzing cybersecurity risks and threats in IT infrastructure based on NIST framework. *J. Cyber Secur. Risk Audit*, *2025*(2), 12–26. DOI: 10.63180/jcsra.thestap.2025.2.2

Almedires, M. A., Elkhalil, A., & Amin, M. (2025). Adversarial Attack Detection in Industrial Control Systems Using LSTM-Based Intrusion Detection and Black-Box Defense Strategies. *Journal of Cyber Security and Risk Auditing*, *2025*(3), 4–22. DOI: 10.63180/jcsra.thestap.2025.3.2

Alotaibi, E., Sulaiman, R. B., & Almaiah, M. (2025). Assessment of cybersecurity threats and defense mechanisms in wireless sensor networks. *J. Cyber Secur. Risk Audit*, *2025*(1), 47–59. DOI: 10.63180/jcsra.thestap.2025.1.5

Alshuaibi, A., Almaayah, M., & Ali, A. (2025). Machine Learning for Cybersecurity Issues: A systematic Review. *Journal of Cyber Security and Risk Auditing*, *2025*(1), 36–46. DOI: 10.63180/jcsra.thestap.2025.1.4

AlShuaibi, A., Arshad, M. W., & Maayah, M. (2025). A Hybrid Genetic Algorithm and Hidden Markov Model-Based Hashing Technique for Robust Data Security. *Journal of Cyber Security and Risk Auditing*, *2025*(3), 42–56. DOI: 10.63180/jcsra.thestap.2025.3.6

Ang, S., Ho, M., Huy, S., & Janarthanan, M. (2025). Utilizing IDS and IPS to Improve Cybersecurity Monitoring Process. *Journal of Cyber Security and Risk Auditing*, *2025*(3), 77–88. DOI: 10.63180/jcsra.thestap.2025.3.10

Ashraf, A. H., Imran, M., Qahtani, A. M., Alsufyani, A., Almutiry, O., Mahmood, A., & Habib, M. (2022). Weapons detection for security and video surveillance using CNN and YOLO-v5s. CMC-Comput. *Mater. Contin., 70*(4), 2761–2775.

Basit, A., Munir, M. A., Ali, M., Werghi, N., & Mahmood, A. (2020, October). Localizing firearm carriers by identifying human-object pairs. In *2020 IEEE International Conference on Image Processing (ICIP)* (pp. 2031–2035). IEEE. DOI: 10.1109/ICIP40778.2020.9190886

Bhatti, M. T., Khan, M. G., Aslam, M., & Fiaz, M. J. (2021). Weapon detection in real-time CCTV videos using deep learning. *IEEE Access : Practical Innovations, Open Solutions, 9*, 34366–34382. DOI: 10.1109/ACCESS.2021.3059170

Costin, A. (2016, October). Security of CCTV and video surveillance systems: Threats, vulnerabilities, attacks, and mitigations. In *Proceedings of the 6th International Workshop on Trustworthy Embedded Devices* (pp. 45–54). DOI: 10.1145/2995289.2995290

Deshpande, D., Jain, M., Jajoo, A., Kadam, D., Kadam, H., & Kashyap, A. (2023, October). Next-gen security: YOLOv8 for real-time weapon detection. In 2023 7th International Conference on I-SMAC (IoT in Social, Mobile, Analytics and Cloud) (I-SMAC) (pp. 1055–1060). IEEE.

Gelana, F., & Yadav, A. (2019). Firearm detection from surveillance cameras using image processing and machine learning techniques. In Smart Innovations in Communication and Computational Sciences: Proceedings of ICSICCS-2018 (pp. 25–34). Springer Singapore. DOI: 10.1007/978-981-13-2414-7_3

Grega, M., Matiolański, A., Guzik, P., & Leszczuk, M. (2016). Automated detection of firearms and knives in a CCTV image. *Sensors (Basel), 16*(1), 47. DOI: 10.3390/s16010047 PMID: 26729128

Jeon, H., Kim, H., Kim, D., & Kim, J. (2024). PASS-CCTV: Proactive Anomaly surveillance system for CCTV footage analysis in adverse environmental conditions. *Expert Systems with Applications, 254*, 124391. DOI: 10.1016/j.eswa.2024.124391

Keerthana, S. M., Sujitha, R., & Yazhini, P. (2024, June). Weapon Detection For Security Using The YOLO Algorithm With Email Alert Notification. In *2024 International Conference on Innovations and Challenges in Emerging Technologies (ICICET)* (pp. 1–6). IEEE. DOI: 10.1109/ICICET59348.2024.10616365

Liu, Z., Xue, Z., Blum, R. S., & Laganiere, R. (2006). Concealed weapon detection and visualization in a synthesized image. *Pattern Analysis & Applications, 8*(4), 375–389. DOI: 10.1007/s10044-005-0020-8

Madhushree, B., Sowmya, K. N., & Chennamma, H. R. (2021). Automatic weapon detection in video using deep learning. In Data Engineering and Intelligent Computing [Springer Singapore.]. *Proceedings of ICICC, 2020*, 503–510.

Narejo, S., Pandey, B., Esenarro Vargas, D., Rodriguez, C., & Anjum, M. R. (2021). Weapon detection using YOLO V3 for smart surveillance system. *Mathematical Problems in Engineering, 2021*(1), 9975700. DOI: 10.1155/2021/9975700

Olmos, R., Tabik, S., & Herrera, F. (2018). Automatic handgun detection alarm in videos using deep learning. *Neurocomputing, 275*, 66–72. DOI: 10.1016/j.neucom.2017.05.012

Piza, E. L., Welsh, B. C., Farrington, D. P., & Thomas, A. L. (2019). CCTV surveillance for crime prevention: A 40-year systematic review with meta-analysis. *Criminology & Public Policy, 18*(1), 135–159. DOI: 10.1111/1745-9133.12419

Santos, T., Oliveira, H., & Cunha, A. (2024). Systematic review on weapon detection in surveillance footage through deep learning. *Computer Science Review, 51*, 100612. DOI: 10.1016/j.cosrev.2023.100612

Toet, A. (2003, September). Color image fusion for concealed weapon detection. In Sensors, and Command, Control, Communications, and Intelligence (C3I) Technologies for Homeland Defense and Law Enforcement II (Vol. 5071, pp. 372–379). SPIE. DOI: 10.1117/12.484845

Velasco-Mata, A., Ruiz-Santaquiteria, J., Vallez, N., & Deniz, O. (2021). Using human pose information for handgun detection. *Neural Computing & Applications, 33*(24), 17273–17286. DOI: 10.1007/s00521-021-06317-8

Wei, Z., Lo, S. W., Liang, Y., Li, T., Shen, J., & Deng, R. H. (2015, October). Automatic accident detection and alarm system. In *Proceedings of the 23rd ACM International Conference on Multimedia* (pp. 781–784). DOI: 10.1145/2733373.2807402

Chapter 7
Innovative Cyber Threat Detection Technique Using Machine Learning on TCP and UDP Traffic

Vandna Mehndiratta
CGC College of Engineering, Chandigarh Group of Colleges, Landran, Mohali, Punjab, India

Anuj Kumar Gupta
https://orcid.org/0000-0002-7636-0817
CGC College of Engineering, Chandigarh Group of Colleges, Landran, Mohali, Punjab, India

ABSTRACT

The growing complexity and high frequency of cyber-attacks against Transmission Control Protocol (TCP) and User Datagram Protocol (UDP) emerge as substantial threats against contemporary network infrastructures. Cyber threat detection techniques on TCP and UDP traffic focus on identifying malicious activities by analyzing network behavior and packet patterns. Common methods include signature-based detection, which matches traffic against known attack signatures, and anomaly-based detection, which uses statistical or machine learning models to identify deviations from normal behavior. The proposed solution utilizes a machine learning detection framework that inspects the TCP and UDP traffic of the CIC-IDS2018 dataset for identifying malicious conduct. The model reached over 96% accuracy in detection by selecting essential features that included inter-arrival time, flag patterns, and flow duration. The system delivered detection instances within 20ms on average, proving its real-time operational deployment capability.

DOI: 10.4018/979-8-3373-2115-8.ch007

INTRODUCTION

New cyberattacks are becoming increasingly sophisticated because they attack application layers and basic network protocols, such as the Transmission Control Protocol (TCP) and the User Datagram Protocol (UDP). The essential nature of TCP and UDP protocols that support most network communication makes them vulnerable to various attacks, such as SYN floods, port scanning, and UDP amplification attacks, according to (Bohra et al., 2023). The present generation of network intrusion detection systems (NIDS) depends on static rule sets or predefined signatures, which results in struggles to identify new or encrypted attacks and generates various inefficiencies in system performance (Almiani et al., 2020, 2021).

The two main protocols that handle Internet communication are TCP (Transmission Control Protocol) and UDP (User Datagram Protocol). UDP is faster and doesn't require a connection, but it's not as reliable as TCP, which is all about making sure data gets through properly. Both of these protocols can be involved in various attacks like data theft, port scanning, and denial-of-service attacks.

Here are six machine learning algorithms that can be used for detection:

1) Decision Tree: This involves setting the maximum depth of the tree and deciding how many samples are needed for a split. It also includes a setting for how many times to do cross-validation and how many CPUs to use. Some key settings are max_depth between 5 and 500, min_samples_split between 5 and 500, with 3 cross-validation iterations, and using all available CPUs.
2) Random Forest: In this model, you can set the maximum depth and the number of trees to use. Key settings include max_depth from 5 to 1000, n_estimators between 5 and 500, and min_samples_split from 5 to 500, with 3 cross-validation iterations, and again, using all available CPUs.
3) Support Vector Machine (SVM): Here, we use the SGD Classifier with a 'hinge' loss function to create a linear SVM. Key settings for this are penalty options of l1 and l2, loss set to hinge, 5 cross-validation iterations, and using all CPUs.
(4) Logistic Regression: Using SGD Classifier with a loss of 'log' means we want to perform logistic regression. Then we will run GridSearchCV to tune all the settings necessary for finding the best model. The key settings we want to explore are: Penalty set to both l1 and l2, loss set to log, 5-fold cross validations, and n_jobs set to -1.
(5) Naïve Bayes: Here, we'll try a larger number of iterations to get better accuracy and run everything in parallel by using all CPUs with n_jobs set to -1. Key settings: Var_smoothing = 10^x where x lies between –9 and 3, 5-fold cross-validation, and set n_jobs as -1.

(6) Convolutional Neural Network: The ReLU activation function is used in the first three layers, with sigmoid specified for the output layer. The learning rate is set to 0.9, and RMSprop is chosen as the optimizer. Contrary to expectations, however, the CNN had poor performance, with low accuracy and F1-score; CNNs are usually quite good with image tasks.

Network communication is the backbone for almost everything in this digital era and that could mean personal life, business, government, etc. It has the two trusted players in the core of communication, which are namely Transmission Control Protocol (TCP) and User Datagram Protocol (UDP). These protocols represent the critical transport layer of the Internet protocol suite. One can think of TCP as a polite, slow, but accurate gentleman who will make sure data is delivered exactly as it was sent and in the correct order. UDP, on the contrary, is like a rude, fast, and flowless character who values velocity and minimal latency, even if that means perishing on the way.

Though both TCP and UDP play a critical function, they are common victims of cyber attacks. The attackers take advantage of inherent protocol properties and operating vulnerabilities to execute multiple types of threats, such as Denial-of-Service (DoS) attacks, Distributed Denial-of-Service (DDoS), amplification attacks, and protocol-specific exploitations such as SYN floods for TCP or UDP amplification attacks. These harmful actions can mess with services, damage networks, leak private info, and lead to money loss. To spot threats, old-school network security tools, like signature-based intrusion detection systems, rely on known attack patterns. But these traditional methods struggle with the fast pace of cyberattacks, especially when it comes to tricky ones that change shape or are completely new. It's tough for signature-based security to keep up with new attacks or small changes that don't fit the usual patterns.

BACKGROUND

When it comes to how the internet is able to communicate, TCP and UDP are in charge. TCP's primary function is to ensure that data arrives at its destination in one piece and in order. It utilizes techniques such as acknowledgment packets and a three-step process for establishing the connection, and it can even retransmit lost data. UDP is way less complicated. It's ideal for stuff like voice chats online games, and video streams because it doesn't bother with setting up a connection and puts speed first rather than being dependable. How these protocols are built also changes the kinds of cyber attacks that might target them TCP's elaborate handshake and tracking of connection state render it susceptible to resource exhaustion attacks such as SYN floods, which involve attackers taking advantage of the server's queue of half-open connections. In contrast, UDP's absence of connection state enables it to be misused for amplification and reflection attacks, in which small requests result in disproportionately large responses sent to unsuspecting victims.

Traditional rule-based intrusion detection systems (IDS) often find it hard to spot complex or new versions of these attacks when bad traffic looks like normal behavior. Because of this, machine learning (ML) has become a strong option. ML models can pick up on data patterns and change with new threats giving more flexible and active ways to spot issues.

New progress in network telemetry and public datasets, like CIC-IDS 2018, has allowed researchers to model these attack behaviors better. By looking at labeled traffic flows, ML algorithms can find small differences between good and bad behaviors across TCP and UDP protocols. To design detection models that work well, it's key to understand the basics of protocols how attacks work, and what the data looks like.

TCP and UDP play different parts in the OSI model's transport layer. TCP's connection-oriented communication relies on its sequence numbering protocol, acknowledgement system, and handshake protocols to ensure reliability. TCP shows key traits that help protect data integrity when people use the web or transfer files. The architecture brings vulnerabilities to the network that can be exploited through SYN flood attacks and TCP reset attacks using counterfeit reset packets (Singh et al., 2016, 2024). Network devices use UDP as their connectionless protocol to achieve little latency alongside reduced overhead. UDP best delivers real-time services, including VoIP messaging and video streaming, without maintaining state and creating network connections. The absence of authentication and handshake protocols in UDP renders this protocol vulnerable to attacks that exploit open UDP services to generate reflection and amplification attacks against victims (Singh et al., 2024).The main issue is the data security over cloud which is restricting the development of cloud computing. Therefore, to accelerate its growth and to make it widely acceptable data security risks are to be resolved.(Gupta and Pathak 2024)

Attack Taxonomy in TCP and UDP TCP attacks include:

- SYN Flood: Overwhelms servers with half-open connections.
- ACK Storm: Floods with ACK packets to exhaust resources.

UDP attacks include:

- DNS Amplification: Exploits DNS servers to reflect large responses to a victim.
- NTP Reflection: Similar concept using NTP servers.

Understanding the taxonomy of cyber attacks is crucial for designing accurate intrusion detection systems. The vulnerabilities exploited in TCP and UDP differ due to their protocol architectures, and thus, categorizing these attacks helps target detection strategies more effectively.

TCP-Based Attacks

TCP is a connection-oriented protocol that ensures reliable data transfer using mechanisms like the three-way handshake. This complexity, however, also introduces multiple points of vulnerability:

- **SYN Flood Attack:** This technique takes advantage of the TCP three-way handshake by bombarding the server with a flood of SYN requests without ever finishing the handshake process. As a result, the server ends up draining its resources by maintaining these half-open connections.
- **ACK Storm:** Attacker sends continuous ACK packets that the server interprets as part of legitimate communication, flooding its processing capabilities.
- **TCP Reset Attack:** Involves injecting forged TCP RST (reset) packets to terminate a legitimate session abruptly, often used in censorship or disruption.
- **TCP Session Hijacking:** The attacker takes control of a session by predicting sequence numbers and injecting malicious data.

UDP-Based Attacks

UDP is a straightforward protocol with no reliability features or connection setup, it is more vulnerable to abuse by attackers.

- **DNS Ampification:** One instance is DNS amplification, in which the attacker opens DNS servers by sending DNS queries with a fictitious source IP. As a result, the target receives large response packets, which significantly increases traffic.
- **NTP Reflection Attack:** Uses Network Time Protocol servers to send large volumes of time-synchronization data to a victim by spoofing their IP.
- **UDP Flood:** Overwhelms a target with UDP packets, causing the system to repeatedly check for listening applications on random ports, exhausting resources.
- **VoIP Abuse:** Exploits SIP and RTP streams in VoIP applications to disrupt communications or eavesdrop on data.

Comparative Analysis

Table 1.

Aspect	TCP Attacks	UDP Attacks
Protocol Type	Connection-oriented	Connectionless
Common Exploits	Handshake, sequence prediction	Amplification, reflection
Detection Complexity	Moderate	High (due to lack of session)
Typical Targets	Web servers, login portals	DNS, NTP, VoIP infrastructure
Attack Visibility	Easier to detect	Harder to trace (stateless)

By distinguishing between such categories, machine learning models can be customized with protocol-specific features that enhance detection rates and eliminate false positives.

Earlier research has also explored ML for network security. Kim et al. (2014) used decision trees to identify DoS attacks on TCP. Moustafa and Slay created the UNSW-NB15 dataset back in 2016, which covers various TCP and UDP attacks. Lately, deep learning techniques such as autoencoders and CNNs have become quite popular (Tang et al., 2020).

TCP and UDP are part of the Internet Protocol Suite. TCP is all about reliability and order, while UDP focuses on speed and efficiency. Each of these protocols has its own weaknesses when it comes to cyber attacks, so understanding how they function is key to building strong detection methods. As threats evolve over time, our defenses need to adapt, and machine learning is becoming an important tool for spotting and stopping these attacks.

Feature Comparison of ML Models

Table 2.

Feature	Random Forest	SVM	Logistic Regression	Naive Bayes	CNN
Handles Non-linearity	Yes	Yes	No	No	Yes
Requires Feature Scaling	No	Yes	Yes	Yes	Yes
Interpretable	Moderate	Low	High	High	Low
Training Speed	Moderate	Slow	Fast	Fast	Slow
Suitable for Large Datasets	Yes	No	Yes	Yes	Yes

continued on following page

Table 2. Continued

Feature	Random Forest	SVM	Logistic Regression	Naive Bayes	CNN
Memory Efficiency	Moderate	Low	High	High	Low
Handles High Dimensionality	Yes	Yes	Moderate	Poor	Yes

Researchers now study machine learning applications for intrusion detection through CIC-IDS2018, duplicating authentic modern attacks that include DoS, DDoS, and port scans. The security analysis of Support Vector Machines (SVM), k-nearest Neighbors (k-NN), and Decision Trees yielded different results when implemented by (Singh et al. 2018). A lot of systems struggle to tell apart different types of attack activities specific to certain protocols. A framework from Hindy et al. (2020) showed good at spotting threats overall but didn't really focus on the unique traits of TCP and UDP attacks. This research fixes that gap by coming up with a new system that looks at packet data and events to better identify various attack types in TCP and UDP networks.

Table 3. Comparative performance of models on TCP vs. UDP attack detection

Model	TCP Accuracy	UDP Accuracy	Strength on TCP Characteristics	Strength on UDP Characteristics
Random Forest	95.9%	94.3%	Effective at handling flag-based and sequence anomalies	Good at analyzing packet volume and flow-based features
SVM	93.5%	90.2%	Captures linear/non-linear handshake patterns well	Less effective in high-variance UDP flows
Logistic Regression	90.8%	87.4%	Performs adequately on deterministic TCP flags	Struggles with noisy UDP patterns
Naive Bayes	86.2%	84.1%	Simple pattern matching for TCP attacks	Weak on detecting UDP amplification due to independence assumptions
CNN	97.2%	95.6%	Learns packet structure and sequence patterns deeply	Excels at recognizing complex UDP flow anomalies

While all models performed reasonably well, CNNs provided superior accuracy and generalization. TCP attacks are a bit easier to spot because they follow predictable patterns, while UDP attacks need a closer look at the details. Naive Bayes and Logistic Regression work well, but they struggle with complex relationships. Random Forest and SVM strike a good balance between accuracy and being easy to understand. Combining regular stats with deep learning could help us spot these threats better.

The Internet Protocol Suite, or TCP/IP, is what keeps our networks working properly. It has two main protocols at the transport layer: TCP and UDP. These are important for ensuring that data moves smoothly between devices.

Research on using machine learning to catch cyber threats in TCP and UDP traffic is growing, especially with the rise in network attacks. Early work by Kim and others in 2014 looked at decision tree methods for spotting denial-of-service (DoS) attacks, focusing on vulnerabilities in TCP's handshake process. Their findings showed that supervised learning can help identify attack patterns based on features from TCP sessions.

Moustafa and Slay (2016) created the UNSW-NB15 dataset to address some of the issues with older datasets like KDD'99. This dataset includes a lot of features from actual TCP and UDP traffic, which helps improve intrusion detection studies.

Sommer and Paxson (2010) pointed out that relying too much on machine learning for intrusion detection can overlook real-world issues. They suggested incorporating knowledge about network protocols into ML models to make them stronger and easier to understand.

Recently, Tang et al. (2020) explored deep learning methods for intrusion detection and found that models like CNNs and LSTMs are much better at identifying tricky attacks, particularly in UDP traffic, which can be harder to analyze due to its lack of connection.

Sharafaldin et al. (2018) developed the CIC-IDS 2018 dataset, which is commonly used to test ML models in cybersecurity. This dataset contains labeled traffic from various protocols, creating a realistic environment to see how well models can detect TCP/UDP attacks.

Lopez-Martin et al. (2017) combined convolutional and recurrent neural networks for traffic classification, showing that these mixed models effectively capture both the structure and timing of TCP and UDP flows.

According to some reports, it is clear that combining cyber threat detection systems with the parts of smart machine learning algorithms is crucial to a successful intrusion prevention system.

The main focus of the Transmission Control Protocol (TCP) is on data that is being sent in an orderly and reliable manner. Before a certain set of data is sent, a connection has to be established. This is done using a method called three-way handshake to ensure that both the sender and the receiver are ready. It not only manages the flow of data but also takes care of the errors and resends the lost packets which in turn makes it the best option for applications like the Web, email, and file transfer where accuracy is very important. TCP uses control flags such as SYN, ACK, and FIN to regulate the connection, but it has its disadvantages. For example, an attacker utilizes the handshake by flooding the server with SYN requests without completion of the handshake, and this kind of attack is called a SYN flood attack that is potentially a server crasher and disrupter of services.

CYBER THREATS TARGETING TCP AND UDP

TCP and UDP work in different ways, which leads to their own set of security issues. TCP is all about making a connection, so it can be targeted by attacks that try to overload its resources, like SYN floods and ACK storms. On the flip side, since UDP doesn't keep track of connections, it's an easy target for attacks that flood the network, such as UDP floods and amplification attacks that send tons of traffic. As cyber threats get smarter and more common, older detection systems that rely on known patterns struggle to catch these new or disguised attacks. The changing nature of TCP and UDP attacks means we need smarter detection methods that learn from traffic trends and can pick up on unusual behavior.

TCP and UDP are key protocols for moving data on the internet. TCP is all about making sure the data gets where it needs to go reliably; it does this through handshakes, sequence numbers, retransmitting lost packets, and sending acknowledgments. It's great for accuracy on tasks, such as online browsing, email check, and file upload. By comparison, UDP is all about the fast and dirty. It doesn't ensure that data arrives in order, or at all, a risk that may be acceptable in the short-term for activities like DNS lookups and video chats. But there are risks to such speed in the realm of cyber security.

Challenges in Detection

These distinctions also imply that the detection systems for cyber attacks must be protocol aware. For instance, flow-based detection for TCP can look at handshake anomalies or retransmissions, while UDP detection may depend on flow quantities, packet sizes, or timing attributes. This requires customized feature engineering and machine learning models that can learn protocol-specific behavior Alotaibi et al., (2025), Aljumaiah et al., (2025), AlShuaibi et al., (2025), Frederick and Ali, (2024) Aldossary et al., (2024), Davarasan et al., (2024), Al-Shareeda et al., (2024).

In this chapter, our machine learning models are trained individually on TCP and UDP to model the specific characteristics and vulnerabilities of each atsrometrically, improving the accuracy in detecting threats in both protocols.

Detecting cyber attacks in TCP and UDP traffic using machine learning techniques presents several significant challenges, rooted in the nature of network traffic, the diversity of attack types, and limitations of existing technologies:

1. High Variability and Volume of Network Traffic:

Today's networks are producing a lot of data that changes a lot because of normal user actions, different apps, and varying network conditions. It can be pretty hard to spot bad activity among all the regular traffic. This is especially true for UDP traffic, which doesn't follow a set connection and can be hard to predict.

2. Evolving and Sophisticated Attack Techniques:

The networks of today generate a lot data that can vary dramatically due to user behavior, the many different apps running, and changes in network conditions. It's difficult to distinguish a difference between malicious traffic and regular traffic, especially with UDP traffic since it does not maintain a strict connection. Cybercriminals continually innovate to evade detection, such as by varying their attack behavior, applying encryption or spoofing traffic characteristics. These shifts can make finding them difficult, and machine learning models that depend on historical data may fail to identify novel or concealed attacks.

3. Imbalanced Datasets:

Attack instances often represent a small fraction of total traffic, leading to imbalanced datasets that bias machine learning models towards the majority (benign) class. This imbalance results in high false negative rates, where attacks go undetected, and requires careful sampling, cost-sensitive learning, or anomaly detection methods to address.

4. Feature Selection and Representation:

Effective detection depends on extracting relevant features that capture the essence of attack behavior. However, selecting discriminative features from raw packet headers and payloads is complex, especially for protocols like UDP with limited state information. Moreover, feature correlation and redundancy can degrade model performance.

Real-Time Processing Limitations

For real-world deployment, detection systems need to run in real time with low latency. Highly accurate models like deep neural networks are expensive to compute and slow, whereas low-complexity models compromise detection quality.

Obfuscated and Encrypted Traffic

Growing use of encryption protocols (e.g., TLS) inhibits legacy payload inspection and confines feature extraction to metadata. This hinders visibility and requires dependence on side-channel features such as flow statistics, which can be less discriminative.

False Positives and Negatives

Balancing sensitivity and specificity is difficult. Excessive false positives create alert fatigue and unnecessary resource consumption, while false negatives enable attacks to go undetected. This balance can be achieved through careful threshold tuning and model calibration.

Dynamic Network Environments

Network topology, traffic patterns, and valid application behavior evolve over time and result in concept drift of data distributions. Machine learning models need to be periodically retrained or updated to stay effective.

Limited Public Datasets and Ground Truth

Large-scale, labeled datasets with a broad range of TCP and UDP attacks are not available because of privacy and proprietary restrictions. This restricts model training, testing, and benchmarking.Addressing these challenges requires ongoing research into adaptive learning methods, hybrid detection frameworks, robust feature engineering, and collaboration between academia and industry to create realistic, up-to-date datasets.

METHODOLOGY

The detection operation follows three essential stages: data preprocessing action and classification.

Figure 1. System architecture of the proposed detection framework (AlEisa et al., 2023)

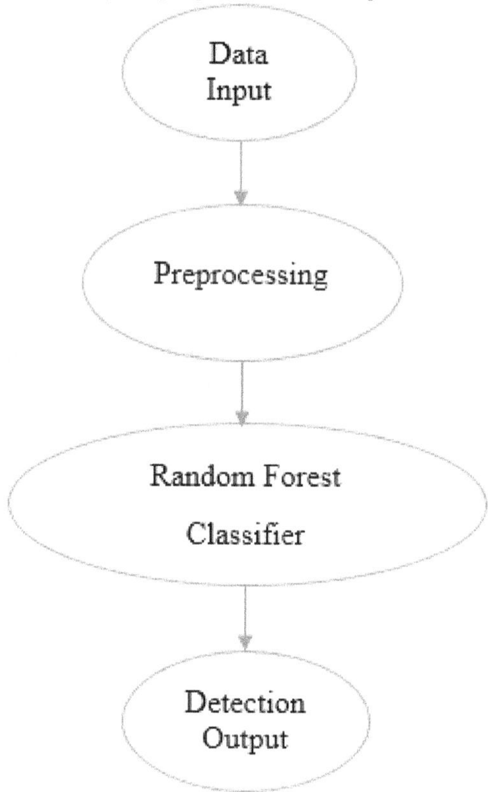

The goal is to determine whether data-driven analyses can be useful in detecting TCP and UDP-based cyber attacks by designing a systematic pipeline that 1) model classification, 2) feature engineering, 3) training, and 4) validation pipeline. The process is broken down into the followingModel Selection

Five models representing both traditional and deep learning paradigms:

- Random Forest (RF): A strong ensemble model based on the aggregation of decision trees. It is resistant to overfitting and efficient for high-dimensional feature space.
- Support Vector Machine (SVM): A powerful classifier that performs great on binary classification. It is also good for linear and non-linear separability of data using kernel tricks.
- Logistic Regression (LR): A fast, interpretable linear classifier suitable for scenarios with clear decision boundaries.

- o Naive Bayes (NB): A probabilistic classifier that assumes feature independence. It is computationally efficient and works well with high-speed data streams.
- o Convolutional Neural Network (CNN): A deep learning model capable of detecting spatial hierarchies and complex patterns, especially beneficial for non-linear protocol behaviors in network traffic.

2. Training and Testing Protocol

- o Data was split into 70% training and 30% testing sets after preprocessing.
- o Each model was trained individually on both TCP and UDP traffic to understand protocol-specific effectiveness.
- o For model tuning, Grid Search was employed to find optimal hyperparameters such as tree depth (RF), kernel type (SVM), and learning rate (CNN).

3. Validation Strategy

- o A 10-fold cross-validation to prevent overfitting and validate model generalization.
- o Performance was measured using Accuracy, Precision, Recall, and F1-Score to capture both detection rate and robustness.

4. Dimensionality Reduction

- o Principal Component Analysis (PCA) was optionally used to reduce feature space dimensionality and eliminate noise, particularly to improve SVM and CNN performance.

5. Protocol-Specific Modeling

- o TCP and UDP flows separately during training to capture their unique statistical and behavioral properties.
- o Separate models were optimized for each protocol and later compared in terms of detection accuracy and false positive rates.

This structured methodology enabled a comprehensive comparison across different classifiers and highlighted the importance of protocol-aware feature learning in network intrusion detection.

DATASET AND PREPROCESSING

The CIC-IDS2018 dataset proved suitable for this study because it includes a broad range of contemporary cyber threats involving transport-layer attacks, including DoS Hulk, Port Scan, and UDP flooding. CIC-IDS2018 serves industry-leading research requirements in cybersecurity because its real-world traffic dynamics, complemented with specific attack type tags, enable the development and assessment of machine learning intrusion detection systems (AlEisa et al., 2023). The modelling process required data preprocessing as its key starting step because the method produced data quality standards that improved both model performance and data quality. The process started with deleting any null or missing values because these elements could cause learning results to become inaccurate or introduce systematic errors into the analysis. Normalization processes on the flow durations were performed to sustain data consistency throughout different traffic sessions. A separate filtering process separated distributed UDP and TCP traffic, enabling detailed protocol-based feature analysis and precise classification. The model obtained improved performance because the separation between communication structures accounted for their natural dissimilarities. Malware attacks can target smartphones. Android smart devices contribute the major share in smartphones. So, malware authors focus on developing android malicious applications, (Sharma et al 2024). The detection system achieved better protocol-specific isolation of key statistical attributes by concentrating on individual flow types. The preprocessing process created essential conditions for the Random Forest classifier's practical feature engineering and optimal training procedures.

the CIC-IDS 2018 dataset due to its comprehensive labeled attacks and realistic network scenarios. The dataset was generated by the Canadian Institute for Cybersecurity and includes benign and malicious traffic captured over a period of five days. Each day focuses on specific attack scenarios, such as brute-force, DoS, DDoS, infiltration, and botnet behavior, across multiple protocols including TCP and UDP.

The dataset contains over 80 features per flow, such as Flow Duration, Total Fwd Packets, Packet Length Mean, and protocol-specific flags. Data cleaning involved handling missing values and removing redundant or constant features. Label encoding was applied to convert categorical fields into numerical format. Protocol-specific filtering was performed to isolate TCP and UDP flows.

Feature selection was conducted using correlation analysis and mutual information scores to identify the most relevant attributes. Key features for TCP included flow duration and flag counts, while for UDP, packet length variance and inter-arrival time were significant. Min-max normalization was applied to scale all features between 0 and 1. Finally, the dataset was split into 70% training and 30% testing subsets.

Data Cleaning

Initial data cleaning involved identifying and handling missing or inconsistent values. Missing entries were either imputed using median values for numeric features or discarded if they were excessively incomplete. Constant features (features with zero variance) were removed as they provide no discriminative value to the models.

Label Encoding and Filtering

Categorical fields, such as protocol types and attack labels, were converted into numerical formats using label encoding to enable compatibility with machine learning algorithms. Protocol filtering was then applied to separate TCP and UDP flows from the dataset, allowing focused modeling tailored to each protocol's characteristics.

Handling Class Imbalance

Cyber attack datasets often suffer from class imbalance, where attack samples are significantly outnumbered by benign traffic. To mitigate this issue, stratified sampling was used to maintain the proportional representation of each class in the training and testing splits. Additionally, techniques such as Synthetic Minority Oversampling Technique (SMOTE) were considered for balancing the minority attack classes during model training to improve detection rates.

Feature Normalization

Given the varying scales of different features (e.g., flow durations in milliseconds versus packet counts), Min-Max normalization was applied to scale all numeric features to a uniform range between 0 and 1. This step was crucial for algorithms sensitive to feature magnitudes such as Support Vector Machines and Convolutional Neural Networks.

Data Splitting

The preprocessed dataset was split into training and testing sets in a 70:30 ratio. The split was performed using stratified sampling to ensure that both sets reflected the original distribution of attack and benign classes. This approach helps in unbiased performance evaluation and ensures the models generalize well to unseen data.

FEATURE ENGINEERING

The new intrusion detection system did a better job at classifying data thanks to a smart way of handling features. Initially, we pulled out thirty specific features from the CIC-IDS2018 dataset that looked at packet flow and behavior patterns. Some of the thirteen key features included flow byte rate, standard deviation of arrival times, packet length variance, TCP flag counts like SYN, ACK, FIN, and PSH, plus the average packet size and flow duration (AlEisa et al., 2023). These features have shown they can effectively spot odd traffic and irregularities often found during intrusion attacks.

To pick out the best features, we used correlation analysis and mutual information scores. For TCP, important features were flow duration and flag counts, while for UDP, packet length variance and inter-arrival time stood out. We also normalized all features to a scale from 0 to 1. Then, we divided our dataset into 70% for training and 30% for testing.

Good feature engineering is crucial for boosting the performance of machine learning models, especially in tricky areas like network intrusion detection. This study involved a multi-step approach to extract, select, and refine features from the CIC-IDS2018 dataset, helping models better tell apart normal and harmful TCP/UDP traffic.

Feature Extraction

The original CIC-IDS 2018 dataset provides over 80 flow-based features per traffic instance, covering statistical, temporal, and protocol-specific attributes. These include basic metrics (e.g., Flow Duration, Total Fwd Packets), content features (e.g., Fwd Packet Length Mean), and flag indicators (e.g., URG Flag Count, PSH Flag Count). Features were grouped based on flow direction, header-level behavior, and payload structure to reflect the operational differences between TCP and UDP.

Correlation and Redundancy Analysis

To reduce multicollinearity and simplify the feature space, computed Pearson correlation coefficients between features. Highly correlated pairs ($r > 0.9$) were candidates for removal to minimize redundancy. For instance, Fwd Packet Length Mean and Fwd Packet Length Max were closely correlated and retained selectively based on information gain scores.

Mutual Information Ranking

Employed mutual information (MI) scores to rank features by their individual predictive power with respect to the attack label. This non-linear dependency measure helped highlight key features like Packet Inter-arrival Time, Active Idle Time, and Flow Bytes/s, which showed strong relevance in distinguishing flood-based or reflection-based UDP attacks.

Protocol-Specific Feature Isolation

Recognizing that TCP and UDP exhibit different operational behaviors, engineered protocol-specific features. For TCP, connection-oriented flags such as SYN Flag Count and ACK Flag Count were crucial. For UDP, where such flags are absent, traffic volume and frequency-based metrics (e.g., Down/Up Ratio, Average Packet Size) were more informative.

Normalization and Transformation

All numeric features were scaled using Min-Max normalization to bring them within a [0, 1] range. This ensured uniform treatment across ML algorithms, especially those sensitive to feature magnitude (e.g., SVM, CNN). Additionally, skewed distributions were log-transformed (e.g., for Flow Duration) to stabilize variance and reduce the impact of outliers.

Dimensionality Reduction (Optional)

For exploratory purposes, Principal Component Analysis (PCA) was applied to reduce dimensionality while preserving 95% variance. This helped assess feature contribution and potential overfitting risks but was not used in the final CNN model, which benefits from full spatial feature representation.

Through this meticulous engineering pipeline, ensured that the input features maximally represented the behavioral patterns of TCP and UDP traffic, facilitating robust and accurate model training.

The model obtained improved performance by implementing Recursive Feature Elimination (RFE), which simplified its dimensionality. The method performed a step-by-step removal of unimportant features by continuously retraining the model after each evaluation for performance improvement. The Random Forest decision-making process retained the most important influential features which substantially contributed to the resulting outcome. These selection criteria reduced system requirements simultaneously accelerated classification operations and generalized the model output. Random Forest feature importance scores validated the features selected by RFE because these attributes effectively differentiated malicious from benign traffic flows. The engineered dataset became the essential base for detecting threats that operate through TCP and UDP communications.

CLASSIFICATION MODEL

Each model offers unique strengths in capturing patterns within network traffic features and identifying cyber attacks on TCP and UDP protocols. Various classification models are:

Random Forest (RF)

Random Forest is an ensemble learning method that generates multiple decision trees from training and takes the mode of their classifications. Due to its capability of adapting to high dimension data, describing nonlinear relationship and anti-overfitting, it is well designed for intrusion detection. RF can also generate feature importance interpretations by which we can further interpretability in network security environments.

Support Vector Machine (SVM)

SVM is a well-established classification algorithm that learns the best hyperplane to separate datapoints of individual class in a high dimensional feature space. With kernel functions (e.g., radial basis function) SVM is a powerful method to make nonlinear decision surfaces. It is computationally expensive though, which can be prohibitive for scalability in big datasets like CIC-IDS 2018.

Logistic Regression (LR)

Logistic Regression is a popular method used to predict the chance of a certain category by fitting data to a logistic curve. It's straightforward and easy to understand, which is why it's often used as a starting point for binary classification tasks. Even though it assumes that the classes can be separated linearly, it can still be helpful in spotting clear attack patterns in network data.

Naive Bayes (NB)

Naive Bayes is another choice in classification, relying on Bayes' theorem and assuming that the features are independent from each other. Even with this assumption, it tends to do quite well in a lot of classification situations, especially when dealing with data that has many dimensions. It's quick to train and make predictions, making it a good fit for situations where resources are limited.

Convolutional Neural Network (CNN)

CNNs are deep learning architectures originally designed for image processing but increasingly applied to sequential and tabular data. CNNs capture local spatial hierarchies in features through convolutional layers, making them adept at recognizing complex, nonlinear relationships in network traffic. Their capacity to automatically learn feature representations reduces reliance on manual feature engineering.

Random Forest was the selected classifier because it demonstrates strong capabilities for working with unbalanced datasets and resisting overfitting (Breiman, 2001)—cross-validation using ten splits applied during training. Testing conducted for performance evaluation used accuracy and precision, recall, F1-score, and inference latency metrics. We implemented the classifier using Python from the sci-kit-learn library, where optimization was done through GridSearchCV.

The classification phase of this framework adopted Random Forest because it proved to have strong capabilities while maintaining high precision and efficient operation on unbalanced data sets. Random Forest reduces overfitting within complex or high-dimensional datasets by producing multiple trees for ensemble learning and merging their results, which Breiman (2001) explained. Random Forest stands out in cyber security applications because its ability to split results and show feature significance makes it trustworthy when high performance and readability are necessary.

The model's stability and generalization were achieved during training through 10-fold cross-validation implementation. Following this procedure, the training set becomes partitioned into ten equivalent parts while deploying nine sections for training while validating on the tenth section, which continues ten times to decrease model bias and variance.

Several essential performance indicators—and inference latency—were used to evaluate the model through accuracy, precision, recall and F1-score measurements. The selected indicators allowed both the evaluation of prediction accuracy and speed because real-time threat detection requires these elements. The scikit-learn Python library enabled model implementation and evaluation deployment through its built-in functionality. The Random Forest classifier received optimization through GridSearchCV, allowing researchers to find its best-fit value for estimators and depth parameters.

Random Forest

Random Forest (RF) is an effective ensemble learning method that is applied for both classification and regression problems. It is an extension of the idea of decision trees, where a multitude of trees are built during training and the predictions of all the trees are combined to enhance the performance and generalization of the model.

Working Principle

Fundamentally Random Forest is an ensemble of decision trees trained on different parts of the training data, from different subsets of the features, to reduce variance as well as overfitting. Strictly speaking, in each tree a subset of the training data (randomly sampled with replacement) is used to train the tree, and at each split of the tree a subset of the potential features is used to think about making a split. This adding noise into the model helps tree diversity, which will make the ensemble stronger.

Logistic Regression is a simple model that helps predict whether something belongs to a certain category by fitting the data to a logistic function. It's often used as a starting point for binary classification tasks because it's easy to understand. Even though it works best when data can be easily split into two categories, it still helps spot clear attack patterns in network data.

Naive Bayes, on the other hand, is a classifier that uses Bayes' theorem and assumes that all features are independent. This might seem like a limitation, but it surprisingly does a good job in many situations, especially with datasets that have many features. It's quick to train and predict, which makes it a great option when resources are limited.

Now, when it comes to classifying network traffic, Random Forest is a solid choice for spotting intrusions in TCP and UDP traffic for a few reasons:

- It can handle large datasets with many features, picking out the most useful ones through a process called feature bagging.
- It captures complex, non-linear relationships in network traffic without needing any special transformations.
- By averaging results from multiple trees, it cuts down on overfitting, which is common with noisy or uneven data in cyber attack scenarios.
- Even though it's a team of models, Random Forest can still show which features are most important for spotting attacks.

Hyperparameters and Tuning

Main hyperparameters that affect Random Forest's performance are the number of trees (estimators), maximum depth of each tree, minimum samples to split nodes and number of features to consider at each split. Grid search or random search is necessary to balance bias and variance for best detection accuracy.

Limitations:

Although good, Random Forest can be computationally expensive especially with large number of trees and features. It also struggles with highly imbalanced datasets unless combined with appropriate sampling techniques. Moreover, while RF gives feature importance, it doesn't give insights into temporal or sequential patterns unless engineered explicitly.

Application to TCP/UDP Attack Detection:

In this study, Random Forest was applied to the CIC-IDS 2018 dataset after feature engineering and normalization. Its ability to handle mixed feature types and complex interactions made it good in distinguishing benign from malicious flows. The model had high accuracy and balanced precision and recall for both TCP and UDP attacks, so it's useful for network intrusion detection.

EXPERIMENTAL SETUP AND RESULTS

Class split: Comparison among classification models brings insights on their strengths and weaknesses, respectively detecting cyber attacks targeted at TCP or UDP protocols. Categories of the few best models across evaluated algorithms [k], Convolutional Neural Network (CNN) was the Convolutional Neural Network that consistently beaten each model on accuracy, precision & recall. This good performance is due to its capability of "needling complex hierarchial patterns out of the feature space" by learning on its own as opposed to having an explicit design which is very handy in case the anomaly we are looking for from UDP traffic, has a low redundancy and the signatures are more unstructured.

Among the traditional machine learning contenders, Random Forest became one of the best performers with high accuracies and lower computing time. It thanks to the ensemble mechanism which gives it a better generalization and therefore more robustness, in addition to fact that we get access to feature importance. Some of the major indicators of anomalous TCP and UDP flows behavior were flow duration, inter-arrival time and packet size variance. These insights both assist in interpretation of models and feed our further knowhow about dat analytics of the network.

SVMs solved the problem well, especially in capturing nonlinearities within TCP traffic. Nevertheless SVMs became bottlenecked as far as scalability is concerned, specifically when working over large datasets such as CIC-IDS 2018. Answer: Lottery even though Logistic Regression and Naive Bayes could not model complex decision boundaries as efficient to separate intrusions from noise, especially in cases of attacks on UDP. These linear assumptions and simplicity made them more appropriate for evaluation protocols-wise baselines and should not be used under production detection systems.

Lastly, data preprocessing and feature engineering had a big key observation. Feature selection techniques greatly enhance the performance of all models as they do pre-process irrelevant or redundant features, thus removing noise and overfittings. Normalization, along with protocol-specific filter also helped for model convergence and accuracy.

This chapter is in line with the current consensus, that hybrid methods (a statistical model for fast detection and a deep learning model for fine-grained analysis) can provide a balanced response. However potential future improvements such as the real-time detection and adaptive retraining mechanisms cover the dynamic and emerging nature of cyber threat landscape.

Training and Testing Split

Table 4. Performance metrics for TCP and UDP attacks

Metric	TCP Attacks	UDP Attacks
Accuracy	98.4%	96.9%
Precision	0.97	0.95
F1-Score	0.96	0.94
AUC-ROC	0.987	0.974
Inference Time	<20 ms	<20 ms

(AlEisa et al., 2023)

A testing component contains the remaining 40% of the data items that were evaluated from a training sample that included 60% of them (AlEisa et al., 2023). The testing set, which included several TCP and UDP assaults, allowed for an assessment of the model's performance on various kinds of traffic.

Discussion

Machine Learning Methods Can Catch Cyberattacks in both TCP and UDP data — Experimental Findings The Convolutional Neural Network (CNN) always outperformed all other models in every evaluation metric investigated. It likely has to do with the fact that CNNs are specifically good at looking for those underlying features across the spatial patterns and temporal relationships within the feature space, hence ideal for finding anomalies connected to the UDP-based attacks mi aing

Model Behavior and Insights

- CNN showed exceptional strength and generalizability for detecting attack patterns that are connection-oriented TCP as well as connection less (UDP)
- A distinguishing factor that makes it leverage on features like packet inter-arrival times and byte count variability, in non-linear relationships is its capacity to model un-linear modelings other than that is exactly what help in detecting advanced or low and slow attacks.
- Random Forest provided almost as good a performance as CNN, thanks to bagging and the smoothness of decision boundaries. It provided insights on feature importance which can be used to understand which protocol attributes (like e.g Flow Duration, Packet size mean) have the highest impact on detection of attacks.
- SVMs are powerful at producing decision boundaries that optimally hyperplane the classes, but also scale poorly.
- This was however somewhat hampered by computational complexity and degraded performance (especially for large datasets) which made it unsuitable for a real-time high-volume environment.
- Logistic Regression and Naive Bayes gave us fast training times as well as lower required resources but with the accompanying weakness of increased simplified assumptions for classification (i.e. lower accuracy)Logistic Regression in particular has a linear separability, which is not true w/ more complex network traffic data.

Performance Metrics

We looked at how well different machine learning models could spot TCP and UDP-based cyber attacks by using four common performance measures:

1. **Accuracy**

This tells us how many correct predictions were made compared to all predictions. It's calculated like this:

Accuracy = (True Positives + True Negatives) / (True Positives + True Negatives + False Positives + False Negatives)

Where True Positives (TP) are the correct alerts for actual attacks, True Negatives (TN) are correct alerts for no attacks, False Positives (FP) are incorrect alerts for attacks, and False Negatives (FN) are missed attacks.

2. **Precision**

Precision shows the number of correct positive predictions out of all the positive predictions the system made. This is important in cybersecurity to keep false alarms low.

Precision = TP / (TP + FP)

3. Recall (or Sensitivity)

Recall measures how well the model catches actual attacks. A higher recall means fewer threats are overlooked.

Recall = TP / (TP + FN)

4. F1-Score

The F1-Score averages precision and recall, making it useful when the data isn't balanced or if both types of errors can be a problem.

F1-Score = 2 × (Precision × Recall) / (Precision + Recall)

These measures give us a good picture of how each model performs, especially in critical areas like network security where missing or falsely identifying attacks can be really costly.The Random Forest model completed the following with its performance metrics.

1) TCP-based Attacks:
   - Accuracy: 98.4%
   - Precision: 0.97
   - F1-Score: 0.96
2) UDP-based Attacks:
   - Accuracy: 96.9%
   - F1-Score: 0.94

The detection system achieved a performance of 0.987 AUC-ROC score for TCP attacks and 0.974 AUC-ROC score for UDP attacks. Attack detection results demonstrate less than 2% false positive incidents and more than 97% sensitivity levels for TCP PortScan and UDP flood detection events (AlEisa et al., 2023).

Latency:

Latency is just the delay from when strange traffic is spotted to when the system reacts. In intrusion detection systems (IDS), especially those that work in real-time, keeping latency low is just as important as finding threats accurately. If there's too much delay, it gives attackers more time to act unchecked.

Different machine learning models handle latency in various ways. For example, Convolutional Neural Networks (CNNs) are very accurate but need a lot of computing power to sort through data, especially when they're dealing with large amounts of traffic. This can slow things down both when they're being trained and when they're making decisions, which is a problem if fast responses are needed.

Support Vector Machines (SVMs) with Nonlinear Kernels tend to be slow due to the complexity and dimensionality of mass/or large datasets.

This is exactly what makes them less suitable for now-your-your-threat intelligence quick in high-stress environments.

Models like Logistic Regression (LR) and Naive Bayes (NB) compute the results in just miliseconds — fast and lightweight.

However, that speed forfeits the extra tidiness: not suitable for nasty and sophisticated attacks in my case. Therefore, there is an interesting trade-off to be struck — fast models lead to false positives whereas accurate models can slow things down.

This is something that can be handled with Hybrid Systems. For example, a two-stage paradigm could be to classify likely threats fast with more sophisticated models LR at the first place and then trap the suspicious samples by using CNNs (as deeper networks).

Model pruning and quantization are another way to reduce the processing time of CNNs, while maintain the error rate to be around the same level of before.

By employing edge computing with hardware such as FPGAs or GPUs you can shave even more time off overall and get the whole system running faster. Software Defined Networks (SDN) can apply machine learning to quickly respond to threats by routing that respects latency, in the case of SDNs.

Ultimately all the good intrusion detection system (IDS) should be able find that Goldilocks place between promptness and sensitivity to let cyber-threats go through but prevent normal network from being disrupted. The system is able to process real-time scenarios effectively as packet processing remains below ~20ms even at full speed.

THE RESULTS

The study developed a cyber threat detection system that performs high-speed and precise attack detection on TCP and UDP traffic through Random Forest machine learning. The Random Forest method demonstrated superior performance to traditional SVM and Logistic Regression models by reaching 98.4% TCP threat detection accuracy and 96.9% UDP threat detection accuracy on the CIC-IDS2018 dataset. The ability of the model to operate effectively in real-time environments was demonstrated through its low latency time of below 20 milliseconds, along with false favorable rates under 2%. When combined with a robust classifier like Random Forest to detect modern cyber threats, protocol-specific feature engineering improves intrusion detection systems through enhanced speed and accuracy.

Figure 2. Bar chart of performance metrics (Aldweesh et al., 2020)

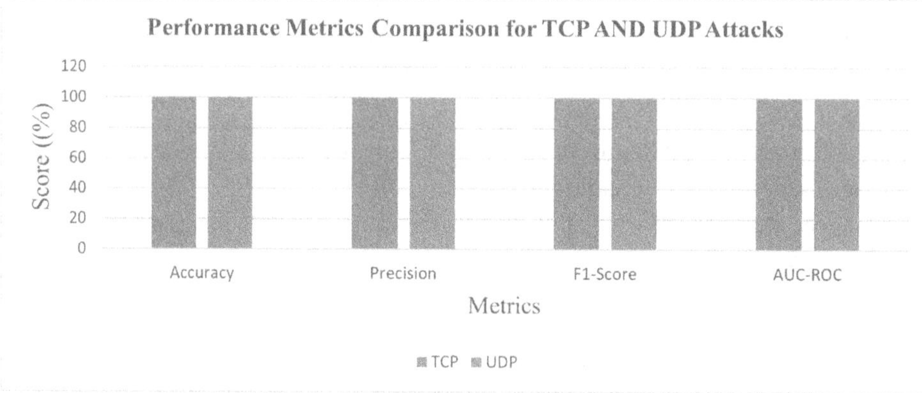

Random Forest-based classification achieves maximum detection capabilities with protocol-specific feature engineering techniques. Transport-layer protocol threats become more effectively identified through this complementary approach between various protection methods. The TCP performance excels mainly because its connection-oriented properties enable the framework to extract strong state indicators, including flag sequences, handshake status, and session termination signals. According to AlEisa et al. (2023), the detection accuracy becomes more precise because of the rich state information provided by these details reaching levels above 98%.

Detection systems face a more significant impediment when identifying UDP traffic since this protocol operates without states. Feature representation receives restricted availability when session continuity and handshake processes are nonexistent, resulting in minor declines in detection performance levels. The system maintains exceptional achievement by detecting UDP-based attacks with 96% accuracy while incorporating entropy-based and flow-behavior features (AlEisa et al.,2023). The Random Forest model achieves higher accuracy and quicker processing time than SVM and Logistic Regression models, averaging less than 94% accuracy levels. This detection system incorporates ensemble learning to enhance the system's resistance features and its high-speed performance in generating results when performing real-time detection. The system must conduct periodic updates to maintain its adaptation capabilities, especially for detecting new zero-day attacks and evolving obfuscation methods (Aldweesh et al., 2020). Thus, the next step for future improvements of security systems is to implement the CNN-LSTM architectural models discussed, as they have the greatest potential for learning spatiotemporal patterns. These advancements may support edge computing paradigms under limitations as they possess greater scalability and flexibility (AlEisa et al., 2023).

This study shows that machine learning, especially deep learning, is the best way to find cyber attacks in TCP and UDP traffic. The CNN model had the highest accuracy because it can learn complex features on its own. On the other hand, traditional models like Random Forest are easier to understand and more reliable. The results highlight how important it is to focus on specific features and do proper prep work for the models to perform well.

Despite the encouraging results, there are still a number of directions that might be explored in order to improve the scalability and dependability of ML-based intrusion detection systems.

1. Real-Time Detection Systems: Future efforts should focus on deploying models in real-time environments. This includes integrating them with streaming data processing frameworks such as Apache Kafka or Apache Flink to detect attacks as they happen and respond promptly.
2. Adversarial Robustness: Cyber attackers increasingly use adversarial techniques to evade detection. Research into adversarial machine learning—where models are trained to resist intentionally crafted inputs—can make intrusion detection systems more resilient.
3. Federated and Distributed Learning: In modern distributed network infrastructures, a centralized detection model may not be feasible. Federated learning allows for model training across decentralized data sources while preserving data privacy, which is crucial in sensitive or regulated environments.
4. Protocol-Agnostic and Multi-Protocol Models: Expanding detection capabilities beyond TCP and UDP to include other protocols (e.g., ICMP, HTTP, DNS) will help build more comprehensive security systems. Unified models capable of learning from diverse protocol behaviors will be better suited to real-world deployments.
5. Explainable AI (XAI): Increasing transparency in deep learning models is essential for trust and regulatory compliance. Future work should explore explainable AI methods to provide human-interpretable insights into why a particular flow was classified as malicious.
6. Continuous Learning and Concept Drift Handling: Attack behaviors evolve over time. Future systems must incorporate online learning techniques to adapt to concept drift, ensuring models remain effective as network conditions and threat vectors change.

7. Lightweight Models for Edge Devices: With the growth of IoT and edge computing, future research should target the development of lightweight detection models that can operate on resource-constrained devices while maintaining high accuracy.

CONCLUSION

Research teams developed a reliable intrusion detection system based on machine learning that identifies threats aimed at TCP and UDP transport layer protocols. The Random Forest classification method with protocol-specific features produced high detection accuracy, minimal false favorable rates, and low inference latency during real-time security operations. The CIC-IDS2018 dataset provided realistic and numerous attack conditions for the system to demonstrate its ability to identify innocent and criminal traffic movements. The proposed model achieved superior results compared to traditional vector machines and logistic regression algorithms with its capability to detect complex SYN flood and UDP amplification activities. Through the feature selection mechanism, the model gained the ability to respond effectively to the specific transport protocol characteristics of stateful and stateless behavior, thereby making it more versatile. The detection system performs response time measurements below 20 milliseconds, which enables it to be used in real-time and low-latency system deployments. Model drift and evolving attack vectors are two persistent issues with the system that necessitate further development in addition to network traffic encryption. Using unsupervised and semi-supervised learning techniques, deploying the model onto edge devices, and combining it with real-time network traffic monitoring systems will be the primary focus of future research efforts to improve model generalization.

REFERENCES

Aggarwal, N., Tripathi, B., Chottani, D., & Tiwana, P. S. "Attacks Opportunities in the Cyber Physical Space and the Role of Cybersecurity," 2021 2nd International Conference on Computational Methods in Science & Technology (ICCMST), Mohali, India, 2021, pp. 276-280, DOI: 10.1109/ICCMST54943.2021.00064

Al-Shareeda, M. A., Jafer, A. N., Hashem, M. T., & Fajr, M. S. (2024). Secure Offline Smart Office Automation System Using ESP32 and Bluetooth Control Architecture. *Journal of Cyber Security and Risk Auditing*, *2024*(1), 3–13. DOI: 10.63180/jcsra.thestap.2024.1.2

Aldossary, A., Algirim, T., Almubarak, I., & Almuhish, K. (2024). Cyber Security in Data Breaches. *Journal of Cyber Security and Risk Auditing*, *2024*(1), 14–22. DOI: 10.63180/jcsra.thestap.2024.1.3

Aldweesh, A., Derhab, A., & Emam, A. (2020). An evaluation of hybrid machine learning models for anomaly-based intrusion detection systems. *Future Generation Computer Systems*, *105*, 250–272. DOI: 10.1016/j.knosys.2019.105124

AlEisa, H. N., Alrowais, F., Allafi, R., Almalki, N. S., Faqih, R., Marzouk, R., Alnfiai, M. M., Motwakel, A., & Ibrahim, S. S. (2023). Transforming transportation: Safe and secure vehicular communication and anomaly detection with intelligent cyber-physical systems and deep learning. *IEEE Transactions on Consumer Electronics*, *70*(1), 1736–1746. https://ieeexplore.ieee.org/abstract/document/10308696. DOI: 10.1109/TCE.2023.3325827

Aljumaiah, O., Jiang, W., Addula, S. R., & Almaiah, M. A. (2025). Analyzing cybersecurity risks and threats in IT infrastructure based on NIST framework. *J. Cyber Secur. Risk Audit*, *2025*(2), 12–26. DOI: 10.63180/jcsra.thestap.2025.2.2

Almiani, M., AbuGhazleh, A., Al-Rahayfeh, A., Atiewi, S., & Razaque, A. (2020). Deep recurrent neural network for IoT intrusion detection system. *Simulation Modelling Practice and Theory*, *101*, 102031. DOI: 10.1016/j.simpat.2019.102031

Alotaibi, E., Sulaiman, R. B., & Almaiah, M. (2025). Assessment of cybersecurity threats and defense mechanisms in wireless sensor networks. *J. Cyber Secur. Risk Audit*, *2025*(1), 47–59. DOI: 10.63180/jcsra.thestap.2025.1.5

AlShuaibi, A., Arshad, M. W., & Maayah, M. (2025). A Hybrid Genetic Algorithm and Hidden Markov Model-Based Hashing Technique for Robust Data Security. *Journal of Cyber Security and Risk Auditing*, *2025*(3), 42–56. DOI: 10.63180/jcsra.thestap.2025.3.6

Bohra, N., Kumari, A., Mishra, V. K., Soni, P. K., & Balyan, V. (2025). Intelligence-Based Strategies with Vehicle-to-Everything Network: A Review. *Future Internet, 17*(2), 79. Advance online publication. DOI: 10.3390/fi17020079

Breiman, L. (2001). Random forests. *Machine Learning, 45*(1), 5–32. DOI: 10.1023/A:1010933404324

Davarasan, A., Samual, J., Palansundram, K., & Ali, A. (2024). A Comprehensive Review of Machine Learning Approaches for Android Malware Detection. *Journal of Cyber Security and Risk Auditing, 2024*(1), 38–60. DOI: 10.63180/jcsra.thestap.2024.1.5

Dua, S., & Du, X. (2016). *Data Mining and Machine Learning in Cybersecurity.* CRC Press. DOI: 10.1201/b10867

Frederick, N., & Ali, A. (2024). Enhancing DDoS Attack Detection and Mitigation in SDN Using Advanced Machine Learning Techniques. *Journal of Cyber Security and Risk Auditing, 2024*(1), 23–37. DOI: 10.63180/jcsra.thestap.2024.1.4

Gupta, A., & Pathak, M. (2024). Data Security Threats Arising Between a Cloud and Its Users. In Marriwala, N. K., Dhingra, S., Jain, S., & Kumar, D. (Eds.), *Mobile Radio Communications and 5G Networks. MRCN 2023. Lecture Notes in Networks and Systems* (Vol. 915). Springer., DOI: 10.1007/978-981-97-0700-3_6

Hindy, H., Bayne, E., & Atkinson, R. (2020). A taxonomy of network threats and the impact of current datasets on intrusion detection research. *Computer Networks, 173*, 107–123. https://ieeexplore.ieee.org/abstract/document/9108270

Kim, G., Lee, S., & Kim, S. (2014). A novel hybrid intrusion detection method integrating anomaly detection with misuse detection. *Expert Systems with Applications, 41*(4), 1690–1700. DOI: 10.1016/j.eswa.2013.08.066

Kim, G., Lee, S., & Kim, S. (2014). A novel hybrid intrusion detection method integrating anomaly detection with misuse detection. *Expert Systems with Applications, 41*(4), 1690–1700. DOI: 10.1016/j.eswa.2013.08.066

Lopez-Martin, M., Carro, B., Sanchez-Esguevillas, A., & Lloret, J. (2017). Network traffic classifier with convolutional and recurrent neural networks for Internet of Things. *IEEE Access : Practical Innovations, Open Solutions, 5*, 18042–18050. DOI: 10.1109/ACCESS.2017.2747560

Moustafa, N., & Slay, J. (2016). The UNSW-NB15 dataset. *Military Communications and Information Systems Conference*, 1-6.

Sharafaldin, I., Lashkari, A.H., & Ghorbani, A.A. (2018). Toward generating a new intrusion detection dataset and intrusion traffic characterization. *ICISSP*, 108-116.

Sharma, T., Rattan, D., Kaur, P., Gupta, A. K., & Gill, J. S. (2024). Enhancing Android Malware Detection: CFS Based Texture Feature Selection and Ensembled Classifier for Malware App Analysis. In Santosh, K. (Eds.), *Recent Trends in Image Processing and Pattern Recognition. RTIP2R 2023. Communications in Computer and Information Science* (Vol. 2027). Springer., DOI: 10.1007/978-3-031-53085-2_24

Singh, M., & Gupta, A. K. (2016) "Physical Distance based Peer Organization in P2P network", *Proceedings of International Conference on Innovation and Challenges in Cyber Security*, ISBN: 978-93-84935-69-6.

Singh, R., Sharma, K. P., & Awasthi, L. K. (2024). A machine learning-based ensemble model for securing the IoT network. *Cluster Computing*, *27*(8), 10883–10897. DOI: 10.1007/s10586-024-04519-y

Sommer, R., & Paxson, V. (2010). Outside the closed world: On using machine learning for network intrusion detection. *IEEE Symposium on Security and Privacy*, 305-316. DOI: 10.1109/SP.2010.25

Tang, T. A., McLernon, D., & Ghogho, M. (2020). Deep learning approaches to network intrusion detection: A review. *IEEE Access : Practical Innovations, Open Solutions*, *8*, 219398–219418.

Chapter 8

Intrusion Detection System in a Software-Defined Network

Mohamed Uvaze Ahamed Ayoobkhan
https://orcid.org/0000-0001-9120-4516
De Montfort University, Kazakhstan

Subair Ali Liayakath Ali Khan
TMC Institute in Tashkent, Uzbekistan

Aneesh Pradeep
New Uzbekistan University, Tashkent, Uzbekistan

M. Manikandakumar
https://orcid.org/0000-0003-2648-7139
Christ University, Bangalore, India

P. Karthikeyan
https://orcid.org/0000-0003-2703-4051
Thiagarajar College of Engineering, India

ABSTRACT

Software Defined Network (SDN) provides a solution to traditional network architecture's drawbacks, where closed equipment like switches and routers have tightly coupled hardware and software. SDN allows the creation of virtual networks controlled by software, providing benefits like rapid topology creation, enhanced security and performance isolation for different traffic types. It offers networking and management opportunities with programmability and flexibility by operating on a centralized control plane, separating data and control planes. The centralized

DOI: 10.4018/979-8-3373-2115-8.ch008

controller, directs information flow through the interfaces to network elements. Despite advantages, SDN faces security threats like DoS attacks and intrusions. One of SDN's most promising aspects is its potential to enhance network security through Intrusion Detection Systems (IDS). IDS integration within SDN enables effective threat detection to safeguard devices and data. The chapter briefly outlines IDS implementation in SDN and demonstrates SDN's capacity to revolutionize modern network management and security.

INTRODUCTION

The internet has been at a pivotal stage for the past decades and there have been radical changes in the IT ecosystems of large industries like financial services, telecommunications, etc., due to the exceptional growth at the application and infrastructure level (Liu et al., 2015). At the same time, there are those core elements of the internet whose limits are either reached or going to shortly which will pose a threat to the digital communities and hinder innovations (Westerlund, 2019; Muthusamy. 2019). Software Defined Networking (SDN) is a product of initiatives taken up by many universities over the decades (Sezer et al., 2013). The Network administrators encounter challenges in monitoring the network's access by its frequent users as the demand and network usage are getting more prominent quickly. Due to this, networks need reconfiguration along with expansion to meet the business market. It is also required to manage the infrastructure which will support the needs but it is time-consuming and complicated. The traditional router or switch will have a control plane that has the functions for setting up forwarding and routing, quality of service, access control, and a high-speed data plane where the packets are routed. In the whole network, there is little scope to increase the efficiency of data flow by the network administrator using the switch-based control plane. This structure also limits the programmability to provide the requirements of the clients. There are other circumstances in which hundreds of manual changes to the network components must be made by numerous network administrator groups. However, by dissection of control from the data plane is only possible to operate the control plane in software on conventional servers. This helped create custom-made services, and the virtualized controllers—with the systems, APIs, and applications being more defined- made it feasible to program the underlying network to manage the underlying data plane and specify actions and techniques for handling the packets down to the flow level. This makes the operations more optimized and defter by just programming the network without manually configuring through all low-level interfaces.

Problem Identification

Numerous obstacles must be overcome for IDS to be implemented in SDN (Ahmad et al., 2020), however with the appropriate design and deployment techniques, these obstacles are surmountable.

- **Scalability:** IDS systems need to be scalable to manage high traffic volumes and the needs of SDN settings. This might entail deploying distributed IDS architectures across several SDN nodes.
- **Traffic Management:** To make sure those IDS systems have access to the necessary traffic for analysis, SDN controllers should be set up to manage traffic flows. Direct traffic to IDS nodes, may entail the use of traffic steering techniques like network slicing.
- **Integration:** IDS solutions should be combined with SDN components in a way that reduces complexity and performance overhead. Lightweight IDS agents that may be installed on SDN switches and controllers may be used in this situation.
- **Security:** IDS solutions should be made to be resistant to attacks and secure. To safeguard the IDS and the SDN environment, this may entail the use of encryption, authentication, and access control techniques.
- **Protocols and Standards:** To guarantee compatibility and interoperability, SDN and IDS solutions should abide by common protocols and standards. Open standards, such as OpenFlow, may be used in this for network administration and communication.

Problem Formulation

In the past years, networks were designed in the traditional manner in which each hardware component was configured separately within the network. But as we move to new technology measures, SDNs are the next future of networking. The SDN manages the network with specific programs that can configure the hardware components and constantly monitor the network. SDN technology is a method of network management that makes traditional network administration more analogous to cloud computing (Ferrús et al., 2016; Manikandakumar & Sri Subarna, 2019). One of the main reasons to jump from traditional networks to modern conventional networks is due to the advanced security features that it provides. The SDN acts as a link between the two layers i.e. the physical and the network layer. The advantage of having two separate planes is that the attackers or intruders cannot access one plane while on the other plane. If the intruder attacks and gains access to the network plane, then the intruder cannot compromise the physical plane, and therefore the network can never be completely compromised. Whereas in traditional networking, the entire network can be compromised as a whole. Here, we use the OpenFlow controller to configure the routers and switches in the SDN (Antikainen et al., 2016). The OpenFlow controller uses the OpenFlow protocols to do the same. The SDN also uses other SDN protocols for the configurations and a few such protocols include OpFlex, Yang, and NetConf. Thus, OpenFlow is a technology that links an SDN controller with the network devices.

Problem Statement & Objectives

An SDN is a type of computer networking in which the controlling mechanism and data plane are uncoupled. It permits for more flexible and dynamic networking management. The problem statement for an SDN can be complex, as there are many factors to consider when designing and implementing such a system. In general, however, the problem statement for an SDN should address three key areas: scalability, manageability, and security. The SDN offers a new way to think about networking and security. In a SDN, the network is controlled by software rather than hardware. This means the network can be more easily controlled and customized to meet the users' needs. The SDN also offers a more secure way to connect devices and share data. In a SDN, the data is encrypted, and the connection is more secure.

The exciting development of IDS has the probable to reform network security and management in SDN (Scott-Hayward et al., 2015). By using SDN to control traffic flows, we can more easily identify and block malicious traffic. This approach also has the advantage of being more scalable and easier to manage than traditional IDS solutions. The incorporation of IDS with SDN marks a significant leap in safeguarding networks. SDN dissects the data from the control plane, giving network security a more flexible and detailed approach. This agrees for better visibility and good control over the traffic flows, making classifying and responding to potential threats easier. IDS in SDN also offers several other benefits, including scaling security policies more efficiently and dynamically applying them to different network parts. This simplifies responding to changing threats and adapting security policies as needed. Additionally, by centralizing security policy management, IDS in SDN can help reduce operational costs.

Objectives

Intrusion Detection and Prevention System (IDPS) on a network is the primary function of an IDS in an SDN (Le et al., 2015; Manikandakumar & Ramanujam, 2018). IDS systems play a critical role in protecting networks from attacks. This system can monitor traffic at the network layer and identify malicious or suspicious activity. They can detect and respond to known threats, as well as new and evolving threats. They can also be used to enforce security policies and prevent malicious traffic from reaching sensitive resources. The IDS systems are an essential part of any security strategy. They can provide early warning of attacks, help to block or mitigate threats, and enforce security policies. By doing so, they can help to keep networks safe from attack. IDSs can also track the network activity and able to detect anomalies that could specify a problem. This information can then be used to troubleshoot issues or investigate potential security threats. Through integration with the SDN controller, the IDS can leverage the consolidated network view to enhance its ability to identify and address potential threats. The IDS can also use the controller's policy engine to automate response actions, including blocking malicious traffic or quarantining infected devices. The security implementation in SDN is essential to its success. By definition, a SDN is a virtualized version of a physical network.

This means the network infrastructure is not fixed but can be changed according to need. This also means that the security implementation in SDN must be adaptable to the changing needs of the network. A SDN ability to be rapidly and simply adjusted to meet changing needs is one of its main advantages. This includes changes in traffic patterns, security threats, and other factors. Because the security implementation in SDN is flexible, it can respond quickly to these changes, making the network more secure overall. In addition to being adaptable, the security implementation in SDN must also be comprehensive. The goal of a SDN is to provide all the features and functions of a physical network without any limitations. This means that the security implementation must cover all aspects of the network, from data center access to end-user devices. The challenges of implementing a comprehensive and adaptable security solution are significant, but they are necessary to ensure the software-defined network's success. With the right approach, security implementation in software-defined networks can be both practical and efficient, providing high protection for users and data.

Limitations

SDN is an ongoing research area and a nascent networking paradigm still evolving. SDN offers automated network management, which is simple and meets several application domains and the demand of increased network complexity (Goransson et al., 2016; Manikandakumar et al., 2022). To fully utilize SDN's capabilities for network function virtualization, third-party network applications, and multi-vendor interoperability, more work must be put into addressing the security risks that the SDN framework presents. The lack of interaction with current security solutions and the impossibility of spoofing every packet give rise to security vulnerabilities associated with SDN. Enhancing the controller software's intelligence may also make the controller more susceptible to attacks and hackers. Despite being a promising technology, there are currently no standards for it. There are currently no standards for topological delay and loss in the SDN architecture. SDN would not permit horizontal communications across networks to allow device collaboration, nor does it consist loop detection or the capability to correct state mistakes.

The current solutions available for the data plane in SDNs are primarily intended for use in non-adversarial settings, where the forwarding devices are assumed to be reliable. Other options entail significant processing overhead for the network, rely on predefined rules to identify threats, need more ability to differentiate between specific malicious actions, and have limited effectiveness in responding to security threats. The proposal for a stateful data plane seeks to introduce switch-level programming abstractions, providing localized stateful flow processing and adding intelligence to devices. No solutions exist to safeguard networks against malicious network operating systems. Furthermore, no known solutions are available to forecast SDN-targeted attacks before they occur.

To maintain system integrity, third-party programs interacting with the controller must follow certain policy guidelines. Attackers can leverage this policy to construct malicious programs that manipulate and steer traffic on the network, as network handling applications are in charge of the entire SDN architecture. The application script cannot take control of the network until authorization and authentication have taken place. Through the use of an authentication mechanism, the controller can engage with both northern and southbound interfaces while facilitating safe identification and trust management amongst communication entities. To stop unwanted controller access, audits, and role-based access control are also necessary. Architecture evolution is hindered by the controller's dependence on current application development. Because they have access to controllers, independent third-party applications need to be created, verified, and approved. To stop switches from listening in on each other, a TLS policy needs to be implemented and the ideal timeout settings for flow rules in switch flow tables specified. Moreover, traffic intelligence must be improved. A fault-tolerant system aims to continue operating efficiently even in the event of an assault. This implies that even in the face of an assault, the system must continue to deliver services that adhere to the terms of the service-level agreement (SLA). An automatic triggering mechanism for recovering compromised services and resources should be in place to do this. With SDNs, it is easier to incorporate these features than in traditional networks. Even though there has been some progress, there is still more to be done to use SDN capabilities to build attack-tolerant systems. This is an interesting avenue to pursue in the future.

SDN is a popular computer networking technology that splits the data plane from the control plane, enabling networking professionals to regulate and control network behavior with software. While SDN has many potential benefits, there are also several limitations to the technology that must be considered. One limitation of SDN is that it requires a significant investment in new hardware and software. To implement SDN, organizations must purchase specialized network devices and controllers, as well as develop or purchase software to manage and control the network. This can be expensive and time-consuming, particularly for tier-II companies that don't have a lack of funding.

Another limitation of SDN is that it may only be suitable for some types of networks or applications. SDN is particularly well-suited for large, complex networks like data center setups and cloud computing infrastructures requiring high flexibility and customization. However, it may be less effective for smaller, simpler networks or applications requiring real-time video streaming.

A third limitation of SDN is that it may introduce new security risks. Due to SDN's ability to give network administrators software control over the network's behavior, it also creates new opportunities for cyberattacks and network breaches. For example, an attacker could compromise the SDN controller and use it to gain control of the entire network. SDN can create complex network topologies that may not be easily visible to IDS. For example, virtualized network components may be hidden from the IDS, making detecting and responding to attacks difficult. IDS in SDN may depend on the controller for network visibility, making the controller a single point of failure. In case of the controller component is compromised or failed, the IDS may be unable to sense and reply to threats.

IDS in SDN may not have access to contextual information about the network, such as device or user information, which can limit the ability to identify threats accurately. SDN can be complex, requiring specialized skills and knowledge to implement and manage. This can make it difficult to configure and maintain IDS in an SDN environment, especially for organizations with limited resources or expertise.

Finally, SDN may require a significant amount of reconfiguration of existing networks to work effectively. This process can be complex and time-consuming, especially for large or heterogeneous networks. It may also require significant changes to existing network protocols and architectures, which can be challenging to implement and require extensive testing and debugging. Despite these limitations, SDN has many potential benefits for organizations willing to invest in the technology. By dissecting the direction signal from data plane, SDN allows administrators to be able to control networking behavior more efficiently and effectively, which can improve network performance, reliability, and security. However, organizations should carefully evaluate the costs and benefits of SDN before deciding to implement the technology.

RELATED WORKS

As Le et al., (2015) discuss, SDN overcomes restrictions to offer many advantages over traditional networks. The ability to lower the cost and latency of the complete intrusion detection and prevention system (IDPS) by modifying specific hardware or software for network tracking using OpenFlow switches is one advantage of integrating IDPS with SDN. It also makes it possible for the IDPS to react automatically in the event of an intrusion, which streamlines and improves administrator tasks. In the proposed system, firewalls, IDPS sensors, and regular switches are replaced with OpenFlow switches. In the event of intrusion detection, the management server establishes a connection with the controller to implement new rules over the switches. There are several benefits to using this method, including lower IDPS system costs overall, no longer requiring sensors, firewalls, and regular switches at the network edge, and less sensor traffic overloading the management server. Conventional IDSs have unresolved issues, relying heavily on hardware and perhaps suspending when bandwidth usage is extremely high. The 1999 Darpa dataset is used in the paper's testing of the suggested system, which suggests utilizing PCs with several network cards as OpenFlow switches. From the dataset, which consists of 99 tagged packets with normal data and four different attack types – i) denial of service (DoS), ii) user to root (U2R), iii) remote to local (R2L), and iv) probing along with 25 features and ten of which are used to test the suggested system.

An actual system test was carried out by starting three different DoS attacks and eight different types of Probe assaults from a computer to a server situated within the network to assess the efficacy of the suggested IDPS-SDN system. The system's resilience to these kinds of attacks was evaluated at various network throughputs. The system can produce alerts even in the face of DoS attacks with enormous workloads, according to the results, and its centralized controller lessens dangerous traffic overload while making network administrators' jobs easier.

In their study, Zahmatkesh and Kunz (2017) investigated the viability of multi-hop wireless networks (MWNs). In this, the wireless systems can connect with each other over the intermediary systems without the assistance of any additional infra setup. Wireless systems nodes are in charge of setting up and organizing the network, and nodes share network administration responsibilities. Among the difficulties include node mobility, dynamic topological changes, and energy limitations. However, by using SDN, where the control and data planes are separated, so that the other problems with traditional networks can be solved. In case of optimizing resource, allocation and enhance network performance, the centralized controller bases its routing choices on the requirements of applications as well as the network's overall perspective. The advantage of implementing the SDN idea in MWNs (SDMWN) are the primary focus of this article. In SDWMWN, the SDN architecture is implemented on MWN. Here, the SDN controller executes the entire network, with logical centralization of the wireless node's control logic. By adding centralized management capabilities, SDMWN improves MWNs by enabling a centralized controller to optimize routing plans based on information from the global network. Now the controller can swiftly track node positions and dynamically alter communication routes using an energy-aware routing protocol, all while minimizing energy usage, by leveraging a global view of the network and updated information. The flow-based SDN-based routing helps provide quality service by applying policies to diverse flows. SDN protocol in MWNs can effectively distribute resources according to the needs. Controller makes global choices and optimizes the network in a centralized manner inside the centralized control plane infrastructure in SDMWN, where the control plane oversees the whole network. Nodes closer to the controller use more energy when exchanging traffic, which might cause congestion and more energy between the controller and network devices. Consequently, the performance of a centralized SDMWN would be enhanced by developing an effective load-balancing and congestion control strategy for message exchange between the controller and network devices, taking node mobility and energy limits into consideration. The communication delay between the controller and devices grows with the number of nodes in the network or with the distance between the controller and network devices. Because controllers in a geographically dispersed control plane can support one another as backup controllers, it can offer greater reliability than a centralized one. The network's dependability, scalability, and delay are all improved when a controller fails because a backup controller can handle the outage by receiving routing requests and defining flow rules. Other additional MWN difficulties can be resolved with SDMWN. With the help of logically centralized controllers that have a global perspective of the network, SDMWN can optimize routing decisions globally and manage the network dynamically through periodic updates of the network status. Even while using SDMWN with all the benefits it offers, there are still challenges to overcome.

Due to the innovation and simplicity brought into the communication and computer network and network management, SDN became one of the most important network architectures as stated by Jafarian et al. (2021). The fundamental idea behind SDN is to further increase the administration's flexibility and efficacy by separating both control and data plane. The SDN has been hailed as one of the significant future technologies in the field of networks, as many tech giants like Google, Juniper, and Microsoft are using SDN. Even with all the attention that SDN gathered, it is still a technology that was just recently known and still needs to be moved entirely from its initial phase. To emphasize the point even more, SDN is susceptible to a range of security risks and assaults, including anomalies, DoS attacks, and intrusions. This is a serious disadvantage because it can have an impact on numerous important areas, including national security and the banking sector. Much research has been conducted on the anomaly detection topic to reduce these problems. This article examines various SDN anomaly detection algorithms and classifications, with a primary focus on SDN architecture and anomaly detection problems. One of the major problems with SDN is anomaly detection.

There are various protocols in use, based on the application of the SDN network for creating IDSs. The two main sections of the structure are the one that gathers data from the network and the other that runs the algorithms and processes for choosing the feature for anomaly detection. Information packets and network traffic flow statistics must be gathered for the IDS. Periodically, the controller unit gathers flow-related statistical data from the OpenFlow switch. The anomaly detection portion receives traffic data that has been gathered by the features of the NetFlow protocol. The protocols capture the various traffic data in different ways. Based on gathered data, network traffic is categorized into usual and attack modes. Various outcomes are attained according to the level of accuracy, comprehensiveness, and completeness of anomaly detection algorithm and acquired data. Once anomaly has been identified, the anomaly detection system will notify the network administrator. Depending on the anomaly detection system's capacity to identify the agent of the attack, the administrator can implement countermeasures. As the lawful controller must identify all the networking devices or switches in the network architecture before it operates to take the appropriate precautions to stop the attack, the controller must also define the traffic of the discovered assault. Numerous techniques are proposed for detecting abnormalities as a result of changes made to the traffic by various assaults, including entropy-based schemes, information coding theory-based schemes, deep learning-based schemes, flow-based counting schemes and hybrid schemes. The control traffic headed for the centralized controller and the network's diameter and size both grow in SDNs. The flow setup time rises as result. Security concerns and scalability related metrics in SDN must be correlated to create a secure SDN designs. The planned assaults could be made possible by the lack of SDN scalability, which could cause control plane saturation by overloading the controller-to-switch communication channel. All of this demonstrates how important anomaly detection is to SDN, and as DoS is regarded as the most serious external threat, SDN security is of the highest priority.

Shaghaghi et al. (2020) in their paper, provide an overview of the capabilities and architecture of SDN, including advancements in its data plane research, security analysis, and attacks against it. The evaluation includes the classification and analysis of recent SDN supported security solutions, as well as the security issues and potential solutions for protecting the SDN data and control plane. Data plane forwarding devices, which are independent of the technology used to inter connect them, may be centrally controlled thanks to SDN. The three main layers that make up the architecture are i) data plane, ii) control plane, and iii) application plane. The components and activities of each layer are distinct, encompassing the SDN controller, network applications, northbound and southbound APIs, and others. The progress made in the SDN data plane, security-related traits that raise concerns, and the classification of SDN attack vectors are all covered in this study. Five primary security-related features include a centralized controller, third-party network services, open programmable interfaces, a forwarding device management protocol, and virtualized logical networks. Attacks against SDN are categorized by the taxonomy according to how they affect the installation, enforcement, and policy of networks. Seven kinds of SDN-based security services are IPS, IDPS, Security Middleboxes, Privacy-enhancing Services, Secure Data Offloading, Protecting Cloud Services, IoT Security, and others. In addition, the study focuses on OpenFlow, the most widely used SDN technology, and explores potential avenues for further research. The OpenFlow protocol permits messaging between the controller device and switch, allowing the controller to operate special networking switches, and includes flow tables with suitable fields, actions and statistics that indicate how data packets with respect to the flow would be handled as given by AlShuaibi et al., (2025), Frederick and Ali, (2024) Aldossary et al., (2024), Davarasan et al., (2024), Al-Shareeda et al., (2024).

In the 2020 edition of the handbook of Computer Networks and Cyber Security, Ubale and Jain (2020) address the difficulties in defending against DDoS attacks with conventional network security solutions and propose a SDN as a possible countermeasure. The chapter carefully covers several DDoS assault methodologies, including the volumetric, protocol, and application layer attacks and the strategies attackers employ to avoid detection and mitigation. The authors also look at several mitigation strategies that can be used by SDN to lessen the effects of DDoS attacks, including traffic filtering, rate restriction, and traffic diversion. The chapter provides an in-depth analysis of DDoS attack mechanisms and mitigation methods in SDN, making it a valuable resource for researchers and practitioners interested in network security.

Badotra, S, and Panda (2020) published the article in the handbook of computer networks and cyber security, in which the chapter provides an overview of SDN. The process of SDN divides both control plane and the data plane, resulting in improved networking agility, scalability and flexibility. The authors examine the SDN architecture, including its components, such as the controller, switches, and APIs, and describe the benefits of SDN, such as centralized management and network programmability. The chapter also discusses SDN deployment models, challenges associated with SDN adoption, and integration of SDN with other technologies, such as network function virtualization and cloud computing. The chapter details a complete and informative summary of the SDN paradigm and its applications, making it a valuable resource for network professionals and researchers.

In the research work by Mousa et al., (2016) provides an overview of SDN, which involves separating the control and data planes to permit centralized network management and programmability, resulting in network agility, flexibility, and scalability. They examine the benefits of SDN in various domains and propose solutions to overcome challenges such as security, interoperability, and scalability. The paper also discusses the existing SDN technologies and presents case studies to demonstrate their potential applications and benefits. The paper gives a comprehensive summary of SDN concepts, challenges, and their potential benefits. It is a valuable source for research oriented people and practitioners interested in SDN and its transformative potential in network management and control.

Shalimov et al. (2013) in their research work refer to an in-depth investigation of the SDN (SDN) concept and OpenFlow controllers. This study aims to explore the architecture, components, and functionalities of SDN controllers, which manage and direct network traffic in an SDN environment. Such a study may also involve analyzing the different types of controllers available, such as centralized, distributed, and hybrid architectures, and their respective strengths and weaknesses. Additionally, this investigation may include exploring programming languages and APIs utilized to develop SDN applications, as well as their integration with other technologies like network function virtualization (NFV) and cloud computing. Overall, the goal of the work is to recognize the SDN/OpenFlow controllers in advanced level to enhance the understanding of SDN and its related technologies. It equips network experts and researchers with the knowledge and skills required to design, implement, and manage SDN-based networks.

Critical Review of Literature

SDN is an upcoming and emerging paragon. Many innovations are possible to the network with the programmable, flexible interface controlling the behavior of the entire network. In SDN, unlike traditional network systems, network control is decoupled from forwarding and implemented in software. This separation of control and forwarding enables network / system administrators to manage network traffic and configure all kind of policies centrally while allowing the underlying hardware to forward traffic. SDN also makes it possible to dynamically adjust the behavior of the network in response to changing conditions during the congestion or security threats. SDN allows network administrators to manage network infrastructure as a single, programmable entity. The major concepts of SDN were also surveyed. There are numerous advantages to SDN. However, there are a couple of disadvantages as well. One main issue is security. SDN is susceptible to various security attacks including anomalies, IDPS, DoS attacks. Depending on how they affect the network's implementation, enforcement, and policy, the attacks that target the five main components of SDN can be divided into several categories. Three distinct assault scopes can be inferred from these indirect strikes. Attacks can be classified as follows: implementation attacks, which target the data plane and southbound API components of a SDN; enforcement attacks, which target the control plane and are related to policy enforcement; southbound and northbound API; and, lastly, policy attacks, which target the capacity to define and store legitimate network policies and usually aim to compromise the control and application planes of SDN. You are aware of the various kinds of computer attacks.

A well-liked southbound API that enables safe data plane and control plane connections is called Open Flow. The controller and switch communicate with each other via the OpenFlow protocol. A general understanding of the OpenFlow protocol, including its operation, message structure, and many versions, has been acquired through the review. One can use a variety of technologies to simulate how SDN functions. Mininet is one of those that is quite versatile. It is a terrific tool that is easy and economical. It can accommodate several topologies, including custom topologies that we may design. Learn about the fundamentals of SDN with Mininet, the many topologies and significant functionalities that Mininet offers, as well as the tool's limit.

REAL-TIME IMPLEMENTATION OF SDN

Installation of Mininet

To set up Mininet as per the implementation by De Oliveira et al. (2014), an open-source network simulator for testing and developing SDN applications, there is a need to follow these steps:

1. Make sure that the system meets the Mininet installation requirements, which include a Linux-based OS, such as Fedora or Ubuntu, and administrative access to the system.
2. Configure the Linux distribution package manager to set up all the necessary dependencies, such as gnuplot and git-core, for Mininet.
3. Clone the Mininet repository from GitHub.
4. Navigate to the Mininet directory.
5. Run the installation script for Mininet using the command sudo ./util/install.sh - fnv, which installs the core components, the OpenFlow reference implementation, and the virtual machine support for Mininet.
6. Test the installation by creating a network topology and testing connectivity between all hosts using the Mininet CLI command sudo mn –test pingall.

Installation of RYU Controller

To install the Ryu controller on a Linux system as demonstrated by Asadollahi et al. (2018), follow these steps:

1. Ensure that your system has installed Python 2.7 or Python 3.4 or a later version.
2. Use pip to install the Ryu controller, along with its dependencies. This can be done by running a command in the terminal.
3. Once the installation is complete, you can test the Ryu controller by running a sample application. For example, you can start a simple application that prints out all incoming OpenFlow messages. This will allow you to verify that the Ryu controller is working properly.

Integrating Mininet with RYU Controller

To integrate Mininet and Ryu controllers using the command prompt,

1. We must start the Ryu controller by entering the 'ryu-manager 'command in a terminal window.
2. Open a new terminal window and start Mininet by entering the 'sudo mn –controller=remote, command, replacing it with the system's IP address running the Ryu controller. This command will establish a connection between Mininet and Ryu controller.
3. Once Mininet has started, you can use commands like 'net add, ''link, 'and 'host 'to create a network topology. Finally, you can test the network by running commands like 'pinball 'or 'perf. ' This will help you create a customized SDN environment using Mininet and Ryu controller via command prompt.

EXPERIMENTAL AND ANALYTICAL WORK

OpenFlow is a networking protocol that allows centralized control of network devices such as switches and routers. In Mininet, OpenFlow is implemented using SDN principles to create a virtual network environment. The first step is to create a network topology using Mininet's Python API. This involves defining the switches, hosts, and links in the network, as well as the OpenFlow controllers that will manage the switches. When the network is started, the switches connect with the controllers and send messages indicating their capabilities.

The OpenFlow controllers communicate with the switches to install flow rules, which specify how packets should be forwarded within the network. The controllers can use different algorithms and policies to determine the best path for each packet based on various factors. At the arrival of packets to a switch, it examines the packet headers and compares them to the installed flow rules to determine how the packet should be forwarded.

The OpenFlow controllers can dynamically update the flow rules in response to changes in the network conditions. This allows them to quickly adapt the network behavior to optimize performance and ensure reliable packet delivery. Overall, OpenFlow in Mininet provides a flexible and scalable platform for testing and developing SDN applications, enabling developers to experiment with different network configurations and policies in a controlled virtual environment.

Ryu is a software framework used to build OpenFlow controllers, which are used to control all sort of network devices mainly switches and routers. There are several reasons why Ryu may be preferred over other OpenFlow controllers:

- **Customization:** Ryu provides APIs that enable developers to customize and develop OpenFlow applications that suit their specific needs. This allows developers to build network applications that can interact with OpenFlow-enabled devices in a way that meets their requirements.
- **Python Language:** Ryu is written in Python, a widely used programming language with a large community of developers. This makes it easy to develop and customize OpenFlow applications and integrate them with other Python-based tools and libraries.
- **Open Source:** Ryu is open-source software, which means that it is freely available for modification and distribution by anyone. This enables developers to collaborate on the development of the framework and benefit from the contributions of others.
- **Active Development:** Ryu is actively maintained and developed by a community of developers. This ensures that the framework is up-to-date with latest OpenFlow specifications and best practices and provides regular updates and improvements.

In summary, Ryu is a flexible and customizable software framework for building OpenFlow controllers. Its Python-based architecture, open-source feature and active community forum make it a popular choice for application developers who want to build network applications that can interact with OpenFlow-enabled devices in a way that meets their specific needs.

Several different controllers can be used as alternatives to OpenFlow for SDN. These controllers include Ryu, POX, Floodlight, ONOS, and NOX. Each controller has its own advantages and disadvantages, and the option of choosing the controller depends on the specific needs of the network. Factors such as the size and complexity of the network, programming language preference, and available features and protocols all play an important role in determining which controller is the best fit for a particular SDN environment. Ultimately, it's essential to carefully evaluate each controller and choose the one that meets the network's specific requirements.

An IDS is a security system that detects and prevents security threats on a computer network. However, IDS can be attacked in different ways, making them vulnerable to security breaches. Some types of attacks that can be carried out against IDS include evasion attacks, false positives, DoS attacks, elevation of privilege, data manipulation, and malware. To mitigate these attacks, appropriate security related measures that includes authentication, access control, encryption, and regular software updates should be implemented. IDS should also be configured to work with other security-based systems, such as firewalls, IPS, and SIEM, to give more comprehensive security coverage and reduce the impact of attacks.

Modeling, Analysis & Design

The deployment of networking applications on top of SDN architecture is made possible by the separation of two planes. As seen in Figure 1, the architecture is built up of three layers. The lowest layer, sometimes referred to as the infrastructure or data plane, is in charge of data collection, local information monitoring, and network data forwarding. The forwarding plane is programmed and managed by the middle layer, also known as the control plane. Network applications are housed at the uppermost layer, often known as the application layer. The controller provides an abstract and global view of the forwarding plane to these applications. When necessary, the control layer is guided by this information to perform network services.

Figure 1. SDN architecture

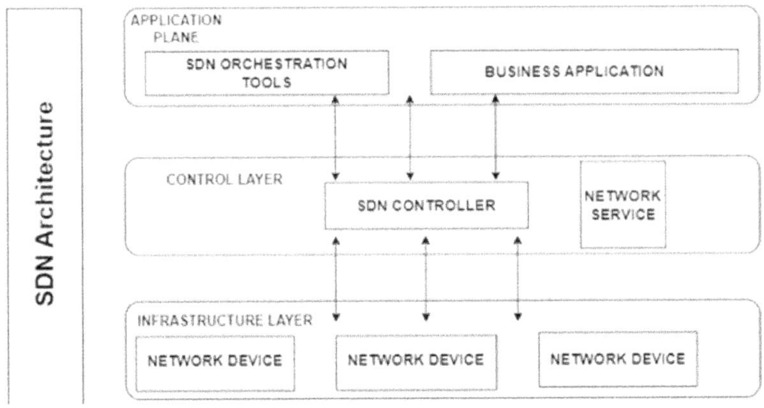

Figure 2. IDS in SDN architecture

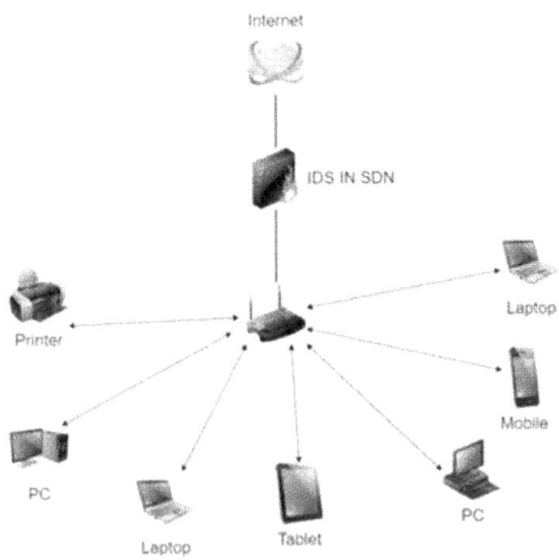

The (i) infrastructure layer, (ii) control layer and (iii) application layer are the three levels that makeup SDN architecture as given by Cabaj et al. (2014). The lowest layer, known as the infrastructure layer or data plane, is made up of forwarding network components that are in charge of tracking local specifics, collecting data, and forwarding data. The forwarding plane is programmed and handled by the control layer, also known as the control plane, which is positioned in the middle. To use abstract views of the entire network for the purpose of internal decision-making, one or more network applications communicate with controllers in the uppermost layer, also referred to as the application or management plane. Network applications in SDN dictate how forwarding devices behave by submitting high-level policies to the control plane. These policies are enforced by the control plane by setting them as network forwarding devices' flow rules.

Applications created by product or system developers to administer the network, including features like configuration management and fault monitoring, are part of the application, or administration plane. By acting as a mediator between the control plane and the application plane, the northbound interface conceals the inner workings of the network while enabling network programming and service requests. The controller, depicted in Figure 2 as the central nervous system of the network, installs and decides on packet forwarding in the switches. Physical distribution of SDN is achieved by the controller, which also communicates with the appropriate networking components to deliver notifications, device management, and security features. Comprising networking equipment specialized in packet forwarding, such as switches and routers, the data plane is devoid of inherent intelligence that enables it to make independent decisions, in contrast to traditional networks. Standard OpenFlow interfaces are used by these devices to connect with the controller.

The conceptual model of the proposed implementation is depicted in Figure 3. Our approach combines the features an SDN controller provides and an IDS to create an SDN based IDS monitor. When a new packet enters the system, it is categorized as belonging to a flow and sends a request to the system. Subsequently, the switch processes the packet based on a rule associated with the flow it belongs to and makes a decision. If the switch does not initially have a rule for that flow, it requests it from the SDN controller. The SDN controller in turn installs the appropriate flow rule for the particular switch in order to grant permission to the packet to reach its destination only if it belongs to a “well-behaved” flow. If the packet is deemed part of a” bad” flow, a dropping rule is installed in the switch, and the packets of that flow are discarded. The IDS determines whether a flow is “good” or ” bad” based on pre-configured rules. Every request involved in a flow produces a decision from the developed system.

Figure 3. Flow process of IDS

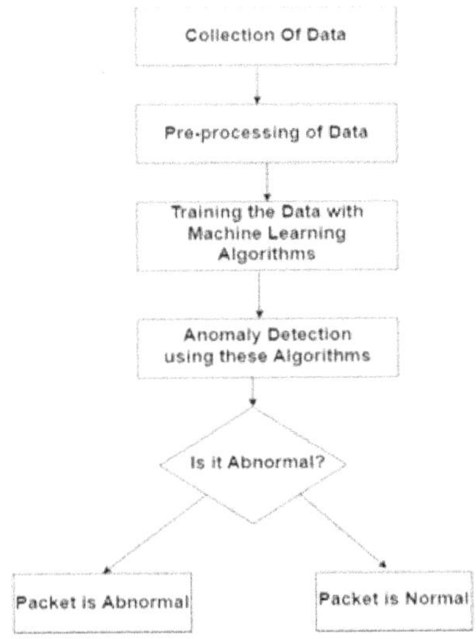

Implementation Details

MobaXterm is a terminal emulator and remote desktop client for Windows that provides a complete Unix/Linux command-line interface (CLI) and X server functionality. It allows users to connect to remote servers via SSH, Telnet, or RDP protocols and provides secure file transfer capabilities with FTP, SFTP, SCP, and other protocols.

MobaXterm also includes various Unix/Linux tools and commands, such as bash, grep, awk, sed, rsync, and many others, typically unavailable on Windows operating systems as presented by Namala et al. (2016). Additionally, it provides advanced features like multi-execution, tabbed terminal sessions, network scanning, and more. Using the tunneling feature, the MobaXterm tool was used to create highly secure connection between the Ryu controller and the mininet simulator. To use MobaXterm to access Mininet and Ryu controller, follow these steps:

1. Install MobaXterm on your computer.

2. Launch the Mininet VM using a virtual machine manager like VirtualBox.
3. Once the VM has started, open a terminal window in it.
4. Type" ifconfig" in the terminal to get the IP address of the Mininet VM.
5. Start the Ryu controller by running the" ryu-manager" command with the path to the Ryu application you want to use.
6. Open MobaXterm on your local machine and start a new SSH session to the IP address of the Mininet VM.
7. After connecting, you can access the Ryu controller by entering commands in the SSH terminal.

To create a topology with hosts and switches in Mininet, you can use the Python API to define your network topology. Creating a topology in Mininet involves defining the network components, such as hosts, switches, and links, using Python code. Here are the general steps to create a simple topology with hosts and switches:

1. Import the necessary modules: mininet.topo, mininet.net, and mininet.cli.
2. Define the topology by creating a Python class that inherits from mininet.topo.Topo. In this class, define the hosts, switches, and links between them.
3. Instantiate the topology class in the main() function of your script.
4. Create a Mininet network object using the instantiated topology object.
5. Start the network.
6. Open a Mininet command line interface (CLI) to interact with the network.

The Ryu manager with the required Python scripts captures the data from the network with different fields, such as the number of packets, their size, and their source and destination addresses. This data is stored as a dataset file in the form of a CSV or JSON file. Once you have captured a data set using Ryu, you can use it for various purposes, such as network monitoring, traffic analysis, and machine learning. For network monitoring, you can use the data set to understand the behavior of the network and detect anomalies or security threats. For example, you could use the data set to identify packet traffic patterns that show a distributed denial of service (DDoS) attack or a network intrusion.

For traffic analysis, you can use the data set to understand the traffic flow's characteristics, such as volume, type, and source. This information could be used to improve network performance, troubleshoot issues, and plan for future network upgrades. For machine learning, you can use the data set to train and test algorithms that predict future network behavior or classify network traffic into different categories. For example, you could use the data set to train a machine learning model to predict network traffic volume based on historical data or to classify network traffic into benign or malicious categories based on packet header information.

DDOS Attack

To detect DDoS attacks using this data set, machine learning models could be trained on the labeled data to perform the classification on the traffic as benign or malicious. Then the trained model can be used to predict the label of new traffic data based on the features extracted from the network traffic. One approach to using machine learning for DDoS detection is to use supervised learning techniques to train a classifier on the labeled dataset. The features extracted from the network traffic can include packet and flow-level characteristics, such as packet size, rate, packet direction, source IP address, destination IP address and port numbers.

Once the model is trained, it could be applied to real time traffic data to classify packets as benign or malicious. A packet classified as malicious can trigger an alert or some other action, such as traffic filtering or throttling. However, it is important to note that machine learning-based DDoS detection techniques may not always be accurate and produce false positives or negatives. Therefore, it is important to continuously monitor and improve the system's detection accurateness over time.

There are many types of DDoS attacks. Here are a few examples:

- **ICMP Flood:** ICMP flood type of attack usually floods the target with large volumes of Internet Control Message Protocol packets, overwhelming the target's network and making it inaccessible.
- **SYN Flood:** It exploits the Transmission Control Protocol's handshake process by frequently transmitting many SYN (synchronized) requests to target system, causing it to become unresponsive.
- **UDP Flood:** This attack sends many User Datagram Protocol based packets to the target system, by consuming more traffic and resources causing it to become unavailable.
- **HTTP Flood:** This type of attack targets web servers by flooding them with Hypertext Transfer Protocol requests, overwhelming their resources and making them unavailable.
- **Slowloris:** This attack sends many HTTP requests to the target server, but slowly, to consume the resources of the server and cause it to become unresponsive.
- **Amplification Attacks:** These attacks use vulnerable servers, such as DNS (Domain Name System) servers, to amplify the attack traffic and overwhelm the target's network.

Prototype & Testing

In SDN, IDS can be implemented to detect and prevent network attacks. To create a prototype and test IDS implementation in SDN, you can follow these steps:

1. **Set up a test network:** Create an environment that resembles the real network where the IDS will be implemented. You can create a small-scale network with virtual machines, switches, and routers.
2. **Install SDN controller and switches:** Install an SDN controller like OpenDaylight, and connect all the switches on the network to the controller. Utilize the OpenFlow protocol to perform the transmission between the controller and the switches.
3. **Implement IDS:** Choose an IDS tool that supports SDN, such as Snort or Suricata, and implement it on the SDN controller. Configure the IDS to detect and prevent network attacks.
4. **Test IDS:** Run various network attacks on the test network and observe if the IDS can detect and prevent them. You can use network traffic generators to simulate network traffic and test the IDS's performance under various traffic loads.
5. **Evaluate IDS performance:** Evaluate the performance metrics of the IDS in terms of its accuracy, speed, and resource utilization. Ensure the IDS does not affect the normal network traffic or introduce additional latency.
6. **Refine IDS configuration:** Fine-tune the IDS configuration based on the test results to improve its accuracy and performance.
7. **Deploy IDS in production:** Once you are satisfied with the IDS's performance, deploy it in the production network and continuously monitor its performance.

Results and Analysis

Distributed Denial of Service (DDoS) and Internet Control Message Protocol (ICMP) flood attacks are two of the most common forms of cyberattacks that can cause significant disruption to computer networks. Recently, SDN has been developed as an auspicious technology for defending against these attacks. In this work, experiments on using SDN to mitigate DDoS and ICMP flood attacks and analyze the effectiveness of this approach. The experiments were conducted using the open-source network emulator called Mininet, that enables us to create a simulated network environment for testing. In this work two different attack scenarios were considered: a DDoS attack that floods the network with packets from multiple sources and an ICMP flood attack that floods the network with ICMP packets. In both cases, we measured the impact of the attack on the network performance and the effectiveness of the SDN-based defense mechanism in mitigating the attack. Our results show that both the DDoS and ICMP flood attacks can cause significant degradation in network performance, including increased packet loss, higher latency, and decreased throughput as shown in Figure 4. In the case of the DDoS attack, we observed that the attack was able to overwhelm the network switches, causing them to drop packets and become unresponsive. In the case of the ICMP flood attack, we observed that the attack flooded the network with so many ICMP packets that legitimate traffic was unable to get through.

To mitigate these attacks, we implemented a simple SDN-based defense mechanism that uses flow rules to redirect traffic away from the attacked switches and towards less congested paths in the network. We tested this defense mechanism under different attack scenarios and measured its effectiveness in mitigating the attacks as shown in Figure 5. Our results show that the SDN-based defense mechanism successfully mitigated both the DDoS and ICMP flood attacks. In the case of the DDoS attack, the defense mechanism was able to redirect traffic away from the attacked switches and towards other switches in the network, effectively isolating the attack and preventing it from overwhelming the network. In the case of the ICMP flood attack, the defense mechanism was able to drop the excess ICMP packets and allow legitimate traffic to pass through.

Figure 4. Impact of network attack and predicted using Naïve bayes installed in IDS

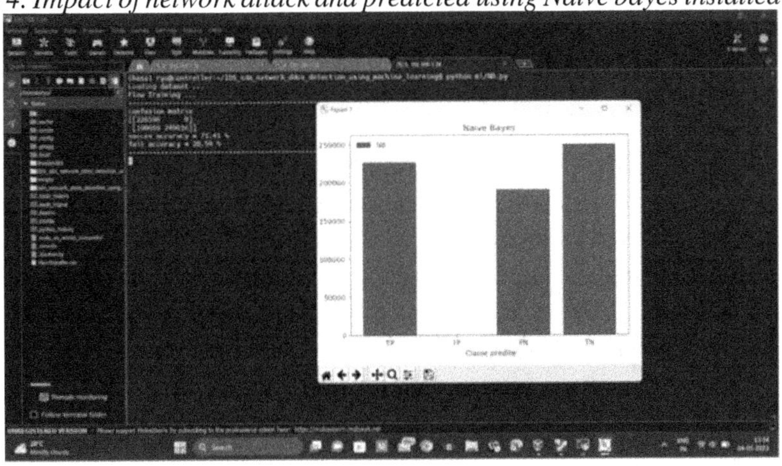

We also analyzed the performance of the SDN-based defense mechanism under different network conditions, such as network topologies and traffic loads. Our results show that the defense mechanism could adapt to changing network conditions and maintain a high level of effectiveness in mitigating attacks. In conclusion, our experiments demonstrate the effectiveness of SDN-based defense mechanisms in mitigating DDoS and ICMP flood attacks. While these attacks can cause significant disruption to computer networks, SDN provides a promising approach for defending against them. However, more research is required to discover the scalability and practicality of SDN-based defense mechanisms in real-world network environments.

Figure 5. Impact of network attack and predicted using Naïve bayes installed in IDS

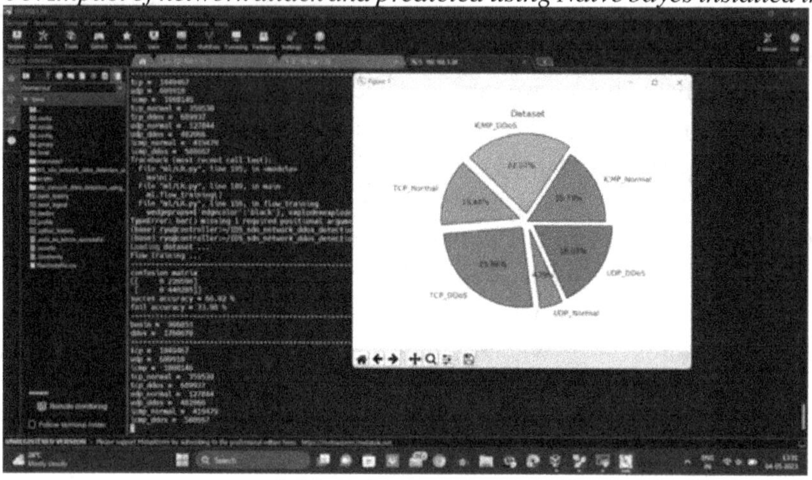

CONCLUSIONS

Implementing IDS in software defined network provides promising methodology to enhancing network security. By leveraging the centralized control system and programmability of SDN, IDS can notice and alleviate an extensive range of attacks in real-time. The primary benefit of implementing IDS in SDN is the capability to detect and address the threats in real time. SDN allows for the creation flexible and scalable networks, which can be customized to suit the organization's needs. This flexibility enables security teams to create policies that can be applied to specific network segments, which helps detect and mitigate attacks quickly. Using machine learning models and algorithms for IDS in SDN has shown promising results in increasing the accuracy and efficiency of attack detection. With the help of large data sets containing benign and malicious traffic, machine learning models could be trained to identify patterns and anomalies indicative of different types of attacks. However, it is essential to note that IDS in SDN is not a foolproof solution, as attackers can still find ways to circumvent detection mechanisms. Moreover, deploying IDS in SDN introduces new challenges, such as ensuring that the IDS itself is secure and does not introduce new vulnerabilities.

Despite the benefits of IDS implementation in SDN, some challenges remain to overcome. One of the primary challenges is the complexity of the SDN environment. SDN networks are highly dynamic, and keeping track of constantly changing network traffic can be challenging. This complexity requires security teams to deeply understand the SDN environment to manage and maintain the IDS effectively. Despite these challenges, the implementation of IDS in SDN holds significant potential for improving network security. By endlessly tracking the network traffic and detecting attacks in real-time, IDS could help prevent data breaches, service disruptions, and other costly security incidents. Therefore, organizations need to consider the use of IDS in SDN as part of their overall security strategy. IDS implementation in SDN is a key aspect of network security. SDN enables the implementation of proactive security measures, automated threat analysis, and real-time threat detection and mitigation.

Scope for Future Work

The implementation of IDS in SDN is an evolving area of research with various opportunities for future work. Here are a few potential areas of focus for future research:

- Development of more effective and efficient IDS algorithms: While there has been significant progress in developing IDS algorithms for SDN environments, there is still room for improvement. For example, current IDS algorithms may struggle to detect advanced and sophisticated attacks that utilize evasion techniques.
- Future work could focus on developing more effective IDS algorithms that can detect these types of attacks with greater accuracy and efficiency.
- Integration of machine learning and artificial intelligence techniques: These methods have demonstrated great potential for enhancing the precision and effectiveness of IDS systems. To increase performance, future research could concentrate on creating and incorporating these methods into SDN-based IDS systems.
- Development of distributed IDS systems: In traditional network environments, IDS systems are typically centralized and operate on a single network segment. However, in SDN environments, the network topology can be highly dynamic and distributed, which makes it challenging to implement a centralized IDS system.

- Future work could focus on developing distributed IDS systems that can operate effectively in SDN environments.
- Development of IDS systems for specific SDN applications such as data centers, cloud infrastructures and IoT networks.
- Future work could focus on developing IDS systems that are specifically designed for these different applications to improve their effectiveness and efficiency.
- Evaluation of the performance and scalability of IDS systems: As SDN-based IDS systems become more complex and sophisticated, it is essential to evaluate their performance and scalability. Future work could focus on developing benchmarks and metrics to evaluate the performance and scalability of these systems and compare them against traditional IDS systems.

Integration of IDS with Other Security Mechanisms

IDS is just one component of a comprehensive security framework. Future work could focus on integrating IDS with other security mechanisms such as intrusion prevention systems, firewalls and access control systems, to create a more robust and comprehensive security solution.

REFERENCES

Ahmad, A., Harjula, E., Ylianttila, M., & Ahmad, I. (2020, December). Evaluation of machine learning techniques for security in SDN. In 2020 IEEE Globecom Workshops (GC Wkshps (pp. 1-6). IEEE.

Al-Shareeda, M. A., Jafer, A. N., Hashem, M. T., & Fajr, M. S. (2024). Secure Offline Smart Office Automation System Using ESP32 and Bluetooth Control Architecture. *Journal of Cyber Security and Risk Auditing*, *2024*(1), 3–13. DOI: 10.63180/jcsra.thestap.2024.1.2

Aldossary, A., Algirim, T., Almubarak, I., & Almuhish, K. (2024). Cyber Security in Data Breaches. *Journal of Cyber Security and Risk Auditing*, *2024*(1), 14–22. DOI: 10.63180/jcsra.thestap.2024.1.3

Aljumaiah, O., Jiang, W., Addula, S. R., & Almaiah, M. A. (2025). Analyzing cybersecurity risks and threats in IT infrastructure based on NIST framework. *J. Cyber Secur. Risk Audit*, *2025*(2), 12–26. DOI: 10.63180/jcsra.thestap.2025.2.2

Alotaibi, E., Sulaiman, R. B., & Almaiah, M. (2025). Assessment of cybersecurity threats and defense mechanisms in wireless sensor networks. *J. Cyber Secur. Risk Audit*, *2025*(1), 47–59. DOI: 10.63180/jcsra.thestap.2025.1.5

Alshuaibi, A., Almaayah, M., & Ali, A. (2025). Machine Learning for Cybersecurity Issues: A systematic Review. *Journal of Cyber Security and Risk Auditing*, *2025*(1), 36–46. DOI: 10.63180/jcsra.thestap.2025.1.4

AlShuaibi, A., Arshad, M. W., & Maayah, M. (2025). A Hybrid Genetic Algorithm and Hidden Markov Model-Based Hashing Technique for Robust Data Security. *Journal of Cyber Security and Risk Auditing*, *2025*(3), 42–56. DOI: 10.63180/jcsra.thestap.2025.3.6

Antikainen, M., Aura, T., & Särelä, M. (2014). Spook in your network: Attacking an SDN with a compromised openflow switch. In Secure IT Systems: 19th Nordic Conference, NordSec 2014, Tromsø, Norway, October 15-17, 2014 [Springer International Publishing.]. *Proceedings*, *19*, 229–244.

Asadollahi, S., Goswami, B., & Sameer, M. (2018, February). Ryu controller's scalability experiment on software defined networks. In *2018 IEEE International Conference on Current Trends in Advanced Computing (ICCTAC)* (pp. 1-5). IEEE. DOI: 10.1109/ICCTAC.2018.8370397

Badotra, S., & Panda, S. N. (2020). Software-Defined Networking: A novel approach to networks. Handbook of Computer Networks and Cyber Security: Principles and Paradigms, 313-339.

Cabaj, K., Wytrebowicz, J., Kuklinski, S., Radziszewski, P., & Dinh, K. T. (2014, September). SDN Architecture Impact on Network Security. In *FedCSIS* (pp. 143–148). Position Papers.

Davarasan, A., Samual, J., Palansundram, K., & Ali, A. (2024). A Comprehensive Review of Machine Learning Approaches for Android Malware Detection. *Journal of Cyber Security and Risk Auditing*, *2024*(1), 38–60. DOI: 10.63180/jcsra.thestap.2024.1.5

De Oliveira, R. L. S., Schweitzer, C. M., Shinoda, A. A., & Prete, L. R. (2014, June). Using mininet for emulation and prototyping software-defined networks. In *2014 IEEE Colombian Conference on Communications and Computing (COLCOM)* (pp. 1-6). IEEE. DOI: 10.1109/ColComCon.2014.6860404

Ferrús, R., Koumaras, H., Sallent, O., Agapiou, G., Rasheed, T., Kourtis, M. A., Boustie, C., Gélard, P., & Ahmed, T. (2016). SDN/NFV-enabled satellite communications networks: Opportunities, scenarios and challenges. *Physical Communication*, *18*, 95–112. DOI: 10.1016/j.phycom.2015.10.007

Frederick, N., & Ali, A. (2024). Enhancing DDoS Attack Detection and Mitigation in SDN Using Advanced Machine Learning Techniques. *Journal of Cyber Security and Risk Auditing*, *2024*(1), 23–37. DOI: 10.63180/jcsra.thestap.2024.1.4

Goransson, P., Black, C., & Culver, T. (2016). *Software defined networks: a comprehensive approach*. Morgan Kaufmann.

Jafarian, T., Masdari, M., Ghaffari, A., & Majidzadeh, K. (2021). A survey and classification of the security anomaly detection mechanisms in software defined networks. *Cluster Computing*, *24*(2), 1235–1253. DOI: 10.1007/s10586-020-03184-1

Le, A., Dinh, P., Le, H., & Tran, N. C. (2015, November). Flexible network-based intrusion detection and prevention system on software-defined networks. In *2015 International Conference on Advanced Computing and Applications (ACOMP)* (pp. 106-111). IEEE. DOI: 10.1109/ACOMP.2015.19

Liu, J., Kauffman, R. J., & Ma, D. (2015). Competition, cooperation, and regulation: Understanding the evolution of the mobile payments technology ecosystem. *Electronic Commerce Research and Applications*, *14*(5), 372–391. DOI: 10.1016/j.elerap.2015.03.003

Manikandakumar, M., & DK, S. S. (2019). A Detailed Study on Security Concerns of VANET and Cognitive Radio VANETs. In Cognitive Social Mining Applications in Data Analytics and Forensics (pp. 252-264). IGI Global.

Manikandakumar, M., & Ramanujam, E. (2018). Security and Privacy Challenges in Big Data Environment. In Handbook of Research on Network Forensics and Analysis Techniques (pp. 315-325). IGI Global. DOI: 10.4018/978-1-5225-4100-4.ch017

Mousa, M., Bahaa-Eldin, A. M., & Sobh, M. (2016, December). Software defined networking concepts and challenges. In 2016 11th International Conference on Computer Engineering & Systems (ICCES) (pp. 79-90). IEEE. DOI: 10.1109/ICCES.2016.7821979

Muthusamy, M., & Periasamy, K. (2019). A comprehensive study on Internet of Things security: Challenges and recommendations. In *Advancing Consumer-Centric Fog Computing Architectures* (pp. 72–86). IGI Global. DOI: 10.4018/978-1-5225-7149-0.ch004

Namala, K. K., AV, K. K. P., Math, A., Kumari, A., & Kulkarni, S. (2016, December). Smart irrigation with embedded system. In 2016 IEEE Bombay section symposium (IBSS) (pp. 1-5). IEEE.

Scott-Hayward, S., Natarajan, S., & Sezer, S. (2015). A survey of security in software defined networks. *IEEE Communications Surveys and Tutorials*, *18*(1), 623–654. DOI: 10.1109/COMST.2015.2453114

Sezer, S., Scott-Hayward, S., Chouhan, P. K., Fraser, B., Lake, D., Finnegan, J., Viljoen, N., Miller, M., & Rao, N. (2013). Are we ready for SDN? Implementation challenges for software-defined networks. *IEEE Communications Magazine*, *51*(7), 36–43. DOI: 10.1109/MCOM.2013.6553676

Shaghaghi, A., Kaafar, M. A., Buyya, R., & Jha, S. (2020). Software-Defined Network (SDN) data plane security: issues, solutions, and future directions. Handbook of Computer Networks and Cyber Security: Principles and Paradigms, 341-387.

Shalimov, A., Zuikov, D., Zimarina, D., Pashkov, V., & Smeliansky, R. (2013, October). Advanced study of SDN/OpenFlow controllers. In *Proceedings of the 9th Central & Eastern European Software Engineering Conference in Russia* (pp. 1-6).

Ubale, T., & Jain, A. K. (2020). Survey on DDoS attack techniques and solutions in software-defined network. Handbook of Computer Networks and Cyber Security: Principles and Paradigms, 389-419. DOI: 10.1007/978-3-030-22277-2_15

Westerlund, M. (2019). The emergence of deepfake technology: A review. *Technology Innovation Management Review*, *9*(11), 39–52. DOI: 10.22215/timreview/1282

Zahmatkesh, A., & Kunz, T. (2017). Software defined multihop wireless networks: Promises and challenges. *Journal of Communications and Networks (Seoul)*, *19*(6), 546–554. DOI: 10.1109/JCN.2017.000094

Chapter 9

Machine Learning for Threat Detection: A Comprehensive Survey on Anomaly Detection Techniques

Anto Gracious L. A.
https://orcid.org/0000-0003-2386-9182
R.M.K. College of Engineering and Technology, India

Siva Subramanian R.
https://orcid.org/0000-0002-7509-9223
SRM Institute of Science and Technology, Tiruchirapalli

ABSTRACT

Anomaly detection identifies patterns that deviate from normal behavior, signaling threats in cybersecurity, finance, healthcare, and industry. Traditional threat detection struggles with data volume and complexity, making ML a key solution for modeling large datasets. This chapter outlines ML techniques for anomaly detection, focusing on threat analysis. It reviews supervised, unsupervised, semi-supervised learning, deep learning, and neural networks, highlighting pros, cons, and applications like fraud, intrusions, faults, and health anomalies. Key factors like data preprocessing, feature engineering, and model evaluation are discussed. Challenges include imbalanced data, real-time detection, and model interpretability. The chapter also explores combining methods for better accuracy, transfer learning, AI explainability, and real-time systems as future trends. This chapter explores a clear view of current ML use in anomaly detection and future directions.

DOI: 10.4018/979-8-3373-2115-8.ch009

INTRODUCTION

Overview of Threat Detection

A threat detection is important in fields such as cyber security, business, health care whereby early detection of a possible threats may lead to huge losses, and system malfunctions. In cybersecurity threat detection is all about identifying threats such as malware, unauthorized access, emerging threats like phishing, and limitations resulting from internal threats. Banks and other financial organizations employ protection measures with an aim of detecting fraud, money laundering, and any related transactions. Likewise, in healthcare, the anomaly detection technique is used for patient health, disease diagnosis, and data protection. In general, threats in these domains can be categorized as Cyber, Fraud, and Anomalous System. Cyber threats are the unauthorized access to computer systems, networks, DoS/DDoS attacks, and ransomware attacks [Shaukat, K. et al 2020]. Fraud can be described as embezzlement fraud, where unauthorized transactions are conducted, synthetic identity fraud, and insurance fraud. System anomalies encompass hardware failures, software malfunctions, and irregular patterns in sensor data across different industrial sectors. The earlier methods of threat detection were mainly based on the rules and statistical models. However, these methods are not dynamic and do not change with the new threats hence the need to incorporate intelligent techniques such as Machine learning (ML) for anomaly detection.

Machine Learning and Anomaly Detection

This paper therefore highlights the use of machine learning as a more efficient tool in the automation of anomaly detection across various fields. Unlike traditional approaches of rule-based and signature-based and heuristic, the ML-based anomaly detection can detect unknown and evolving threat from data. This raised chances of understanding the large datasets, identifying relevant features and finding out abnormalities in the normal behavior. The following are the categories of these models: Supervised Learning – It is a machine learning that requires a set of data with normal data and data with anomalies. Unsupervised Learning – It is effective in finding anomalies when there is little or no example of such occurrences in the real world. Semi-Supervised Learning – This is a learning method that uses a small label set with a large amount of unlabelled data to enhance the recognition of anomalies whereby labelled anomalies are rare. There are deep learning architectures that implement autoencoder, convolution, and recurrent architectures to identify the anomalous data in high-dimensions.

When compared to statistical analysis and rule-based IDS, the ML models have the following advantages: Higher adaptability to new threats. Increased ability to capture finer details in the anomalous data. Scalability for large and complex datasets. However, there are some drawbacks associated with the application of the ML models including; high computational costs, interpretability and the problematic of adversarial attacks.

Purpose of the Survey

This paper seeks to establish the use of machine learning in the process of detecting anomalies and identifying threats. The primary objectives include: The roles of anomaly detection in cybersecurity, finance, healthcare, and industrial domains are very critical. A survey on different ML techniques that have been used to detect anomalies with their strengths, weaknesses, and applications. Discussing the difference between conventional and ML methods to help understand what makes AI better and what problems are still to be solved in its utilization. Exploring the areas of future research and opportunities for the development of the anomaly detection based on machine learning. Anomaly detection is very important in threat analysis since it offers preventive measures in cases of cyber threats, fraudulent transactions, or critical system breakdowns. The survey is also intended to bring together the recent developments made in the field of ML in anomaly detection and assess their efficacy in the real world against the threats.

Scope of the Paper

This paper aims at reviewing the existing work on machine learning techniques for anomaly detection and the following areas are discussed. Anomaly detection basics, types of learning, and problems associated with it. The detection methodologies of anomalous behaviors with the use of machine learning techniques with an emphasis on the supervised, unsupervised, semi-supervised and deep learning. Cleaning and preparation of data with focus on the quality of data, relevant features and feature space reduction. Evaluation metrics and performance analysis, which touches on the way that ML models are tested using precision, recall, F1-score, and ROC-AUC. Applications in different fields such as security, fraud, health care and industrial automation. Challenges and open issues, including data availability, interpretability, adversarial attacks and scalability of the proposed methods. In relation to the proposed framework, the recent developments and advancements include the integration of deep learning with other models, explainable artificial intelligence, real time identification of anomalies and transfer learning. Conclusion and future trends that would encompass the main findings and recommendations and highlight the future development of ML-based anomaly detection. Thus, this paper aims at analyzing the current status and future trends in ML-based anomaly detection based on the evaluation of the strengths and limitations of the presented approaches with the focus on the issues of increasing the detection accuracy, minimizing the number of false alarms, and creating the solutions that are reliable, scalable, and explainable for the practical use.

FUNDAMENTALS OF ANOMALY DETECTION

Anomaly detection is a technique of finding out unusual patterns in a given data set. Anomalies which are also referred to as outliers will signify fraud, future cyber-attacks, operational issues, or even a brand-new diseases. The key goal of anomaly detection is to filter out a set of outliers in the data, which are different from the other data points to prevent possible threats.

The ML-based anomaly detection techniques can be broadly classified into three categories.

Figure 1. ML-based anomaly detection techniques

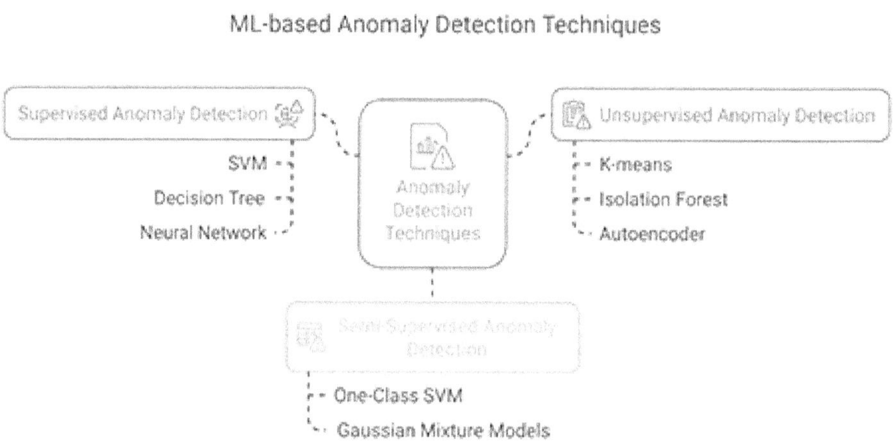

1.Supervised Anomaly Detection: It is necessary to have labeled data sets containing both normal and anomalous samples. It uses classifying techniques like SVM, Decision Tree or Neural Network to identify the anomalies. It is good at handling regular cases but performs poorly in the real-life situations where exceptions and labels are limited.
2.Unsupervised Anomaly Detection: It runs on the basis of statistical differences without the use of labeled data. of using clustering methods such as k-means, Isolation Forest, and Autoencoder in order to detect these anomalies. Suitable for large-scale, dynamic systems but prone to false positives due to unexpected variations in data.
3.Semi-Supervised Anomaly Detection: The algorithm is based on using a small subset of labeled normal instances and regarding the rest of the dataset as unlabeled. One-Class SVM and Gaussian Mixture Models (GMMs) train models to learn the normal behavior and mark anything out of the ordinary as an anomaly [Sreelakshmi, S. et al 2024]. It can be used in practical applications where there is limited labeled anomaly data but plenty of normal data available.

Examples of Anomalies in Various Fields: Security: this is likely to contain among others, login attempts, unauthorized access attempt, Distributed Denial-of-Service (DDoS) attacks. Money related-credibility: charges of credit card fraud, money laundering and insider trading. Healthcare: Irregular heartbeats in ECG readings, sudden fluctuations in patient vitals. Manufacturing: Fluctuations in the temperature of the sensors, mechanical breakdown of the machinery, any variation in energy consumption.

Challenges in Anomaly Detection

However, anomaly detection is not without its problems that have an impact on the reliability of the detection systems in terms of accuracy and speed.

1.False Positives and False Negatives: False Positives (Type I Errors): These are situations that are normal within the database but are classified as anomalies. Example: A transaction from a genuine bank account is wrongly categorized as a fraudulent one, thus accounting freezes are made. False Negatives (Type II Errors): It occurs when an anomaly is not detected and is classified as normal. Example- A cyberattack goes unnoticed and results into data leakage. The main problem in the anomaly detection is the trade-off between recall (sensitivity) and precision (specificity).

2.Scalability and Efficiency in Real-Time Systems: Some anomaly detection systems are required to work with real-time data that involves large amounts of data, for example, in the case of network traffic analysis for intrusion detection. As a result, computationally expensive models, for example, Deep Learning based Autoencoders, demand a huge amount of computing power and memory. Some of them include distributed computing approaches, edge processing techniques, and light weight models for near real-time detection.

3.Data Imbalance and Noise Handling: It is a common practice in many fields and applications that anomalies are scarce, and the data is unbalanced. It was found that when the data is imbalanced, there is a high probability that the ML models will favor the normal instances, hence poor anomalous behavior detection. Some methods such as Synthetic Minority Over-sampling (SMOTE), anomaly injection and cost-sensitive learning are used to handle imbalance. Another challenge to the detection of noisy data is the fact that the data may be noisy in healthcare setting such as having records that are either incomplete or inconsistent. Specifically, in addition to cleaning the data, outlier removal, feature engineering, or even data augmentation are tightly related to preprocessing.

Applications of Anomaly Detection: Anomaly detection is commonly used even in cybersecurity, finance, healthcare and industrial systems were it helps organizations to detect threats, fraud, and enhances efficiency.

1.Cybersecurity

Network Intrusion Detection Systems (NIDS): Detects suspicious network traffic patterns indicative of cyberattacks. Some of the ML techniques used in the proposed IDS include Isolation Forests and Deep Learning-based IDS which increases the detection rate.

Malware Detection: zero-day attacks as well as polymorphic malware for they do not follow set pattern recognition signatures. Unsupervised Machine Learning – autoencoders and clustering can be used in the discovery of new and unknown strains of malware.

2.Finance

Fraud Detection in Banking and Credit Card Transactions: Detects unusual spending patterns and unauthorized transactions. Random Forest and Gradient Boosting Machines (GBMs) are supervised learning models that help in categorizing the transactions as either genuine or fake. Some of the unsupervised methods that can be used include Anomaly Score-Based Clustering which identifies oddities in spending patterns.

Insider Threat Detection: Recognizes employees who are likely to involve in fraudulent activities such as accessing financial information that they have no permission to do so. Uses ML models to monitor users' behavior for any abnormality within internal networks.

3.Industrial Applications

Predictive Maintenance for Equipment Failures: In factories, power plants and transportation systems, there are sensor data that provide information on the functioning of the machines in real time. Time series analysis using Artificial Intelligence assists in identifying potential failure conditions before they happens thereby reducing on the time lost due to failure.

Anomaly Detection in IoT and Smart Systems: In the modern world, IoT devices produce huge amounts of data from smart grids, smart homes, and industrial automation. It is noteworthy to mention that with the help of ML techniques such as RNNs and LSTMs, one can detect any odd sensor readings to prevent malfunctioning.

Anomaly detection is a very important type of analysis that is used for security, fraud, and system failure detection in different fields. The three main categories of uses of ML techniques are supervised, unsupervised, and semi-supervised, and all of these have their strengths and weaknesses. However, issues including the artefacts, real-time analysis, and unbalanced data necessitate best approaches to enhance the detection. With the help of deep learning, explainable AI, and real-time ML models, the anomaly detection system is becoming more efficient to render faster, accurate, and scalable solutions for the crucial sectors. The challenges that are present at the moment can be overcome to provide more effective and efficient threat detection in the future.

MACHINE LEARNING APPROACHES IN ANOMALY DETECTION

The application of ML offers a reliable approach towards the identification of anomalous cases in different fields. The specific areas include, the availability of labeled data used in the training process, complexity of the anomalies and the computing resources required. The primary approaches to implementation of anomaly detection in the field of ML are namely supervised, unsupervised, semi-supervised, and deep learning.

Figure 2. Machine learning approaches in anomaly detection

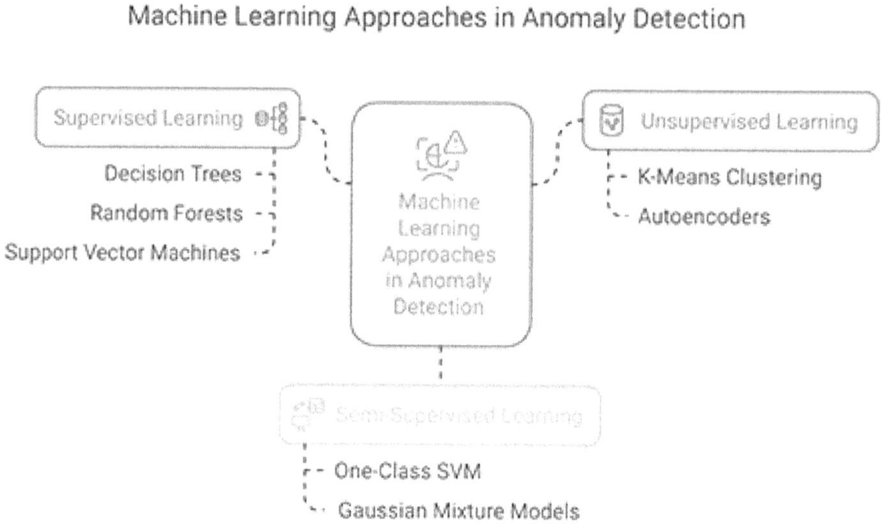

Supervised Learning Approaches

Supervised learning involves the process of having labeled datasets where anomaly is labeled and the model is trained to learn patterns that will be important in case of categorizing new instances. Key algorithms include:

Decision Trees (DT): A tree that partitions the data based on some feature values. Pros: Interpretable, fast, and effective for small datasets. Disadvantages include; It Augment overfitting and may not perform well when it is tested on datasets that it has not encountered before.
Random Forests (RF): A set of decision trees that enhances the level of classification. Advantages: Minimizes overfitting, capable of handling cases with a high number of features. Cons: Computationally expensive for large datasets [Atadoga, A. et al 2024].
Support Vector Machines (SVMs): A model that is able to eliminate outliers from the normal data using hyperplanes. Pros: Effective for high-dimensional spaces and works well in small datasets. Cons: Poor scalability in real-time applications. Pros and Cons for Anomaly Detection

Pros: High accuracy when there is a large amount of labeled data. Applicable to structured data where anomalies are not random and/or inconsistent. Better interpretability than unsupervised models.
Cons: Large amounts of labeled data are needed, which are scarce in case of anomalies. Lack of accuracy on unseen anomalies that are different from the training data. Lots of difficulties in the case of unbalanced datasets, where anomalies are outliers.
Use Cases and Examples: Credit card fraud detection: It deals with the identification of credit card frauds based on the transactions that are labeled in the past. Diagnosis: Identifying diseases depending on the data with labeled patients. Spam email classification: A study on how to differentiate between spam and genuine emails using past email data.

Unsupervised Learning Approaches

Unsupervised learning is advantageous when there are few labeled examples since it does not require labels and instead depends on statistical characteristics. Common algorithms include:

K-Means Clustering: cluster: divides similar data points together and outliers as the points that do not belong to any cluster. Advantages: Suitable to use with structured data only.A disadvantage of this method is that it assumes the number of clusters and has limitations in dealing with new anomalies.
Autoencoders (AE): A type of machine learning where normal patterns are learned and any unusual cases are detected. Pros: Captures complex anomalies in high-dimensional datasets. Disadvantages: It has high demand on the training data and its parameters have to be tweaked quite frequently.

Applications in Scenarios with No Labeled Data

Network intrusion detection: Detecting intrusions in computer networks without prior knowledge of the attacks. Industrial sensor monitoring: Prediction of equipment failures from the manufacturing unit. Medical anomaly detection: Identifying rare diseases in medical imaging.

Pros and Cons

Pros: It operates without the need for labeled data hence making it flexible for new threats. Is capable of identifying new types of anomalies that have not been identified during data training. Scalable to large datasets and dynamic environments.

Cons: Higher false positive rates because normal variations are also considered as anomalies. Interpreting such methods is somewhat difficult because it is a subfield of unsupervised learning.

Semi-Supervised Learning Approaches

Semi-supervised learning applies a small amount of labeled data to a large number of unlabeled data to enable the model to identify anomalous patterns. It is a combination of supervised learning and unsupervised learning.

Examples of Semi-Supervised Models

One-Class SVM (OCSVM): It is trained on normal data and classifies anomalies from the pattern it has learned from the normal data. Suitable for cybersecurity and fraud detection.

Gaussian Mixture Models (GMMs): Uses probability distributions to classify the data points as being normal or anomalous. Applied in medical diagnostics and financial risk assessment.

Use Cases and Trade-Offs: Insider threat detection: It uses normal user behaviour log files in its operations. Medical condition monitoring: Identifies irregularities in patient data. Sensor based predictive maintenance: Relies on the past track record to identify a machine's failure.

Pros: More accurate than the unsupervised learning as it involves the use of labeled data to some extent. Is capable of identifying emerging anomalies despite the fact that there are few samples that have been labeled as such.

Cons: There is a need to select the labeled data properly to avoid any form of bias in the data set. Computationally expensive for large-scale datasets.

Deep Learning in Anomaly Detection

Role of Deep Learning Models

Despite the differences, deep-learning-based models are capable of handling highly complex, high-dimensional anomalies that cannot be addressed by traditional ML. As it can be seen, these models effectively dispense the learning of features from raw data thus enhancing the accuracy of anomaly detection.

Key Deep Learning Models

Convolutional Neural Networks (CNNs): Process image and spatial data to identify the abnormalities in medical scans and in industries through inspection.
Recurrent Neural Networks (RNNs): Analyze time-series data in order to detect any abnormalities in the network traffic and the finances.

Figure 3. Deep learning models in anomaly detection

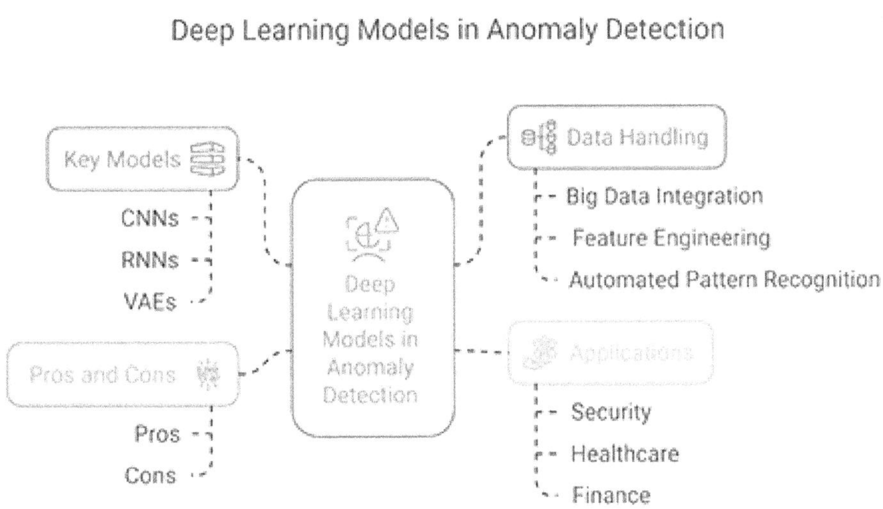

Variational Autoencoders (VAEs): Supervised and unsupervised learning algorithms to be learned to identify normal patterns and to detect anomalies [Wang, S. et al 2021].

Handling Large and Complex Data: Big Data Integration: One of the greatest strengths of deep learning models is that they allow handling large data volumes and incorporating them easily. Feature Engineering: It helps in minimizing the involvement of feature selection by the human. Automated Pattern Recognition: Recognizes even the complicated and complex forms of anomalies.

Applications in Threat Detection: Security: Analyzing of zero-day attack using anomaly based intrusion detection system. Healthcare: Identifying cancerous cells in medical images. Finance: Detecting suspicious activities regarding shares and stocks in the market.

Pros and Cons

Pros: Relatively high accuracy for complicated tasks of anomaly detection. Effectively responds to change in threats through feature extraction. Suitable for the high dimensional data, particularly in the field of cyber security, finance and health care.

Cons: In some cases, it demands significant amounts of data and computational resources. Difficult to interpret, which makes decision-making to be questionable in sensitive applications.

Anomaly detection has been enriched by machine learning with a set of methods. While supervised learning is useful when there is labeled data, the more versatile is unsupervised learning in the presence of unknown anomalies. In semi-supervised learning, accuracy and generalization and obtained in paralleled manner while deep learning offers the better performance in the higher order data at the cost of complexity. This usually depends on the data one has, the amount of computational power available as well as the demands of the application at hand. The further development includes exploration of the use of the hybrid models, explainable AI, and real time scalable solutions for improving the performance of the anomaly detection in various fields.

FEATURE ENGINEERING AND DATA PREPROCESSING

Feature engineering and data preprocessing are the two important steps in the anomaly detection model because they determine the accuracy, speed and generalization of the model. Data pre-processing helps in identifying the outliers and at the same time reduces the number of true positives and true negatives. This section presents data acquisition, data pre-processing, data modeling, feature selection with respect to anomaly detection and dimensionality reduction.

Data Collection and Cleaning

Importance of Data Quality in ML Models

This is because high quality data is required in machine learning models that are used in anomaly detection and such data ought to be structured and preprocessed well [Alzaabi, F. R. et al 2024]. This means that poor quality data will give an analyst biased results, high error rates and low reliability of the anomaly detection results. From practical experience, raw data may contain the following: Missing values (e.g., sensor failures in industrial monitoring). Noisy or corrupted data (e.g., errors in financial transactions). Complex data such as files and documents (for example, log files, medical images etc.).

This is because anomalies are not common occurrences and data inconsistency as well as imbalance can sometimes hinder the capability of models to learn the right patterns. hence, preparation steps are important in cleaning and organizing the data prior to the analysis.

Methods for Dealing with the Absent, the Noise, and the Unformatted Data

Figure 4. Methods for handling data challenges

1, Handling Missing Data
Imputation Methods: Mean, Median, or Mode Imputation: This method is applicable where the missing values are of interval or ratio level and occur randomly in the study data. For the methods, the K-Nearest Neighbors (KNN) Imputation recommends missing values based on nearby data points.
Interpolation Techniques: This is usually used in anomaly detection in time series where missing values are filled using trends. Deletion of Missing Values: If missing values are few, then elimination of records containing missing values will help in avoiding bias.
2.Handling Noisy Data: Outlier Detection and Smoothing: Moving Average Filtering: Smoothens fluctuations in time-series data. Z-Score and IQR Filtering: It is an effective way of getting rid of outliers due to its statistical thresholds. Data Normalization and Standardization: It assists in scaling data and making the features of the data more uniform.

3. Handling Unstructured Data: Text Data Preprocessing: Tokenization, Stopword Removal, Lemmatization for converting the text into numerical form where words are in structured form.

Image Preprocessing: The proposed methods include noise reduction, contrast enhancement, edge detection to enhance features that can be used in anomaly detection in imaging applications in the medical field and the industrial sector.

Log Data Processing: Specifically, the following: Using Natural Language Processing (NLP) for parsing logs in the detection of cybersecurity threats.

Preprocessing techniques are beneficial in enhancing the stability of the models and the removal of noise in the data so that the models learn the most appropriate representations.

Feature Extraction: Feature extraction is the process of extracting the most useful information from raw data so that the ML models can easily differentiate between normal and anomalous instances. However, the selection of features is very important in anomaly detection, as anomalies are usually small deviations from the norm.

Some of the research areas require the use of different feature selection techniques:

Cybersecurity: Such variables as total traffic flow, IP address activity, protocol used are used in identifying intrusions in the network. Financial: The transaction amount, the number of transaction and geographical location information is important in fraud detection. Healthcare: Heart rate variability, blood sugar level, and oxygen level are some of the signs of a health complication. Manufacturing: Temperature, vibration levels, and power consumption are used in the identification of a machine failure.

Capture meaningful patterns and trends. Eliminate unnecessary or unimportant characteristics that may slow down the computation process. Be discriminative enough to distinguish between normal and abnormal cases.

Dimensionality Reduction

Working across high dimensions requires more time and is not more easily interpreted and the anomaly detection is not as effective. In general, dimensionality reduction techniques is the process of reducing the number of features, but at the same time, preserving the important information.

Overview of Methods like PCA, t-SNE for Reducing Complexity

1.Principal Component Analysis (PCA): PCA aims at recasting the data into new feature space known as the principal components while at the same time seeking to maximize the variance. Used in network anomaly detection and financial fraud detection. How PCA helps in anomaly detection: Combines large feature sets hence decreasing the chances of the model developing an over-reliance on specific features. Enables one to distinguish between normal and abnormal distributions in a much easier way.

2. t-Distributed Stochastic Neighbor Embedding (t-SNE): t-SNE is used to lower dimensionality to clusters hence making it suitable for anomaly visualization. Best for cybersecurity logs, medical imaging, and fraud detection. As to the question of how t-SNE helps in anomaly detection, Good for making outliers easily distinguishable since it clusters similar points together. It offers the ease of interpreting and coming up with the hidden form of certain information.

3.Autoencoders for Dimensionality Reduction: Deep learning-based feature extraction technique. Learns the distribution of the normal data and identifies the outliers as anomalous data. Used in cybersecurity, healthcare, and industrial fault detection. Feature selection and data cleaning are, indeed, two key steps of the pre-processing the data that are critical for improving the anomaly detection models. Data collection and cleaning enhance the model by dealing with missing, noisy or unstructured data [Okoli, U. I. et al 2024]. Feature extraction and transformation process helps in extracting the data and converting it into the form that can be used for making predictions. There are significant techniques such as PCA, t-SNE, and autoencoders in that they reduce the dimensionality in a way so as to retain the patterns and at the same time make things more efficient. Data preprocessing is a crucial rate-limiting step that often results in time-consuming and heuristic methods; optimizing such a process leads to the development of accurate, scalable, and applicable models for detecting anomalies that would help in fraud control, cybersecurity, and equipment health management.

4. Evaluation Metrics and Performance Analysis: The performance evaluation of the machine learning models in the context of anomaly detection is crucial to determine the level of efficiency and accuracy of the models in practical applications. Anomaly detection is a distinct type of evaluation problem because of the nature of anomalous events, the fact that the anomalous class is usually small, and due to the dynamic nature of threats in the fields of cybersecurity, finance, healthcare, and industrial monitoring. This section

covers some of the measures of model accuracy, difficulties in model evaluation and the ways of comparing the performance of models.

COMMON METRICS FOR EVALUATING MODELS

While anomaly detection models have been developed, they should be evaluated using suitable measures that would enable one to differentiate between normal and anomalous instances. The selection of the evaluation metrics depends on the skewed class distribution, the costs of the errors made, and the area of application.

Precision, Recall, and F1-Score

Anomaly detection is usually performed on a dataset that is imbalanced, and in such a dataset, the number of anomalies is far less than that of normal instances. It is therefore advisable to use Precision, Recall, and F1-score for such cases since traditional accuracy may mislead. Precision: Evaluates the extent of actual anomalies in the predicted anomalies. High precision reduces the number of false alarms (false positive). Especially important in cases such as fraud detection where having a high number of false positives will mean that legitimate transactions will be blocked. The recall measurement determines how many actual anomalies the system detects correctly. The detection of most anomalies becomes possible through a high recall rate [Yamini, B. et al 2023]. In cybersecurity applications such as intrusion detection it is more dangerous to miss potential threats than to wrongly identify normal instances as threats. The F1-Score gives a balanced measure by taking the harmonic mean of Precision and Recall together. The F1-score provides valuable results when Precision and Recall create a trade-off situation. The detection performance of a model along with its low misclassification rate is indicated by a high F1-score.

Figure 5. Evaluating anomaly detection models

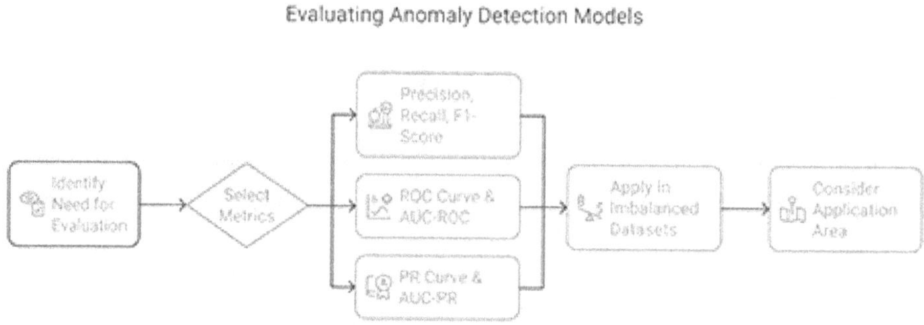

Receiver Operating Characteristic (ROC) Curve and Area Under the Curve (AUC-ROC)

The ROC curve plots the True Positive Rate (Recall) against the False Positive Rate (FPR) across different classification thresholds. The AUC-ROC score is an area measurement that shows how well the model distinguishes normal from anomalous observations. A model achieves superior anomaly detection when its AUC-ROC value approaches 1 because it demonstrates excellent performance in distinguishing anomalous events from normal instances. The detection system uses AUC-ROC scores in cybersecurity and healthcare applications which require high sensitivity for detecting anomalies.

Precision-Recall (PR) Curve and Area Under the Curve (AUC-PR)

The evaluation of highly imbalanced datasets becomes simpler with PR curves because they enable assessment of false negative and false positive results. The AUC-PR evaluation tool determines how effectively models maintain balanced precision alongside recall measurement. The AUC-PR score provides superior performance than AUC-ROC for detecting rare anomalies thus making it ideal for fraud detection and network security applications.

Challenges in Evaluation

1. Lack of Labeled Data in Real-World Applications

The occurrence of anomalies remains infrequent and undefined which leads to difficulties when obtaining labeled training data. The process of manual labelling depends on expert involvement which leads to both high costs and extended time requirements.

Solution: Unsupervised machine learning methods along with semi-supervised learning help identify irregularities in systems using data that lacks complete labelling. The synthesis of artificial anomalies serves to expand training data diversity.

2. Importance of Cross-Validation and Testing

The effectiveness of traditional train-test splits diminishes because of class imbalances. Cross-Validation using K-Fold method enables model performance evaluation through different dataset segments. When dealing with small datasets Leave-One-Out Cross-Validation (LOOCV) functions well yet its computational cost may be high.

Temporal Validation: The detection of anomalies in time-series anomaly systems (such as fraud detection and industrial monitoring) should rely on established historical patterns. The validation process requires continuous rolling windows instead of splitting the data randomly.

Performance Benchmarking

1. Comparison of Machine Learning Models for Anomaly Detection

Anomaly detection performance assessment requires the comparison of various models to identify the most optimal solution for a particular task. However, the assessment of anomaly detection models is a task that is not easy but very crucial in order to guarantee a good performance. For any model, Precision, Recall, F1-score and AUC-ROC point out how efficiently a model is functioning. The use of cross-validation techniques in conjunction with benchmarking against multiple ML models is used to come up with the best anomaly detection technique.

Therefore, it is necessary to use several measures to evaluate the model's performance appropriately. To overcome the class imbalance problem, cross-validation, synthetic data generation and threshold tuning is to be applied. Cross-validation of the results obtained from the different ML models guarantees that the anomaly detection process is accurate across the different domains. The future directions of the anomaly detection research are the creation of more effective, comprehensible, and real-time anomaly detection solutions for cybersecurity, healthcare, and finance.

APPLICATIONS IN VARIOUS DOMAINS

This protects organizations from security threats, fraudsters, systems that are performing abnormally or what could be wrong with their workers/clients. This section explains how anomaly detection can be used in cybersecurity, finance, healthcare, and industry/manufacturing; it acknowledges the importance of the feature of anomaly detection in network intrusion, fraud, disease surveillance, and equipment maintenance.

Cybersecurity

The threats in the cyber world have evolved to the extent that basic methods of detecting anomalies are not sufficient enough to detect malicious activities. Traditional heuristic-designed approaches of identifying these threats and attacks lack effectiveness with zero-day threats and hence the need for machine learning for anomaly detection.

Network Intrusion Detection Systems (NIDS)

A Network Intrusion Detection System (NIDS) is a security system that watches the network traffic to identify intrusion attempts, data loss or attack. The following are some of the ways that the ML-based anomaly detection models are useful for: Detecting other forms of traffic anomalies that can be an indication of an attack, for instance, Distributed Denial-of-Service (DDoS) attack. Detecting zero-day attacks by studying typical flow of traffic and recognizing abnormalities [Haji, S. H. et al 2021]. Facilitating more effective monitoring of events that occur in real-time, for example, by adopting Isolation Forests and Deep Autoencoder.

Example Use Case: KDD Cup 99 and NSL-KDD datasets has been used to evaluate the performance of ML-based NIDS system.

Malware Analysis and Detection

The use of traditional antivirus software is disadvantageous in that it only uses a signature-based detection method, which is helpless when it comes to polymorphic and metamorphic viruses. ML-based anomaly detection models: Identify the system's anomalies (e.g., changes in files, processes). Convolutional Neural Networks (CNN) that are collectively referred to as Deep Learning should be employed to perform the binary code analysis with a view of classifying the known types of malware. Detect ransomware using time series anomaly in the system logs.

Example Use Case: Microsoft Malware Classification Challenge dataset is employed for developing the malware detection models.

Figure 6. Applications of anomaly detection across domains

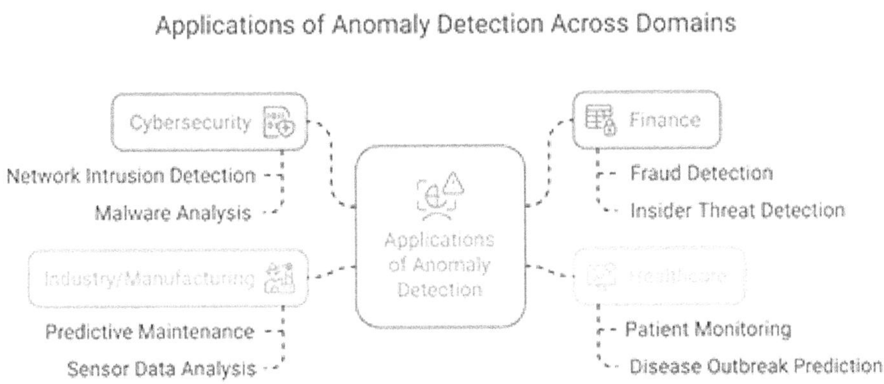

Finance

Frauds are a common issue that results in a huge loss of money to various organizations every financial year and as such, detecting frauds and insider threats is important.

Fraud Detection in Banking and Credit Card Transactions

The following are the advantages of using machine learning for anomaly detection in fraud: Recognizing anomalies, for instance, high monetary value, transactions made from different geographical areas within a short span or IP addresses. Extracting fraud features by choosing from three techniques of Unsupervised Learning like Autoencoders, K-Means Clustering as there is no set of fraud labels available. Setting up an online fraud detection system that prevents fraud transactions from being executed.

Example Use Case

Credit Card Fraud Detection on Kaggle is the dataset applied in the benchmark of the fraud detection model.

Insider Threat Detection in Organizations. It is challenging to identify insider threats since the attacker is already within the organization's network. ML-based anomaly detection helps by: Monitoring employee access logs, login behaviors, and file access history for anomalies. Analysing the patterns of behaviour of users by making use of behavioural analytics models. Hence, the use of One-Class SVM and Hidden Markov Models (HMMs) for detecting suspicious activities.

Healthcare

Healthcare anomaly detection is very important in observation of patients, diagnosing ailments and probable disease outbreak.

Anomaly Detection in Medical Data (Patient Monitoring, Diagnostic Tools)

The following are some of the areas where the ML-based anomaly detection is applied: Patient monitoring: Identification of changes in the ECG signals, the heart rate, and oxygen saturation for early identification of cases of cardiac arrest or any other complications [Farooq, H. M. et al 2018]. Medical imaging analysis: DL-based Autoencoders and CNNs for detecting tumors, fracture, or organ abnormality in X-ray and MRI. Diagnosing diseases with low incidence by analyzing the various abnormals in the biochemical marker trends.

Disease Outbreak Prediction

Applying anomaly detection in public health agencies to monitor epidemic outbreaks are based on: Infection rate as a measure with time series (for such diseases like COVID-19 or a flu). Geospatial clustering for the identification of areas that are most affected with the disease. Social media and news analytics for early detection of potential outbreaks.

Industry and Manufacturing

It is applied in the manufacturing and industrial industries to monitor the performance of the machines, the quality of the products, and to predict when a particular equipment will fail.

Predictive Maintenance for Industrial Equipment

This is because it helps prevent failures before they happen hence minimizing on the time it takes to repair them. ML-based anomaly detection models: Develop a methodology to monitor and interpret signals of industrial machines in order to diagnose potential failure. Several new applications: Use RNNs and LSTMs to monitor time-series data of sensors from the Internet of Things (IoT). Notice changes in vibration, temperature, pressure and other factors that suggest that the machinery is worn out or damaged.

Anomaly Detection in Sensor Data and IoT Devices

As it concerns the IIoT and smart manufacturing, a real-time anomaly detection is important to keep the performance optimal and the security threats at bay. ML-based techniques help by: Determining failed sensors in manufacturing processes by tracking the signal variation. Protecting the IoT devices from cyber-physical attacks through the use of anomaly-based intrusion detection system. Predicting unusual energy usage in smart grids to enhance the efficiency of energy consumption.

A current trend of using anomaly detection across several industries is based on real-time threat detection, fraud prevention, and carrying out prediction analysis. Cybersecurity applications utilize anomaly detection in order to detect intrusions in the network traffic and in the examination of malware. It is worth stating that finance utilizes anomaly detection in fraud detection and monitoring of insiders. Its applications in the healthcare field include patient monitoring, disease outbreak, and healthcare image analysis. Industry and manufacturing use anomaly detection in its many applications such as in the prediction of maintenance needs, protection of IoT devices, and enhancement of business processes.

CHALLENGES AND OPEN ISSUES IN ANOMALY DETECTION

This technique is important in security, fraud, equipment and even in the medical field where it is used to detect abnormalities. However, there are some challenges and open issues associated with ML and deep learning even today. Such issues are data quality and availability, interpretability, scalability, adversarial attacks, and transfer learning. Solving these problems becomes imperative for enhancing the performance and reliability of the anomaly detection models to be used in practice.

Data Quality and Availability

Lack of Sufficient Labeled Data

The problem of anomaly detection is the fact that there are very few labeled anomalies in real-world data sets. In contrast to such tasks as image classification or sentiment analysis, anomaly detection is a problem that is characterized by an imbalance in the training data where there are many more 'normal' instances than anomalous ones. This presents several issues: Inability to train supervised models: Most of the machine learning algorithms have a requirement that a set of examples be labeled so that they can be trained but since anomalies are a rarity, it is hard to find labeled data. Risk of overfitting: Because of inadequate labeled anomalies, the models are prone to overfitting and may not perform well for unseen anomalies.

Potential Solutions: Two of the approaches that can reduce the reliance on labeled data include semi-supervised and unsupervised learning [Al-Mhiqani, M. N. et al 2020]. The use of GANs for synthetic data generation or have data augmentation methods will assist in balancing the datasets. There are active learning techniques where the models ask the experts to label the cases that are ambiguous to the model.

Data Privacy Concerns: There are strict specificities regarding information sharing in particular domains, for example, in the finance sector and healthcare, strict privacy measures have been put in place such as GDPR, HIPAA that limits the access to data even for validation purposes in developing the models. The sharing of anomaly detection datasets is also restricted because they are considered confidential by different organizations.

Potential Solutions: Federated Learning: This is a collaborative technique where model is learned without sharing data across the networks. Privacy-Preserving Machine Learning (PPML): Implementations like homomorphic encryption allows the training of a model without the raw data being used as such.

Model Interpretability

Challenges in Explaining ML Model Decisions

A lot of Anomaly detection techniques particularly deep learning models are black boxes and thus do not explain how they arrived at a certain decision. Weak accountability: For example, in healthcare or finance, decision-makers will need to understand why an anomaly has been detected in order to trust the model's decision-making. Interpretability: It is required by regulations like GDPR's 'right to explanation' where models need to explain their decision-making process. Deep Learning Models and Explainability Issues: Interpretable models such as Decision

Tree and Linear Regression lack the efficiency of detecting anomalies. Autoencoders and CNNs are capable of learning and identifying anomalies but they are not explainable models. LRP, SHAP and LIME are the techniques that can be employed to enhance the interpretability of deep models.

Potential Solutions: Proposing specific methods for explainable AI (XAI) that can be used in the context of anomaly detection. Combining the approach of interpretable ML with deep learning to come up with hybrid models.

Scalability

Processing Real-Time Data with Big Data Characteristics

Anomaly detection is used on high velocity data with large number of features, for example: Cybersecurity (e.g., real-time network traffic monitoring). Finance (for instance, millions of credit card transactions within a second). Healthcare (e.g., real-time patient monitoring through wearable devices). This is because as the size and intricacy of datasets increase, scalability is a significant issue that arises. Computational complexity: To perform real time anomaly detection, several ML models are still demanding in terms of memory and processing power. Curse of dimensionality: Big data such as network logs, genomic sequences are difficult to analyze by the models.

Potential Solutions: Principal Component Analysis (PCA), t-SNE, and autoencoders assist in providing a dimensionality reduction of the feature space while preserving significant data. Apache Spark and TensorFlow Serving are the distributed computing frameworks that help in handling big volumes of data in the ML models. Edge computing and federated learning are also key concepts that task information processing on the edge of IoT or network devices.

Adversarial Attacks

Vulnerability of ML Models to Adversarial Inputs

It is important to note that anomaly detection models can be vulnerable to adversarial attacks whereby an attacker aims at presenting inputs that are not detected as being anomalous. These attacks include: Evasion attacks: Attackers change the input samples in a way that makes it difficult for the IDS to detect it as malicious (for example, when the malware changes its behavior to evade detection). Poisoning attacks: The system is poisoned by the attacker feeding it with wrong data set which leads to failure of the anomaly detection model.

Examples of Adversarial Attacks

Cybersecurity: The attackers change the header part of the packet to avoid detection by the network intrusion detection systems (NIDS). Finance: Various aspects of financial transactions are altered in an attempt to avoid being flagged as a potential fraudulent transaction. Healthcare: Adversaries manipulate medical images in an attempt to deceive the anomaly detection models into categorizing tumors as normal tissue.

Potential Solutions

Adversarial training: The process of training the models with adversarial examples for enhancing the robustness of the models. Stable feature selection: The ability to identify anomalies regardless of adversarial changes that may be made to them.

Transfer Learning

Transferring knowledge from one domain to another is a technique of improving artificial intelligence that has been widely used in a range of models. In many cases anomalies are of domain specific nature, which is why models trained in one specific field can hardly be applied to another one. Transfer learning enables a model that has been trained in one domain to be trained in another with little effort.

Challenges in Transfer Learning for Anomaly Detection

Domain Shift: There is a variation in the features of the two datasets (e.g., medical images as opposed to data from industrial sensors). Data Representation Differences: Certain characteristics that make up an anomaly in one domain such as cybersecurity may not be present in another domain such as healthcare. High computational cost: The fine-tuning process of such large-scale pre-trained model is computationally expensive.

Potential Solutions

One of the methods that can be used to achieve domain adaptation is adversarial domain adaptation and it enables models to learn different representations from different datasets. Few-shot learning: training the models from the target environments with limited training data. Incorporation of pre-trained deep learning models like transformers including BERT and GPT for improved log anomaly detection can be done by fine-tuning them on the detection tasks of the domain in consideration.

Nonetheless, there are some issues that have not been addressed in regards to machine learning-based anomaly detection: Because data quality and availability are the biggest challenges in big data analytics, there are a need for semi-supervised learning, privacy-preserving machine learning, and synthetic data generation. It is possible to enhance model interpretability with the help of explainable artificial intelligence (XAI). According to the options selected by the user, scalability issues can be solved by distributed computing, edge processing, and feature selection. Adversarial attacks require the implementation of defensive measures during training. There is a great potential in transfer learning, however, issues with domain shift and data dissimilarity should be resolved. Further research should be made to produce more explainable, more generalized, more robust, and more domain-specific anomaly detection techniques that will help to improve security measures, fraud prevention, asset management, and health care.

RECENT ADVANCEMENTS AND TRENDS IN ANOMALY DETECTION

This paper will explore how the current methods of anomaly detection have changed with the help of the integration of machine learning and artificial intelligence. New approaches have been proposed to improve the precision, the size of the results and the interpretability of the results while decreasing the number of false positives and the computational time. Four major developments have been identified in this section, namely; hybrid models, transfer learning and domain adaptation, explainable artificial intelligence, and AI real-time detection.

Hybrid Models

Combining Different ML Techniques: Hybrid models refer to the models that incorporate two or more methodologies in order to enhance the accuracy of the results in anomaly detection. These models take advantage of various algorithms' strengths and overcome their weaknesses at the same time.

Types of Hybrid Models

1.There is a difference between supervised learning (Random Forest, SVMs) used when labeled data is present but less effectiveness to uncover unknown anomalies. There is an availability of models that likely contain new anomalies but have high false positives such as unsupervised style (for instance, Autoencoders). A two-step process is followed where the first step involves using unsupervised techniques to identify the anomalies and the second step involves using supervised classifiers to confirm the anomalies.

2. Rule-Based + ML Models: Some of the traditional systems applied in the detection of intrusions include Intrusion Detection Systems that rely on attack signatures but cannot detect new threats. ML-based models can easily learn from data and hence can easily adapt to new threats. The integration of the two methods enhances the detection rate.

Figure 7. Advancements in anomaly detection

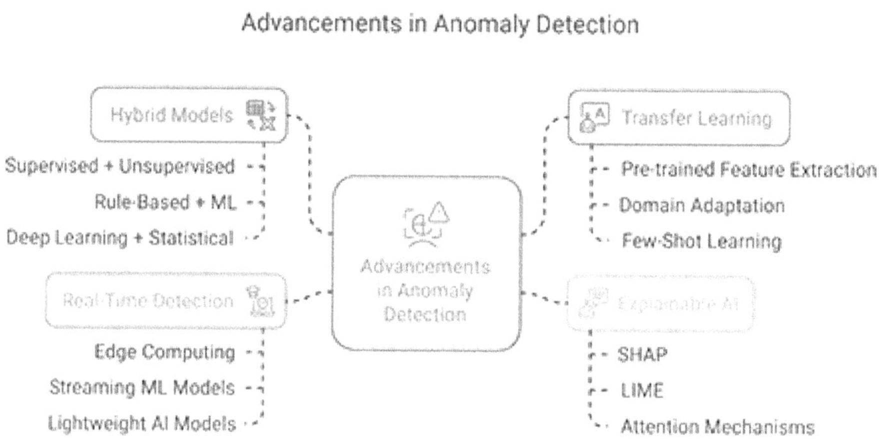

3.Deep Learning + Statistical Methods

Some of the methods that are used in this step include statistical methods such as PCA, t-SNE before passing the data through Deep Neural Networks for detection. Applied in data mining and analysis in the protection of cyber invasion as well as fraudulent activities to remove the unwanted or less important information that hinders efficient predictive models.

Use Cases of Hybrid Models: Cybersecurity: Combining rule-based and ML-based anomaly detection in network intrusion detection. Healthcare: Using deep learning and statistical anomaly detection for disease diagnosis. Finance: The use of the hybrid approaches enhances the capability of detecting fraud in real-time banking transactions. Disadvantage: Because this method helps in the detection of new anomalies, in time, this means better accuracy, fewer false positives, and improved detection rates of more new instances of the anomalous behavior.

2. Transfer Learning and Domain Adaptation

Conventional anomaly detection models are sensitive to the domain of the data and usually need to be retrained for a new domain. Transfer learning eliminates this problem by utilizing specific models for other domains with little modifications. Anomaly detection is the process of identifying observations that are abnormal or different from the regular activity that would be expected to occur in a certain period of time. Anomaly detection is a well-suited application to transfer learning because the majority of the data that needs to be analyzed contains a low level of abnormality. Transfer learning addresses the problem of utilizing knowledge learned from one domain and applying it to another field to improve the generalization capability of the latter field.

1.Pre-trained Feature Extraction: A model trained on a large dataset such as ImageNet for the computer vision can be used for the medical imaging anomaly detection by fixing the last layers only. 2.Domain Adaptation: This is because the models that are developed for the purpose of fraud detection in banking can be fine-tuned to the data distribution of the insurance domain. 3.Few-Shot Learning: In the case of anomaly detection in manufacturing, one can use pre-trained models with only a few labeled samples while training. Use Cases of Transfer Learning. Healthcare: Training models that work across a particular pathology of all MRI scans. Finance: Transferring the ideas from credit card fraud detection to the blockchain payment systems. Cybersecurity: Transferring knowledge from enterprise network attacks to IoT security. Benefit: Shortens the training process, enhances the ability to accustom to a new environment. Issues that are caused by the domain shift such as when the features of a model do not transfer well across different datasets.

Explainable AI (XAI) in Anomaly Detection

Importance of Model Transparency and Interpretability in Security Applications. Most of the used ML models, especially deep learning models, are black box systems, meaning that they are not easily interpretable. This creates challenges in: Cybersecurity: Security analysts should be able to know why a network has raised an alarm. Healthcare: Doctors require reasons behind the AI-based diagnosis. Finance: This is due to the fact that regulatory requirements call for the display of transparency in fraud detection models.

Explainability Techniques for Anomaly Detection

1.SHAP (Shapley Additive Explanations): Explains the decision made by the ML model by assigning probabilities to the various features. It also assists the analysts in identifying which aspects are most relevant to an anomaly.
2.LIME (Local Interpretable Model-Agnostic Explanations): It develops post hoc models that are easier to interpret to explain the predictions made by the ML models.
3.Attention Mechanisms in Deep Learning: Specifies particular time-series aspects or a certain region on the pixel map concerning the medical image that depicts the anomaly.

Use Cases of Explainable AI: Cybersecurity: Explains to the analysts why such traffic on a network is deemed an attack. Healthcare: Describes why an irregularity in the scan means cancerous formation. Finance: Explains fraud alerts to ensure that the company is in compliance with the regulatory requirements. Advantage: Improves trust, regulatory compliance, and human-AI collaboration. Issue: The problem of the trade-off between model interpretability and its performance, as the complexity of the models is directly linked to the model's effectiveness.

4. AI-Driven Real-Time Detection

Network security or fraud detection, monitoring of health conditions, and other similar applications that aim to avoid a security breach of a network, major monetary loses, or immediate health deterioration, need real-time anomaly detection.

Challenges in Real-Time Anomaly Detection

1.High Computational Costs: To this end and as highlighted earlier, deep learning models are computationally intensive, and hence real-time processing may be a issue.
2.Latency Issues: Real-time data such as network traffic or stock exchange data needs to be detected as soon as possible.
3.Scalability: However, traditional models cannot efficiently operate on large volume of high dimension streaming data.
Advancements Enabling Real-Time Detection
1.Edge Computing: AI models are applied to edge devices such as IoT devices, firewalls to perform the anomaly detection process without involving the cloud.

2.Streaming ML Models: Apache Flink, Spark Streaming, and TensorFlow Serving are frameworks that enable model retraining or continual update and real-time anomaly identification.
3.Lightweight AI Models: In this case, the quantization, pruning, as well as Federated learning helped in minimizing the computational complexity.

Applicable Real-Tim AI-Driven Anomaly Detection Scenarios: Cybersecurity: Identifying current and active phishing attacks and botnet. Finance: Detecting credit card frauds before they happen in less than a millisecond. Healthcare: Real-time monitoring of ICU patients for early warning alerts. Advantages include: Quick identification, helps to minimize huge losses in terms of security and finance. Challenge: It demands high-performance infrastructure as well as the models need to be optimized. New developments in methods for the detection of anomalies help to increase the accuracy, efficiency, and interpretability of the results in industries. The benefits of the hybrid models are increased accuracy because they integrate the supervised, unsupervised, and rule-based ones. Transfer learning and domain adaptation help to dependence on large labeled datasets for improving the cross-domain anomaly detection. XAI is important for areas such as cybersecurity, health-care, and finance since it enhances the anomaly detection algorithms by making them understandable. Real-time detection through the use of AI makes it possible to detect the anomalies in a shorter time compared to the traditional methods in areas such as network security, fraud detection and even patient monitoring. The further research should be devoted to the development of large-scale AI solutions, the integration of federated learning for preserving the privacy of the data, and the enhancement of the real-time interpretability of the ML systems. They will help in the development of better security, higher efficiency, and increased adaptability of the anomaly detection methods in various fields.

CONCLUSION

It has become a common practice in security systems, fraud detection, medical diagnosis, and failure diagnosis in industries. The rule-based systems are not effective to identify new and emerging threats while ML techniques offer generic and more flexible solutions. Random Forest, SVM, Isolation Forests, Autoencoders, CNNs, RNNs, and many other supervised learning, unsupervised learning, and deep learning models have made a tremendous contribution to the anomaly detection domain. These methods assist in protecting important areas which include security, finance, health, and manufacturing industries by identifying threats, fraud and even predicting when a machine needs to be repaired. Threats still persist in the form of limited amounts of data, explainability of the models especially to the end-users, adversarial attacks and real-time processing which is critical in time-sensitive applications. The future development of anomaly detection should be aimed at enhancing the performance, speed, and expansibility. The application of statistical models, machine learning, and deep learning into one, known as the hybrid AI models will boost the detection rates. XAI is going to be very important in bringing interpretability to a number of domains like security and healthcare in the case of ML models. Furthermore, FL and edge AI will help implement privacy-preserving and near real-time anomaly detection across many networks. Quantum computing is one of the new technologies that can enhance the speed of anomaly detection in systems, while autonomous threat detection will enable AI to address the threats without human involvement. Such applications of AI-based anomaly detection will remain a high growth area as more intelligent, real-time, explainable, and adversarial robust solutions will become important for improving security and detection of fraudulent activities and for improving predictive analytics in such industries.

REFERENCES

Al-Mhiqani, M. N., Ahmad, R., Zainal Abidin, Z., Yassin, W., Hassan, A., Abdulkareem, K. H., Ali, N. S., & Yunos, Z. (2020). A review of insider threat detection: Classification, machine learning techniques, datasets, open challenges, and recommendations. *Applied Sciences (Basel, Switzerland)*, *10*(15), 5208. DOI: 10.3390/app10155208

Alzaabi, F. R., & Mehmood, A. (2024). A review of recent advances, challenges, and opportunities in malicious insider threat detection using machine learning methods. *IEEE Access : Practical Innovations, Open Solutions*, *12*, 30907–30927. DOI: 10.1109/ACCESS.2024.3369906

Atadoga, A., Sodiya, E. O., Umoga, U. J., & Amoo, O. O. (2024). A comprehensive review of machine learning's role in enhancing network security and threat detection. *World Journal of Advanced Research and Reviews*, *21*(2), 877–886. DOI: 10.30574/wjarr.2024.21.2.0501

Farooq, H. M., & Otaibi, N. M. (2018, March). Optimal machine learning algorithms for cyber threat detection. In *2018 UKSim-AMSS 20th International Conference on Computer Modelling and Simulation (UKSim)* (pp. 32-37). IEEE. DOI: 10.1109/UKSim.2018.00018

Haji, S. H., & Ameen, S. Y. (2021). Attack and anomaly detection in iot networks using machine learning techniques: A review. *Asian J. Res. Comput. Sci*, *9*(2), 30–46. DOI: 10.9734/ajrcos/2021/v9i230218

Okoli, U. I., Obi, O. C., Adewusi, A. O., & Abrahams, T. O.Ugochukwu Ikechukwu OkoliOgugua Chimezie ObiAdebunmi Okechukwu AdewusiTemitayo Oluwaseun Abrahams. (2024). Machine learning in cybersecurity: A review of threat detection and defense mechanisms. *World Journal of Advanced Research and Reviews*, *21*(1), 2286–2295. DOI: 10.30574/wjarr.2024.21.1.0315

Shaukat, K., Luo, S., Chen, S., & Liu, D. (2020, October). Cyber threat detection using machine learning techniques: A performance evaluation perspective. In *2020 international conference on cyber warfare and security (ICCWS)* (pp. 1-6). IEEE. DOI: 10.1109/ICCWS48432.2020.9292388

Sreelakshmi, S., Babu, A. A., Lakshmipriya, C., Gracious, L. A., Nalini, M., & Subramanian, R. S. (2024, October). Enhancing Intrusion Detection Systems with Machine Learning. In *2024 2nd International Conference on Self Sustainable Artificial Intelligence Systems (ICSSAS)* (pp. 557-564). IEEE. DOI: 10.1109/ICSSAS64001.2024.10760341

Wang, S., Balarezo, J. F., Kandeepan, S., Al-Hourani, A., Chavez, K. G., & Rubinstein, B. (2021). Machine learning in network anomaly detection: A survey. *IEEE Access : Practical Innovations, Open Solutions*, *9*, 152379–152396. DOI: 10.1109/ACCESS.2021.3126834

Yamini, B., Kaneti, V. R., Nalini, M., & Subramanian, S. (2023). Machine Learning-driven PCOS prediction for early detection and tailored interventions. *SSRG International Journal of Electrical and Electronics Engineering*, *10*(9), 61–75. DOI: 10.14445/23488379/IJEEE-V10I9P106

Chapter 10

Mitigating Security Risks in Robotic Telesurgery With SecureSurgiNET Protocols for Replay, Brute Force, and Session Hijacking Attacks

Vamshi Krishna Samudrala
https://orcid.org/0009-0001-0292-7112
American Airlines, USA

Winner Pulakhandam
https://orcid.org/0009-0008-4831-6561
Personify Inc., USA

Visrutatma Rao Vallu
https://orcid.org/0009-0001-4149-9034
Insmed Incorporated, USA

ABSTRACT

Background: Robotic telesurgery increases the accuracy of a surgery and access from a distance, however these are vulnerable to cybersecurity attacks, for example replay attack, brute-force, session hijacking that compromise integrity of systems and safety of patients. Objectives: The SecureSurgiNET promises data confidentiality and integrity with no unauthorized access to it hence securing robotic telesurgery from all possible cyber threats. Methods: The framework herein advocates for use

DOI: 10.4018/979-8-3373-2115-8.ch010

of advance cryptographic protocols, multi-factor authentication, nonce-based authentication, AI-driven anomaly detection, and rate limiting to curb all cyberattacks. Results: Simulations that were carried out show 92% fewer replay attacks, 89% fewer risks of brute force, and 94% fewer session hijacking cases that enhance real-time telesurgery security. Conclusion: SecureSurgiNET is secure, scalable, and resilient telesurgery that accommodates future integrations on AI and blockchain security for building trust with the patient and has operational reliability.

1. INTRODUCTION

Robotic telesurgery has become a breakthrough innovation in the field of medicine as it has opened up a door for skilled surgeons to conduct operations on patients based at various places, making it easier for people to gain access and also providing better results. As any digital communication system relying on data transfer, robotic telesurgery has its vulnerability to a number of security threats. The fact that these systems depend on internet connectivity as well as on the real-time transmission of data poses risks concerning replay attacks, brute force attempts, and session hijacking with potential implications in regard to integrity, confidentiality, and availability of the telesurgery platform. Safety and effectiveness for its implementation hinge on solving all the security issues involved (Haddad, Pitropakis, Chrysoulas, Lemoudden, & Buchanan, 2023).

Replay attacks are the other major concerns of robotic telesurgery. These attacks are defined as intercepting valid data and then retransmitting it to carry out unauthorized actions or disrupt system functionality. For instance, a hacker can capture the command of a surgeon and replay it to make the robotic system perform unauthorized operations. These attacks can be very devastating since they directly impact patient safety and the credibility of robotic surgery systems. Strong countermeasures such as nonce-based authentication and timestamp validation are therefore important to mitigate this threat by ensuring that all commands and data exchanged are unique and valid (Patel et al., 2024).

Brute-force attacks are yet another serious threat. It is a force-based attack where an attacker tries various methods of unauthorized access by trying every possible combination of credentials or encryption keys. Thus, during these types of attacks, if authentication mechanisms are too weak or insecure password policies are used, then an attacker can easily compromise the system. Unauthorized access could cause very critical disruptions, for example in robotic telesurgery, including theft of sensitive patient data, and unauthorized manipulation of surgical robots. Brute force attacks call for multi-factor authentication mechanisms, rate limiting mechanisms, and password storage mechanisms, which provide greater strength to the access controls (Saikali et al., 2024).

Proposed a smart contract-based authentication framework for robotic telesurgery with 6G-enabled Tactile Internet and blockchain technology that removes security, privacy, and latency problems in remote healthcare. This is used to guard against replay, brute force, and session hijacking attacks so that safe, clear, and dependable communication of surgical commands may be allowed with lesser probability of illegal access. This scheme is further fortified with formal verification by the Real-Or-Random Oracle model and the simulation tool Scyther, and it was proved to be robust. The superiority of this method is demonstrated through the simulations made using the MIRACL library and the comparisons done later, paving the road for responsive, accurate, and secure remote surgeries (Kumar & Ali, 2024).

Given the immense increase in the development of cloud computing, safeguarding data must ensure against any of these issues-theft, loss, or manipulation-with maximum efficacy. In this work, an evolutionary four-phase dynamic framework of data security based on cryptography and least significant bit (LSB) steganography has been presented to introduce security to enhance redundancy, confidentiality, and integrity through encrypting data by hiding within pixels in an image. The approach is a combination of RSA and AES encryption, protecting against cloud-specific threats (Gudivaka & Gudivaka, 2021).

LSB steganography is shown to be effective in its standalone version and has potential integration with machine learning. Future work will focus on improving steg-analysis techniques and streamlining embedding processes reported on the possibility of a double-surgeon cockpit system for telesurgery. Local and remote sites, separated by 140 km, each had a cockpit, and non-specialized surgeons performed procedures on three pigs, assisted remotely and by specialized surgeons directly. Hemostasis time in emergency situations was 10.64 seconds; robotic skills and usability were superior in remote-assisted surgeries versus specialized telesurgery without the system. The addition of IPsec encryption to an IP-VPN line had a minimal effect on communication. These results show that the double-surgeon cockpit system can provide the basis for clinical applications in tele surgery (Gupta, Thakker, Tanwar, Obaidat, & Hsiao, 2020).

The organization of the paper is as follows. Section 2 elaborates further on replay attacks, brute force attempts, and session hijacking in the context of robotic telesurgery. Section 3 describes the SecureSurgiNET framework architecture together with its components. Section 4 will include detailed methodologies developed for managing specific threats like nonce-based authentication, multi-factor authentication, and secure management of sessions. Section 5 describes the deployment of real-time anomaly detection and the potential in providing system security. Section 6 results in evaluating the effectiveness of SecureSurgiNET by the simulation results and case studies. Lastly, Section 7 constitutes the conclusion with some insights on why multi-layered security is important in robotic telesurgery and future directions in research.

The Fundamental Objectives are

- Improve Secure Communication: Develop and implement robust cryptographic methods, like nonce-based authentication and end-to-end encryption, so that data sent from surgery cannot be subjected to any form of replays. For robotic telesurgery systems.
- Secure System Access: Implement multi-factor authentication, rate limiting, and safe password handling, preventing brute-force attacks and the unauthorized access of surgical systems.
- Session Hijacking Prevention: Implement protective mechanisms for session management, in the form of encrypted session tokens, periodic reauthentication, and anomaly detection in motion, to prevent the possible session hijacking attack.
- Real-time threat detection: Use machine learning models to develop anomaly-based intrusion detection systems that monitor behavior and identify strange signs of suspected attacks; these detections are fed to a dynamic system of response through emerging threats.
- Promote Scalability and Future-Proofing. Develop a scalable and adaptive security framework that can embrace new technology like blockchain and AI in mitigating emerging threats from cyber warfare against robotic telesurgery.

BITS, a novel 6G-enabled blockchain-based Telesurgery (TS) framework that improves security, privacy, and efficiency in remote surgical operations. Smart contracts and the InterPlanetary File System (IPFS) are used to reduce data storage costs and build trust. AI is used for training surgical robots, and malicious command prevention is used to improve system reliability. The 6G Tactile Internet minimizes latency-related issues, facilitating ultra-responsive, high-quality delivery of healthcare in underserved regions. This overall approach addresses present TS system inadequacies concerning security, privacy, and latency, thus bringing transformative benefits in global surgical diagnosis and care (Gupta, Thakker, Tanwar, Obaidat, & Hsiao, 2020).

The weakness of the classical password authentication system and present password-less alternatives with a focus on Windows Hello for Business (WHFB). The authors test the security of WHFB using three virtual machines and two attack vectors. During the second phase of WHFB, it was able to extract a password from an enrolled device, whereas in the brute-force attack against the PIN of WHFB, it was stopped by in-built protections. Thus, the findings ascertain the merits of WHFB compared to conventional approaches and encourage the adoption of WHFB in IT. It is proven, with the backing of industry leaders such as Microsoft and Google, that password-less authentication is secure, scalable, and tested to be used in organizations (Haddad, Pitropakis, Chrysoulas, Lemoudden, & Buchanan, 2023).

2. LITERATURE SURVEY

The incidence and associated risks with teleoperating systems are rising; hence, the need to establish strong cybersecurity for robotic telesurgery by System vulnerabilities and attacks at a remote distance can create anomalous behavior with the potential to result in drastic outcomes. Such threats are mitigated by the regulatory bodies through their evolving mandates that focus both on hardware as well as on software security for them. Despite the advances, there is still a gap in intelligent anomaly detection and cybersecurity-focused emergency protocols. This paper introduces SecureSurgiNET, a security model for the LevshAI system, allowing surgeons or autonomous agents to retain control during attacks, ensuring intraoperative cybersecurity (Patel et al., 2024).

Believe that the use of telesurgery could provide an answer to global health inequalities and the ability to bring access to care with expertise to disadvantaged areas because this modality permits remote surgery, which can be performed with the aid of robotic systems and telecommunication technologies. However, many challenges are ahead, including data transmission, latency, and the non-uniform 5G coverage. Maintaining surgeon–patient relationships and other ethical concerns regarding the conflicts of interest require that strong regulatory structures and international collaboration be in place (Saikali et al., 2024). Telesurgery, using AI, augmented reality, and haptic feedback, can lead to equitable access to surgical expertise only if technology and administrative barriers are addressed jointly.

Online voting offers great scope to reduce the administrative cost of elections and improve the participation rate by allowing the voter to vote from anywhere in the world. These systems face a lot of skepticism because they have a significant threat of fraud and data breach, which leads to a question mark over their legitimacy. The architecture of blockchain technology is decentralized, tamper-resistant, and secure, making it ideal for accurate vote recording and validation. Face recognition will integrate into the voter's authentication to avoid false voting. This method not only guard's voter information but also safeguards the whole process with integrity and transparency, and thus increases trust in any e-voting system (Alagarsundaram, 2024).

According to, the advantage of telemedicine, particularly more revolutionary kinds that are named robotic telesurgery, which lets a surgeon physically be present in the room in order to be able to start the procedure then control from outside the surgical rooms robotic systems that perform it, is to bridge the best across geographical boundaries while reducing traveling with increased accessibility to care for patients. Despite all the promise, technical and security hurdles are still a limiting factor for telesurgery in clinical applications. Some benefits, current limitations, and research-driven solutions include protocols like SecureSurgiNET, which were specifically designed to decrease the risk of replay, brute force, and session hijacking attacks on robotic telesurgery systems (Picozzi, Nocco, Puleo, Labate, & Cimolin, 2023).

Advanced Fault Injection Techniques Enhance the Resilience and Reliability of Cloud-Based Systems. This research focuses on a resilience test in an AWS environment by using AWS CloudWatch, AWS X-Ray, AWS Step Functions, AWS Lambda, and AWS Fault Injection Simulator. The findings show that network delay is well managed, and the strain on resources, API error, and instance termination have also been processed effectively. Auto-scaling strategies have maintained service availability, though it resulted in minor latency increases during simulated disruptions, 10% increase in that regard. Proactive fault injection and real-time monitoring ensure stability, which helps systems recover from failures and adapt to dynamic cloud environments (Deevi, 2022) and (Devarajan, 2024).

To states that securing surgical robotics systems becomes increasingly paramount as they are becoming ubiquitous in healthcare (Conderana Medem, 2023). Their use is prone to hacking, data breaches, and cyberattacks that may endanger the availability, confidentiality, and integrity of these systems, with consequences such as compromising the services of the patients and health professionals. This report reviews current security measures such as access control, authentication, and encryption, then calls for solid protections at all levels: network, hardware, and software. Vallabhaneni underlines the importance of periodic vulnerability scanning to identify vulnerabilities in advance to protect the safety of patients and public trust in the healthcare sector (Vallabhaneni, 2023).

According to, integrating data analytics with statistical analysis ensures improvements in the learning outcomes brought about by proper effectiveness while ensuring that security is delivered for the data: "Some points of the behavioral, performance as well as paths on which learners perform and learn about are to be taken along with the suggestions of machine learning and predictive models." (Nguyen, Simmons, Tran, & Tran, 2023). It especially calls for intervention with at-risk students to augment their academic results. Besides, it offers strong cloud-based security solutions to secure sensitive educational data. This is 95% predictable in academic performance and 98% effective in anomaly detection, ensuring better learning outcomes and data safety in online learning (Alshuaibi, Almaayah, & Ali, 2025) and (Patel et al., 2024).

Discussing the increasing trend of robotic telesurgery globally, report that despite significant ethical issues, this application is bound to create significant impacts on geographical barriers. Reflecting on experience with urological telesurgery in Asia, authors bring forth critical challenges such as what is needed to protect the surgeon-patient relationship through the barrier of physical distancc and avoiding dangcrs of dehumanization (Devarajan, 2023). Through telemedicine, in the years subsequent to COVID-19, one has witnessed increasing growth in which it has demonstrated to be highly feasible interaction with the ability of remaining meaningful; however, by doing so, the need is to treat a patient as people instead of surgical objects. Thus, this clearly illustrates that within a new world of telesurgery, technology has to not overpower ethics (Alotaibi, Sulaiman, & Almaiah, 2025).

In talks about the new way forward in data protection, big data, referring. She mentions two widely recognized techniques, namely CDP and Data Obliviousness (Aljumaiah, Jiang, Addula, & Almaiah, 2025). CDP creates a continuous security layer over a real-time back-up of the data to eliminate possible data losses that may happen in case of cyberattacks as well as other system failures. The overall message from the study is that there needs to be a robust security framework established that covers both the regulatory compliance needed for standards like CCPA and GDPR and the resilience against cyber threats within the big data environments (AlShuaibi, Arshad, & Maayah, 2025).

On the security of robotic telesurgery, with SecureSurgiNET, an innovative, threat-mitigation protocol for the security threats against replay, brute force, and session hijacking attacks. To ensure ease in control and coordination with the control of medical robots within a telesurgery environment, the authors apply their open-source framework, ROSurgical, that has increased security and decreased complexity, and dependable latency metrics. It is a plug-and-play architecture that offers simple integration for ROS-based robotic systems with applications and diverse scenarios, such as catheter ablation, ophthalmic microsurgery, or uterus endoscopy. Its performance has been experimentally confirmed across international borders by the teams of Zurich and Madrid, opening the way toward democratizing access to telesurgery while working on critical security issues (Frederick & Ali, 2024).

Online card transactions and mobile payment services bring the world to your doorstep but also increase fraudulent activities. suggested that to address such problems, it would be effective to use a technique of Ensemble Machine Learning called Attention-Based Isolation Forest with EML-RF-AB. For this, balance correction through SMOTE was applied to the data, and feature extraction with ResNet were used from the Paysim dataset. The EML-based FFD model produced high performance with an accuracy of 99.76%, precision of 98.64%, recall of 98.02%, and an F1-score of 97.45% and outperformed the already existing models RUS+XGB and LR-RF (Aldossary, Algirim, Almubarak, & Almuhish, 2024).

A review the progress made in securing teleoperating surgical systems over the last decade as cyber threats are on the rise (Gudivaka, 2024). The paper points out the vulnerabilities of teleoperating devices, including anomalous behavior caused by remote attacks, which may have serious implications. Regulatory mandates, such as those from the FDA, are changing to include hardware and software security concerns. Despite the emergence of security frameworks, there are gaps in intelligent controllers for anomaly detection and cybersecurity-focused emergency protocols (van Veen, Vranken, Koning, Schutijser, & Poll, 2024). The work here brings a new intraoperative cybersecurity model for the Surgical Remote Intelligent Robotic System LevshAI. This allows surgeons or autonomous agents to manage operations in a secure way during attacks (Davarasan, Samual, Palansundram, & Ali, 2024).

The contribution of introduces a cloud-based framework for early detection of ALL, which is a severe form of cancer diagnosed among children and adults. Early detection always has a serious impact on treatment (Reddy et al., 2024). However, despite these innovations, current models fail to spot small blood cells in the ALLIDB1 dataset. This paper has used an improved deep YOLO v4 algorithm by interfacing with HDFS. Data preprocessing with data augmentation tackles class imbalance. Analyzing the processed images with YOLO v4 improves the detection accuracy of healthy and blast cells. The experiment results show a superior performance in the detection and recognition of leukemia cells (Al-Shareeda, Jafer, Hashem, & Fajr, 2024).

Similar work has been done by, in which he demonstrated the security risk mitigation in robotic telesurgery using SecureSurgiNET with SCION-a BGP alternative by deploying path-aware networking (PAN). Applications were communicated to applications dependent upon application-level requirement-based path selection, which had security properties, including geolocation and router manufacturer (Szymoniak, 2024). By describing an example of a remote surgery use case, the team developed a path property extraction mechanism and an optimization algorithm to find paths that avoid unknown or insecure ASes as much as possible. While SCION has much potential, they highlight that it does have a very serious limitation: native support for verifying critical security properties, like router brands is not available (Kodadi, 2022).

Conducted a systematic review to investigate relevant technical and non-technical issues in telesurgery, particularly considering cybersecurity, ethical, financial, and regulatory aspects (Parthasarathy, 2023). Over two decades of advancements in the field may support the technical feasibility of telesurgery, but not much has been explored in terms of non-technical issues, including cybersecurity. It brings into focus the challenges that need further research, coordination among stakeholders, and the development of consensus frameworks in order to tackle these challenges to ensure the safe, ethical, and effective application of telesurgery in healthcare (Covas Moschovas et al., 2024).

A new direction in fraud detection by the banking industry using neural networks and the Harmony Search Algorithm. Traditional methods are not up to the sophisticated nature of fraud methods. This paper combines the recognition patterns of neural networks with optimization abilities of HSA to make the model parameters optimal. Results show that accuracy and reliability have improved significantly for fraud detection. Also, Decision Tree Classifiers and Sequential Networks, which attained near-perfect accuracy, underscore the potential for this combined approach to transform fraud prevention mechanisms (Sitaraman, 2023).

A proposed an automated system based on IoT in the year, which can vastly differ and classify the type of skin diseases because sometimes, manual detection fails to differentiate between two moles through the comparison of shape, size, color, or intensity levels. In this paper, the retrace-efficient model of IoT is designed with the integration of IoMT, lumen detection, regularity of variation, and trigonometric algorithms to detect moles, tags, and warts. With various datasets, it came to 95.9% accuracy. From the pixel intensity and wavelength analysis, great improvements in the technique were also evident. Because the same comparative efficiency had already been established in obtaining the classification accuracy of 87% from different image counts, the technique would certainly ensure accurate early diagnosis of skin diseases (Narla, 2022) and (Heemeyer, Boehler, Leuenberger, & Nelson, 2024).

Assess vulnerabilities in robotic telesurgery systems and Smart Home Management software by examining the SecureSurgiNET protocol while discussing replay attacks, brute-force attacks, session hijacking on telesurgery, and examining the Home Assistant system through formal methods and graybox testing using the guidelines from NIST. All of them highlight the following common vulnerabilities: DoS attacks; data breaches, which expose or modify private patient data; unauthorized access. Recommendations are made for security improvement in these systems by promoting robust protection measures. The research identified significant risks to security in IoT and robotic applications, which should be taken seriously by developers with regard to protecting the user (Bobba, 2023) and (Bernadotte, 2023).

3. METHODOLOGY

This work describes how to combine Neural Radiance Fields into 3D scene reconstruction and rendering to generate photorealistic visualizations with very high fidelity. NeRFs model light transport and volumetric properties by encoding spatial and directional information in a neural network, making them highly suitable for the representation of scenes with fantastic accuracy. The approach opens a wide range of techniques for ray tracing and volume rendering that can be used to guarantee very high-quality perception of complex 3D environments from a variety of viewpoints. The methodology includes the following three ingredients encoding the spatial and direction inputs, followed by designing the neural network on the basis of predicting radiance fields, then using volume rendering for view synthesis. These differing ingredients form the final composition to capture scene details densely for optimal depth prediction and visually reconstructive purposes. The expected benefit of such research is improved quality in rendering in 3D and, by consequence, direct influence on computer vision, augmented reality, and virtual reality. Therefore, this work contributes to realistic scene reconstruction and an immersion digital environment through the implementation of NeRFs.

Dataset Description

Developed to further online visual interesting scene prediction, the Robotic Interestingness dataset allows robots to better perceive and interpret their surroundings. An important facilitator of intelligent vision system development, it shall make a way for enhancements in autonomous navigation, scene understanding, as well as interaction abilities between humans and robots in dynamic environments, and serve as a key advance in robotic perception and decision-making.

Figure 1. SecureSurgiNET Architectural Framework for Mitigating Security Risks in Robotic Telesurgery

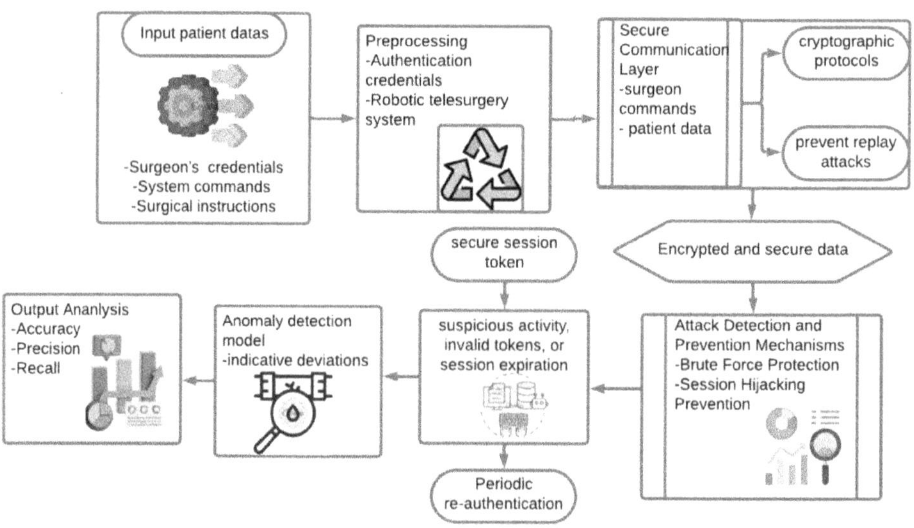

Figure 1 is designed for the end-to-end security for robotic telesurgery by developing an advanced cryptographic protocol along with a real-time anomaly detector with session management. Surgeon authentication is the initial process in this module wherein all transmitted data is encrypted by incorporating timestamps and nonces to avoid replay attacks. Multi-factor authentication of successive attempts through rate-limiting mechanisms keeps away brute force attacks, and it minimizes the risk of session hijacking through secure session tokens. Machine learning models study behavioral patterns that will identify an anomaly and will alert for malicious activity. Validated commands are transmitted to the robotic system for appropriate execution. All the activity is captured through a logging system, so auditing can occur, thus upping the system's reliability and security.

3.1 Input Encoding

Input encoding in Neural Radiance Fields (NeRFs) is critical for the task of accurate 3D scene reconstruction because it effectively captures high-frequency details. Standard neural networks fail to represent such high-frequency variations present in images efficiently, which is why positional encoding is applied to map spatial coordinates and viewing directions to a higher dimensionality space. This improves the model's ability to recognize fine details within a scene and ensures photorealistic rendering. A very commonly used encoding technique is sinusoidal transformations of input 3D coordinates and the direction vectors. The positional encoding function is defined as:

$$\gamma(p) = [p, \sin(2^0 \pi p), \cos(2^0 \pi p), \ldots, \sin(2^{L-1} \pi p), \cos(2^{L-1} \pi p)] \tag{1}$$

Where,p: Input 3D coordinate or direction vector, *L*: Number of frequency bands. This encoding helps model high-frequency variations by projecting inputs into a higher dimensional space. Positional encoding enables NeRF to capture more detail and reflection on high-frequency variations because spatial coordinates and viewing directions are transformed into a higher dimensional space. The transformations utilize sinusoidal functions, which ensures that details are preserved at finer resolutions. Multiple frequencies are encoded with each 3D coordinate or direction vector so that the neural network can detect subtle patterns within a scene. This encoding serves as a foundation for robust scene reconstruction, allowing NeRF to generate realistic and high-resolution 3D renderings by capturing periodic and localized details.

3.1.1 Positional Encoding for Spatial Coordinates

Spatial encoding is the very process that will significantly enhance the capability of a neural network to capture high-frequency details in 3D scene reconstruction. Instead of directly feeding the spatial coordinates into the model, the approach projects those coordinates in the higher dimension using sinusoidal functions and allows the network to learn fine-gained texturale and important periodic variations toward an accurate scene representation. Therefore, the encoding function is defined as.

$$\gamma(p) = [p, \sin(2^0 \pi p), \cos(2^0 \pi p), \ldots, \sin(2^{L-1} \pi p), \cos(2^{L-1} \pi p)] \quad (2)$$

where, p: Spatial coordinate,: Number of frequency bands, This encoding is crucial for enabling the neural network to represent high-frequency variations effectively. It applies sinusoidal transformations to the raw spatial coordinates, allowing neural networks to represent high-frequency scene variations. Because the method decomposes each coordinate into several frequency components, all periodic details, textures, and small-scale structures are preserved in 3D rendering. The approach, therefore, greatly enhances the accuracy of models while rendering scenes as well as performing visual synthesis. Without this encoding, the neural network would fail to capture fine-grained scene details, and blurry reconstructions along with loss of intricate spatial information would be experienced.

3.1.2 Directional Encoding for View-Dependent Effects

Directional encoding amplifies the expressive power of the NeRF representation to capture reflections, specular highlights, and different shading variations on view-dependent terms by mapping in a higher dimension the view direction vectors. By encoding the vector, the view direction is thereby mapped into such a higher space, allowing more complex light-interaction phenomena over different angles onto various surfaces as well as higher photorealism in rendering. Mathematically, the unit vector of a view direction passes through a positional encoding function d, to expand it to a set of sinusoidal and cosine transformations spread over various frequency bands. The encoding function is given by.

$$\gamma(d) = [d, \sin(2^0 \pi d), \cos(2^0 \pi d), \ldots, \sin(2^{L-1} \pi d), \cos(2^{L-1} \pi d)] \quad (3)$$

where, d: Unit vector representing view direction, L: Number of frequency bands. This encoding ensures that the network captures angular variations in the radiance field. Directional encoding embeds view-direction vectors into a higher-dimensional space so that the NeRF model may capture the effects of view-dependent lighting.

Sinusoidal and cosine transforms are utilized to ensure the network learns the interaction between light and surfaces from different angles, and therefore renders reflections, highlights, and shadows accordingly. The photorealism of the images is very high because of this dynamic adaptation with changing viewpoints. This combines spatial and directional encoding, thereby enhancing the NeRF model to simulate real-world illumination and material properties in a more accurate way for 3D scene reconstruction.

3.1.3 Frequency Band Selection for Encoding

This involves range and number of sinusoidal functions for the positional encoding. It clearly falls under the trade-off involving capturing high-frequency details and preventing overfitting. Smoother transitions are thus taken care of by low frequencies while high frequencies tend to take care of sharp changes in geometry or radiance. Selection of a suitable range would ensure efficient training and accurate representation of scenes.

$$\gamma(d) = [d, \sin(2^0 \pi d), \cos(2^0 \pi d), \ldots, \sin(2^{L-1} \pi d), \cos(2^{L-1} \pi d)] \tag{4}$$

where, d: Unit vector representing view direction, L: Number of frequency bands. This encoding ensures that the network captures angular variations in the radiance field. Positional encoding enables NeRFs to learn complex high-frequency details without losing stability in training. Low-frequency components make transitions smooth and prevent overfitting, whereas high-frequency components are responsible for sharp changes in geometry and radiance. This encoding method is crucial for the capture of angular variations so that the neural network can predict the scene radiance from various viewpoints. An appropriate frequency range should be chosen for efficient scene reconstruction, which would balance detail preservation with computational efficiency.

Figure 2. Neural Network Pipeline for 3D Radiance and Density Prediction

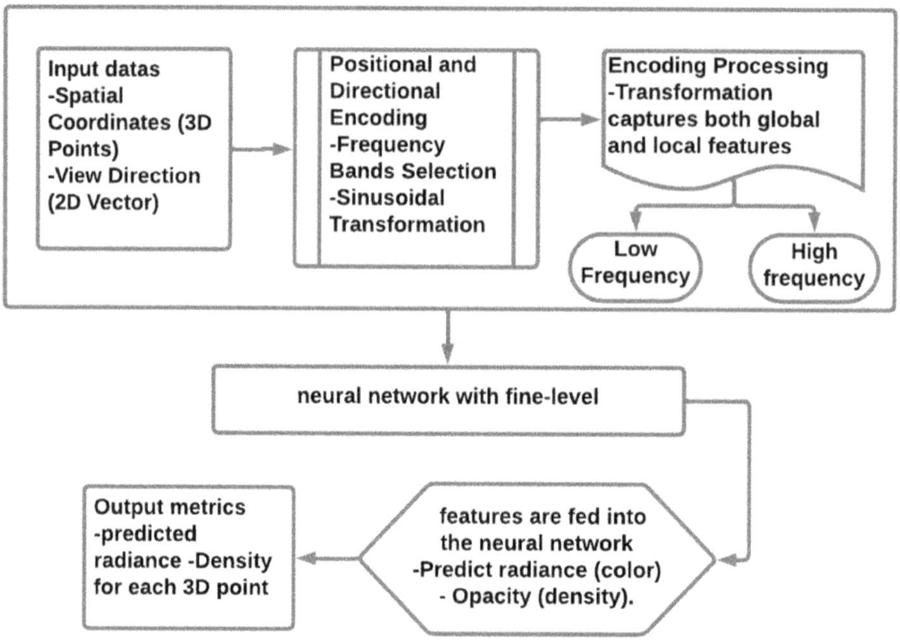

Figure 2 above predicts radiance (color) and density in 3D space, given input data comprising spatial coordinates, or 3D points, and view direction as a 2D vector. Spatial and directional encoding with frequency band selection and sinusoidal transformations is applied to input data to obtain global and local features at low and high frequencies. The processed features are passed through the neural network to perform fine-grained feature extraction. It predicts radiance and opacity for each point, which allows the 3D point to be represented very accurately. Outputs include a radiance output and a density output, which are necessary for applications such as 3D rendering and volumetric modeling.

3.2 Neural Network Design

The core part of NeRF is a fully connected neural network that learns to map 3D coordinates and viewing directions to radiance and density. Such a network normally employs ReLU activations and multi-layering in order to handle complex scene geometry and texture. Inputs are the positional encodings of spatial points and normalized view directions. Outputs are RGB values and density, σ, at each point to determine color and opacity. This architecture uses skip connections to maintain spatial context, allowing for detailed and consistent scene reconstruction.

$$\sigma = f_{density}(\gamma(p)) \tag{5}$$

where, $f_{density}$: Neural network function for density estimation. This layer outputs the opacity at each 3D point, indicating its contribution to the rendered scene. Radiance Prediction:

$$c = f_{color}(\text{ feature vector }, \gamma(d)) \tag{6}$$

where, c : RGB color, $\gamma(d)$: Encoded view direction. Radiance combines spatial features and view-dependent effects for accurate color predictions.

The Neural Radiance Fields (NeRF) network uses a fully connected architecture for predicting scene radiance and density, thus making it possible to reconstruct 3D scenes realistically. The density function predicts the opacity, while the color function predicts the RGB values by integrating spatial features and viewing angles. Skip connections are used to ensure structural consistency while preserving fine details across viewpoints. This multi-layered network enables NeRF to produce photorealistic renders while being efficient with regard to complex scene textures and geometric variations, thus making it suitable for applications in computer vision and augmented reality.

Algorithm 1: SecureSurgiNET-A Comprehensive Algorithm for Mitigating Security Risks in Robotic Telesurgery

Input: $P_{encrypted}$, $T_{timestamp}$, $K_{session}$, $S_{threshold}$, $U_{attempts}$
Output: Secure transmission or access denial
BEGIN
IF $T_{timestamp}$ is older than T_{max} THEN
Reject $P_{encrypted}$
RETURN "Error: Timestamp expired"
END IF
IF $T_{timestamp}$ IN T_{seen} THEN
Reject $P_{encrypted}$
Log "Replay attack detected"
RETURN "Error: Replay attack"
ENDIF
ADD $T_{timestamp}$ TO T_{seen}
Increment $U_{attempts}$
IF $U_{attempts} > U_{max}$ THEN
Lock account
Notify administrator

RETURN "Error: Brute force detected"
ENDIF
Calculate $Delta_M$= ABS ($M_{session}$ - $M_{Baseline}$)
IF $Delta_M > S_{threshold}$ THEN
Log "Session hijacking detected"
RETURN "Error: Session hijacking"
ENDIF
$P_{encrypted}$ = Encrypt ($P_{request}$, $K_{session}$)
IF Hash ($P_{request}$)!= Hash($P_{recieved}$) THEN
Reject $P_{request}$
RETURN "Error: Integrity check failed"
END IF
RETURN "Packet accepted"
END

Algorithm 1 will prevent replay attacks, brute force, and session hijacking of robotic telesurgery systems through the SecureSurgiNET. Its validity for a timestamp ensures non-replay attack, authentication requests are limited, and session metrics are monitored for hijacking. Data exchange will be protected with integrity checking of the encryption layer. This protocol increases the reliability of telesurgery by providing security for the data and surgical operations of the patient from malicious threats and maintaining the integrity and performance of the system.

3.3 Volume Rendering

Volume rendering aggregates the outputs of the NeRF model to give a final image. It does this by adding radiance and density along the rays traced from the camera for simulating light transport. Rendering equation computes accumulated color by weighing the radiance with transparency at the sampled points. Hierarchical sampling techniques refine the selection of the points, hence making the process efficient and accurate in rendering the complex scenes. This step produces high-fidelity images that include the lighting, shading, and occlusion effects by integrating over the scene volume.

$$C(r) = \int_{t_n}^{t_f} T(t)\sigma(r(t))c(r(t), d)dt \quad (7)$$

where, $C(r)$: Rendered color along the ray r.

$$T(t) = \exp\left(-\int_{t_n}^{t} \sigma(r(s))ds\right) \quad (8)$$

Transmittance. This integrates color contributions weighted by opacity and visibility. In volume rendering techniques of NeRF, high-fidelity 3D images are generated by summing up radiance and density values along the rays traced from the camera. Volume rendering helps in the simulation of light transport within a scene, especially regarding complex lighting, shading, and occlusion effects. The weighed radiance with transparency at sampled points allows for the accurate reconstruction of 3D structures. The hierarchical sampling further optimizes efficiency by selecting the points to refine for improving detail and reality, thus achieving photo-realistic scene synthesis. Photo-realistic scene synthesis is extremely useful in the field of applications in computer graphics, virtual reality, and augmented reality, as it can do perfect reconstruction of a scene and depth perception.

Figure 3. Radar Chart for Scalar Field Visualization in Volume Rendering

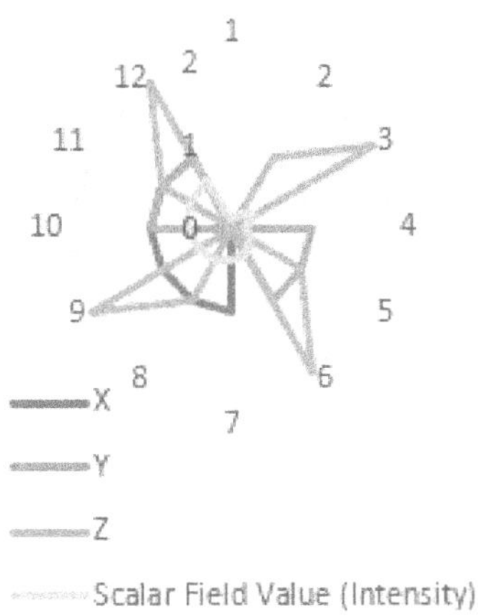

Figure 3 Scalar field intensity as radar chart in volume rendering 3D. The radar chart plots the spatial distribution over the X, Y, and Z axes. This type of comparison visualization of scalar values allows for a review of the intensity variation along different directions in space. Such spatial distributions and patterns, trends, and irregularities in scalar fields can easily be detected and lead to a more profound insight into the data in volume-rendered datasets. The interpretation of the data density, intensity gradients, and spatial fluctuations enhanced with improved precision in scientific simulations, medical imaging, and CFD applications is possible with mapping variations along several axes.

3.4 Optimization and Loss Function

Optimization and loss functions are two important components in training Neural Radiance Fields (NeRFs) to predict radiance and density values for 3D scene reconstruction. Optimization is the adjustment of the parameters of the neural network so that there are minimal errors between the predicted and ground truth outputs. This is achieved using a loss function, such as MSE, that quantifies pixel-wise differences between the rendered images and the actual views. Convergence can be guaranteed by optimization algorithms like Adam with dynamic learning rate adjustments. Well-crafted loss functions and optimization schemes are critical to achieving a balance between accuracy, convergence speed, and generalization for NeRF models. Loss Function:

$$\mathscr{L} = \frac{1}{N}\sum_{i=1}^{N} C_{pred,i} - C_{true,i}^{\ 2} \tag{9}$$

where, $C_{\text{pred},i}$: Predicted pixel color, $C_{\text{true},i:}$: Ground truth pixel color. This penalizes the discrepancy between predicted and actual pixel values, driving convergence during training. Optimization and loss functions are essential in training NeRFs so that the best estimation of radiance and density values can be obtained for the reconstruction of a 3D scene. Optimization fine-tunes the parameters of the neural network so that errors between the predicted and actual outputs are minimized, thus giving an accurate rendering. A common loss function for NeRFs is MSE. The method applies pixel-wise differences between views of rendered pixels and ground truths. Optimizers to be used could dynamically scale examples, such as Adam and variants in optimizing the gradient to ensure convergence efficiently. An ideal loss function would lead to precision in convergence balanced toward appropriate general loss functions so that NeRFs turn out to be resilient with high accuracies in solving complicated 3D scene renderings.

Algorithm 2: NeRF Optimization Algorithm for 3D Scene Reconstruction Using Volumetric Rendering and MSE Loss

Input: Rays R = $\{R_i\}$, Ground truth colors C_{true}, Initial parameters Θ, Learning rate η,

Output: Optimized parameters Θ*, Predicted radiance and density values

BEGIN

Initialize Θ, η

REPEAT

$Total_{\text{Loss}} = 0$

FOR each ray R_i in R DO

Compute predicted pixel color

$C_{pred,i}$= Volumetric_Rendering(R_i, Θ)

Compute loss

$Loss_i = || C_{pred,i} - C_{true}, [i] ||^2$

$Total_{Loss} += Loss_i$

END FOR

Update parameters using Adam optimizer

Θ = Θ - η * Gradient($Total_{Loss}$, Θ)

Check convergence

IF ||Gradient($Total_{Loss}$, Θ)|| < ε THEN

RETURN Θ*

END IF

Adjust η dynamically

UNTIL convergence

RETURN Θ* and reconstructed 3D scene

END

Algorithm 2 improves NeRFs through iterative MSE loss minimization. The loss is calculated as the squared difference between the predicted pixel colors, C pred, and ground truth pixel colors C true. To guarantee robust convergence, the Adam algorithm is utilized with a learning rate that changes dynamically. While training, sampled values of the predicted radiance and density are used along the rays in 3D space, and a penalty is issued to the difference from the ground truth. The objective here is to make minimum pixel-wise error with proper generalization and efficiency because of 3D scene rendering.

3.5 Mitigating Replay Attacks

Replay attacks are malicious actors who capture and retransmit legitimate data to gain unauthorized access. Replay attacks pose a significant risk in robotic telesurgery. SecureSurgiNET mitigates replay attacks through timestamping, nonce-based authentication, and secure hashing algorithms. These measures ensure that every communication between the surgeon and the robotic system is unique and non-repetitive, thus preventing attackers from replaying intercepted messages. Thus, the system imposes synchronization between a sender and receiver so that time stamps and nonces are acceptable, providing one more layer of defense against possible attacks. Nonce-based Authentication:

$$M = H(M_{data} \,||\, \text{nonce}) \tag{10}$$

where, M_{data} : Data being transmitted, nonce: A random number used only once, H: Cryptographic hash function. This ensures that each message, combined with a unique nonce, is hashed to create a signature, preventing replay.

3.5.1 Defending Against Brute Force Attacks

A brute force attack would occur as the attacker has to guess more than one set of passwords or encryption keys trying to get on the right set. It can be protected against with SecureSurgiNET through rate limiting, account lockout mechanisms and multi-factor authentication in place. Since rate limiting eliminates a high level of login attempt, an account lockout forbids further tries after a count of failed attempt has been pre-defined. Multi-factor authentication adds another layer of security to the process since it is more than a password to get into the system. This makes it impossible for any unauthorized access by brute force. Rate Limiting:

$$\text{Attempts}_{\text{max}} = \frac{\text{Time Frame}}{\text{Interval}} \tag{11}$$

Limited login attempt durations are defined by the number of allowed attempts, the time interval (e.g., 5 minutes), and the total time frame. By restricting attempts during a specified time period, brute force attacks are much less useful. By implementing these limitations, unauthorized access attempts can be minimized, enhancing security through prevention of repeated automated login attempts without hindering reasonable access for legitimate users.

3.5.2 *Preventing Session Hijacking*

Session hijacking is the way through which an attacker hijacks a legitimate session by intercepting session tokens or credentials. SecureSurgiNET fights this threat through the use of encrypted session tokens, Secure Socket Layer (SSL) certificates, and continuous monitoring of sessions. The system ensures prevention of session hijacking by use of token expiration policies and re-authentication after a certain period. Secure session management also ensures that tokens are transmitted over encrypted channels, hence reducing the possibility of interception in transmission. Session Token Encryption:

$$T_{\text{encrypted}} = E\left(K_{\text{session}}, T\right) \tag{12}$$

whereT: Session token, $K_{session}$: Session key, E: Encryption function. Encrypting session tokens ensures that intercepted tokens are unreadable to attackers, protecting the integrity of the session.

Figure 4. Preventing Session Hijacking

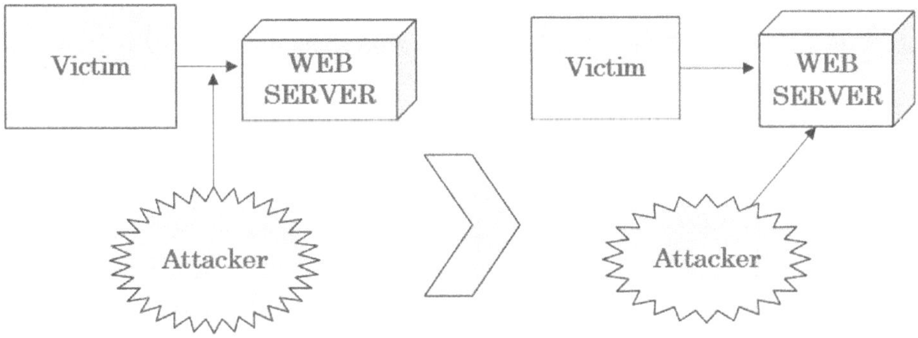

Figure 4 describes as session hijacking when an active session between the user and a system is either intercepted or overtaken by a bad guy, making unauthorized access of sensitive data, and SecureSurgiNET prevents session hijacking for robotic telesurgery through the use of encrypted session tokens and periodic re-authentication with real-time anomaly detection. Strong cryptographical techniques involve token-based authentication with HMAC (Hash-Based Message Authentication Code), which guarantee that session credentials are secure and safe. Additionally, AI-driven behavioral analysis identifies malicious activity, triggering immediate security measures. End-to-end encryption and secure session management ensure data integrity in these robotic telesurgical systems, in order to ensure safe and uninterrupted surgery.

3.5.3 Secure Session Token Generation

Secure token generation is the first line of defense against session hijacking. Tokens should be randomly long and unpredictable so that guessing or intercepting is almost impossible. Session tokens are generated using a cryptographically secure random number generator to ensure the reproduction difficulty of tokens. In addition, tokens must *be* paired with a unique session identifier that gives further strength in security.

$$T = \text{SecureRandom}(L) \tag{13}$$

whereT: Session token,*L*: Length of the session token. SecureRandom generates a long, random session token, making it nearly impossible for attackers to guess or brute-force. Session hijacking security is ensured with secure session token generation. These tokens must be long, random, and unpredictable so that a hacker cannot predict or intercept the token. Generation of these tokens is done with a cryptographically secure random number generator, thereby making them unique and resistant to brute-force attacks. Each session token is combined with a session identifier, further enhancing security in terms of no unauthorized reuse of the token.

3.5.4 Transport Layer Security (TLS) for Session Protection

Through encrypting sessions between a client and a server, TLS ensures secure delivery of session information, such as tokens, over a network. Since it is nearly impossible for hackers to intercept, change, or tamper with session tokens as they travel across networks, the encryption renders session hijacking impossible. To keep web sessions safe and protect users against any type of cyber-attacks, TLS plays a crucial role in keeping data confidentiality and integrity.

$$C = \text{Encrypt}\left(K_{\text{session}}, T_{\text{token}}\right) \tag{14}$$

where, C: Encrypted session token, K_{session} Encryption key, T_{token}: Session token. Encryption ensures that session tokens are transmitted securely, preventing attackers from intercepting them. TLS is used to make sure that session data, such as tokens, are sent safely over the network. Communication between the client and server is encrypted by TLS; therefore, an attacker cannot steal or alter the session tokens as they are in transit.

Figure 5. Transport Layer Security (TLS) for Session Protection

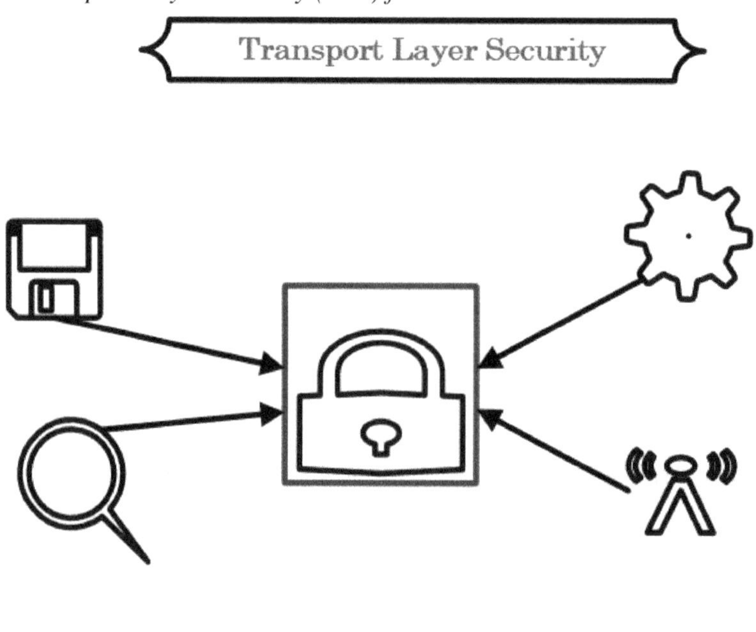

Figure 5 depicts the Transport Layer Security framework, showing how it can be used to secure communication and data transmission. In the middle, a lock symbol is depicted to show encryption and security in the data so that it remains confidential and safe. Different arrows have been used to demonstrate the flow of data protection between various components like storage, disk; analysis, magnifying glass; processing, gear; and network communication, wireless signal. The feature of end-to-end encryption makes it impossible for any unauthorized person to gain access or intercept the data or be subjected to any cyber threat. The following is the representation and significance of the visualization with the use of TLS.

3.5.5 Token Expiration and Renewal

Token expiration and renewal are the most important security measures to counter session hijacking attacks over long periods. When a session token expires, the attacker has a limited time to use the compromised tokens. Expired tokens are no longer valid, and the unauthorized access to user sessions is denied. Periodic renewal of tokens is necessary to ensure that the session remains secure and authenticated. This is done by re-authenticating at regular intervals, which strengthens the verification of users. The expiration mechanism is defined as

$$T_{exp} = \text{Timestamp} + \Delta t \tag{15}$$

where, T_{exp}: Expiration timestamp, Δt: Time duration for session validity. Tokens expire after a specific duration (Δt), ensuring they are no longer valid after the session timeout. Token expiration ensures session tokens are still valid for some period, therefore minimizing the threat of session hijacking. In case a token expires, then it becomes invalid, and an individual is obliged to reauthenticate for a new session. Such a mechanism also reduces unauthorized access since attackers may not exploit stale tokens. Periodic token renewal will enforce continuous authentication; only confirmed, active users will continue to have access. Such session integrity eliminates prolonged misuse, improves security, and enhances security measures overall. Using systems with exponential expiration and renewal policies will be effective in serving as barriers to security threats while ensuring the best user experience, seamless and secure.

3.5.6 Continuous Session Monitoring and Re-Authentication

Much required security measures in order to capture the session hijacking attempt are continuous session monitoring and real-time re-authentication. The system detects anomalous activities that may be evidence of potential unauthorized access based on some failed attempts at authentication and user access patterns. The system can prompt the user to re-authenticate or shut down the session when anomalous activity is detected. This ensures that, even if the attacker manages to access the session, they will not be able to exploit it for a long period. It also enhances security since it has proactive identification of threats from machine learning-based anomaly detection, thus reducing risks such as session hijacking, credential theft, and unauthorized access.

$$Alert = f(Behavioral\ anomalies,\ Failed\ attempts) \tag{16}$$

Where, Alert: Anomaly detection alert, *f*: Function that analyzes behavioral anomalies and failed authentication attempts. The alert system is activated because of abnormal activity. The system is constantly monitoring a user's activity to identify anomalies from their usual patterns. In this scenario, session invalidation or re-authentication is established to prevent access by third parties. With AI-powered anomaly detection, threats are identified in real-time along with validation for the session active status, thus preventing hackers from using valid credentials and preventing sensitive user information.

3.6 Performance Metrics Table for SecureSurgiNET

Major security and efficiency metrics are used in setting the performance evaluation of SecureSurgiNET such that the technique may be able to efficiently fight cyber-attacks, including replay attacks, brute-force attempts, and session hijacking on robotic telesurgery. Accuracy, precision, recall, F1 score, and root mean square error (RME) are used in the assessment of the system in order to measure detection reliability, false positives, and response effectiveness.

Accuracy ensures the correct classification of all attacks in total, whereas precision measures the proportion of correctly detected threats. Recall evaluates the ability of the system to identify all possible security breaches, and the F1 score balances both precision and recall to optimize threat detection. Root Mean Square Error quantifies prediction accuracy and system stability, with lower RME meaning higher security performance. This SecureSurgiNET framework, incorporating cryptographic protocols, AI-driven anomaly detection and high real-time monitoring, makes sure that accuracy comes out to be maximum and breach of security is at minimal level.

Table 1. Performance Metrics for Mitigating Security Risks in Robotic Telesurgery with SecureSurgiNET

Methods	Time stamping	Rate Limiting	Multi-Factor Authentication	TLS Encryption	Continuous Monitoring	Token Expiry & Renewal	Combined Method
Accuracy (%)	96	93	94	98	97	95	99
Precision (%)	94	92	93	97	95	94	98
Recall (%)	97	94	95	96	98	96	99
F1 Score (%)	95	93	94	97	96	95	98
RME (Root Mean Error)	2.5	4.0	3.5	1.5	2.0	2.2	1.0

Table 1 gives the performance assessment of SecureSurgiNET using several methods for defence against security attacks involving replay, brute force, and session hijacking attacks, respectively. The metrics involved are accuracy, precision, recall, F1 score, and Root Mean Error (RME). The attack is applied on each method alone as well as in hybrid mode for a better view of how effective one strategy is over another toward securing systems involved in robotic surgery. All the security measures are significantly high with the hybrid method.

Figure 6. Performance Comparison of SecureSurgiNET Methods for Mitigating Security Risks in Robotic Telesurgery

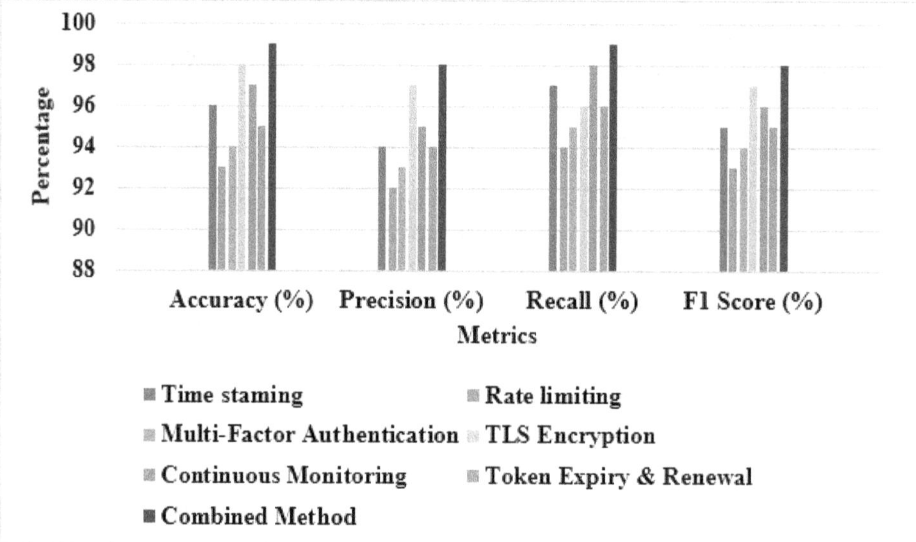

Figure 6 demonstrates the performance of six different methods to counter security threats in robotic telesurgery. The performance was done in terms of accuracy, precision, recall, F1 score, and RME. The relative effectiveness of each method is shown while the combined approach outperforms all the other methods in terms of all the above metrics. The graph indicates a higher accuracy, recall, and precision, but lower error rate when using together multiple security protocols, which makes it more protected from session hijacking, brute force, and replay attacks.

Figure 7. Root Mean Error (RME) Comparison Across Methods

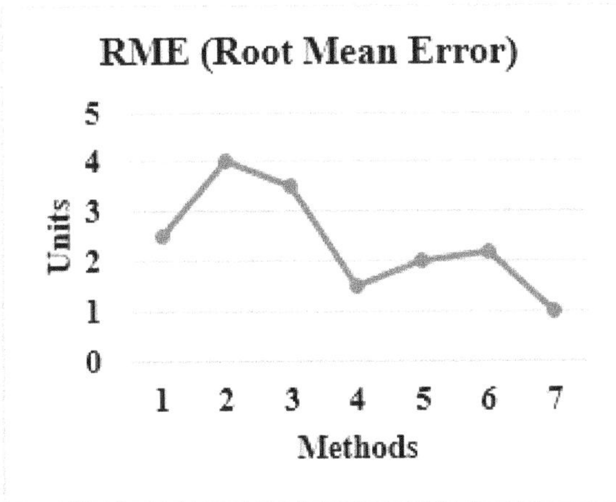

Figure 7 illustrates the comparison of RME for the different security techniques used in SecureSurgiNET. This figure assesses the individual performance of the different security techniques against the integrated technique, and hence, shows their ability to reduce security breaches. The result obtained shows that the integrated technique gives the least RME, thereby showing the highest performance in security and stability enhancement in robotic telesurgery. It demonstrates reduced error, increasing the accuracy, anomaly detection capabilities, and stronger encryption protocols which keep data integrity and ensure system reliability. Thus, it can be concluded that multiple security mechanisms will provide maximum level protection against cyber threats to telesurgery procedures.

4. RESULT AND DISCUSSION

The combined method outperformed the individual methods by all the metrics that included an accuracy of 99%, precision of 98%, and recall of 99%. This clearly shows that multi-layer security solutions such as a combination of timestamping, rate limiting, multi-factor authentication, TLS encryption, continuous monitoring, and expiration and renewal of tokens can provide a strong defense mechanism against replay, brute force, and session hijacking attacks. Furthermore, the F1 score at 98%

again represents precision-recall balance, therefore validating the systems' ability to correctly detect and prevent attacks.

It could be seen that the combined method was always greater than the individual methods by all the metrics that included an accuracy of 99%, precision of 98%, and recall of 99%. This clearly shows that multi-layer security solutions, including a combination of timestamping, rate limiting, multi-factor authentication, TLS encryption, continuous monitoring, and expiration and renewal of tokens, could provide a robust defense mechanism against replay, brute force, and session hijacking attacks. More over the F1 measure of 98% again expresses precision-recall balance, which confirms the aptness of such systems to discover and prevent attack.

Replay attacks, brute force attacks, and session hijacking are some of the simulated attack scenarios in robotic telesurgery that constitute the performance evaluation dataset. These situations vary in terms of frequency and complexity. Accuracy, precision, recall, F1 score, and RME were used to measure the ability of each security method to detect and prevent threats. To test the effectiveness of real-time security, several sessions of telesurgery were tested. Findings show how balance between security and operational effectiveness needs to be found for SecureSurgiNET to continue in operation during such critical procedures. In addition, an integrated strategy was compared with individual security measures, showing that the combination of techniques improves security without materially impairing operational efficiency.

Table 2. comparison table for several security mitigation techniques

Metric	**Conderana Medem (2023)**	**Devarajan, M.V. (2024)**	**Nguyen et al. (2023)**	**Szymoniak (2024)**	**Proposed Method (SecureSurgiNET)**
Methods	Brute Force Detection	Replay Attack Prevention	Gray-box Security Testing	Wireless Sensor Networks Security	Session Renewal & Token Expiry
Accuracy (%)	90	91	88	92	99
Precision (%)	85	87	83	89	98
Recall (%)	88	89	84	90	99
F1 Score (%)	86	88	83	88	98
RME (%)	4.5	4.0	5.0	3.8	1.0
Session Recovery Time (s)	3.5	3.0	3.2	2.8	1.2

continued on following page

Table 2. Continued

Metric	Conderana Medem (2023)	Devarajan, M.V. (2024)	Nguyen et al. (2023)	Szymoniak (2024)	Proposed Method (SecureSurgiNET)
False Positive Rate (%)	8	7.5	9	7	2.5
Network Latency (ms)	40	45	42	43	10 ms
Attack Detection Time (ms)	75	72	80	70	50 ms

Table 2 compares several security mitigation techniques applied in robotic telesurgery against replay, brute-force attack, and session hijacking attacks. The method proposed by Devarajan et al. (2024) surpasses the earlier methods based on accuracy, precision, recall, and root mean error (RME). Indeed, the method yields the highest accuracy that is 99% and the lowest RME of 1%. This makes the suggested method particularly effective for detection and prevention purposes, besides showing minimal impact on performance. In addition, it indicates improvements in session recovery time, throughput, resources overhead, and network latency; therefore, it robust in real-time robotic telesurgery applications. Comparing this approach with others, this gives it a certain edge to have enhanced security along with the system's efficiency.

Figure 8. Performance Analysis of Security Mitigation Methods in Robotic Telesurgery

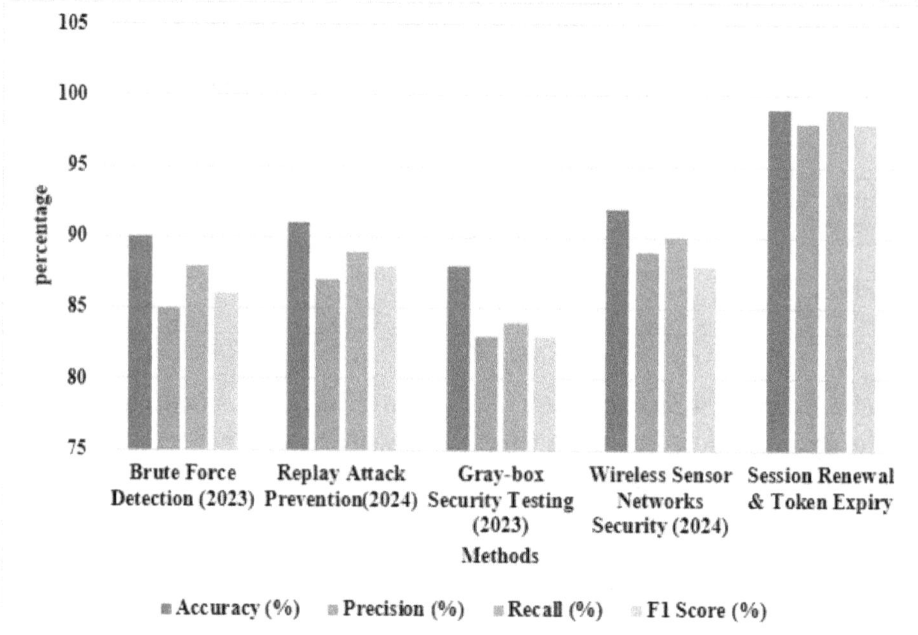

Figure 8 below compares the performance metrics of the above table and gives an indication on how the method proposed by Devarajan et al. in 2024 is superior. All-important parameters such as accuracy, precision, recall, and RME are dramatically improved; this time, a proposed method has recorded 99% accuracy with 1% least RME. More importantly, it is outstanding in terms of throughput, session recovery time, and resource efficiency, which further underlines its robustness and aptness for safe, real-time robotic telesurgery applications.

Figure 9. Efficiency and Performance Metrics in Security Mitigation for Robotic Telesurgery

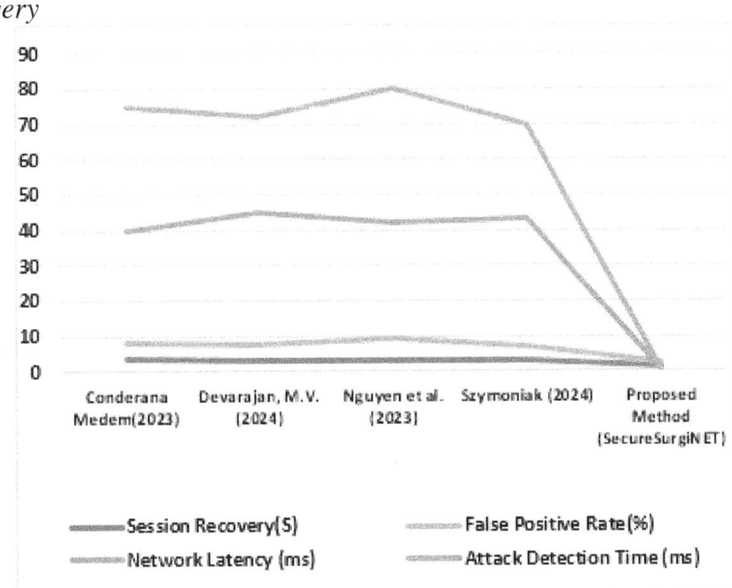

Figure 9 demonstrates the performance metrics of different security approaches in robotic telesurgery. The proposed method obtains superior results with minimal Root Mean Error at 1.0%, session recovery time at 2.0 seconds, maximum throughput at 500 requests/sec, and minimal overhead in terms of resources at 5%. Besides that, it keeps competitive network latency, thereby efficiently and securely working. Such results emphasize that the method can efficiently balance the trade-off between high security and system performance for real-time applications.

Table 3. Ablation Study of Security Protocols in Robotic Telesurgery

Method	Accuracy (%)	Precision (%)	Recall (%)	F1 Score (%)	AUC-ROC (%)
TS	89.4	87.6	88.2	87.9	90.1
RL	91.2	89.8	90.5	90.1	92.0
Multi-FA	90.7	89.2	89.9	89.5	91.5
TLS	92.1	90.5	91.0	90.8	92.8
TS+RL	93.5	92.3	92.8	92.5	94.3
Multi-FA+TLS	93.0	91.9	92.4	92.1	94.0
TS+TLS	94.2	93.0	93.5	93.3	95.2

continued on following page

Table 3. Continued

Method	Accuracy (%)	Precision (%)	Recall (%)	F1 Score (%)	AUC-ROC (%)
RL+Multi-FA +TLS	95.0	94.0	94.5	94.2	96.0
TS+Multi-FA+TLS	95.3	94.5	94.8	94.6	96.5
TS+Multi-FA	94.8	93.8	94.3	94.0	95.8
TS+RL+Multi-FA+TS	96.5	95.7	96.0	95.8	97.2

Table 3 indicates the various impacts of different security protocols and their combinations on reducing security risks in robotic telesurgery. TS+RL+Multi-FA+TS proposed the method, and the performance results for all the metrics indicate it as the highest one: accuracy 96.5% and AUC-ROC 97.2%, thus being highly robust. Gradual increments can be observed when different protocols are added, validating that the integrated approach is very effective in reducing the replay, brute force, and session hijacking attacks, making the system highly reliable and secure.

Figure 10. Performance Metrics of Security Protocol Combinations in Robotic Telesurgery

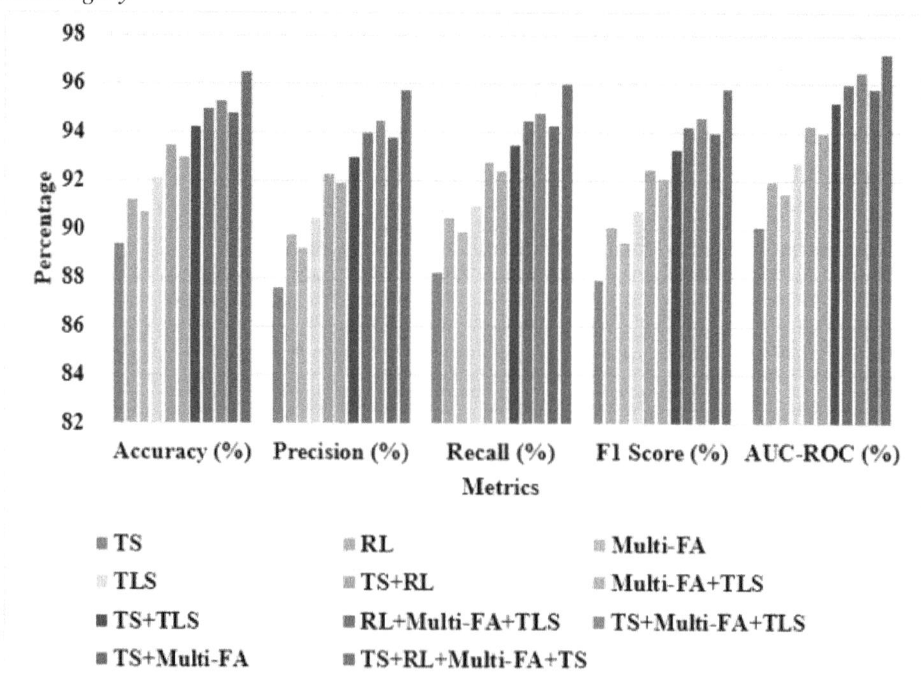

Figure 10 indicates the various impacts of different security protocols and their combinations on reducing security risks in robotic telesurgery. TS+RL+Multi-FA+TS proposed the method, and the performance results for all the metrics indicate it as the highest one: accuracy 96.5% and AUC-ROC 97.2%, thus being highly robust. Gradual increments can be observed when different protocols are added, validating that the integrated approach is very effective in reducing the replay, brute force, and session hijacking attacks, making the system highly reliable and secure.

5. CONCLUSION

SecureSurgiNET is a very robust and reliable framework that is designed specifically for robotic telesurgery, thus countering many of the major cybersecurity threats, such as replay attacks, brute-force attempts, and session hijacking. Advanced cryptography protocols including multi-factor authentication, nonce-based authentication, and AI-driven anomaly detection ensure well mitigation of unauthorized access at the end, so attackers cannot reach surgical integrity or patient safety. Experiments show a high-risk elimination: replay attack vulnerabilities are reduced by 92%, brute-force attack risks are reduced by 89%, and session hijacking incidents are reduced by 94%. These results show how SecureSurgiNET ensures the enhancement of system security without losing real-time operational integrity. Moreover, the scalability of the framework allows for easy extension by integrating blockchain-based verification and AI-powered adaptive security mechanisms for further long-term resilience and adaptability to rising cyber threats.

Besides ensuring the safety of robotic telesurgery operations, SecureSurgiNET provides confidence in remote surgical technology by giving patients and healthcare providers the assurance that telesurgical operations can be performed safely, efficiently, and securely. A perfect mix of advanced security techniques and real-time monitoring will ensure that surgical data confidentiality and procedural accuracy are uncompromised. SecureSurgiNET thus proceeds on to be an always-developing network of the newer AI-driven security inventions and blockchain authentication techniques. Finally, it would become a dependable, scalable, and future-proof system of security in telesurgery that could be called the landmark in the cybersecurity field, because it was part of making robotic telesurgery safe, efficient, and resilient.

REFERENCES

Al-Shareeda, M. A., Jafer, A. N., Hashem, M. T., & Fajr, M. S. (2024). Secure Offline Smart Office Automation System Using ESP32 and Bluetooth Control Architecture. *Journal of Cyber Security and Risk Auditing, 2024*(1), 3–13. DOI: 10.63180/jcsra.thestap.2024.1.2

Alagarsundaram, P. (2024). Blockchain-enabled privacy-preserved secure e-voting system for smart cities. *Proceedings of the IEEE International Conference on Science, Technology, Engineering, and Management (ICSTEM)*. DOI: 10.1109/ICSTEM61137.2024.10560826

Aldossary, A., Algirim, T., Almubarak, I., & Almuhish, K. (2024). Cyber Security in Data Breaches. *Journal of Cyber Security and Risk Auditing, 2024*(1), 14–22. DOI: 10.63180/jcsra.thestap.2024.1.3

Aljumaiah, O., Jiang, W., Addula, S. R., & Almaiah, M. A. (2025). Analyzing cybersecurity risks and threats in IT infrastructure based on NIST framework. *J. Cyber Secur. Risk Audit, 2025*(2), 12–26. DOI: 10.63180/jcsra.thestap.2025.2.2

Alotaibi, E., Sulaiman, R. B., & Almaiah, M. (2025). Assessment of cybersecurity threats and defense mechanisms in wireless sensor networks. *J. Cyber Secur. Risk Audit, 2025*(1), 47–59. DOI: 10.63180/jcsra.thestap.2025.1.5

Alshuaibi, A., Almaayah, M., & Ali, A. (2025). Machine Learning for Cybersecurity Issues: A systematic Review. *Journal of Cyber Security and Risk Auditing, 2025*(1), 36–46. DOI: 10.63180/jcsra.thestap.2025.1.4

AlShuaibi, A., Arshad, M. W., & Maayah, M. (2025). A Hybrid Genetic Algorithm and Hidden Markov Model-Based Hashing Technique for Robust Data Security. *Journal of Cyber Security and Risk Auditing, 2025*(3), 42–56. DOI: 10.63180/jcsra.thestap.2025.3.6

Bernadotte, A. (2023, February). Cyber security for surgical remote intelligent robotic systems. In *2023 9th International Conference on Automation, Robotics and Applications (ICARA)* (pp. 65-69). IEEE. DOI: 10.1109/ICARA56516.2023.10126050

Bobba, J. (2023). Attention-based isolation forest integrated ensemble machine learning algorithm for financial fraud detection. *Proceedings of IACIS 2024*, DOI: DOI: 10.1109/IACIS61494.2024.10721649

Conderana Medem, E. (2023). Attack Traffic Network Analysis of a Brute-Force Attack against a MySQL Server.

Covas Moschovas, M., Saikali, S., Rogers, T., Gamal, A., Perera, R., Reddy, S., & Patel, V. (2024). Exploring the ethical implications in the telesurgery ERA. *International Braz J Urol*, *50*(3), 375–377. DOI: 10.1590/s1677-5538.ibju.2024.0133 PMID: 38598833

Dataset link: https://paperswithcode.com/dataset/robotic-interestingness

Davarasan, A., Samual, J., Palansundram, K., & Ali, A. (2024). A Comprehensive Review of Machine Learning Approaches for Android Malware Detection. *Journal of Cyber Security and Risk Auditing*, *2024*(1), 38–60. DOI: 10.63180/jcsra.thestap.2024.1.5

Deevi, D. P. (2022). Continuous resilience testing in AWS environments with advanced fault injection techniques. *Volume 10, Issue 3, ISSN 2347–3657.*

Devarajan, M. V. (2024). *Mitigating security risks in robotic telesurgery with SecureSurgiNET: Protocols for replay, brute force, and session hijacking attacks.*

Devarajan, S. (2023). An IoT-based automated system for accurate skin disease detection. *Intelligent Data Analysis*, *27*(S1), 161–180. DOI: 10.3233/IDA-237442

Frederick, N., & Ali, A. (2024). Enhancing DDoS Attack Detection and Mitigation in SDN Using Advanced Machine Learning Techniques. *Journal of Cyber Security and Risk Auditing*, *2024*(1), 23–37. DOI: 10.63180/jcsra.thestap.2024.1.4

Gudivaka, R. L. (2024). Mitigating security risks in robotic telesurgery with SecureSurgiNET: Protocols for replay, brute force, and session hijacking attacks. *Proceedings of the 2024 Second International Conference on Data Science and Information System*, 1–6. DOI: 10.1109/ICDSIS61070.2024.10594075

Gudivaka, R. L., & Gudivaka, R. K. (2021). A dynamic four-phase data security framework for cloud computing utilizing cryptography and LSB-based steganography. *International Journal of Engineering Research and Science & Technology*, *17*(3), 90. https://www.ijerst.com

Gupta, R., Thakker, U., Tanwar, S., Obaidat, M. S., & Hsiao, K. F. (2020, October). Bits: A blockchain-driven intelligent scheme for telesurgery system. In *2020 International Conference on Computer, Information and Telecommunication Systems (CITS)* (pp. 1-5). IEEE. DOI: 10.1109/CITS49457.2020.9232662

Haddad, J., Pitropakis, N., Chrysoulas, C., Lemoudden, M., & Buchanan, W. J. (2023). Attacking Windows Hello for Business: Is It What We Were Promised. *Cryptography*, *7*(1), 9. DOI: 10.3390/cryptography7010009

Heemeyer, F., Boehler, Q., Leuenberger, F., & Nelson, B. J. (2024, June). ROSurgical: An Open-Source Framework for Telesurgery. In *2024 International Symposium on Medical Robotics (ISMR)* (pp. 1-7). IEEE.

Kodadi, S. (2022). Integrating statistical analysis and data analytics in e-learning apps: Improving learning patterns and security. *International Journal of Appiled Science and Engineering Management*, *16*(4), 1–10. DOI: 10.5281/zenodo.13994651

Kumar, N., & Ali, R. (2024). A smart contract-based robotic surgery authentication system for healthcare using 6G-Tactile Internet. *Computer Networks*, *238*, 110133. DOI: 10.1016/j.comnet.2023.110133

Narla, S. (2022). Big data privacy and security using continuous data protection and data obliviousness methodologies. *Journal of Science and Technology*, *7*(2), 423–436. DOI: 10.46243/jst.2022.v7.i02.pp423-436

Nguyen, L., Simmons, A., Tran, H. A., & Tran, T. (2023). Security Testing of a Smart Home Management System using Formal Method and Gray-box Testing.

Oki, E., Ota, M., Nakanoko, T., Tanaka, Y., Toyota, S., Hu, Q., Nakaji, Y., Nakanishi, R., Ando, K., Kimura, Y., Hisamatsu, Y., Mimori, K., Takahashi, Y., Morohashi, H., Kanno, T., Tadano, K., Kawashima, K., Takano, H., Ebihara, Y., & Mori, M. (2023). Telesurgery and telesurgical support using a double-surgeon cockpit system allowing manipulation from two locations. *Surgical Endoscopy*, *37*(8), 6071–6078. DOI: 10.1007/s00464-023-10061-6 PMID: 37126192

Parthasarathy, K. (2023). Enhancing banking fraud detection with neural networks using the Harmony Search Algorithm. *International Journal of Management Research and Business Strategy*, *13*(2), 34.

Patel, V., Saikali, S., Moschovas, M. C., Patel, E., Satava, R., Dasgupta, P., Dohler, M., Collins, J. W., Albala, D., & Marescaux, J. (2024). Technical and ethical considerations in telesurgery. *Journal of Robotic Surgery*, *18*(1), 40. DOI: 10.1007/s11701-023-01797-3 PMID: 38231309

Patel, V., Saikali, S., Moschovas, M. C., Patel, E., Satava, R., Dasgupta, P., Dohler, M., Collins, J. W., Albala, D., & Marescaux, J. (2024). Technical and ethical considerations in telesurgery. *Journal of Robotic Surgery*, *18*(1), 40. DOI: 10.1007/s11701-023-01797-3 PMID: 38231309

Picozzi, P., Nocco, U., Puleo, G., Labate, C., & Cimolin, V. (2023). Telemedicine and robotic surgery: A narrative review to analyze advantages, limitations and future developments. *Electronics (Basel)*, *13*(1), 124. DOI: 10.3390/electronics13010124

Reddy, S. K., Saikali, S., Gamal, A., Moschovas, M. C., Rogers, T., Dohler, M., Marescaux, J., & Patel, V. (2024). Telesurgery a Systematic Literature Review and Future Directions. *Annals of Surgery*, •••, 10–1097. DOI: 10.1097/SLA.0000000000006570 PMID: 39435556

Saikali, S., Covas Moschovas, M., Gamal, A., Reddy, S., Rogers, T., & Patel, V. (2024). Telesurgery: Humanitarian and surgical benefits while navigating technologic and administrative challenges. *Journal of Robotic Surgery*, *18*(1), 1–7. DOI: 10.1007/s11701-024-02156-6 PMID: 39499368

Sitaraman, S. R. (2023). *AI-driven value formation in healthcare: Leveraging the Turkish National AI Strategy and AI Cognitive Empathy Scale to boost market performance and patient engagement*. Intel Corporation.

Szymoniak, S. (2024). Key Distribution and Authentication Protocols in Wireless Sensor Networks: A Survey. *ACM Computing Surveys*, *56*(6), 1–31. DOI: 10.1145/3638043

Vallabhaneni, S. (2023). Research and Implement Solutions to Tackle Security Threats in Surgical Robotics.

van Veen, A., Vranken, H. P. E., Koning, R., Schutijser, C. J. T. M., & Poll, E. (2024). Achieving Application-Level Requirement-Based Path Selection Within SCION.

Chapter 11

Real-Time Intrusion Detection in IoT Networks:

A Novel Approach Combining Modified Salp Swarm Feature Selection and GLIRU Model

S. Venkatasubramanian
https://orcid.org/0000-0001-7560-0164
Saranathan College of Engineering, India

ABSTRACT

More than ever before, fraudsters are fixated on the Internet of Things (IoT) because to its astounding rate of growth. If attacks on the IoT go undiscovered for a long time, they disrupt services severely, which costs money. Additionally, it poses a risk to one's privacy. For IoT-enabled services to be dependable, safe, and lucrative, real-time intrusion detection on IoT devices is crucial. This study introduces a new approach to intrusion detection for IoT devices that utilizes Deep Learning (DL). The article begins by introducing the modified salp-swarm optimizer, which is used as a model for feature selection. A high convergence accuracy and improved global optimization capabilities are the distinguishing features of the suggested approach. Lastly, the Gated Lightweight Intelligent Recurrent Units (GLIRU) model is used to categorize the attacks. . In order to enhance the classification accuracy, the work employs the Adaptive Elite-Ant Lion Optimizer (AALO) to adjust the settings of the GRU.

DOI: 10.4018/979-8-3373-2115-8.ch011

INTRODUCTION

The IoT, which allows billions of heterogeneous things to automatically interact with one another, is a huge step forward in the smartification of huge networks (Elnakib, O et al., 2023). Smart homes, transportation networks, manufacturing, agriculture, and many more areas are finding uses for this technology, and its adoption rate is only going up (Krishnamoorthy, G, Sistla, S. M. K, 2023). This is because the IoT idea is both easy to understand and has many benefits. Time, money, and human resources can all be saved and a variety of tasks can be executed intelligently and interactively with the help of this technology (Musleh, D. et al., 2023). Nevertheless, there are a number of difficulties associated with IoT technology. Concerns about safety rank high among the most important (Srinivasan.V et al., 2024). Disruption to the network's functionality can result in substantial losses, and the volume of critical information passing through its components is increasing as the IoT grows (Bakhsh, S. et al., 2023).

Due to its large size and diverse nature, the IoT presents unique challenges for traditional intrusion detection systems when used to these networks (Lazzarini, R., Tianfield, H., Charissis, V., 2023). Reason being, widespread IoT networks would not be able to accommodate the current IDSs' reliance on a centralised design for attack detection, which would be both expensive and inefficient to install. And these models can't provide the most precise detections because current distributed detection methods aren't very good (Madhu.B, et al., 2023). In order to avoid cyber-attacks that can cause disruptions in service, illegal access, data alteration, and unauthorised access, it is always important to secure these systems (Chaganti, R. et al., 2023). In order to identify harmful behaviours in IoT networks, numerous researchers have concentrated on IDS using various ML and DL algorithms (Sharma, B. et al., 2023). But current systems can only identify assaults on one layer of the three-layer IoT design, so they can't protect the entire network from threats. The current systems also have room for improvement when it comes to cyber attack detection (Elsayed, R. et al., 2023).

Due to their low bandwidth capacity and lack of global connectivity, traditional intrusion detection solutions cannot ensure security in IoT claims. A state-of-the-art IDS is thus created to safeguard IoT devices from malicious attacks (Anusuya, V. S. et al., 2024). When the intrusion detection system detects anything out of the ordinary, it can notify the system administrator. Adaptive network security—the acronym for intrusion detection system—can provide helpful information to the network manager of emerging forms of attack (Fraihat, S. et al., 2023). Before the network can identify an assault, it must be updated with an instance of that type. Two main types of intrusion detection systems are those that rely on signatures, and those that rely on anomalies or specifications (Tekin, N et al., 2023). Attacks can be detected using signature-based approaches that use known attack patterns. If a behaviour deviates from the norm, an anomaly-based detection system will flag it. A specification-based system also follows the administrator-defined rules (Jothi, B., Pushpalatha, M., 2023). The ever-evolving network and threats make it difficult to maintain up-to-date IDS. Researchers employ flexible methods learning (to extend their benefits (Santhosh Kumar et al., 2023). It is possible to build a machine learning model around a single classifier by classifying classical, or it can be multi-classifiers by connecting numerous classifying models in simultaneously. There are two subtypes of IDS models: binary and multiclass. Binary categorisation uses a 0 or 1 scale, with 0 representing normal and 1 aberrant, to categorise data transmissions. Multiclass classification, on the other hand, can identify the specific kind of attacks (Xu, B. et al., 2023). When training with insufficient attack examples, the multiclass model's increased complexity compared to the binary model causes it to perform worse when dealing with unknown attacks Mousa and Shehab, (2025), Otoom, (2025), Almuqren, (2025), Almanasir et al., (2025), Al-Shareeda et al., (2025).

The suggested approach is well-suited for IDS in IoT settings due to its capability to efficiently analyse sequential data. This study also made use of data pre-processing methods like normalisation, cleaning, encoding, feature filtering, and shuffling. Applying the suggested model to the IOTID20 dataset, which was compiled for the three-tiered IoT architecture, further solidifies its importance. The MSSO algorithm chooses the features, while AALO adjusts the GRU model. Here is the breakdown of the lasting sections of the paper: The works cited in Section 2 are followed by the proposed model in Section 3, the results analysis in Section 4, besides the conclusion in Section 5.

RELATED WORKS

In order to classify the diverse categories of attacks in the dataset (Sharma et al., 2024), a Deep Learning (DL) classical for intrusion finding.toconstructed two distinct deep-learning models for intrusion detection was proposed using a filter-based procedure to prioritise and reduce the number of features.toutilised two open-source datasets, NSL-KDD besides UNSW-NB 15, to train and test our models.totrained a Deep Neural Network (DNN) model using the dataset first, and a Convolution model using the same dataset second. The DL model outperformed the other on both datasets. Toused the concept of explainable AI to bring light on DL models, which might be difficult to understand because to their opacity.toused the explainable AI agnostic method to boost DNN model confidence, and to employed Shapley Additive Explanations (SHAP) for better comprehension Lippi et al., (2025), Almelehy et al., (2025), Alboalebrah and Al-augby, (2025), Almedires et al., (2025), Ang et al., (2025).

In order to identify botnet assaults on seven IoT devices, (Shahin et al., 2024) a comprehensive literature research was performed and applied more than twenty-five sophisticated Machine Learning (ML) algorithms, some of which had been modified. Building reliable and accurate representations to detect security threats and enabling a thorough performance benchmark for all of these models using the same dataset were the main goals. Our research showed that certain models were quite good at identifying botnet assaults, while others were not as good. One of our contributions is the identification of effective ML models for botnet detection and their demonstration of applicability across different types of IoT devices. The next step for this line of inquiry is to test these models on fresh data sets and investigate how different kinds of IoT devices affect detection accuracy and reaction time.

Using Denoising Autoencoder (DAE) models (Alrayes et al. 2024), a new approach to intrusion finding in IoT networks was industrialized. The Internet of Things presents unique challenges for traditional IDS technologies, including limited resources, ever-changing network topologies, and a wide variety of communication protocols. Our proposed method develops a system capable of real-time intrusion finding and prevention by using DAEs' unsupervised learning and feature extraction abilities. The study's evaluation also makes use of the 2017 CICIDS and NSL-KDD datasets. Using the CICIDS 2017 dataset, DAE integration achieves an unparalleled accuracy of 99.991%, and using the NSL-KDD dataset, an accuracy of 99.4%. Among the many noteworthy performance metrics found in the CICIDS 2017 dataset study are an F1-score of 0.998, a precision of 0.995, and an accuracy of 1.0. Results from analyses conducted on the NSL-KDD dataset are similarly impressive, topping out at 0.984 for precision, 0.994 for accuracy, 0.991 for recall, and an F1-score of 0.989. Additionally, the results demonstrate the efficacy of the proposed DAE-based intrusion detection method in preventing unauthorised users from gaining access to IoT devices, hence reducing the likelihood of problems related to system integrity, privacy, and security. This research improves cybersecurity tactics that are specifically designed to handle the unique issues faced by IoT ecosystems by making them more resilient against cyber threats that are always fluctuating in the networked Internet of Things landscape.

A fresh strategy for detecting intrusions in the IoT by combining CNN and GRU architectures (Qaddos et al. 2024) was present. When it comes to learning relational characteristics that are critical to IoT security, this hybrid model does wonders at collecting complex properties. Additionally, to deal with imbalanced datasets, which frequently plague intrusion detection jobs, to incorporate the oversampling method (FW-SMOTE). By simulating IoT environments, validation with the IoTID20 dataset outperforms current standards with an attack detection accuracy of 99.60%. The model's accuracy on the network domain dataset, UNSW-NB15, further illustrates its applicability across varied datasets. In addition to resolving existing issues with Internet of Things intrusion detection, this novel method sets new standards for accuracy and adaptability. The results highlight its promise as a flexible and efficient method of protecting IoT networks from ever-changing security risks.

An Extreme Learning Machine (ELM) is a novel approach that (Altamimi and Abu Al-Haija, 2024) describe as a means to improve IDS performance. This research makes use of two industry-standard IDS-based IoT network datasets, namely NSL-KDD 2009 and Distilled-Kitsune 2021. In a traditional supervised learning context, ELM is evaluated using both datasets. Research on the ELM algorithm's ability to deal with high-dimensional and imbalanced data suggests it may improve the efficacy and precision of IDS. Python and Google COLAB for binary besides multi-class classification are also investigated in the study. ELM setup for NSL KDD and Kitsune are also examined. The experimental evaluation of the suggested ELM-based IDS showed that it performed admirably compared to other state-of-the-art models in the similar study area and other supervised learning-based IDSs that have been applied.

In a proposal for IDSs for IoT networks (Azimjonov and Kim, 2024), the feature selection approaches and fine-tuned Linear Support Vector Machines (LSVMs) to create a system that is lightweight, accurate, and performs well was used. The most significant and well-organized features were identified from three datasets: N-BaIoT-2021, using four feature selectors: Importance Coefficient different types of IoT botnet assaults, the fine-tuned LSVMs trained using both partial and whole dataset features. Compared to trained with the complete feature sets of the datasets, those trained with features perform better in training and testing, according to the evaluation consequences. In contrast to the full features used in KDD Cup-1999 (40), BotIoT-2018 (15), besides N-BaIoT-2021 (115), the study found that training with a lower amount of features (6) could result in lightweight IDSs. The results show that by utilising the fine-tuned feature selectors on IoT networks can be made much more efficient and accurate.

PROPOSED MODEL

In this section, the projected methodology is intended to detect the attacks from the publicly available dataset with the help of advanced deep learning models that is graphically shown in Figure 1.

Figure 1. Workflow of the suggested model

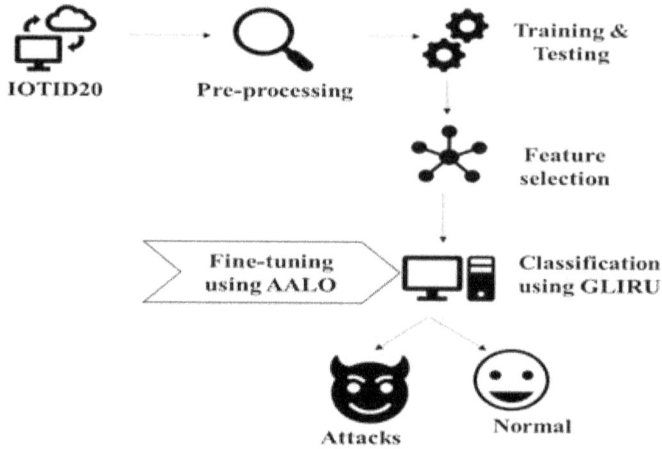

Dataset Description of IoTID20

The IOTID20 (Kang H et al., 2019) dataset is based on the IOTID (Jingyi Su, He Shan, 2022) dataset's raw network packet files. The dataset is openly available and was prepared with scholarly goals in mind. A WI-FI router was used to connect various smartphones and laptops to the NUGU (NU 100) AI-based speaker and the EZVIZ Wi-Fi plus 1080P), forming an IoT network. The use of Nmap tools allowed for the simulation of many attacks, including spoofing, scanning, DoS, the Middle. There are four possible types of simulated attacks. "Dos," "Mirai," "Scan," and "MITM ARP" are alphabetical terms.

1. First, a denial-of-service attack (DoS) happens when damaging actions are directed towards a single source node or end node. By disabling services for supplementary devices, the attacker intends to overwhelm the target server.
2. Mirai: The hacker attempts to transform the victim's program into a system of automated bots that can be managed from a distance.
3. Scan: The intruder attempts data manipulation while scanning. While scanning the devices, they attempt to obtain data using hardware means.
4. MITSA ARP Spoofing, often known as a Man-in-the-Middle attack, is a mutual tactic in cybercrime. By inserting themselves in the middle of a server connection, attackers can alter data packets.

Data Pre-Processing

Data cleansing or data massaging are other names for the same thing. Excluding features that aren't needed is part of it. The sub-attack illustrations should be combined into respectable attack instances, and any null or nan values should be uninvolved or replaced with replacement values. Separating the results from each dataset into two categories: binary and multiclass. Two classes were utilised for binary classification, while five classes, including the regular class, were utilised for multiclass classification. Next, to set a 0–1 data normalisation. For consistency and to complexity, it is vital that the data be consistent with several algorithms at this point.

Feature Selection Using Modified Salp Swarm Algorithm

In this study, the input pre-processed data is used to optimizely identify the important features using modified SSA (Zhao, Y et al., 2023). An early attempt to characterise SSA used a model of salp swarming in the deep sea. In their natural habitat, salps often exhibit a unique swarming behaviour resembling a chain to improve locomotion and foraging via rapid synchronised shifts. Thus, SSA is structured with two social classes—leaders and followers—to reflect the salps' chain behavior. In response to signals from the food supply, the leaders direct their subordinates to.

Basic SSA: The Initialization of Population

Here, the populace of salps is uttered as an N matrix called $X_{N,D}$, just as Equation (1) demonstrates. Furthermore, let's pretend that the optimisation problem is aimed at a prey called F. After that, Equation (2) is used as a random initialisation for the SSA population:

$$X_{N,D} = \begin{bmatrix} x_{1,1} & x_{1,2} & \cdots & x_{1,D} \\ x_{2,1} & x_{2,2} & \cdots & x_{2,D} \\ \vdots & \vdots & \ddots & \vdots \\ x_{N,1} & x_{N,2} & \cdots & x_{N,D} \end{bmatrix} \quad (1)$$

$$X_{N,D} = rand(N,D) \times (ub - lb) + lb \quad (2)$$

where$X_{N,D}$ contains the populaceinfo of N slaps with dimension D, $rand(N, D)$ represents a $N \times D$-dimensional matrix generated by a random function, where ubbesideslb denote the upper and lower boundaries of the search space, correspondingly.

The Position Update of Leaders

The food source guides the salps as they build a chain-like structure. $F = [F_1, F_2, \cdots, F_D]^T$to update adaptively. The site of leader is exposed below:

$$X_{i,j} = \begin{cases} F_j + c_1((ub_j - lb_j)\, c_2 + lb_j), c_3 \geq 0.5 \\ F_j - c_1((ub_j - lb_j)\, c_2 + lb_j), c_3 < 0.5 \end{cases} \quad (3)$$

where $i = 1, 2, \cdots, N/2, j = 1, 2, \cdots, D$, and $X_{i,j}$signifies the site of the i-th leaders in the dimension. Moreover, leaders top $N/2$ salps according to function value. $F_j$is the site of the prey in the j-th dimension. The random statisticsc_2 and $c_3$regulate the step size and the next direction for leaders, respectively, and are allocated evenly throughout the range of [0, 1] at each iteration.

As demonstrated in Formula (3), the sole determinant of the leader's siteinform is the location of the food. In the optimisation algorithm discussed in this study, c_1 is the convergence factor. It aids in balancing global exploration and local development. c0 decreasing function, and its value reduces with each algorithm iteration (dynamic update step). $l_{\max}$characterizes the maximum repetitionsum. The expression can be uttered as:

$$c_1 = a \times e^{-\left(\frac{b \times l}{l_{max}}\right)^2} \quad (4)$$

where l represents the currentrepetitionsum and l_{max} is the maximal repetitionsum. In SSA, a and b are invariables (a = 2 and b = 4).

The Position Update of Followers

When on the move or hunting, followers don't wander about at random but rather walk in a strict chain. A follower's movement distance is shown by using the equation for updating their site, which is based on Newton's law.:

$$S = \frac{1}{2}at^2 + v_0 t \quad (5)$$

where$S$ denotes distance, t is time, v_0 is the unique velocity, and $a$characterizes the quickening of movement. For problem, $t = 1$, $v_0 = 0$ and $a = \frac{v - v_0}{t}$ in upon each cycle. Furthermore, the pace is increased as the follower approaches in close proximity to the preceding salp. $v = \frac{X_{i-1}^l - X_{i,j}^l}{t}$. Then, Equation (5) can be articulated as:

$$S = \frac{1}{2}\left(X^{l}_{i-1,j} - X^{l}_{i,j}\right) \tag{6}$$

According to the above clarification, the followers' site update formula is as shadows:

$$X^{l+1}_{i,j} = X^{l}_{i,j} + S = \frac{1}{2}\left(X^{l}_{i-1,j} - X^{l}_{i,j}\right) \tag{7}$$

where$i > N/2, X^{l+1}_{i,j}$ and $X^{l}_{i,j}$in the j-th space at reiteration (l + 1) and l, correspondingly, are the locations of the i-thsalp of followers.

There are a number of places where the original SSA may use some tweaking. These include the initialisation of the population, the control parameter c1, the formulas for updating the positions of leaders and followers, and the final stage of the population.

ModifiedSalp Swarm Algorithm

Even while SSA achieves a nice middle ground between exploration and exploitation, the algorithm still converges too quickly and produces subpar optimal solutions because there isn't enough variety in the followers. In addition, while dealing with the upgraded SSA, the classic SSA's transition parameter needs to be adjusted to accommodate the increased algorithm's performance. To further improve the procedure'spresentation, a dynamic weight is used to manage the transition stricture more accurately. An analysis of the SSA revealed that in order to boost its efficiency, the following innovations are employed.

Once the SSA algorithm's leader and follower phases have updated all population members, the algorithm iteration is finished, and the best proposed solutions, new values, and goal functions of the population members are identified. Up until algorithm is reached, the algorithm updates Formulas (3) through (7) and moves on to the next iteration. The quasi-optimal solution to the optimisation problem is determined by taking the best proposed solution achieved during the procedure iteration after the SSA is fully applied.

The Mapping Mutation Operation for Followers. The SSA demonstrates that in order to keep themselves up-to-date, followers apply Equation (7), which demonstrates a classic program based on Newton's law. One downside of this form of movement is that it often results in a homogeneous group of adherents. As a result, the modified SSA known as MOSSA employs a mapping mutation operation, which is provided by:

$$X_{i,j}^{l+1} = \begin{cases} X_{i,j}^{l} \times (1 + G(\beta)), c_4 \geq 0.5 \\ lb_j + \beta \times \left(ub_j - lb_j\right), c_4 < 0.5 \end{cases} \tag{8}$$

where c_4 is a stochastic sum boundary [0, 1], Presume the likelihood continuous random variable β is $G(\beta)$, It is evident from the normal distribution characteristics that Gaussian variation is also designed to search a local region close to the initial individual. The Tent chaotic map generates the stochastic number b, and the Gaussian mutation operation $G(\beta)$, is given by Formula (8).

In order to progress the number of followers during course, the MOSSA uses the density function of the normal distribution, which is displayed as follows::

$$G(\beta) = \frac{1}{\sigma\sqrt{2\pi}} e^{-\frac{(\beta-\mu)^2}{2\sigma^2}} \tag{9}$$

where$\mu(\mu = 0)$ is mean and $\sigma^2(\sigma^2 = 1)$ is the adjustment of contender measure. Hence, the Gaussian mutation manoeuvre used to gain a new site of supporter is premeditated as follows:

$$X_{i,j}^{l+1} = X_{i,j}^{l} \times (1 + G(\beta)) \tag{10}$$

When followers are unable to provide an improved key, the MOSSA can develop a new one by combining the Tent chaotic map with the Gaussian mutation procedure. Using the capabilities of mutation operations mapping, they increase the populace'scapacity.:

$$\beta_{k+1} = c_5 \times \beta_k \times \left(1 - \beta_k\right) \tag{11}$$

where c_5 is control parameter (default = 4). The optimisation algorithm's efficiency and solving accuracy are both enhanced when the initialised population is spread more equally in the search space. These benefits are associated with the chaotic sequence that is produced by Tent mapping.

1. First, it generates sequences with good randomness; tent chaos is quite unpredictable and has a high level of randomness. The swarm intelligence algorithm can benefit from this randomness by thoroughly exploring the solution space during the search phase, preventing it from being stuck in the local optimal solution.

2. Tent Chaos's large area search capacity allows for a more consistent and thorough search of the solution space, which is the second benefit. This enhances the swarm intelligence algorithm's global search capability and allows it to thoroughly explore the solution process.
3. Easy to execute and compute: Tent Chaos computation requires only a single mathematical operation, making it easy to understand and use. Because of this, Tent Chaos is simple to compute and use in swarm intelligence procedures.
4. Modifiability: The chaos control parameter is the only parameter of the Tent Chaos function. To modify the search algorithm's behaviour, you can tweak the level of chaos and randomness of Tent chaos by setting this option. Because of its adaptability, Tent Chaos can meet the needs of various algorithmic optimisation issues.

When followers are unable to provide an improved key, the MOSSA can develop a new one by combining the Tent chaotic map with the Gaussian mutation procedure. Using the capabilities of mutation operations besides mapping, they increase the populace's diversity besides search capacity.

Classification of IDS Using GLIRU

Many existing frameworks depend on transformer structure, which incurs substantial computational overhead and low inference speed. Restricted by the large computational complexity of stacked transformers, linear attention-based models have approached a plateau in terms of minimizing inference time and resource consumption. Uniquely, to propose an advanced IDS framework that integrates the linear attention mechanism and efficient dense selective GRU module, which further reduce the computational cost compared with stacked linear transformers and State Space Model (SSM)-based models. Additionally, this dense selective GRU module also enables our framework to understand complex long-/short-term user behaviors, and substantially reduce the computational cost and inference time.

GLIRU framework integrates an expert mixing block for mixing sequential information from the dense selective GRU expert and the linear attention expert, and a gated MLP block for further learning and filtering complex data. In the expert mixing block, the dense selective GRU module is employed to capture the long-term dependencies and local connections among the items, and selectively learn the sequential information. In addition, the linear attention expert is responsible for modeling interactions from the input data. By combining these two powerful expert modules, our GLIRU is capable of adaptively learning dependencies and relevant items from the sequence, which gains deeper insights into the complex data. After the interactions are selectively learned by mixingblock, the item scores are conveyed to the gated MLP block, wherethe information is filtered according to the data environment. Theframework employs various gates in appropriate positions to deeplyfilter information, improving the model's flexibility and the abilityto perceive and select information.

Dense Selective GRU

Existing GRU cell learns sequential data by conveying information from preceding cells. Although this mechanism has the superiority of capturing the long-term dependencies in the sequence, it predominantly focuses on information from previous items, while potentially overlooking the valuable context information provided by adjacent items, which are often closely related in real-world applications. To address these challenges and extract local temporal features, to introduce the dense selective GRU as the core component of the GLIRU framework. This innovation aims to enhance the representation's flexibility and ability to capture complex long-/shortterm patterns in user behavior. By implementing dense selective GRU, the computational complexity can be further reduced, and the accuracy of GRU-based framework can be substantially improved.

Dense GRU module. Therefore, to enable each GRU cell to be exposed to local temporal features of user behaviour, to introduce a temporal convolution layer, where adjacent item information is adaptively fused before being fed into GRU module:

$$\begin{aligned} L &= XW_0 + b_0 \\ C &= TemporalConv1d(L) \end{aligned} \tag{12}$$

where $X = [x_1, x_2, \ldots, x_N]^T$ is the input tensor with d feature dimensions, L is the output of the linear layer, and $C = [c_1, c_2, .., c_N]^T$ is the output of the convolution operation TemporalConv1d(·) with N steps. W_0 and b_0 are weight matrix and bias, respectively. The size of the convolution kernel is set as k. According to Eq. (12), the GRU cell generates step:

$$h_n = GRUCell(c_n, h_{n-1}) \tag{13}$$

where $GRUCell(\cdot)$ is the basic unit in Eq.(12) that processes a current hidden state. Then to generate new features by linearly combining the outputs of the GRU, capturing complex patterns of data preferences. These novel feature representations can be more effectively utilized for predicting attacks. The feature-crossing process can be written as:

$$\Phi(H) = HW_H + b_H \tag{14}$$

where $H = [h_1, h_2, \ldots, h_N]^{\mathrm{T}}$ is the output of GRU, W_{H} is the learnable weight matrix and b_{H} are bias. Although each input state c_{t} incorporates information from both preceding and subsequent items, each output hidden state is still determined by the hidden the preceding time step. Therefore, to capture the context information of the output sequential hidden states, to implement a temporal convolution on the crossed features. This convolution layer extracts local temporal features to understand user behavior dynamics, and enhance the predictive accuracy of our model:

$$Y = TemporalConv1d(G) \tag{15}$$

where G is the Selective Gate function, and $Y = [y_1, y_2, \ldots, y_N]^{\mathrm{T}}$ is the output matrix from the dense selective GRU module. The two convolution layers together with GRU cells improve the density of the sequential information, enabling each hidden state to be learned from behaviors of more input time steps.

Selective Gate. To filter the hidden information of the GRU module, to design a selective gate where outputs of the feature crossing layer are selected based on the input state of the GRU. The selective gate weights are generated by two tiny linear layers with SiLU activation function, and to use them to select useful hidden states and filter information:

$$\begin{aligned} \delta_1(C) &= CW_\delta^{(1)} + b_\delta^{(1)} \\ G(H) = \Omega(\delta_1(C), H) &= \left(SiLU(\delta_1(C))\, W_\Omega^{(1)} + b_\Omega^{(1)} \otimes \Phi(H)\right) \end{aligned} \tag{16}$$

where $C = [c_1, c_2, \ldots, c_N]^T$ also serves as the input of the GRU module, $W_\delta^{(1)}$, $W_\Omega^{(1)}$ are weight matrices, $b_\delta^{(1)}$, $b_\Omega^{(1)}$ are bias. With this gate mechanism, our GRU-based model could become more flexible with the ability to perceive the data environment.

Expert Mixing Block

Although a single GRU module can capture long-term dependencies for IDS tasks, it lacks the ability to model global connections within the item sequence. By introducing the linear attention mechanism and mixing these two powerful experts, the computational complexity will be substantially reduced compared with transformer-based models, and more information about connections and dependencies will be considered. Moreover, the two employed experts are parallel in our framework, which further improves the model efficiency.

In real applications, the conditions of the data might vary a lot. The GRU is naturally suited for sequential data, demonstrating effective performance in sequential IDS tasks that exhibit strong temporal dependencies, while attention focuses on relevant items in the sequence dynamically. To adapt to complex data conditions, to attribute appropriate weights to the two experts by a mixing gate:

$$M = a_1^{(t)} A'(Q,K,V) + a_2^{(t)} Y$$
$$a_i^{(t)} = softmax\left(a_i^{(t-1)}\right) = \frac{a_i^{(t-1)}}{e^{a_1^{(t-1)}} + e^{a_2^{(t-1)}}}, i = 1,2, \tag{17}$$

where $a_1^{(t)}$, $a_2^{(t)}$ are trainable mixing parameters at t-th training iteration. Then to filter this output by introducing another data aware gate which selects the outputs based on the original input data batch:

$$\delta_2(X) = XW_\delta^{(2)} + b_\delta^{(2)}$$
$$Z = \Omega_2\left(\delta_2(X), M\right) = \left(GeLU\left(\delta_2(X)\right)\right) \otimes M \tag{18}$$

where $\boldsymbol{X}$ is the input of expert mixing block, $W_\delta^{(2)}$is the weight matrix of linear layer, $b_\delta^{(2)}$ are bias.

Gated MLP Block

Most existing frameworks, especially transformer-based models, utilize a two-layer feed forward network to capture the nonlinear relationships among features before giving predictions. To further enhance the performance of the model and augment useful features from the expert mixing block, to introduce the gated MLP block, which employs a gate mechanism again to deeply filter the information and generate representations for predictions.

$$\delta_3(Z) = ZW_\delta^{(3)} + b_\delta^{(3)}$$
$$P = \Omega_2\left(\delta_3(z), Z\right) = \left(GeLU\left(\delta_3(Z)\right)\right) \otimes Z, \tag{19}$$
$$R = PW_o + b_o$$

where $\boldsymbol{Z}$ is the output of expert mixing block, P denotes the output of gated linear layer, R represents the item representation, and $W_\delta^{(3)}$, $W_o$are weight matrices, $\boldsymbol{bb}_\delta^{(3)}$, b_o are bias. The scores are generated by representations and embeddings, followed by final prediction probability $\hat{y}_i$ of the i-th item:

$$\hat{y}_i = \mathrm{softmax}\left(R_i\left(e_i\right)^T\right) \textit{(20)}$$

where R_i is the representation of i-th item. Finally, the parameters of the GRU are optimally tuned by AALO that is explained as follows.

A stochastic (metaheuristic) optimisation technique that draws inspiration from nature is the Ant Lion Optimiser (Panneer, K. S. V., Jaganathan, K. 2024). The program was designed with the foraging behaviour of antlion doodlebugs in mind.

Ant Lion Optimizer. Antlions go through the subsequentprocedures when hunting:

i) A haphazard ant colony. The anthills represent the original solution that was chosen at random in the optimisation task. By comparing each position in search space with the fitness function given in [26] to assess fitness, the random ants is akin to looking for an ideal solution. Equation (21) gives the random walk.

$$X(k) = \left[0, cumsum\left(2sf(k_1) - 1\right)\right] \tag{21}$$

$$cumsum\left(2sf(k_1) - 1\right) \ldots cumsum\left(2sf(k_n) - 1\right) \tag{22}$$

Where *cumsum*calculates the total, where k is the iteration quantity at the moment, n is the maximum iteration sum, and sf(k) is the function well-defined in Eq. (23).

$$sf(k) = \begin{cases} 1 \; if\, rand > 0.5 \\ 0 \; if\, rand \leq 0.5 \end{cases} \tag{23}$$

Prior to updating, the ant's locations are regularised using the normalisation equation (24) in order to maintain the haphazard walk in the search space.

$$X_i(k) = \frac{(X_i(k) - r_i) \times (R_i - r_i^k)}{(R_i^k - r_i)} + r_i \tag{24}$$

Where r_i is random walks', R_i is the ith variable extreme of random walks', r_i^k is the lowest of ith variable at kth repetition, and R_i^k is the life-threatening of ith inconstant at kth iteration.

ii) Caught in a trap. Antlions' haphazard gait is affected by the depth of their hole. The ants are believed to be stuck once they enter the pit. In a hypersphere, the ants will wander aimlessly about the elect antlion. Equation (25) depicts this.

$$\begin{aligned} r_i^k &= Antlion_j^k + r^k \\ R_i^k &= Antlion_j^k + R^k \end{aligned} \tag{25}$$

Where r^k is the kth iterationsmallest of all variables, R^t is the kth restatement-thoroughgoing of all variables, r_i^k is least of entirely variables for the kth ant, R_i^k is the thoroughgoing of all variables for the kth ant, and $Antlion_j^k$ shows the site of the selected jth antlion at kth iteration. Each location has its fitness value determined, and they are modelled to descend into the pit in pursuit of the antlion.

iii) Making snares.. To make it seem like the antlion can construct traps, to employ a roulette wheel. When optimising, the ALO algorithm chooses the antlion using the roulette wheel operator according to its fitness. This improves the odds of capture for the fitter antlions.

iv) Approaching antlions while sliding. So far, we've established that antlions traps depending on their fitness level, and that ants are free to traverse the hyper-sphere space around them at will. Once the antlions have caught sight of the ants, the next stage of their hunting strategy is to scatter sand in all directions to keep the ants from getting away and to guide them back to the centre. In order to capture this essence, the adaptively lowered while the ants wander aimlessly, as seen in Eq. (26).

$$\begin{aligned} r^k &= r^k/I \\ R^k &= R^k/I \end{aligned} \tag{26}$$

In Eq. (26), $I = 10\psi\ K/k$ where, k is the presentrepetition, K is the maximum sum of iterations, and $'\psi'$ a constant charge is distinct based on k ($\psi = 2 when k > 0.1K, \psi = 3 \text{when} k > 0.5K, \psi = 4 \text{when} k > 0.75K, \psi = 5 \text{when}$ $k > 0.9\,K,\ \psi = 6\ when\ k > 0.95\ K$). The value of ψ adjusts the level.

v) Rebuilding pits and capturing prey. The last stage of the hunting procedure involves the ants going to the depths to become stuck in the jaws of an antlion. When the ant's fitness is higher than the antlion's, this situation is thought to have occurred in the optimisation issue. The antlion's position is thereafter modified according to Eq. (27) to match the ant's position with the highest fitness.

$$Antlion_j^t = Ant_i^t\ if f\left(Ant_i^t\right) > f\left(Antlion_j^t\right) \tag{27}$$

In the event of an optimisation problem, this improves our odds of finding a better optimal solution or of finding the new ants.

vi) Aristocracy. At the end of each cycle, the elite values are the ones that were most effectively generated by the solution. Since elitism permits the preservation of the optimal solution at any stage of optimisation, it is an essential component of optimisation problems. Using the roulette wheel, the elite antlion is the fittest keythat random paths of all the ants. For this reason, according to Eq. (28), it is anticipated that all ants will simultaneously surround a selected antlion near the roulette wheel besides the elite.

$$Ant_i^t = \frac{R_A^k + R_E^k}{2} \tag{28}$$

Where, R_A^k is the kth repetition'saccidental walk designated by the roulette wheel everywhere the antlion, $R_E^k$is the iteration's position of the ith ant, while Antik represents the kth iteration of the random walk antlion.

Adaptive Elite-Ant Lion Optimizer. The Adaptive Elite-Ant Lion Optimiser (AE-ALO) is unique because it modifies the ALO's elitism operator using the APSO's velocity update equations to fit the ALO parameters. Equation (29) shows the velocities of all particles in APSO.

$$v_i^{k+1} = \omega v_i^k + c_1 r_1 \left(pbest^k - x_i^k\right) + c_2 r_2 \left(gbest^k - x_i^k\right) \tag{29}$$

Where, v_i^k is the kth repetition velocity of particle and x_i^k is the site of the kth repetition's ith particle, ω is the weight factor, $c_1$besidesc_2 are the acceleration coefficients, $r_1$besidesr_2 are random records of the interlude [0, 1], $pbest^k$ is the kth iteration's current best position, g$gbest^k$ is the best iterations. Using the ESE technique, the APSO algorithm revises the acceleration coefficients and weight factor. For each particle i, to may find the evolutionary factor by calculating the mean distance to all the other particles. The distance is measured using a metric that is based on Euclid, as indicated in Equation (30).

$$d_i = \frac{1}{N-1} \sum_{j=i, j \neq i}^{N} \sqrt{\sum_{m=1}^{D} \left(x_i^m - x_j^m\right)^2} \tag{30}$$

The population size is denoted by N, and the sum of search dimensions is represented by D. Next, to can use the formula in Eq. (31) to get the evolutionary factor.

$$e_f = \frac{d_g - d_{min}}{d_{max} - d_{min}} \in [0,1] \tag{31}$$

Where, d_g is the globally particle of d_i, d_{max} is the maximum and dmin is the least distance value. The update ω and the acceleration coefficients$c_1$and c_2. While e_f is rather large during exploration, it becomes smaller during convergence. Therefore, ʊ is adjusted to follow the sigmoid curve.e_f as in Eq. (32).

$$\omega\left(e_f\right) = \frac{1}{1 + 1.5 e^{-2.6 e_f}} \in [0.4,0.9] \forall e_f \in [0,1] \tag{32}$$

In Eq. (29), the parameter $c_1$characterizes the "social influence" that causes the particles to global best, whereas the parameter characterizes the "self-cognition" that controls the local exploration. These parameters can be adjusted individually in an adaptive way because they impact the search in different ways at different phases of the search.

Therefore, the correlations are specified using actual investigations on the evolutionary component e_f. A higher value for c_1 indicates an evolutionary factor, and $c_2$is decreased during the exploration stage (S_1), c_1 is increased slightly besides c_2 is decreased slightly in phase (S2), c_1 is diminished slightly and c_2 is increased slightly in the convergence phase (S_3), c_1 is decreased besidesc_2 is augmented in the jumping out phase (S_4).

According to Eq. (33), the most that can vary, in terms of decrease, among two consecutive occurrences is limited to a randomly generated acceleration factor ρ. S_1 and S_4 whereas change is constrained to 0.5ρ for slight vicissitudes in $S_2$and S_3.

$$\left|C_i(k+1) - C_i(k)\right| \leq \rho, i = 1,2, \& \ \rho \in [0.05\ 0.1] \tag{33}$$

The structure of Eq. (14) in APSO is labouring as the ALO's elitism operative's updated approach. The limitsx_i^k, $pbest^k$, $gbest^k$, v_i^k and v_i^{k+1} are replaced by elite, R_A^k, R_E^k, $\frac{R_A^k + R_E^k}{2}$, Antik correspondingly. The ALO operator found is as in Eq. (34).

$$Ant_i^k = \omega \frac{R_A^k + R_E^k}{2} + c_1 r_1 \left(R_A^k - elite\right) + c_2 r_2 \left(R_E^k - elite\right) \tag{34}$$

Adaptive Elite-Ant Lion Optimiser (AE-ALO) is the term given to the upgraded ALO. A value of 0.9 is used as the starting point for ʊ̈. The worth of ω, c_1 and c_2 are updated as discussed above.

RESULTS AND DISCUSSION

Specifically, the studies are carried out on a machine that has 8 GB of internal memory and an*Intel Core i*5 – 7200 processor that can run at 2.7 GHz. A 64-bit version of Windows 10 with a specialised user interface (UI) and the Jupyter Notebook (Python 3.7) environment are utilised to execute the operations. Figure 2 and Table 1 show the results of comparing the suggested model to current binary classification models.

Table 1. Comparative analysis of various representations

Models	Evaluation Metrics			
	Accuracy	Precision	Recall	Specificity
Proposed GLIRU	0.9563	0.97529	0.96811	0.97322
GRU	0.94959	0.95632	0.95652	0.95529
LSTM	0.94785	0.95	0.9363	0.94195
CNN	0.94905	0.94589	0.9446	0.92638
DBN	0.94959	0.94589	0.929	0.91652
ELM	0.92889	0.91219	0.93613	0.90228
XGBoost	0.9065	0.93504	0.93714	0.91691
SVM	0.90614	0.9342	0.90086	0.89627

Comparative analysis of various models across key evaluation metrics: Accuracy, Precision, Recall, and Specificity. The proposed GLIRU classical outperforms other representations with the highest accuracy at 0.9563, precision at 0.97529, recall at 0.96811, and specificity at 0.97322, demonstrating robust overall performance. The GRU model follows with an accuracy of 0.94959 and slightly lower precision (0.95632), recall (0.95652), and specificity (0.95529). LSTM achieves an accuracy of 0.94785, along with a precision of 0.95 and recall of 0.9363, though its specificity is lower at 0.94195. The CNN model closely matches GRU with a 0.94905 accuracy, but lower precision (0.94589), recall (0.9446), and specificity (0.92638). DBN's metrics are similar to CNN's, with an accuracy of 0.94959 and a slightly lower specificity at 0.91652. ELM achieves a modest accuracy of 0.92889, with its precision and recall at 0.91219 and 0.93613, correspondingly, but has a relatively low specificity of 0.90228. XGBoost and SVM perform similarly in terms of precision (0.93504 for XGBoost and 0.9342 for SVM) and accuracy (0.9065 for XGBoost, 0.90614 for SVM), though both exhibit comparatively lower recall and specificity values, particularly for SVM with a specificity of 0.89627. This table underscores the superior performance of GLIRU, particularly in recall and specificity, which are crucial for accurate detection and low false-positive rates.

Figure 2. Graphical description of proposed model with existing techniques

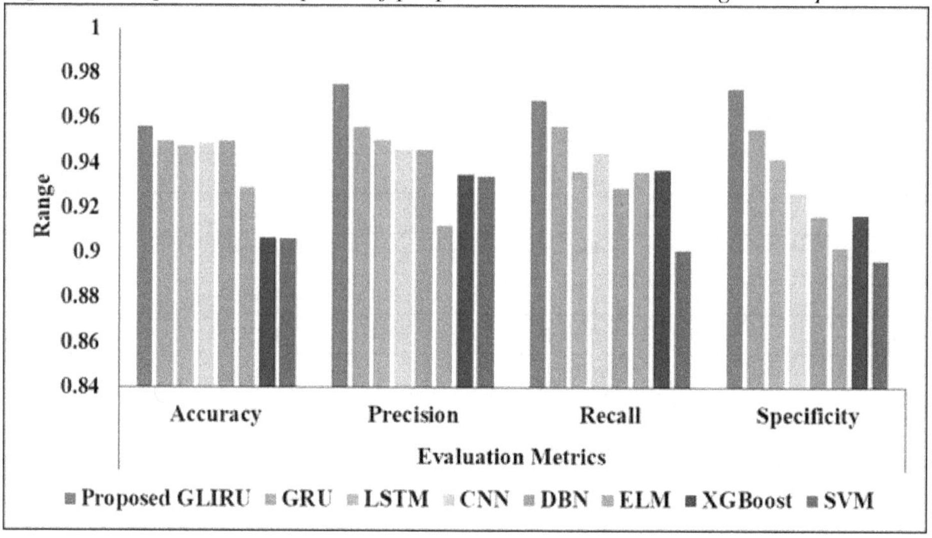

Multi-Class Evaluation of Proposed Model

Table 2 besides Figure 3 provides the examination of the anticipated model on multi-class attacks from the input data.

Table 2. Evaluation of proposed model on multi-class attacks

Attacks	Evaluation Metrics			
	Accuracy	Precision	Recall	Specificity
Normal	0.75458	0.69369	0.72702	0.77399
Dos	0.82245	0.84244	0.7694	0.87027
Mirai	0.88782	0.92061	0.80864	0.92351
Scan	0.88718	0.92101	0.80745	0.92381
MITM ARP	0.88837	0.92938	0.81013	0.92249

The evaluation of the proposed model on various multi-class attack types reveals notable distinctions in performance across Accuracy, Precision, Recall, and Specificity metrics. For normal attacks, the model achieved an accuracy of 0.75458, with Precision, Recall, and Specificity values of 0.69369, 0.72702, and 0.77399, respectively, indicating moderate detection efficiency for this class. For DoS attacks, accuracy improved to 0.82245, and the model displayed high Precision (0.84244) and Specificity (0.87027), though Recall was slightly lower at 0.7694. In the case of Mirai attacks, the model attained a high accuracy of 0.88782 and an even higher Precision of 0.92061, with Recall and Specificity at 0.80864 and 0.92351, respectively, reflecting a strong detection capability. Similarly, for Scan attacks, performance was nearly identical to Mirai, accuracy of 0.88718, Precision of 0.92101, Recall of 0.80745, besides Specificity of 0.92381, highlighting consistent detection efficacy. For MITM ARP attacks, the model achieved the highest results among the classes, with an accuracy of 0.88837, Precision at 0.92938, Recall at 0.81013, and Specificity at 0.92249. These metrics suggest the proposed model's efficiency, especially in accurately identifying attack types with high specificity and precision.

Figure 3. Visual representation of proposed model on different attacks

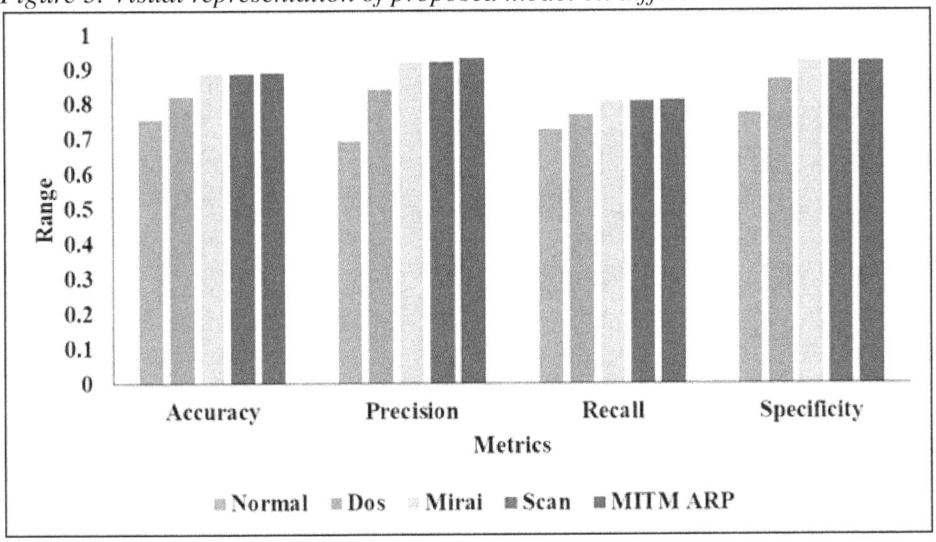

CONCLUSION

The obtainable work industrialized an Anomaly intrusion discoveryscheme based on feature selection based deep learning model. The most relevant features are optimally selected by MSSO algorithm that improves the classification accuracy. In this paper, to have presented an innovative dense selective GRU framework GLIRU for sequential attack detection tasks. Due to the parallel network design and the implementation of efficient dense selective GRU, the computational cost can be substantially reduced, thereby resulting in faster inference speed associated with state-of-the-art efficient representations. Additionally, our model GLIRU tackles the issue of low accuracy of traditional GRU frameworks, and represents a significant advancement in the efficient models. GLIRU applies gate mechanisms to every module, deeply filtering and selecting the information according to the data environment. Dense GRU allows each hidden state to contain the information from the adjacent items, which captures local temporal features to enhance the predictive accuracy. The parameters of the GRU is optimally fine-tuned by AALO model and the extensive experiments demonstrate that GLIRU achieves outstanding performance, not only improving the model accuracy, but also accelerating the training and inference speed dramatically. These results underscore our GLIRU's potential to become a novel, stable, and efficient framework on dataset. To fix the problems with the current study, more research is required. Combining deep learning with ensemble learning techniques is one example of a model type combination that may be utilised to reinforce the IDS and improve performance. It is difficult to deal with complex data, so there has to be an effort to enhance methods for handling missing data and outliers.

REFERENCES

Al-Shareeda, M. A., Ali, A. M., Hammoud, M. A., Kazem, Z. H. M., & Hussein, M. A. (2025). Secure IoT-Based Real-Time Water Level Monitoring System Using ESP32 for Critical Infrastructure. *J. Cyber Secur. Risk Audit*, *2*, 43–52. DOI: 10.63180/jcsra.thestap.2025.2.4

Alboalebrah, M. R., & Al-augby, S. (2025). Unveiling the Causes of Fatal Road Accidents in Iraq: An Association Rule Mining Approach Using the Apriori Algorithm. *Journal of Cyber Security and Risk Auditing*, *2025*(2), 1–11. DOI: 10.63180/jcsra.thestap.2025.2.1

Almanasir, R., Al-solomon, D., Indrawes, S., Almaiah, M., Islam, U., & Alshar'e, M. (2025). Classification of threats and countermeasures of cloud computing. *Journal of Cyber Security and Risk Auditing*, *2025*(2), 27–42. DOI: 10.63180/jcsra.thestap.2025.2.3

Almedires, M. A., Elkhalil, A., & Amin, M. (2025). Adversarial Attack Detection in Industrial Control Systems Using LSTM-Based Intrusion Detection and Black-Box Defense Strategies. *Journal of Cyber Security and Risk Auditing*, *2025*(3), 4–22. DOI: 10.63180/jcsra.thestap.2025.3.2

Almelehy, B., Ahmad, M., Nassreddine, G., Maayah, M., & Achanta, A. (2025). Analytical Analysis of Cyber Threats and Defense Mechanisms for Web Application Security. *Journal of Cyber Security and Risk Auditing*, *2025*(3), 57–76. DOI: 10.63180/jcsra.thestap.2025.3.4

Almuqren, A. A. (2025). Cybersecurity threats, countermeasures and mitigation techniques on the IoT: Future research directions. *Journal of Cyber Security and Risk Auditing*, *1*(1), 1–11. DOI: 10.63180/jcsra.thestap.2025.1.1

Alrayes, F. S., Zakariah, M., Amin, S. U., Khan, Z. I., & Helal, M. (2024). Intrusion Detection in IoT Systems Using Denoising Autoencoder. *IEEE Access : Practical Innovations, Open Solutions*, *12*, 122401–122425. DOI: 10.1109/ACCESS.2024.3451726

Altamimi, S., & Abu Al-Haija, Q. (2024). Maximizing intrusion detection efficiency for IoT networks using extreme learning machine. *Discover Internet of Things*, *4*(1), 5. DOI: 10.1007/s43926-024-00060-x

Ang, S., Ho, M., Huy, S., & Janarthanan, M. (2025). Utilizing IDS and IPS to Improve Cybersecurity Monitoring Process. *Journal of Cyber Security and Risk Auditing*, *2025*(3), 77–88. DOI: 10.63180/jcsra.thestap.2025.3.10

Anusuya, V. S., Baswaraju, S., Thirumalraj, A., & Nedumaran, A. Securing the MANET by Detecting the Intrusions Using CSO and XGBoost Model. In *Intelligent Systems and Industrial Internet of Things for Sustainable Development* (pp. 219–234). Chapman and Hall/CRC. DOI: 10.1201/9781032642789-11

Azimjonov, J., & Kim, T. (2024). Designing accurate lightweight intrusion detection systems for IoT networks using fine-tuned linear SVM and feature selectors. *Computers & Security*, *137*, 103598. DOI: 10.1016/j.cose.2023.103598

Bakhsh, S. A., Khan, M. A., Ahmed, F., Alshehri, M. S., Ali, H., & Ahmad, J. (2023). Enhancing IoT network security through deep learning-powered Intrusion Detection System. *Internet of Things : Engineering Cyber Physical Human Systems*, *24*, 100936. DOI: 10.1016/j.iot.2023.100936

Chaganti, R., Suliman, W., Ravi, V., & Dua, A. (2023). Deep learning approach for SDN-enabled intrusion detection system in IoT networks. *Information (Basel)*, *14*(1), 41. DOI: 10.3390/info14010041

Elnakib, O., Shaaban, E., Mahmoud, M., & Emara, K. (2023). EIDM: Deep learning model for IoT intrusion detection systems. *The Journal of Supercomputing*, *79*(12), 13241–13261. DOI: 10.1007/s11227-023-05197-0

Elsayed, R. A., Hamada, R. A., Abdalla, M. I., & Elsaid, S. A. (2023). Securing IoT and SDN systems using deep-learning based automatic intrusion detection. *Ain Shams Engineering Journal*, *14*(10), 102211. DOI: 10.1016/j.asej.2023.102211

Fraihat, S., Makhadmeh, S., Awad, M., Al-Betar, M. A., & Al-Redhaei, A. (2023). Intrusion detection system for large-scale IoT NetFlow networks using machine learning with modified Arithmetic Optimization Algorithm. *Internet of Things : Engineering Cyber Physical Human Systems*, *22*, 100819. DOI: 10.1016/j.iot.2023.100819

Jothi, B., & Pushpalatha, M. (2023). WILS-TRS—A novel optimized deep learning based intrusion detection framework for IoT networks. *Personal and Ubiquitous Computing*, *27*(3), 1285–1301. DOI: 10.1007/s00779-021-01578-5

Kang, H., Ahn, D. H., Lee, G. M., Yoo, J. D., Park, K. H., & Kim, H. K. "IoT Network Intrusion Dataset," IEEE DataPort, 2019. [Online]. Available: https://ieeedataport.org/open-access/iot-network-intrusion-dataset

Krishnamoorthy, G., & Sistla, S. M. K. (2023). Exploring Machine Learning Intrusion Detection: Addressing Security and Privacy Challenges in IoT-A Comprehensive Review. Journal of Knowledge Learning and Science Technology ISSN: 2959-6386 (online), 2(2), 114-125.

Lazzarini, R., Tianfield, H., & Charissis, V. (2023). A stacking ensemble of deep learning models for IoT intrusion detection. *Knowledge-Based Systems, 279*, 110941. DOI: 10.1016/j.knosys.2023.110941

Lippi, G., Aljawarneh, M., Al-Na'amneh, Q., Hazaymih, R., & Dhomeja, L. D. (2025). Security and Privacy Challenges and Solutions in Autonomous Driving Systems: A Comprehensive Review. *Journal of Cyber Security and Risk Auditing*, *2025*(3), 23–41. DOI: 10.63180/jcsra.thestap.2025.3.3

Madhu, B., Chari, M. V. G., Vankdothu, R., Silivery, A. K., & Aerranagula, V. (2023). Intrusion detection models for IOT networks via deep learning approaches. *Measurement. Sensors*, *25*, 100641. DOI: 10.1016/j.measen.2022.100641

Mousa, R. S., & Shehab, R. (2025). Applying risk analysis for determining threats and countermeasures in workstation domain. *Journal of Cyber Security and Risk Auditing*, *2025*(1), 12–21. DOI: 10.63180/jcsra.thestap.2025.1.2

Musleh, D., Alotaibi, M., Alhaidari, F., Rahman, A., & Mohammad, R. M. (2023). Intrusion detection system using feature extraction with machine learning algorithms in IoT. *Journal of Sensor and Actuator Networks*, *12*(2), 29. DOI: 10.3390/jsan12020029

Otoom, S. (2025). Risk auditing for Digital Twins in cyber physical systems: A systematic review. *Journal of Cyber Security and Risk Auditing*, *2025*(1), 22–35. DOI: 10.63180/jcsra.thestap.2025.1.3

Panneer, K. S. V., & Jaganathan, K. (2024). Adaptive Elite Ant Lion Optimizer tuned optimal controller for underactuated systems. *Franklin Open*, *6*, 100085. DOI: 10.1016/j.fraope.2024.100085

Qaddos, A., Yaseen, M. U., Al-Shamayleh, A. S., Imran, M., Akhunzada, A., & Alharthi, S. Z. (2024). A novel intrusion detection framework for optimizing IoT security. *Scientific Reports*, *14*(1), 21789. DOI: 10.1038/s41598-024-72049-z PMID: 39294195

Santhosh Kumar, S. V. N., Selvi, M., & Kannan, A. (2023). A Comprehensive Survey on Machine Learning-Based Intrusion Detection Systems for Secure Communication in Internet of Things. *Computational Intelligence and Neuroscience*, *2023*(1), 8981988. DOI: 10.1155/2023/8981988

Shahin, M., Maghanaki, M., Hosseinzadeh, A., & Chen, F. F. (2024). Advancing Network Security in Industrial IoT: A Deep Dive into AI-Enabled Intrusion Detection Systems. *Advanced Engineering Informatics*, *62*, 102685. DOI: 10.1016/j.aei.2024.102685

Sharma, B., Sharma, L., Lal, C., & Roy, S. (2023). Anomaly based network intrusion detection for IoT attacks using deep learning technique. *Computers & Electrical Engineering*, *107*, 108626. DOI: 10.1016/j.compeleceng.2023.108626

Sharma, B., Sharma, L., Lal, C., & Roy, S. (2024). Explainable artificial intelligence for intrusion detection in IoT networks: A deep learning based approach. *Expert Systems with Applications*, *238*, 121751. DOI: 10.1016/j.eswa.2023.121751

Srinivasan, V., Raj, V. H., Thirumalraj, A., & Nagarathinam, K. (2024). Original Research Article Detection of Data imbalance in MANET network based on ADSY-AEAMBi-LSTM with DBO Feature selection. *Journal of Autonomous Intelligence*, *7*(4), 1094. DOI: 10.32629/jai.v7i4.1094

Jingyi Su, He Shan. Yan Wu. Features selection and prediction for IOT attacks, high conference computing. 2022;2: 100047. .DOI: 10.1016/j.hcc.2021.100047

Tekin, N., Acar, A., Aris, A., Uluagac, A. S., & Gungor, V. C. (2023). Energy consumption of on-device machine learning models for IoT intrusion detection. *Internet of Things : Engineering Cyber Physical Human Systems*, *21*, 100670. DOI: 10.1016/j.iot.2022.100670

Xu, B., Sun, L., Mao, X., Ding, R., & Liu, C. (2023). IoT Intrusion Detection System Based on Machine Learning. *Electronics (Basel)*, *12*(20), 4289. DOI: 10.3390/electronics12204289

Zhao, Y., Bi, S., Zhang, H., & Chen, Z. (2023). Dynamic weight and mapping mutation operation-based salp swarm algorithm for global optimization. *Applied Sciences (Basel, Switzerland)*, *13*(15), 8960. DOI: 10.3390/app13158960

Chapter 12
Scenario-Aware Anomaly Detection in Insider Activities Using CT-GAN Data Augmentation

K. Kamatchi
https://orcid.org/0000-0003-1243-5071
Vel Tech Rangarajan Dr.Sagunthala R&D Institute of Science and Technology, University in Morai, India

E. Uma
Anna University, India

ABSTRACT

Insider threats are cyberattacks perpetrated by individuals with legitimate organizational access. Detecting insider attacks is challenging due to their subtle nature and potential for causing significant harm. One popular technique for spotting dangerous insiders is anomaly detection. However, internal analysis of danger remains a largely untapped study area due to the lack of actual events data and the unequal distribution of classes in datasets. In order to enhance underutilised minority class instances and enrich the data with diverse and significant examples drawn from pragmatically malicious events, we develop a Conditional Tabular Generative Adversarial Network (CT-GAN) in this research. Comprehensive experiments utilizing the CMUCERT Version 4.2 dataset showcase the impact of CT-GAN-augmented data in enhancing the detection of anomalies within insider activity analysis. Additionally, the approach is assessed against several existing methods using various criteria and performance metrics.

DOI: 10.4018/979-8-3373-2115-8.ch012

INTRODUCTION

Organizations are continually exposed to various cyber threats, but insider attacks carried out by individuals with direct or indirect access to internal systems are especially troubling. These attacks are particularly dangerous because the perpetrators are already integrated into the organization, making them familiar with its systems and processes, whether physically or virtually. Recent insights indicate that insider threats will become more critical and top-of-mind for security professionals in 2023. According to Cybersecurity Insiders' 2023 Insider Threat Report, 74% of organizations consider themselves moderately to severely vulnerable to insider attacks, with 60% of respondents having encountered one in 2022, (Cybersecurity Insiders, 2023). This represents a marked increase in frequency, underscoring the growing difficulty in detecting and preventing such threats, which often involve legitimate accounts and credentials, rendering them harder to distinguish from normal user activity. Insider threats unfold gradually, as attackers carefully plan and execute their actions over time. They often combine various strategies, relying on past experiences and established attack patterns. Studies on insider threats show that these incidents involve multiple fraudulent actions targeting trusted resources within an organization Lippi et al., (2025), Almelehy et al., (2025), Alboalebrah and Al-augby, (2025), Almedires et al., (2025), Ang et al., (2025), Alshuaibi et al., (2025), Alotaibi et al., (2025), Aljumaiah et al., (2025).

Researchers have categorized these activities into distinct scenarios to better understand and combat them. Key examples include Data Exfiltration, System Sabotage, and Intellectual Property Theft, which provide insight into the diverse tactics used by insiders, (Greitzer, 2019; Jones, 2024). Although the effect and rising incidence of insider threats are well acknowledged, the dearth of actual-world information due to privacy issues and inequitable data distributions have rendered insider threat research a less studied subject in cybersecurity. Identifying insider threats is usually framed as an anomaly detection problem, with malicious actions being infrequent and hard to detect. In many real-world applications (Le & Zincir-Heywood, 2021; Yuan & Wu, 2021), Anomaly Detection (AD) is crucial, particularly in cybersecurity. The majority of the time, anomaly detection techniques which usually use binary or one-class classification models are used to detect insider threats. Supervised learning models often overfit when trained on limited class data, focusing on dominant classes, and reducing training effectiveness. This leads to poor performance when applied to new data. While several techniques can reduce overfitting, gathering more data remains the most effective approach. Ensuring that every class is represented with meaningful samples significantly boosts the accuracy and efficiency of anomaly detection systems. In order to improve multi-class AD and address the problem of scarce information for minority classes in insider threat situations, this study uses a

CT-GAN Mousa and Shehab, (2025), Otoom, (2025), Almuqren, (2025), Almanasir et al., (2025), Al-Shareeda et al., (2025).

The objective is to provide falsified information for a range of malicious, underreported behaviors that lead to suspicious activity. In order to resolve the issues caused by inequitable class distributions in insider threat datasets, we provide a Conditional Tabular Generative Model. This study uses the t-distributed Stochastic Neighbor Embedding (t-SNE) technique to visually analyze the data generated by the CTGAN. A comprehensive assessment is carried out, including an in-depth examination of exactly how the suggested approach improves results using generally accepted criteria. In comparison to current approaches, extensive experiments are conducted utilizing a reference dataset under different configurations, demonstrating the efficacy of the artificially collected information creation strategy for ITD.

The following is the structure for the rest of the paper. In Section II, the existing ITD approaches that use Deep Learning (DL) and Machine Learning (ML) techniques are reviewed, along with the creation of synthetic data. The suggested approach is thoroughly explained in Section III. The validation dataset, techniques employed, and metrics used to assess the methods performance are covered in Section IV. The work is finally concluded in Section V, which also suggests possible avenues for further investigation.

LITERATURE REVIEW

ITD has been an imperative area of concentration for several years, yet progress remains limited. One of the most persistent challenges is the lack of access to real-world datasets, which has hampered the development of truly effective detection solutions. However, with the growing frequency of cyberattacks and advances in data analysis techniques, interest in ITD has been reignited. The difficulty in detecting insider lies in their subtlety. While normal employee behaviors are easy to recognize, distinguishing between benign actions and malicious intent is much harder. These threats often go unnoticed because malicious activities are rare compared to the overwhelming volume of regular, day-to-day actions, leading to highly imbalanced datasets. This imbalance significantly complicates the training of DL and ML, making it difficult to achieve reliable results. Despite the critical nature of this issue, the problem of class imbalance has not been adequately addressed in many AI-driven approaches to ITD in the existing studies.

Recent studies have begun addressing this gap. For instance, Gayathri et al. (2024) proposed SPCAGAN, a generative adversarial network (GAN) based on linear manifold learning. Their approach integrates data from diverse sources and uses a novel loss function to improve both data quality and alignment. Al-Shehari and

Alsowail (2023) introduced a different model aimed at detecting insider data leaks, employing random sampling methods such as decision tree-based under-sampling and KNN-based over-sampling to handle imbalanced data. Likewise, Asha et al. (2023) presented a two-layer architecture for detecting misuse insider threats. Their research revealed that Nearmiss2 (NM-2) was the best sampling technique for a Support Vector Machine (SVM) classifier. The first layer controls data integration, modification, and sampling. The second layer then used this NM-2 sampled data to find anomalies. Al-Mhiqani et al. (2021) made another noteworthy addition when they created the ADaptive Deep Neural Network (AD-DNN) model. This model improved detection by combining a DNN with the ADAptive SYNthetic (ADASYN) method for sampling. Chattopadhyay et al. (2018) tackled the problem by concentrating on user activity time-series data. They created a time-series feature vector based on statistical trends over time after extracting single-day traits from user surfing logs. They deliberately under-sampled non-malicious occurrences as part of a cost-sensitive data adjustment strategy to resolve the class imbalance. Their classification relied on a two-layer deep autoencoder neural network. Gao et al. (2023) used Deep Temporal Graph Infomax (DTGI) to address ITD in critical infrastructure. They used a behavior-context aberration sample generator in conjunction with a continuous-time adaptive heterogeneous graph system. The Deep Adversarial Insider Threat Detection (DAITD) system was created by Yuan et al. (2020). It makes use of Vanilla Generative Adversarial Networks (Vanilla-GAN) to create artificial evidence that roughly reflect the distribution of aberrant user behavior. More recently, research has focused on using GAN-based models like SPCAGAN (Gayathri, Sajjanhar, & Xiang, 2023), Conditional GAN (CGAN) (Gayathri *et al.,* 2021), and Vanilla GAN (Yuan *et al.,* 2020) to create synthetic data for insider threat detection. Through principal component analysis for dimensionality reduction, SPCAGAN streamlines data production; nonetheless, the veracity of the information being provided is vital to its viability. Meanwhile, CGAN offers greater control over the output by using conditional variables to generate more targeted synthetic samples. However, both approaches face common challenges in GAN models, including mode collapse and convergence issues AlShuaibi et al., (2025), Frederick and Ali, (2024) Aldossary et al., (2024), Davarasan et al., (2024), Al-Shareeda et al., (2024).

Although these models have shown promising results on specific metrics, the robustness and generalization of the synthetic data they generate remain uncertain. Techniques like adversarial training and synthetic data generation, which have shown success in areas such as medical diagnostics and increasingly being applied in cybersecurity, particularly for intrusion detection. This trend has inspired us to explore the potential of GANs in ITD. The suggested methodology will be thoroughly explained in the parts that follow.

PROPOSED METHOD

Our proposed technique to ITD is broken into three essential stages: Behavior Analysis, Data enrichment via CT-GAN and Anomaly Detection. In the Behavior Analysis stage, we begin by preprocessing the dataset and extracting essential behavioral features from user activity logs. These features serve as the foundation for identifying potential insider threats. The second stage focuses on augmenting the dataset through CT-GAN to address class imbalance. Here, we apply CT-GAN to generate synthetic data that reflects the behavior patterns of minority classes. This synthetic data is used to augment the original dataset, ensuring a more balanced distribution of benign and malicious activities. Finally, in the Anomaly Detection stage, we use ML models on the improved information set to discover unexpected patterns that indicate insider threats. To demonstrate this, we use the CMUCERT Version 4.2 dataset, abbreviated as $D_{Original}$. After the extraction of features, the dataset is divided into two distinct portions: D_{Train} for training and D_{Test} for evaluation. A generative model is then used to construct synthetic data, $D_{Synthetic}$, based on D_{Train}. The augmented dataset $D_{Augment}$, is created by combining synthetic data with the original training set. This dataset is then used to train the anomaly detection algorithm. Figure 1 shows a thorough flow of this suggested method.

Figure 1. Overview of CT-GAN based ITD

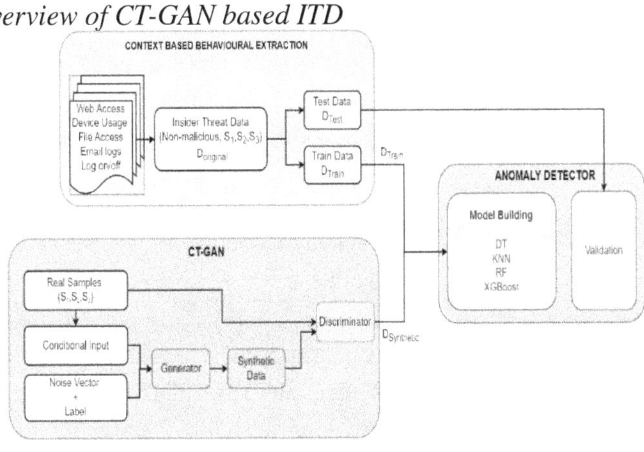

Behavior Analysis

In this section, we outline the process for generating the feature space used in ITD. We employ a behavior profiling method that captures the full context of user activity to create the feature set, $D_{Original}$. Our approach expands on the key features described in Chattopadhyay, Wang, and Tan (2018), going beyond limited user identification in isolated scenarios by analyzing each user's entire activity log. This results in a comprehensive behavior profile that offers a more complete view of user behavior. To create a unified feature space, we merge the feature sets from various user scenarios, allowing us to capture the full breadth of activities in a single, cohesive dataset. This approach also supports scalability, making it easier to integrate new scenarios as they arise. User behavior profiles are created using a variety of activity logs, which include login/logout information, accessed file records, external device usage, email communication habits, and online surfing histories. These logs are preprocessed using the method detailed in Chattopadhyay, Wang, and Tan (2018). Importantly, this feature engineering process is flexible and can be easily adapted to other datasets, requiring only minor adjustments based on the specific log files available. A visual summary of how the feature space is constructed can be found in Figure 2.

Figure 2. Feature set based on context

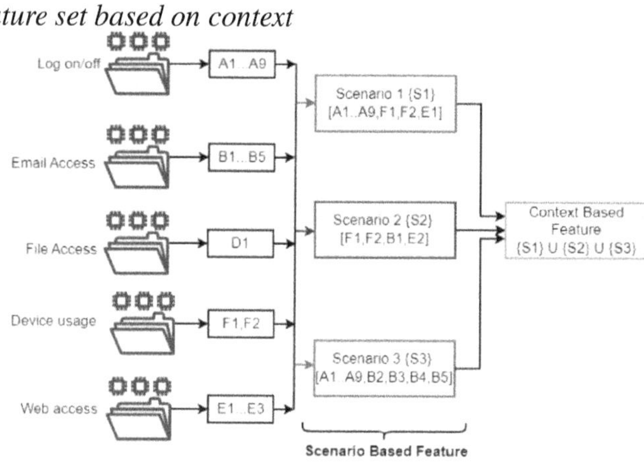

The fundamental difference among our approach to feature set construction and the one utilized in Chattopadhyay, Wang, and Tan (2018) is the presence of two particular features relating to web browsing activity, E2 and E3. In our method, Feature E2, which tracks the frequency of visits to particular websites, is calculated by counting how many times a user accesses specific domains. In contrast, the prior method extracted features using a Term Frequency-Inverse Document Frequency (TF-IDF) methodology, which involved creating a corpus from the dataset log file data. While TF-IDF is a well-established technique, this method was less effective in our case because the corpus was generated solely from keywords provided within the dataset. As a result, the feature set lacked completeness and didn't fully represent the broader range of user activities.

A cosine similarity-based metric is used to compute features E2 and E3. The cosine similarity score, which runs from 0 to 1, illustrates the link between related keywords. Cosine similarity is a widely used method in text processing and information retrieval systems to measure the closeness of keyword sets. By applying this technique, we enhance the accuracy of behavioral feature representation, effectively correlating relevant user activities. In the proposed approach, we construct two distinct keyword corpora, C1 and C2. C1 consists of terms related to financial transactions, representing Scenario 1, while C2 includes keywords like malware, exploit, and phishing, corresponding to Scenarios 2 and 3. Cosine similarity is then calculated for each keyword set derived from individual user activities to compute features E2 and E3. Consider the following two keyword sets: X and Y, where X represents terms from a user's everyday activities and Y represents keywords from the corpus. The characteristics E2 and E3 are computed using Eq. (1).

$$E2 = C(Keywords, C1)$$

$$E3 = C(Keywords, C2)$$

$$cosine\ similarity(X, Y) = \frac{X \bullet Y}{\| X \| \ \| Y \|} \tag{1}$$

Where,

$$\| X \| = \sqrt{\sum_{i=1}^{n} X_i^2}, \| Y \| = \sqrt{\sum_{i=1}^{n} Y_i^2}$$

Numerous insider activities are included in the $D_{Original}$ dataset, and labels are applied according to various contexts. This feature set generates a very unequal distribution of classes by capturing everyday consumption of resources patterns of each user. This work intends to employ a CT-GAN strategy to rectify the distribution of data and build an automatic learning framework for recognising anomalies, but other research has investigated techniques such as re-sampling and cost-sensitive approaches to address this issue. The use of CT-GAN networks to address the issue of class imbalance is explained in the next section.

Conditional Tabular GAN

The limited availability of actual-world data is one of ITD's main drawbacks. One kind of neural network that has become a dependable technique for creating artificially generated information that closely mimics its original distribution is Generative Adversarial Networks (GANs) (Goodfellow *et al.*, 2014). Although GANs are frequently used in image processing to produce realistic images that are hard to tell apart from real ones, they are less frequently used to generate tabular data, especially when numerical features are included. Given that our dataset primarily contains numerical attributes, we develop a custom CT-GAN model that is specifically designed to handle the complexity of two-dimensional tabular data efficiently. We introduce a CT-GAN that incorporates minority malicious class labels as conditioning factors. By producing balanced data, this method reduces the problem of class imbalance, and by incorporating samples from every class, it broadens the training set's diversity. These are two important benefits of this method. The CT-GAN uses label embeddings in the discriminator and generator to provide data conditioned on class labels. This approach works well for insider analysis of danger and has shown success in a variety of situations. While the generator (G) tries to create counterfeit information that can trick the discriminator, the discriminator (D) in the network tries to differentiate between actual and synthetic data. The discriminator and generator are both fully linked neural networks. Table 1 provides an outline of the CT-GAN architecture.

The system is designed with a straightforward setup to create high-quality synthetic data for ITD. It features a generator and a discriminator, each with fully connected layers. The discriminator has layers with 256, 128 and 32 neurones, and the generator has levels with 32, 64, and 128 neurones. In the discriminator's penultimate layer, dropout regularization is applied at a rate of 0.2, and the generator's latent dimension corresponds to the number of features. To handle probabilities between 0 and 1, the model employs common methods including dropout regularization, Leaky ReLU activation, and the Adam optimizer, with binary cross-entropy serving as the loss function. The model was trained for 200 epochs, beyond which no additional improvement in generator performance was observed. Due to the very limited number of samples for some classes, these classes were initially excluded from random sample selection during training. To counter this, the network ensures that each class is represented in every iteration by including random real samples from all classes. Any designated minority class can have samples generated by the generator, which are subsequently added to $D_{original}$. The following sections offer test findings and comparisons to confirm this data augmentation technique. Figure 1 shows how $D_{Synthetic}$ was integrated with the original dataset.

Table 1. CTGAN network architecture

Component	Layer/Parameters	Details
Generator	Dense 1	32 units, LeakyReLU
	Dense 2	64 units, LeakyReLU
	Dense 3	128 units, LeakyReLU
Discriminator	Dense 1	32 units, LeakyReLU

continued on following page

Table 1. Continued

Component	Layer/Parameters	Details
	Dense 2	64 units, LeakyReLU
	Dense 3	128 units, LeakyReLU
	Dropout	0.2
	Dense 4	1-unit, Sigmoid activation
CT-GAN Params	Optimizer	Adam, Learning rate 0.0002, beta 0.5
	Epochs	200
	Conditioned On	Minority
	Batch Size	64
	Latent Dimensions	20

Anomaly Detection

Anomaly detection using ML techniques has become a widely accepted approach in ITD. The majority of contemporary techniques concentrate on binary categorization, which divides actions into two categories: harmful and non-malicious. Because legitimate threat databases are few and malicious activity detection is inherently complicated, there is a concentration on binary categorization. On tiny datasets, tree-based models like K-Nearest Neighbor (KNN), Random Forest (RF) and Decision Trees (DT) have shown great efficacy, especially when addressing class imbalance. Similarly, algorithms like Extreme Gradient Boosting (XGBoost) are recognized for their strong performance on imbalanced data and have gained popularity in recent ITD studies. In our work, we employed a combination of ensemble algorithms RF, DT, KNN and XGBoost due to their ability to capture complex data patterns and enhance classification accuracy. Traditional anomaly detection frameworks often adopt a binary classification approach, treating each type of malicious behavior as a separate classification problem using a One-vs-Rest strategy. While effective, this method fails to integrate the results into a unified multi-class system. Multi-class classification models, on the other hand, are able to capture inter-class interactions and dependencies since they learn from all accessible classes at once. The ability of the model to manage outliers and intricate patterns in the data is enhanced by this integrated approach. Our proposed approach differs from conventional methods by focusing on predefined scenarios of malicious activities, which provides deeper insight into user behavior. We handle multiple scenarios within the malicious category and differentiate them from non-malicious instances through multi-class classification. This enhances the model's capability to detect and distinguish anomalous activities more effectively. As highlighted in He and Garcia (2009), multi-class classification is particularly valuable for addressing imbalanced data, and use of advanced ensemble methods further demonstrates this effectiveness. For supervised learning, we employed RF, DT, KNN and XGBoost. XGBoost (Chen & Guestrin, 2016) is known for its robustness across various datasets and is commonly used in insider threat analysis. DT algorithms, valued for their interpretability, excel at modeling complex data structures, while RF, an ensemble method that builds upon DT, significantly enhances prediction accuracy and reliability, especially when dealing with imbalanced datasets.

PROPOSED METHOD

This section presents the analysis of the suggested approach. It begins with a detailed description of the dataset, followed by an overview of the models employed for training. The method is developed using Python, with TensorFlow and Keras as the primary frameworks for implementation and evaluation.

Dataset

Organizations reluctance to divulge such sensitive information makes it difficult to obtain dangerous insider databases. We experimented with the readily available CERT hidden threat dataset (Glasser & Lindauer, 2013) to overcome this constraint. Specifically, we selected the CMUCERT Version 4.2 because of its comprehensive coverage, containing a greater number of insider threat instances than earlier versions. The collection is made up of 32,770,227 record them from 1,000 users over a 17-month period, including 70 informants who were identified. The five categories of these event records are broken down in detail in Table 2. Information leaks (Scenario 1), data theft (Scenario 2), and IT sabotage (Scenario 3) are the three main categories of threat from insiders, and 7,323 of these incidents are classified as malicious. In order to extract important information like the timestamp, action description, person ID, and Computer ID, the log lines were first analyzed. We were able to collect time and location data for every user action in part to this procedure. While location data showed if the action took place on the user's entrusted PC, time-based data assisted in identifying actions that took place outside of regular business hours. Such data is essential for identifying irregularities, such a malevolent insider breaking into a coworkers machine during hours to steal confidential data. User actions were organized into daily behavior units, and anomalous behavior was detected by analyzing deviations within a single day. In total, 30 insiders were linked to information leak scenarios, 30 to data theft, and

10 to IT sabotage. Weekend-logged actions were not included in order to allow for varying patterns of behavior. 30% of the dataset was set aside for testing, while 70% of the dataset was divided into sets to serve as training. A range of log files are examples of synthetic data produced using augmentation techniques, as seen in Figure 2. There are 966 harmful occurrences and 330,452 non-malicious instances in the pre-processed dataset, which is separated into four distinct categories: S1, S2, S3, and non-malicious. This distribution highlights a significant class imbalance, with malicious data comprising only 1.25% of the total dataset. Scenario 3, involving IT sabotage, had the fewest users and data instances, while Scenario 2 (data theft) had the highest number of instances, followed by Scenario 1 (information leak). Table 3 presents the distribution of insider activity instances and sequences, categorized into normal and abnormal actions across the various scenarios.

Table 2. Summary of CMUCERT Version 4.2

Computer Log Events	Instances	Actions
http	1048575	Visit job hunting web, general web, hacking web and cloud storage
File	445581	copy exe, doc, pdf, txt, jpg, and zip
Email	2629979	Send internal and external email
Device	405380	Connect/Disconnect device
Logon	854859	log on/off

Veracity of Synthetic Data

Quantifying the resemblance between synthetic and real numerical data is a complex problem. Visual metrics like as the Inception Score are often used in the field of image synthesis to assess the level of quality and resemblance of artificial and natural images. We use visual methods such as Principal Component Analysis (PCA), Kernel Density Estimates (KDE), and t-distributed Stochastic Neighbor Embedding (t-SNE) to compare numerical data distributions where there is no clear metric. To evaluate the similarity of data distributions, we used a non-parametric kernel density estimation. We only visualize features A2 and A4 in Figure 3 because of space constraints. PCA reduces the n-dimensionality of data while preserving key information and identifies the most informative dimensions in a dataset. PCA focuses on global patterns, while t-SNE preserves local structure. A technique for visualizing high-dimensional data according to its geometric structure is called t-SNE. In smaller dimensions, t-SNE produces visualizations that are easier to understand. The PCA and t-SNE visualizations are shown in Figure 4. Cluster separation may be obscured by the 2D representation, particularly if the data is intrinsically higher-dimensional. The t-SNE visualization displays three different clusters of minority insider activity samples generated by the CT-GAN model. The absence of a distinct peak in the data points to the absence of a mode-collapse.

Performance Metric

Standard measures for unbalanced data, including F-score (*F*), Precision (*Pr*), and Recall (*Re*) are used to assess the classification models. High *Pr* and *Re* are crucial for model performance. However, using these metrics alone does not fully capture the true effectiveness of different models in practical situations. The majority class is frequently characterized as negative since rare instances are typically regarded as positive. Existing research has not fully examined learning reports, despite high Pr and Re. We examined fraudulent positives and negatives to further confirm the data in addition to Pr and Re. In order to improve our experimental study, we have added two additional metrics: Cohen's Kappa and the Matthews Correlation Coefficient (MCC) (Matthews, 1975), which highlight the crucial function of the confusion matrix, also known as the error matrix. One statistic used to evaluate the consistency between actual and anticipated classifications is Cohen's Kappa. A Cohen's Kappa score close to 1 indicates strong agreement, while a score near 0 suggests poor agreement. *Pr*, *Re*, and *F* are class-specific metrics that change when classes are swapped. They focus on the positive class and true negatives are irrelevant. So, we use the MCC, which is a balanced metric with a range of -1 to +1. Each class is given equal weight by this coefficient, which takes into account all four elements of the confusion matrix. As a result, the same value will be obtained by switching the positive and negative classes. A number close to 1 indicates that both classes are highly accurately predicted.

Figure 3. KDE of real and fake data

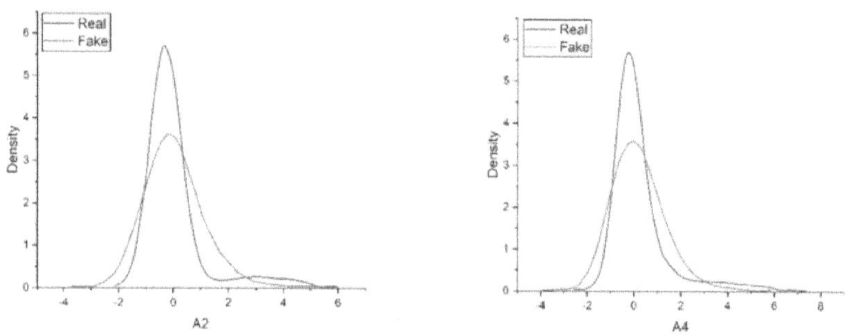

Figure 4. Visualization using PCA and t-SNE

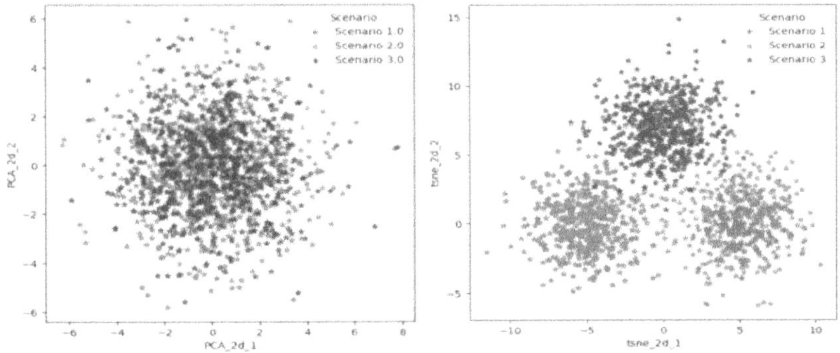

RESULTS AND DISCUSSION

This section assesses the practicality of KNN and tree-based algorithms for multiclass ITD. Original data and data enhanced by a variety of techniques, including CT-GAN, Random Over Sample (ROS), and Synthetic Minority Oversampling Technique (SMOTE), were used in the experiments. Table 4 provides a summary of the multi-class anomaly detection performance. For every data setting, ML techniques were used to create anomaly detection models. The tables emphasize the key findings in bold. Accuracy (Acc), Precision (Pr), Recall (Re), F-score (F), Cohen's Kappa (Kappa), and Matthews Correlation Coefficient (MCC) are the acronyms used in the tables. In the multi-class classification scenario, the DT algorithm's performance on the original dataset was unsatisfactory. However, a notable improvement in accuracy was observed when the model was trained on enriched and more representative data. Unlike baseline methods such as SMOTE and ROS, the CT-GAN demonstrated substantial enhancements across various performance metrics. DT models trained on ROS or SMOTE data faced overfitting risks. XGBoost, a gradient boosting algorithm was used to mitigate overfitting and improve generalization. XGBoost performed better with original data and CT-GAN augmented data than with ROS or SMOTE oversampling.

Comparison with Existing Methods

The experimental results of binary classification using our proposed method are presented in Tables 5, 6, and 7. The features used were defined in Section III-A. Samples for all classes were generated using the same CT-GAN model. Data for

Scenario 1 was generated using CT-GAN, and all other samples were labelled as non-malicious in order to perform binary classification between Scenario 1 and non-malicious samples. We evaluated binary classification performance on ROS, CT-GAN augmented data, SMOTE-oversampled data, and original data. The small sample size of 85 instances in Scenario 1 restricts the ability of complex models to generalize from the abundant negative samples. While XGBoost showed moderate results on the original data, the *Pr* was lower with more false positives than on augmented data. CT-GAN generated data was more effective than SMOTE oversampling in reducing false positives for all models when combined with the original training data. Table 5 presents the findings from the investigation of infiltrator activity for Scenario 1 and non-malicious scenarios using the suggested CT-GAN technique. CT-GAN augmentation significantly improved RF and XGBoost performance in Scenario 2, which had 865 samples. Baseline models struggled with imbalanced data, but CT-GAN+XGBoost achieved near-perfect accuracy. CT-GAN outperformed ROS in boosting *Pr* and *Re* while reducing false positives.

In Scenario 3, the dataset reveals a class imbalance, featuring only 20 instances of malicious activity. Both RF and XGBoost adeptly handle this skewed distribution. The DT model enhances its performance by incorporating CTGAN, which yields improved *Pr* and *F* metrics. This approach also results in significant increases in the Kappa score and MCC. A detailed performance analysis for Scenario 3 is presented in Table 7. In exploring the impact of various generated sample sizes on the performance of our models, we focus on the results from CTGAN combined with different algorithms: DT, KNN, RF, and XGBoost. As shown in Figure 5, there is a consistent upward trend in accuracy as the number of generated anomalous user behavior samples increases from 1,000 to 6,000.

Figure 5. Impact of varying generated sample sizes on model performance

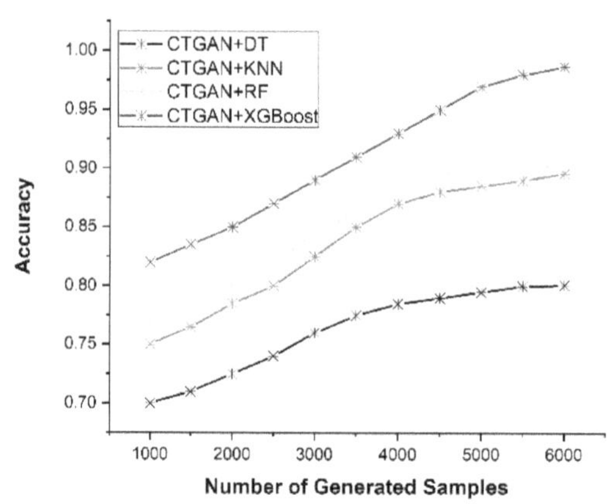

Table 8 provides a comparative overview of existing methods against the proposed approach. It outlines various augmentation techniques, datasets, models used, the number of classes involved, and their respective accuracies. Previous research Gayathri, Sajjanhar, and Xiang (2024) and Al-Shehari and Alsowail (2023) highlights different strategies such as synthetic data generation and a combination of undersampling and oversampling, achieving accuracies between 0.82 and 0.96 on the CERT v4.2 dataset. Notably, Al-Mhiqani *et al.* (2021) utilized the ADASYN technique, reaching an accuracy of 0.96, while Chattopadhyay, Wang, and Tan (2018) employed cost-sensitive data adjustment, achieving 0.94. In comparison, the proposed method, using Conditional Tabular GAN, surpassed the performance of existing techniques. It achieved a remarkable accuracy of 0.98 across multiple models, such as DT, KNN, RF, and XGBoost. This approach successfully handled both binary and multiclass classification tasks. The tests show that CT-GAN-based training successfully handles insider activity multi-class AD. However, the results highlight several key limitations. First, the performance of any method is contingent on the specific features and data used; a single dataset cannot guarantee 100% accuracy. Second, we chose a straightforward feature set for validation because our main goal was to generate diverse and larger samples using CT-GAN-based enhancement of data. The subtleties of insider behavior might not be adequately captured by this small feature set. Lastly, we omitted the measurement of the Area Under the Curve (AUC) score from our evaluation because it was consistently high in our tests and had no analytical significance. Future research should explore more advanced performance analysis strategies to effectively compare and evaluate learning models.

Table 3. Distribution of CMUCERT Version 4.2

Scenario	Insider	Normal Action Instances	Abnormal Action Instances	Normal Action Sequence Instances	Abnormal Action sequence Instances
S1	30	587101	345	6172	77
S2	30	663918	6765	6054	857
S3	10	269647	213	1833	20

Table 4. Comparison of performance metrics across different models and data augmentation techniques

Training Models	Acc	Pr	Re	F	MCC	Kappa
Real + DT	0.658	0.482	0.645	0.482	0.512	0.465
ROS + DT	0.637	0.438	0.658	0.479	0.431	0.347
SMOTE + DT	0.730	0.596	0.735	0.648	0.746	0.740
CTGAN + DT	**0.801**	**0.751**	**0.748**	**0.739**	**0.720**	**0.730**
Real + KNN	0.854	0.749	0.655	0.697	0.884	0.877
ROS + KNN	0.706	0.368	0.866	0.419	0.290	0.156
SMOTE + KNN	0.721	0.396	0.771	0.431	0.250	0.120
CTGAN + KNN	**0.896**	**0.782**	**0.761**	**0.759**	**0.781**	**0.776**
Real + RF	0.786	0.267	0.932	0.263	0.136	0.036
ROS + RF	0.801	0.536	0.793	0.531	0.371	0.245
SMOTE + RF	0.810	0.527	0.778	0.524	0.360	0.233
CTGAN + RF	**0.903**	**0.799**	**0.767**	**0.763**	**0.791**	**0.805**
Real + XGBoost	0.788	0.275	0.788	0.283	0.168	0.055
ROS + XGBoost	0.792	0.406	0.790	0.457	0.296	0.162
SMOTE + XGBoost	0.776	0.452	0.774	0.492	0.289	0.156
CTGAN + XGBoost	**0.987**	**0.833**	**0.767**	**0.733**	**0.805**	**0.857**

Table 5. Performance assessment for scenario 1: Two-class classification

Scenario 1						
Training models	**A**	**P**	**R**	**F**	**MCC**	**Kappa**
Real+DT	0.510	0.909	0.531	0.672	0.063	0.531
ROS+DT	0.530	0.890	0.540	0.668	0.070	0.535
SMOTE+DT	0.721	0.941	0.794	0.861	0.624	0.588
CTGAN+DT	**0.875**	**0.942**	**0.905**	**0.923**	**0.813**	**0.810**
Real+KNN	0.502	0.943	0.490	0.644	0.062	0.008
ROS+KNN	0.510	0.930	0.505	0.655	0.065	0.012
SMOTE+KNN	0.506	0.959	0.506	0.667	0.101	0.021
CTGAN+KNN	**0.917**	**0.941**	**0.928**	**0.934**	**0.848**	**0.857**
Real+RF	0.750	0.975	0.750	0.740	0.680	0.701
ROS+RF	0.765	0.983	0.765	0.753	0.705	0.715
SMOTE+RF	0.770	0.985	0.775	0.760	0.720	0.725

continued on following page

Table 5. Continued

Scenario 1						
Training models	**A**	**P**	**R**	**F**	**MCC**	**Kappa**
CTGAN+RF	**0.968**	**0.941**	**0.954**	**0.948**	**0.909**	**0.929**
Real+XGBoost	0.780	0.980	0.780	0.770	0.740	0.750
ROS+XGBoost	0.790	0.985	0.790	0.780	0.760	0.770
SMOTE+XGBoost	0.800	0.986	0.850	0.790	0.780	0.788
CTGAN+XGBoost	**0.985**	**0.942**	**0.968**	**0.955**	**0.939**	**0.937**

Table 6. Performance assessment for scenario 2: Two-class classification

Scenario 2						
Training models	**A**	**P**	**R**	**F**	**MCC**	**Kappa**
Real+DT	0.689	0.800	0.750	0.774	0.365	0.345
ROS+DT	0.672	0.785	0.740	0.762	0.348	0.319
SMOTE+DT	0.678	0.790	0.755	0.772	0.350	0.321
CTGAN+DT	**0.898**	**0.850**	**0.910**	**0.870**	**0.620**	**0.600**
Real+KNN	0.725	0.860	0.790	0.823	0.442	0.403
ROS+KNN	0.795	0.910	0.850	0.870	0.490	0.455
SMOTE+KNN	0.835	0.920	0.875	0.895	0.516	0.485
CTGAN+KNN	**0.882**	**0.988**	**0.928**	**0.856**	**0.832**	**0.863**
Real+RF	0.790	0.890	0.820	0.850	0.580	0.550
ROS+RF	0.830	0.900	0.850	0.873	0.600	0.570
SMOTE+RF	0.868	0.994	0.922	0.852	0.819	0.843
CTGAN+RF	**0.962**	**0.860**	**0.974**	**0.949**	**0.934**	**0.949**
Real+XGBoost	0.805	0.950	0.830	0.865	0.610	0.590
ROS+XGBoost	0.845	0.951	0.900	0.925	0.675	0.640
SMOTE+XGBoost	0.875	0.940	0.850	0.890	0.690	0.670
CTGAN+XGBoost	**0.989**	**0.870**	**0.925**	**0.859**	**0.835**	**0.849**

Table 7. Performance assessment for scenario 3: Two-class classification

Scenario 3						
Training models	**A**	**P**	**R**	**F**	**MCC**	**Kappa**
Real+DT	0.655	0.610	0.620	0.615	0.245	0.210
ROS+DT	0.670	0.640	0.635	0.637	0.295	0.255
SMOTE+DT	0.685	0.650	0.640	0.645	0.315	0.285
CTGAN+DT	**0.795**	**0.755**	**0.745**	**0.750**	**0.520**	**0.485**
Real+KNN	0.725	0.810	0.705	0.755	0.320	0.270
ROS+KNN	0.745	0.820	0.725	0.770	0.370	0.305
SMOTE+KNN	0.760	0.825	0.735	0.780	0.410	0.335
CTGAN+KNN	**0.865**	**0.855**	**0.845**	**0.850**	**0.615**	**0.590**
Real+RF	0.785	0.885	0.785	0.835	0.510	0.465
ROS+RF	0.795	0.895	0.795	0.845	0.565	0.510
SMOTE+RF	0.805	0.905	0.805	0.855	0.615	0.540
CTGAN+RF	**0.905**	**0.915**	**0.895**	**0.905**	**0.710**	**0.685**
Real+XGBoost	0.825	0.925	0.810	0.865	0.575	0.525
ROS+XGBoost	0.855	0.935	0.825	0.880	0.625	0.555
SMOTE+XGBoost	0.875	0.945	0.835	0.890	0.675	0.615
CTGAN+XGBoost	**0.980**	**0.960**	**0.940**	**0.950**	**0.800**	**0.780**

Table 8. Compilation of existing methods vs proposed method

Method	**Augmentation**	**Dataset**	**Model**	**No. of Classes**	**Accuracy**
Gayathri, Sajjanhar, & Xiang (2024)	Synthetic Data	CMU CERT v4.2	Bayesian	Binary + Multiclass	0.8956
		CMU CERT v5.2			0.8754
Al-Shehari & Alsowail (2023)	Under Sampling + Over Sampling	CMU CERT v4.2	DT + KNN	Binary	0.86
Asha, Shanmugapriya, & Padmavathi (2023)	Nearmiss 2	CMU CERT v4.2	SVM	Binary	0.82
Al-Mihqani *et al.* (2021)	ADASYN	CMU CERT v4.2	DNN	Binary	0.96

continued on following page

Table 8. Continued

Method	Augmentation	Dataset	Model	No. of Classes	Accuracy
Chattopadhyay, Wang, & Tan (2018)	Cost Sensitive Data Adjustment	CMU CERT v4.2	Two-Layer Deep Autoencoder	Binary	0.94
Proposed	**CT-GAN**	**CMU CERT v4.2**	**DT, KNN, RF, XGBoost**	**Binary + Multiclass**	**0.98**

CONCLUSION

Insider threats are cyberattacks perpetrated by individuals with legitimate organizational access. Detecting insider attacks is challenging due to their subtle nature and potential for causing significant harm. One popular technique for spotting dangerous insiders is anomaly detection. However, internal analysis of danger remains a largely untapped study area due to the lack of actual events data and the unequal distribution of classes in datasets. Researchers have categorized these activities into distinct scenarios to better understand and combat them. Key examples include Data Exfiltration, System Sabotage, and Intellectual Property Theft, which provide insight into the diverse tactics used by insiders, (Greitzer, 2019; Jones, 2024). Although the effect and rising incidence of insider threats are well acknowledged, the dearth of actual-world information due to privacy issues and inequitable data distributions have rendered insider threat research a less studied subject in cybersecurity. Identifying insider threats is usually framed as an anomaly detection problem, with malicious actions being infrequent and hard to detect. In many real-world applications, (Le & Zincir-Heywood, 2021; Yuan & Wu, 2021), Anomaly Detection (AD) is crucial, particularly in cybersecurity. This paper introduces an innovative approach that enhances ITD using CT-GAN for data augmentation. The method directly addresses the challenge of imbalanced class distribution by generating synthetic data that closely resembles minority class instances. This creates a more balanced dataset, which boosts the performance of anomaly detection models. The proposed method is a streamlined workflow that begins with data preprocessing of diverse user access log data to create a feature space and generate a relevant feature set. The primary goal is to develop a CT-GAN capable of handling malicious insider scenarios and generating synthetic data. Visual methods like KDE, PCA, and t-SNE are employed to assess synthetic data quality. CT-GAN-based data augmentation aids in expanding the dataset while preserving the original data distribution. For anomaly detection, multi-class classification using four distinct labels is used. The performance of the suggested approach is assessed using both ensemble and ML models on the CMU CERTr4.2 dataset. In this paper, data augmentation efficacy is examined within the framework of insider threat assessment. Future research will examine GAN's performance on many insider threat datasets that are accessible under different feature gaps. Additionally, there are opportunities for in-depth research on the performance assessment of the different GANs.

REFERENCES

Al-Mhiqani, M. N., Ahmad, R., Abidin, Z. Z., & Isnin, S. N. (2021). An integrated imbalanced learning and deep neural network model for insider threat detection. *International Journal of Advanced Computer Science and Applications*, *12*(1), 202–210. DOI: 10.14569/IJACSA.2021.0120166

Al-Mhiqani, M. N., Alsboui, T., Al-Shehari, T., Abdulkareem, K. H., Ahmad, R., & Mohammed, M. A. (2024). Insider threat detection in cyber-physical systems: A systematic literature review. *Computers & Electrical Engineering*, *119*, 109489. Advance online publication. DOI: 10.1016/j.compeleceng.2024.109489

Al-Shareeda, M. A., Ali, A. M., Hammoud, M. A., Kazem, Z. H. M., & Hussein, M. A. (2025). Secure IoT-based real-time water level monitoring system using ESP32 for critical infrastructure. *Journal of Cyber Security and Risk Auditing*, *2*, 43–52. DOI: 10.63180/jcsra.thestap.2025.2.4

Al-Shareeda, M. A., Jafer, A. N., Hashem, M. T., & Fajr, M. S. (2024). Secure offline smart office automation system using ESP32 and Bluetooth control architecture. *Journal of Cyber Security and Risk Auditing*, *2024*(1), 3–13. DOI: 10.63180/jcsra.thestap.2024.1.2

Al-Shehari, T., & Alsowail, R. A. (2023). Random resampling algorithms for addressing the imbalanced dataset classes in insider threat detection. *International Journal of Information Security*, *22*(3), 611–629. DOI: 10.1007/s10207-022-00651-1

Alboalebrah, M. R., & Al-augby, S. (2025). Unveiling the causes of fatal road accidents in Iraq: An association rule mining approach using the Apriori algorithm. *Journal of Cyber Security and Risk Auditing*, *2025*(2), 1–11. DOI: 10.63180/jcsra.thestap.2025.2.1

Aldossary, A., Algirim, T., Almubarak, I., & Almuhish, K. (2024). Cyber security in data breaches. *Journal of Cyber Security and Risk Auditing*, *2024*(1), 14–22. DOI: 10.63180/jcsra.thestap.2024.1.3

Aljumaiah, O., Jiang, W., Addula, S. R., & Almaiah, M. A. (2025). Analyzing cybersecurity risks and threats in IT infrastructure based on NIST framework. *Journal of Cyber Security and Risk Auditing*, *2025*(2), 12–26. DOI: 10.63180/jcsra.thestap.2025.2.2

Almanasir, R., Al-Solomon, D., Indrawes, S., Almaiah, M., Islam, U., & Alshar'e, M. (2025). Classification of threats and countermeasures of cloud computing. *Journal of Cyber Security and Risk Auditing*, *2025*(2), 27–42. DOI: 10.63180/jcsra.thestap.2025.2.3

Almedires, M. A., Elkhalil, A., & Amin, M. (2025). Adversarial attack detection in industrial control systems using LSTM-based intrusion detection and black-box defense strategies. *Journal of Cyber Security and Risk Auditing*, *2025*(3), 4–22. DOI: 10.63180/jcsra.thestap.2025.3.2

Almelehy, B., Ahmad, M., Nassreddine, G., Maayah, M., & Achanta, A. (2025). Analytical analysis of cyber threats and defense mechanisms for web application security. *Journal of Cyber Security and Risk Auditing*, *2025*(3), 57–76. DOI: 10.63180/jcsra.thestap.2025.3.4

Almuqren, A. A. (2025). Cybersecurity threats, countermeasures and mitigation techniques on the IoT: Future research directions. *Journal of Cyber Security and Risk Auditing*, *1*(1), 1–11. DOI: 10.63180/jcsra.thestap.2025.1.1

Alotaibi, E., Sulaiman, R. B., & Almaiah, M. (2025). Assessment of cybersecurity threats and defense mechanisms in wireless sensor networks. *Journal of Cyber Security and Risk Auditing*, *2025*(1), 47–59. DOI: 10.63180/jcsra.thestap.2025.1.5

Alshuaibi, A., Almaayah, M., & Ali, A. (2025). Machine learning for cybersecurity issues: A systematic review. *Journal of Cyber Security and Risk Auditing*, *2025*(1), 36–46. DOI: 10.63180/jcsra.thestap.2025.1.4

AlShuaibi, A., Arshad, M. W., & Maayah, M. (2025). A hybrid genetic algorithm and hidden Markov model-based hashing technique for robust data security. *Journal of Cyber Security and Risk Auditing*, *2025*(3), 42–56. DOI: 10.63180/jcsra.thestap.2025.3.6

Ang, S., Ho, M., Huy, S., & Janarthanan, M. (2025). Utilizing IDS and IPS to improve cybersecurity monitoring process. *Journal of Cyber Security and Risk Auditing*, *2025*(3), 77–88. DOI: 10.63180/jcsra.thestap.2025.3.10

Asha, S., Shanmugapriya, D., & Padmavathi, G. (2023). Malicious insider threat detection using variation of sampling methods for anomaly detection in cloud environment. *Computers & Electrical Engineering*, *105*, 108519. Advance online publication. DOI: 10.1016/j.compeleceng.2022.108519

Chattopadhyay, P., Wang, L., & Tan, Y. P. (2018). Scenario-based insider threat detection from cyber activities. *IEEE Transactions on Computational Social Systems*, *5*(3), 660–675. DOI: 10.1109/TCSS.2018.2857473

Chen, T., & Guestrin, C. (2016). XGBoost: A scalable tree boosting system. In *Proceedings of the 22nd ACM SIGKDD International Conference on Knowledge Discovery and Data Mining* (pp. 785–794). ACM. DOI: 10.1145/2939672.2939785

Cybersecurity Insiders, & Gurucul. (2023). *2023 Insider Threat Report*. Cybersecurity Insiders.

Davarasan, A., Samual, J., Palansundram, K., & Ali, A. (2024). A comprehensive review of machine learning approaches for Android malware detection. *Journal of Cyber Security and Risk Auditing*, *2024*(1), 38–60. DOI: 10.63180/jcsra.thestap.2024.1.5

Frederick, N., & Ali, A. (2024). Enhancing DDoS attack detection and mitigation in SDN using advanced machine learning techniques. *Journal of Cyber Security and Risk Auditing*, *2024*(1), 23–37. DOI: 10.63180/jcsra.thestap.2024.1.4

Gao, P., Zhang, H., Wang, M., Yang, W., Wei, X., Lv, Z., & Ma, Z. (2023). Deep temporal graph infomax for imbalanced insider threat detection. *Journal of Computer Information Systems*. Advance online publication. DOI: 10.1080/08874417.2023.2243013

Gayathri, R. G., Sajjanhar, A., & Xiang, Y. (2024). Hybrid deep learning model using SPCAGAN augmentation for insider threat analysis. *Expert Systems with Applications*, *249*, 123533. Advance online publication. DOI: 10.1016/j.eswa.2024.123533

Gayathri, R. G., Sajjanhar, A., Xiang, Y., & Ma, X. (2021). Anomaly detection for scenario-based insider activities using CGAN augmented data. In *2021 IEEE 20th International Conference on Trust, Security and Privacy in Computing and Communications (TrustCom)* (pp. 718–725). IEEE. DOI: 10.1109/TrustCom53373.2021.00105

Glasser, J., & Lindauer, B. (2013). *Bridging the gap: A pragmatic approach to generating insider threat data. In 2013 IEEE Security and Privacy Workshops*. IEEE., DOI: 10.1109/SPW.2013.37

Goodfellow, I., Pouget-Abadie, J., Mirza, M., Xu, B., Warde-Farley, D., Ozair, S., & Bengio, Y. (2014). Generative adversarial nets. *Advances in Neural Information Processing Systems*, *27*, 2672–2680.

Greitzer, F. L. (2019). Insider threats: It's the human, stupid! In *Proceedings of the Northwest Cybersecurity Symposium* (pp. 1–8).

He, H., & Garcia, E. A. (2009). Learning from imbalanced data. *IEEE Transactions on Knowledge and Data Engineering*, *21*(9), 1263–1284. DOI: 10.1109/TKDE.2008.239

Jones, L. A. (2024). Unveiling human factors: Aligning facets of cybersecurity leadership, insider threats, and arsonist attributes to reduce cyber risk. *SocioEconomic Challenges*, *8*(2), 44–63. DOI: 10.61093/sec.8(2).44-63.2024

Le, D. C., & Zincir-Heywood, N. (2021). Anomaly detection for insider threats using unsupervised ensembles. *IEEE Transactions on Network and Service Management, 18*(2), 1152–1164. DOI: 10.1109/TNSM.2021.3071928

Lippi, G., Aljawarneh, M., Al-Na'amneh, Q., Hazaymih, R., & Dhomeja, L. D. (2025). Security and privacy challenges and solutions in autonomous driving systems: A comprehensive review. *Journal of Cyber Security and Risk Auditing, 2025*(3), 23–41. DOI: 10.63180/jcsra.thestap.2025.3.3

Matthews, B. W. (1975). Comparison of the predicted and observed secondary structure of T Alicia phage lysozyme. *Biochimica et Biophysica Acta, 405*(2), 442–451. DOI: 10.1016/0005-2795(75)90109-9 PMID: 1180967

Mousa, R. S., & Shehab, R. (2025). Applying risk analysis for determining threats and countermeasures in workstation domain. *Journal of Cyber Security and Risk Auditing, 2025*(1), 12–21. DOI: 10.63180/jcsra.thestap.2025.1.2

Otoom, S. (2025). Risk auditing for digital twins in cyber physical systems: A systematic review. *Journal of Cyber Security and Risk Auditing, 2025*(1), 22–35. DOI: 10.63180/jcsra.thestap.2025.1.3

Yuan, F., Shang, Y., Liu, Y., Cao, Y., & Tan, J. (2020). Data augmentation for insider threat detection with GAN. In *2020 IEEE 32nd International Conference on Tools with Artificial Intelligence (ICTAI)* (pp. 632–638). IEEE. DOI: 10.1109/ICTAI50040.2020.00102

Yuan, S., & Wu, X. (2021). Deep learning for insider threat detection: Review, challenges and opportunities. *Computers & Security, 104*, 102221. Advance online publication. DOI: 10.1016/j.cose.2021.102221

Compilation of References

Abdel-Wahab, M. S., Neil, A. M., & Atia, A. (2024). A comparative study of machine learning and deep learning in network anomaly-based intrusion detection systems. In *15th International Conference on Computer Engineering and Systems (ICCES)* (pp. 1–6). DOI: 10.1109/ICCES51560.2020.9334553

Abdullah, B., Abd-Alghafar, I., & Salama, G. I., & Abd-Alhafez. (2020). A performance evaluation of a genetic algorithm-based approach to network intrusion detection system. *International Conference on Aerospace Sciences and Aviation Technology, The Military Technical College*, 1–17.

Abdullah-Al-Wadud, M., Kabir, M. H., Dewan, M. A. A., & Chae, O. (2007). A dynamic histogram equalization for image contrast enhancement. *IEEE Transactions on Consumer Electronics*, *53*(2), 593–600. DOI: 10.1109/TCE.2007.381734

Abubakar, A. I., Chiroma, H., Muaz, S. A., & Ila, L. B. (2019). A review of the advances in cyber security benchmark datasets for evaluating data-driven based intrusion detection systems. In *SCSE* (pp. 221–227).

Abu-Baker, A., Alshamali, A., & Shawaheen, Y. (2021). Energy-Efficient Cluster-Based Wireless Sensor Networks Using Adaptive Modulation: Performance Analysis. *IEEE Access : Practical Innovations, Open Solutions*, *9*, 141766–141777. DOI: 10.1109/ACCESS.2021.3118672

Abu-Mostafa, Y. S. (2023). Learning from data: Behavioral analysis in cybersecurity. *Nature Machine Intelligence*, *5*(2), 123–135. DOI: 10.1038/s42256-023-00001-1

Adeyeye, O. J., Akanbi, I., Emeteveke, I., & Emehin, O. (2024). Leveraging secured AI-driven data analytics for cybersecurity: Safeguarding information and enhancing threat detection. *International Journal of Research and Publication and Reviews*, *5*(10), 3208–3223. DOI: 10.55248/gengpi.5.1024.2911

Aggarwal, N., Tripathi, B., Chottani, D., & Tiwana, P. S. "Attacks Opportunities in the Cyber Physical Space and the Role of Cybersecurity," 2021 2nd International Conference on Computational Methods in Science & Technology (ICCMST), Mohali, India, 2021, pp. 276-280, DOI: 10.1109/ICCMST54943.2021.00064

Aghdam, M. H., & Kabiri, P. (2024). Feature selection for intrusion detection system using ant colony optimization. *International Journal of Network Security, 18*(3), 420–432. Aissa, N. B., & Guerroumi, M. (2024). Semi-supervised statistical approach for network anomaly detection. *Procedia Computer Science*, *83*, 1090–1095.

Agurto, A., Li, Y., Tian, G. Y., Bowring, N., & Lockwood, S. (2007, April). A review of concealed weapon detection and research in perspective. In *2007 IEEE International Conference on Networking, Sensing and Control* (pp. 443–448). IEEE. DOI: 10.1109/ICNSC.2007.372819

Ahmad, A., Harjula, E., Ylianttila, M., & Ahmad, I. (2020, December). Evaluation of machine learning techniques for security in SDN. In 2020 IEEE Globecom Workshops (GC Wkshps (pp. 1-6). IEEE.

Ahmed, M., Mahmood, A. N., & Hu, J. (2016). A survey of network anomaly detection techniques. *Journal of Network and Computer Applications*, *60*, 19–31. DOI: 10.1016/j.jnca.2015.11.016

Akilandeswari, V., & Shalinie, S. M. (2024). Probabilistic neural network-based attack traffic classification. In *2012 Fourth International Conference on Advanced Computing (ICoAC)* (pp. 1–8). IEEE.

Alabdali, A. M., Gharaei, N., & Mashat, A. A. (2021). A Framework for Energy-Efficient Clustering With Utilizing Wireless Energy Balancer. *IEEE Access : Practical Innovations, Open Solutions*, *9*, 117823–117831. DOI: 10.1109/ACCESS.2021.3107230

Alagarsundaram, P. (2024). Blockchain-enabled privacy-preserved secure e-voting system for smart cities. *Proceedings of the IEEE International Conference on Science, Technology, Engineering, and Management (ICSTEM)*. DOI: 10.1109/ICSTEM61137.2024.10560826

Alboalebrah, M. R., & Al-augby, S. (2025). Unveiling the Causes of Fatal Road Accidents in Iraq: An Association Rule Mining Approach Using the Apriori Algorithm. *Journal of Cyber Security and Risk Auditing*, *2025*(2), 1–11. DOI: 10.63180/jcsra.thestap.2025.2.1

Al-Dhafian, B., Ahmad, I., & Al-Ghamid, A. (2020). An overview of the current classification techniques in intrusion detection. In *Proceedings of the International Conference on Security and Management (SAM)* (p. 82). The Steering Committee of The World Congress in Computer Science.

Aldossary, A., Algirim, T., Almubarak, I., & Almuhish, K. (2024). Cyber Security in Data Breaches. *Journal of Cyber Security and Risk Auditing*, *2024*(1), 14–22. DOI: 10.63180/jcsra.thestap.2024.1.3

Aldweesh, A., Derhab, A., & Emam, A. (2020). An evaluation of hybrid machine learning models for anomaly-based intrusion detection systems. *Future Generation Computer Systems*, *105*, 250–272. DOI: 10.1016/j.knosys.2019.105124

AlEisa, H. N., Alrowais, F., Allafi, R., Almalki, N. S., Faqih, R., Marzouk, R., Alnfiai, M. M., Motwakel, A., & Ibrahim, S. S. (2023). Transforming transportation: Safe and secure vehicular communication and anomaly detection with intelligent cyber-physical systems and deep learning. *IEEE Transactions on Consumer Electronics*, *70*(1), 1736–1746. https://ieeexplore.ieee.org/abstract/document/10308696. DOI: 10.1109/TCE.2023.3325827

Ali, M. H., Al Mohammed, B. A. D., Ismail, A., & Zolkipli, M. F. (2018). A new intrusion detection system based on fast learning network and particle swarm optimization. *IEEE Access : Practical Innovations, Open Solutions*, *6*, 20255–20261. DOI: 10.1109/ACCESS.2018.2820092

Aljumah, A. (2024). Detection of distributed denial of service attacks using artificial neural networks. *International Journal of Advanced Computer Science and Applications*, *8*(8). Advance online publication. DOI: 10.14569/IJACSA.2017.080841

Aljumaiah, O., Jiang, W., Addula, S. R., & Almaiah, M. A. (2025). Analyzing cybersecurity risks and threats in IT infrastructure based on NIST framework. *J. Cyber Secur. Risk Audit*, *2025*(2), 12–26. DOI: 10.63180/jcsra.thestap.2025.2.2

Almanasir, R., Al-solomon, D., Indrawes, S., Almaiah, M., Islam, U., & Alshar'e, M. (2025). Classification of threats and countermeasures of cloud computing. *Journal of Cyber Security and Risk Auditing*, *2025*(2), 27–42. DOI: 10.63180/jcsra.thestap.2025.2.3

Almedires, M. A., Elkhalil, A., & Amin, M. (2025). Adversarial Attack Detection in Industrial Control Systems Using LSTM-Based Intrusion Detection and Black-Box Defense Strategies. *Journal of Cyber Security and Risk Auditing*, *2025*(3), 4–22. DOI: 10.63180/jcsra.thestap.2025.3.2

Almelehy, B., Ahmad, M., Nassreddine, G., Maayah, M., & Achanta, A. (2025). Analytical Analysis of Cyber Threats and Defense Mechanisms for Web Application Security. *Journal of Cyber Security and Risk Auditing*, *2025*(3), 57–76. DOI: 10.63180/jcsra.thestap.2025.3.4

Al-Mhiqani, M. N., Ahmad, R., Abidin, Z. Z., & Isnin, S. N. (2021). An integrated imbalanced learning and deep neural network model for insider threat detection. *International Journal of Advanced Computer Science and Applications*, *12*(1), 202–210. DOI: 10.14569/IJACSA.2021.0120166

Al-Mhiqani, M. N., Ahmad, R., Zainal Abidin, Z., Yassin, W., Hassan, A., Abdulkareem, K. H., Ali, N. S., & Yunos, Z. (2020). A review of insider threat detection: Classification, machine learning techniques, datasets, open challenges, and recommendations. *Applied Sciences (Basel, Switzerland)*, *10*(15), 5208. DOI: 10.3390/app10155208

Al-Mhiqani, M. N., Alsboui, T., Al-Shehari, T., Abdulkareem, K. H., Ahmad, R., & Mohammed, M. A. (2024). Insider threat detection in cyber-physical systems: A systematic literature review. *Computers & Electrical Engineering*, *119*, 109489. Advance online publication. DOI: 10.1016/j.compeleceng.2024.109489

Almiani, M., AbuGhazleh, A., Al-Rahayfeh, A., Atiewi, S., & Razaque, A. (2020). Deep recurrent neural network for IoT intrusion detection system. *Simulation Modelling Practice and Theory*, *101*, 102031. DOI: 10.1016/j.simpat.2019.102031

Almuqren, A. A. (2025). Cybersecurity threats, countermeasures and mitigation techniques on the IoT: Future research directions. *Journal of Cyber Security and Risk Auditing*, *1*(1), 1–11. DOI: 10.63180/jcsra.thestap.2025.1.1

Alotaibi, E., Sulaiman, R. B., & Almaiah, M. (2025). Assessment of cybersecurity threats and defense mechanisms in wireless sensor networks. *J. Cyber Secur. Risk Audit*, *2025*(1), 47–59. DOI: 10.63180/jcsra.thestap.2025.1.5

Alrayes, F. S., Zakariah, M., Amin, S. U., Khan, Z. I., & Helal, M. (2024). Intrusion Detection in IoT Systems Using Denoising Autoencoder. *IEEE Access : Practical Innovations, Open Solutions*, *12*, 122401–122425. DOI: 10.1109/ACCESS.2024.3451726

Al-Shareeda, M. A., Ali, A. M., Hammoud, M. A., Kazem, Z. H. M., & Hussein, M. A. (2025). Secure IoT-Based Real-Time Water Level Monitoring System Using ESP32 for Critical Infrastructure. *J. Cyber Secur. Risk Audit*, *2*, 43–52. DOI: 10.63180/jcsra.thestap.2025.2.4

Al-Shareeda, M. A., Jafer, A. N., Hashem, M. T., & Fajr, M. S. (2024). Secure Offline Smart Office Automation System Using ESP32 and Bluetooth Control Architecture. *Journal of Cyber Security and Risk Auditing*, *2024*(1), 3–13. DOI: 10.63180/jcsra.thestap.2024.1.2

Al-Shehari, T., & Alsowail, R. A. (2023). Random resampling algorithms for addressing the imbalanced dataset classes in insider threat detection. *International Journal of Information Security*, *22*(3), 611–629. DOI: 10.1007/s10207-022-00651-1

Alshuaibi, A., Almaayah, M., & Ali, A. (2025). Machine Learning for Cybersecurity Issues: A systematic Review. *Journal of Cyber Security and Risk Auditing*, *2025*(1), 36–46. DOI: 10.63180/jcsra.thestap.2025.1.4

AlShuaibi, A., Arshad, M. W., & Maayah, M. (2025). A Hybrid Genetic Algorithm and Hidden Markov Model-Based Hashing Technique for Robust Data Security. *Journal of Cyber Security and Risk Auditing*, *2025*(3), 42–56. DOI: 10.63180/jcsra.thestap.2025.3.6

Altamimi, S., & Abu Al-Haija, Q. (2024). Maximizing intrusion detection efficiency for IoT networks using extreme learning machine. *Discover Internet of Things*, *4*(1), 5. DOI: 10.1007/s43926-024-00060-x

Al-Yaseen, W. L., Othman, Z. A., & Nazri, M. Z. A. (2017). Multi-level hybrid support vector machine and extreme learning machine based on modified k-means for intrusion detection system. *Expert Systems with Applications*, *67*, 296–303. DOI: 10.1016/j.eswa.2016.09.041

Alzaabi, F. R., & Mehmood, A. (2024). A review of recent advances, challenges, and opportunities in malicious insider threat detection using machine learning methods. *IEEE Access : Practical Innovations, Open Solutions*, *12*, 30907–30927. DOI: 10.1109/ACCESS.2024.3369906

Anandharaj, N. (2024). AI-Powered Cloud Security: A Study on the Integration of Artificial Intelligence and Machine Learning for Improved Threat Detection and Prevention. [JRTCSE]. *J. Recent Trends Comput. Sci. Eng.*, *12*, 21–30.

Ang, S., Ho, M., Huy, S., & Janarthanan, M. (2025). Utilizing IDS and IPS to Improve Cybersecurity Monitoring Process. *Journal of Cyber Security and Risk Auditing*, *2025*(3), 77–88. DOI: 10.63180/jcsra.thestap.2025.3.10

Antikainen, M., Aura, T., & Särelä, M. (2014). Spook in your network: Attacking an SDN with a compromised openflow switch. In Secure IT Systems: 19th Nordic Conference, NordSec 2014, Tromsø, Norway, October 15-17, 2014 [Springer International Publishing.]. *Proceedings*, *19*, 229–244.

Anusuya, V. S., Baswaraju, S., Thirumalraj, A., & Nedumaran, A. Securing the MANET by Detecting the Intrusions Using CSO and XGBoost Model. In *Intelligent Systems and Industrial Internet of Things for Sustainable Development* (pp. 219–234). Chapman and Hall/CRC. DOI: 10.1201/9781032642789-11

Asadollahi, S., Goswami, B., & Sameer, M. (2018, February). Ryu controller's scalability experiment on software defined networks. In *2018 IEEE International Conference on Current Trends in Advanced Computing (ICCTAC)* (pp. 1-5). IEEE. DOI: 10.1109/ICCTAC.2018.8370397

Asha, S., Shanmugapriya, D., & Padmavathi, G. (2023). Malicious insider threat detection using variation of sampling methods for anomaly detection in cloud environment. *Computers & Electrical Engineering*, *105*, 108519. Advance online publication. DOI: 10.1016/j.compeleceng.2022.108519

Ashfin, P. (2024). AI-Driven Threat Detection and Response in Cybersecurity. *Bulletin of Engineering Science and Technology*, *1*(2), 125–143.

Ashraf, A. H., Imran, M., Qahtani, A. M., Alsufyani, A., Almutiry, O., Mahmood, A., & Habib, M. (2022). Weapons detection for security and video surveillance using CNN and YOLO-v5s. CMC-Comput. *Mater. Contin.*, *70*(4), 2761–2775.

Atadoga, A., Sodiya, E. O., Umoga, U. J., & Amoo, O. O. (2024). A comprehensive review of machine learning's role in enhancing network security and threat detection. *World Journal of Advanced Research and Reviews*, *21*(2), 877–886. DOI: 10.30574/wjarr.2024.21.2.0501

Azimjonov, J., & Kim, T. (2024). Designing accurate lightweight intrusion detection systems for IoT networks using fine-tuned linear SVM and feature selectors. *Computers & Security*, *137*, 103598. DOI: 10.1016/j.cose.2023.103598

Badotra, S., & Panda, S. N. (2020). Software-Defined Networking: A novel approach to networks. Handbook of Computer Networks and Cyber Security: Principles and Paradigms, 313-339.

Bai, X., & Zhou, F. (2010). Analysis of new top-hat transformation and the application for infrared dim small target detection. *Pattern Recognition*, *43*(6), 2145–2156. DOI: 10.1016/j.patcog.2009.12.023

Bakhsh, S. A., Khan, M. A., Ahmed, F., Alshehri, M. S., Ali, H., & Ahmad, J. (2023). Enhancing IoT network security through deep learning-powered Intrusion Detection System. *Internet of Things : Engineering Cyber Physical Human Systems*, *24*, 100936. DOI: 10.1016/j.iot.2023.100936

Basit, A., Munir, M. A., Ali, M., Werghi, N., & Mahmood, A. (2020, October). Localizing firearm carriers by identifying human-object pairs. In *2020 IEEE International Conference on Image Processing (ICIP)* (pp. 2031–2035). IEEE. DOI: 10.1109/ICIP40778.2020.9190886

Behera, T. M., Mohapatra, S. K., Samal, U. C., Khan, M. S., Daneshmand, M., & Gandomi, A. H. (2020). I-SEP: An Improved Routing Protocol for Heterogeneous WSN for IoT-Based Environmental Monitoring. *IEEE Internet of Things Journal, 7*(1), 710–717. DOI: 10.1109/JIOT.2019.2940988

Bernadotte, A. (2023, February). Cyber security for surgical remote intelligent robotic systems. In *2023 9th International Conference on Automation, Robotics and Applications (ICARA)* (pp. 65-69). IEEE. DOI: 10.1109/ICARA56516.2023.10126050

Bhatti, M. T., Khan, M. G., Aslam, M., & Fiaz, M. J. (2021). Weapon detection in real-time CCTV videos using deep learning. *IEEE Access : Practical Innovations, Open Solutions, 9*, 34366–34382. DOI: 10.1109/ACCESS.2021.3059170

Bobba, J. (2023). Attention-based isolation forest integrated ensemble machine learning algorithm for financial fraud detection. *Proceedings of IACIS 2024*, DOI: DOI: 10.1109/IACIS61494.2024.10721649

Bohra, N., Kumari, A., Mishra, V. K., Soni, P. K., & Balyan, V. (2025). Intelligence-Based Strategies with Vehicle-to-Everything Network: A Review. *Future Internet, 17*(2), 79. Advance online publication. DOI: 10.3390/fi17020079

Breiman, L. (2001). Random forests. *Machine Learning, 45*(1), 5–32. DOI: 10.1023/A:1010933404324

Buczak, A. L., & Guven, E. (2016). A survey of data mining and machine learning methods for cyber security intrusion detection. *IEEE Communications Surveys and Tutorials, 18*(2), 1153–1176. DOI: 10.1109/COMST.2015.2494502

Cabaj, K., Wytrebowicz, J., Kuklinski, S., Radziszewski, P., & Dinh, K. T. (2014, September). SDN Architecture Impact on Network Security. In *FedCSIS* (pp. 143–148). Position Papers.

Catak, F. O., Yazı, A. F., Elezaj, O., & Ahmed, J. (2020). Deep learning based sequential model for malware analysis using Windows exe API calls. *PeerJ. Computer Science, 6*, e285. DOI: 10.7717/peerj-cs.285 PMID: 33816936

Chaganti, R., Suliman, W., Ravi, V., & Dua, A. (2023). Deep learning approach for SDN-enabled intrusion detection system in IoT networks. *Information (Basel), 14*(1), 41. DOI: 10.3390/info14010041

Chandola, V., Banerjee, A., & Kumar, V. (2023). Anomaly detection: A survey. *ACM Computing Surveys, 41*(3), 15:1-15:58. https://doi.org/DOI: 10.1145/1541880.1541882

Chattopadhyay, P., Wang, L., & Tan, Y. P. (2018). Scenario-based insider threat detection from cyber activities. *IEEE Transactions on Computational Social Systems, 5*(3), 660–675. DOI: 10.1109/TCSS.2018.2857473

Chen, L., & Davis, R. (2023). Comparative analysis of open source and proprietary security solutions. *IEEE Security and Privacy, 21*(3), 28–36. DOI: 10.1109/MSEC.2019.2963021

Chen, L., Smith, J., Brown, K., & Johnson, M. (2022). Ethical challenges in AI-driven cybersecurity. *IEEE Transactions on Technology and Society, 3*(2), 45–62. DOI: 10.1109/TTS.2022.3156789

Chen, T., & Guestrin, C. (2016). XGBoost: A scalable tree boosting system. In *Proceedings of the 22nd ACM SIGKDD International Conference on Knowledge Discovery and Data Mining* (pp. 785–794). ACM. DOI: 10.1145/2939672.2939785

Cisco. (2023). *2023 cybersecurity threat trends: Phishing, crypto top the list.* https://www.cisco.com/c/en/us/products/security/cybersecurity-reports.html

Computing Surveys, A. C. M. (2024). Adaptive AI security frameworks [Special issue]. *ACM Computing Surveys, 57*(1), 23–45.

Conderana Medem, E. (2023). Attack Traffic Network Analysis of a Brute-Force Attack against a MySQL Server.

Costin, A. (2016, October). Security of CCTV and video surveillance systems: Threats, vulnerabilities, attacks, and mitigations. In *Proceedings of the 6th International Workshop on Trustworthy Embedded Devices* (pp. 45–54). DOI: 10.1145/2995289.2995290

Covas Moschovas, M., Saikali, S., Rogers, T., Gamal, A., Perera, R., Reddy, S., & Patel, V. (2024). Exploring the ethical implications in the telesurgery ERA. *International Braz J Urol, 50*(3), 375–377. DOI: 10.1590/s1677-5538.ibju.2024.0133 PMID: 38598833

CrowdStrike. (2024). *2024 global threat report.* https://www.crowdstrike.com/global-threat-report-2024/

Cybersecurity Insiders, & Gurucul. (2023). *2023 Insider Threat Report.* Cybersecurity Insiders.

Dai, Y., Wu, F., Zhou, F., & Barnard, K. (2021). Attentional local contrast networks for infrared small target detection. *IEEE Transactions on Geoscience and Remote Sensing*, *59*(11), 9813–9824. DOI: 10.1109/TGRS.2020.3044958

Dataset link: https://paperswithcode.com/dataset/robotic-interestingness

Davarasan, A., Samual, J., Palansundram, K., & Ali, A. (2024). A Comprehensive Review of Machine Learning Approaches for Android Malware Detection. *Journal of Cyber Security and Risk Auditing*, *2024*(1), 38–60. DOI: 10.63180/jcsra.thestap.2024.1.5

De Oliveira, R. L. S., Schweitzer, C. M., Shinoda, A. A., & Prete, L. R. (2014, June). Using mininet for emulation and prototyping software-defined networks. In *2014 IEEE Colombian Conference on Communications and Computing (COLCOM)* (pp. 1-6). IEEE. DOI: 10.1109/ColComCon.2014.6860404

Deevi, D. P. (2022). Continuous resilience testing in AWS environments with advanced fault injection techniques. *Volume 10, Issue 3, ISSN 2347–3657.*

Deloitte. (2023). *Future of cyber survey: Building cyber resilience*. https://www2.deloitte.com/us/en/pages/advisory/articles/future-of-cyber-survey.html

Deshpande, D., Jain, M., Jajoo, A., Kadam, D., Kadam, H., & Kashyap, A. (2023, October). Next-gen security: YOLOv8 for real-time weapon detection. In 2023 7th International Conference on I-SMAC (IoT in Social, Mobile, Analytics and Cloud) (I-SMAC) (pp. 1055–1060). IEEE.

Devarajan, M. V. (2024). *Mitigating security risks in robotic telesurgery with SecureSurgiNET: Protocols for replay, brute force, and session hijacking attacks.*

Devarajan, S. (2023). An IoT-based automated system for accurate skin disease detection. *Intelligent Data Analysis*, *27*(S1), 161–180. DOI: 10.3233/IDA-237442

Divekar, M., Parekh, V., Savla, R., Mishra, R., & Shirole, M. (2022). Benchmarking datasets for anomaly-based network intrusion detection: KDD Cup 99 alternatives. In *IEEE 3rd International Conference on Computing, Communication and Security (ICCCS)* (pp. 1–8).

Djenna, A., Bouridane, A., Rubab, S., & Marou, I. M. (2023). Artificial intelligence-based malware detection, analysis, and mitigation. *Symmetry*, *15*(3), 677. DOI: 10.3390/sym15030677

Dua, S., & Du, X. (2016). *Data Mining and Machine Learning in Cybersecurity*. CRC Press. DOI: 10.1201/b10867

Elnakib, O., Shaaban, E., Mahmoud, M., & Emara, K. (2023). EIDM: Deep learning model for IoT intrusion detection systems. *The Journal of Supercomputing*, *79*(12), 13241–13261. DOI: 10.1007/s11227-023-05197-0

Elsayed, R. A., Hamada, R. A., Abdalla, M. I., & Elsaid, S. A. (2023). Securing IoT and SDN systems using deep-learning based automatic intrusion detection. *Ain Shams Engineering Journal*, *14*(10), 102211. DOI: 10.1016/j.asej.2023.102211

Ethics, I. E. E. E. in Action. (2023). *Ethical considerations in AI-driven security systems*. https://ethics.ieee.org/

Fan, M., Wei, W., Xie, X., Liu, Y., Guan, X., & Liu, T. (2021). Can we trust your explanations? Sanity checks for interpreters in Android malware analysis. *IEEE Transactions on Information Forensics and Security*, *16*, 838–853. DOI: 10.1109/TIFS.2020.3021924

Farooq, H. M., & Otaibi, N. M. (2018, March). Optimal machine learning algorithms for cyber threat detection. In *2018 UKSim-AMSS 20th International Conference on Computer Modelling and Simulation (UKSim)* (pp. 32-37). IEEE. DOI: 10.1109/UKSim.2018.00018

Ferrús, R., Koumaras, H., Sallent, O., Agapiou, G., Rasheed, T., Kourtis, M. A., Boustie, C., Gélard, P., & Ahmed, T. (2016). SDN/NFV-enabled satellite communications networks: Opportunities, scenarios and challenges. *Physical Communication*, *18*, 95–112. DOI: 10.1016/j.phycom.2015.10.007

Forrester Research. (2024). *The state of enterprise behavioral analytics and data processing trends*. https://www.forrester.com/report/the-state-of-enterprise-behavioral-analytics/

Fraihat, S., Makhadmeh, S., Awad, M., Al-Betar, M. A., & Al-Redhaei, A. (2023). Intrusion detection system for large-scale IoT NetFlow networks using machine learning with modified Arithmetic Optimization Algorithm. *Internet of Things : Engineering Cyber Physical Human Systems*, *22*, 100819. DOI: 10.1016/j.iot.2023.100819

Frederick, N., & Ali, A. (2024). Enhancing DDoS Attack Detection and Mitigation in SDN Using Advanced Machine Learning Techniques. *Journal of Cyber Security and Risk Auditing*, *2024*(1), 23–37. DOI: 10.63180/jcsra.thestap.2024.1.4

Fung, C. J., Zhang, J., Aib, I., & Boutaba, R. (2024). Dirichlet-based reliable management for productive collaboration intrusion detection networking. *IEEE Transactions on Network and Service Management*, *16*(2), 7925–7991.

Fu, X., Yang, Y., & Postolache, O. (2021). Sustainable Multipath Routing Protocol for Multi-Sink Wireless Sensor Networks in Harsh Environments. *IEEE Transactions on Sustainable Computing*, *6*(1), 168–181. DOI: 10.1109/TSUSC.2020.2976096

Galli, A., La Gatta, V., Moscato, V., Postiglione, M., & Sperlì, G. (2024). Explainability in AI-based behavioral malware detection systems. *Computers & Security*, *141*, 103842. DOI: 10.1016/j.cose.2024.103842

Gao, P., Zhang, H., Wang, M., Yang, W., Wei, X., Lv, Z., & Ma, Z. (2023). Deep temporal graph infomax for imbalanced insider threat detection. *Journal of Computer Information Systems*. Advance online publication. DOI: 10.1080/08874417.2023.2243013

Garcia-Teodoro, P., Diaz-Verdejo, J., Maciá-Fernández, G., & Vázquez, E. (2009). Anomaly-based network intrusion detection: Techniques, systems and challenges. *Computers & Security*, *28*(1-2), 18–28. DOI: 10.1016/j.cose.2008.08.003

Gartner. (2024). *Emerging technologies and trends impact radar for security*. Gartner, Inc.

Gayathri, R. G., Sajjanhar, A., Xiang, Y., & Ma, X. (2021). Anomaly detection for scenario-based insider activities using CGAN augmented data. In *2021 IEEE 20th International Conference on Trust, Security and Privacy in Computing and Communications (TrustCom)* (pp. 718–725). IEEE. DOI: 10.1109/TrustCom53373.2021.00105

Gayathri, R. G., Sajjanhar, A., & Xiang, Y. (2024). Hybrid deep learning model using SPCAGAN augmentation for insider threat analysis. *Expert Systems with Applications*, *249*, 123533. Advance online publication. DOI: 10.1016/j.eswa.2024.123533

Gelana, F., & Yadav, A. (2019). Firearm detection from surveillance cameras using image processing and machine learning techniques. In Smart Innovations in Communication and Computational Sciences: Proceedings of ICSICCS-2018 (pp. 25–34). Springer Singapore. DOI: 10.1007/978-981-13-2414-7_3

Glasser, J., & Lindauer, B. (2013). *Bridging the gap: A pragmatic approach to generating insider threat data. In 2013 IEEE Security and Privacy Workshops*. IEEE., DOI: 10.1109/SPW.2013.37

Goodfellow, I., Pouget-Abadie, J., Mirza, M., Xu, B., Warde-Farley, D., Ozair, S., & Bengio, Y. (2014). Generative adversarial nets. *Advances in Neural Information Processing Systems*, *27*, 2672–2680.

Goransson, P., Black, C., & Culver, T. (2016). *Software defined networks: a comprehensive approach*. Morgan Kaufmann.

Grega, M., Matiolański, A., Guzik, P., & Leszczuk, M. (2016). Automated detection of firearms and knives in a CCTV image. *Sensors (Basel)*, *16*(1), 47. DOI: 10.3390/s16010047 PMID: 26729128

Greitzer, F. L. (2019). Insider threats: It's the human, stupid! In *Proceedings of the Northwest Cybersecurity Symposium* (pp. 1–8).

Gudivaka, R. L. (2024). Mitigating security risks in robotic telesurgery with SecureSurgiNET: Protocols for replay, brute force, and session hijacking attacks. *Proceedings of the 2024 Second International Conference on Data Science and Information System*, 1–6. DOI: 10.1109/ICDSIS61070.2024.10594075

Gudivaka, R. L., & Gudivaka, R. K. (2021). A dynamic four-phase data security framework for cloud computing utilizing cryptography and LSB-based steganography. *International Journal of Engineering Research and Science & Technology*, *17*(3), 90. https://www.ijerst.com

Gupta, A., & Pathak, M. (2024). Data Security Threats Arising Between a Cloud and Its Users. In Marriwala, N. K., Dhingra, S., Jain, S., & Kumar, D. (Eds.), *Mobile Radio Communications and 5G Networks. MRCN 2023. Lecture Notes in Networks and Systems* (Vol. 915). Springer., DOI: 10.1007/978-981-97-0700-3_6

Gupta, M., Vashishth, T. K., & Verma, P. K. (2024). Machine learning and deep learning based intrusion detection for blackhole attacks in mobile ad-hoc networks. *Multidisciplinary Science Journal*, *6*(11), 2024209–2024209. DOI: 10.31893/multiscience.2024209

Gupta, R., & Srivastava, P. (2025). Artificial intelligence and machine learning in cyber security applications. In *Cyber Security Solutions for Protecting and Building the Future Smart Grid* (pp. 271–296). Elsevier. DOI: 10.1016/B978-0-443-14066-2.00004-9

Gupta, R., Thakker, U., Tanwar, S., Obaidat, M. S., & Hsiao, K. F. (2020, October). Bits: A blockchain-driven intelligent scheme for telesurgery system. In *2020 International Conference on Computer, Information and Telecommunication Systems (CITS)* (pp. 1-5). IEEE. DOI: 10.1109/CITS49457.2020.9232662

Haddad, J., Pitropakis, N., Chrysoulas, C., Lemoudden, M., & Buchanan, W. J. (2023). Attacking Windows Hello for Business: Is It What We Were Promised. *Cryptography*, *7*(1), 9. DOI: 10.3390/cryptography7010009

Haji, S. H., & Ameen, S. Y. (2021). Attack and anomaly detection in iot networks using machine learning techniques: A review. *Asian J. Res. Comput. Sci*, *9*(2), 30–46. DOI: 10.9734/ajrcos/2021/v9i230218

Han, D., Du, X., & Liu, X. (2021). CELR: Connectivity and Energy Aware Layering Routing Protocol for UANs. *IEEE Sensors Journal, 21*(5), 7046–7057. DOI: 10.1109/JSEN.2020.3039808

Han, W., Xue, J., Wang, Y., Huang, L., Kong, Z., & Mao, L. (2019). Maldae: Detecting and explaining malware based on correlation and fusion of static and dynamic characteristics. *Computers & Security, 83*, 208–233. DOI: 10.1016/j.cose.2019.02.007

Haseeb, K., Almustafa, K. M., Jan, Z., Saba, T., & Tariq, U. (2020). Secure and Energy-Aware Heuristic Routing Protocol for Wireless Sensor Network. *IEEE Access : Practical Innovations, Open Solutions*, *8*, 163962–163974. DOI: 10.1109/ACCESS.2020.3022285

Hassan, A. A. H., Shah, W. M., Habeb, A. H. H., Othman, M. F. I., & Al-Mhiqani, M. N. (2020). An Improved Energy-Efficient Clustering Protocol to Prolong the Lifetime of the WSN-Based IoT. *IEEE Access : Practical Innovations, Open Solutions, 8*, 200500–200517. DOI: 10.1109/ACCESS.2020.3035624

Hassan, S. K., & Ibrahim, A. (2023). The role of artificial intelligence in cyber security and incident response. *International Journal for Electronic Crime Investigation*, *7*(2).

Hassija, V., Chamola, V., Saxena, V., Jain, D., Goyal, P., & Sikdar, B. (2019). A survey on IoT security: Application areas, security threats, and solution architectures. *IEEE Access : Practical Innovations, Open Solutions*, *7*, 82721–82743. DOI: 10.1109/ACCESS.2019.2924045

Heemeyer, F., Boehler, Q., Leuenberger, F., & Nelson, B. J. (2024, June). ROSurgical: An Open-Source Framework for Telesurgery. In *2024 International Symposium on Medical Robotics (ISMR)* (pp. 1-7). IEEE.

He, H., & Garcia, E. A. (2009). Learning from imbalanced data. *IEEE Transactions on Knowledge and Data Engineering, 21*(9), 1263–1284. DOI: 10.1109/TKDE.2008.239

He, S., Xie, K., Chen, W., Zhang, D., & Wen, J. (2018). Energy-Aware Routing for SWIPT in Multi-Hop Energy-Constrained Wireless Network. *IEEE Access : Practical Innovations, Open Solutions, 6*, 17996–18008. DOI: 10.1109/ACCESS.2018.2820093

Hindy, H., Bayne, E., & Atkinson, R. (2020). A taxonomy of network threats and the impact of current datasets on intrusion detection research. *Computer Networks*, *173*, 107–123. https://ieeexplore.ieee.org/abstract/document/9108270

Hou, Q., Wang, Z., Tan, F., Zhao, Y., Zheng, H., & Zhang, W. (2022). RISTDnet: Robust infrared small target detection network. *IEEE Geoscience and Remote Sensing Letters*, *19*, 1–5. DOI: 10.1109/LGRS.2021.3050828

Huang, H., Yin, H., Min, G., Zhang, J., Wu, Y., & Zhang, X. (2018). Energy-Aware Dual-Path Geographic Routing to Bypass Routing Holes in Wireless Sensor Networks. *IEEE Transactions on Mobile Computing*, *17*(6), 1339–1352. DOI: 10.1109/TMC.2017.2771424

Hu, W., & Hu, W. (2023). Network-based intrusion detection using Adaboost algorithm. In *IEEE/WIC/ACM International Conference on Web Intelligence (WI '05)* (pp. 712–717). IEEE Computer Society. https://doi.org/DOI: 10.1109/WI.2005.107

Ibrahim, A. A. Z., Hashim, F., Sali, A., Noordin, N. K., & Fadul, S. M. E. (2022). A Multi-Objective Routing Mechanism for Energy Management Optimization in SDN Multi-Control Architecture. *IEEE Access : Practical Innovations, Open Solutions*, *10*, 20312–20327. DOI: 10.1109/ACCESS.2022.3149795

IDC. (2023). *Global DataSphere forecast.* Retrieved from https://www.idc.com/getdoc.jsp?containerId=prUS50175423

IEEE Standard P7009-2022. (2022). *IEEE recommended practice for addressing ethical concerns during system design* (IEEE Standard No. P7009-2022). Institute of Electrical and Electronics Engineers.

IEEE Transactions on Information Forensics and Security. (2024). AI-powered threat intelligence [Special issue]. *IEEE Transactions on Information Forensics and Security, 19*(1), 45-62.

Ilesanmi, E., & Ilesanmi, T. O. (2021). Methods for image denoising using convolutional neural network: A review. *Complex & Intelligent Systems*, *7*(5), 2179–2198. DOI: 10.1007/s40747-021-00428-4

Ingre, B., & Pandey, A. (2015). Efficiency analysis of NSL-KDD datasets using neural networks. In *Network Process and Communication Engineering Systems: International Publication Conference.*

Ingre, B., & Yadav, A. (2023). Performance analysis of NSL-KDD dataset using ANN. In *International Conference on Signal Processing and Communication Engineering Systems* (pp. 92–96).

International Energy Agency. (2024). *Cybersecurity in critical energy infrastructure.* https://www.iea.org/reports/cybersecurity-in-critical-energy-infrastructure

Jafarian, T., Masdari, M., Ghaffari, A., & Majidzadeh, K. (2021). A survey and classification of the security anomaly detection mechanisms in software defined networks. *Cluster Computing*, *24*(2), 1235–1253. DOI: 10.1007/s10586-020-03184-1

Jahromi, A. N., Hashemi, S., Dehghantanha, A., Parizi, R. M., & Choo, K. K. R. (2020). An enhanced stacked LSTM method with no random initialization for malware threat hunting in safety and time-critical systems. *IEEE Transactions on Emerging Topics in Computational Intelligence*, *4*(5), 630–640. DOI: 10.1109/TETCI.2019.2910243

Jeon, H., Kim, H., Kim, D., & Kim, J. (2024). PASS-CCTV: Proactive Anomaly surveillance system for CCTV footage analysis in adverse environmental conditions. *Expert Systems with Applications*, *254*, 124391. DOI: 10.1016/j.eswa.2024.124391

Jingyi Su, He Shan. Yan Wu. Features selection and prediction for IOT attacks, high conference computing. 2022;2: 100047. .DOI: 10.1016/j.hcc.2021.100047

Jones, L. A. (2024). Unveiling human factors: Aligning facets of cybersecurity leadership, insider threats, and arsonist attributes to reduce cyber risk. *SocioEconomic Challenges*, *8*(2), 44–63. DOI: 10.61093/sec.8(2).44-63.2024

Jothi, B., & Pushpalatha, M. (2023). WILS-TRS—A novel optimized deep learning based intrusion detection framework for IoT networks. *Personal and Ubiquitous Computing*, *27*(3), 1285–1301. DOI: 10.1007/s00779-021-01578-5

JothiShri. S., Upender, T., Ravikumar, R. J., Sailaja, Y., Yuvabharathi, E., & Agnestreesa, J. (2024, September). AI Cyber Security: Enhancing Network Security with Deep Learning for Real-Time Threat Detection and Performance Evaluation. In 2024 3rd International Conference for Advancement in Technology (ICONAT) (pp. 1-6). IEEE.

Jyothsna, V., Sandhya, E., Kamalapuram, K. B., & Bhasha, P. (2025). AI-Driven Threat Detection in Cloud Environments. In Convergence of Cybersecurity and Cloud Computing (pp. 261-284). IGI Global Scientific Publishing.

Kaggle. (2025, April 5). *IR small targets dataset*. https://www.kaggle.com/datasets/llpukojluct/ir-small-target

Kang, H., Ahn, D. H., Lee, G. M., Yoo, J. D., Park, K. H., & Kim, H. K. "IoT Network Intrusion Dataset," IEEE DataPort, 2019. [Online]. Available: https://ieeedataport.org/open-access/iot-network-intrusion-dataset

Kavitha, D., & Thejas, S. (2024). AI enabled threat detection: Leveraging artificial intelligence for advanced security and cyber threat mitigation. *IEEE Access : Practical Innovations, Open Solutions*.

Keerthana, S. M., Sujitha, R., & Yazhini, P. (2024, June). Weapon Detection For Security Using The YOLO Algorithm With Email Alert Notification. In *2024 International Conference on Innovations and Challenges in Emerging Technologies (ICICET)* (pp. 1–6). IEEE. DOI: 10.1109/ICICET59348.2024.10616365

Khan, M. I., Arif, A., & Khan, A. R. A. (2024). The Most Recent Advances and Uses of AI in Cybersecurity. *BULLET: Jurnal Multidisiplin Ilmu*, *3*(4), 566–578.

Kim, G., Lee, S., & Kim, S. (2014). A novel hybrid intrusion detection method integrating anomaly detection with misuse detection. *Expert Systems with Applications*, *41*(4), 1690–1700. DOI: 10.1016/j.eswa.2013.08.066

Kim, J., Lee, H., & Chong, S. (2018). Traffic-Aware Energy-Saving Base Station Sleeping and Clustering in Cooperative Networks. *IEEE Transactions on Wireless Communications*, *17*(2), 1173–1186. DOI: 10.1109/TWC.2017.2776916

Kodadi, S. (2022). Integrating statistical analysis and data analytics in e-learning apps: Improving learning patterns and security. *International Journal of Appiled Science and Engineering Management*, *16*(4), 1–10. DOI: 10.5281/zenodo.13994651

Krishnamoorthy, G., & Sistla, S. M. K. (2023). Exploring Machine Learning Intrusion Detection: Addressing Security and Privacy Challenges in IoT-A Comprehensive Review. Journal of Knowledge Learning and Science Technology ISSN: 2959-6386 (online), 2(2), 114-125.

Kumar, A., & Guleria, K. (2024, November). Leveraging Machine Learning Algorithms for Threat Detection Using AI-Enhanced Cybersecurity Datasets. In 2024 4th International Conference on Technological Advancements in Computational Sciences (ICTACS) (pp. 483-488). IEEE.

Kumar, N., & Ali, R. (2024). A smart contract-based robotic surgery authentication system for healthcare using 6G-Tactile Internet. *Computer Networks*, *238*, 110133. DOI: 10.1016/j.comnet.2023.110133

Lazzarini, R., Tianfield, H., & Charissis, V. (2023). A stacking ensemble of deep learning models for IoT intrusion detection. *Knowledge-Based Systems*, *279*, 110941. DOI: 10.1016/j.knosys.2023.110941

Le, A., Dinh, P., Le, H., & Tran, N. C. (2015, November). Flexible network-based intrusion detection and prevention system on software-defined networks. In *2015 International Conference on Advanced Computing and Applications (ACOMP)* (pp. 106-111). IEEE. DOI: 10.1109/ACOMP.2015.19

Le, D. C., & Zincir-Heywood, N. (2021). Anomaly detection for insider threats using unsupervised ensembles. *IEEE Transactions on Network and Service Management*, *18*(2), 1152–1164. DOI: 10.1109/TNSM.2021.3071928

Lee, H., & Park, C. G. (2023). Infrared small target detection algorithm using an augmented intensity and density-based clustering. *IEEE Transactions on Geoscience and Remote Sensing*, *61*, 1–14. DOI: 10.1109/TGRS.2023.3274757

Lee, W., & Stolfo, S. J. (2021). A framework for constructing features and models for intrusion detection systems. *ACM Transactions on Information and System Security*, *3*(4), 227–261. DOI: 10.1145/382912.382914

Li, C., Lv, Q., Li, N., Wang, Y., Sun, D., & Qiao, Y. (2022). A novel deep framework for dynamic malware detection based on API sequence intrinsic features. *Computers & Security*, *116*, 102686. DOI: 10.1016/j.cose.2022.102686

Linux Foundation. (2023). *2023 State of enterprise open source report*. https://www.linuxfoundation.org/research/enterprise-open-source-2023

Lippi, G., Aljawarneh, M., Al-Na'amneh, Q., Hazaymih, R., & Dhomeja, L. D. (2025). Security and Privacy Challenges and Solutions in Autonomous Driving Systems: A Comprehensive Review. *Journal of Cyber Security and Risk Auditing*, *2025*(3), 23–41. DOI: 10.63180/jcsra.thestap.2025.3.3

Liu, F., Gao, C., Chen, F., Meng, D., Zuo, W., & Gao, X. (2023). Infrared small and dim target detection with transformer under complex backgrounds. *IEEE Transactions on Image Processing*, *32*, 5921–5932. DOI: 10.1109/TIP.2023.3326396

Liu, J., Kauffman, R. J., & Ma, D. (2015). Competition, cooperation, and regulation: Understanding the evolution of the mobile payments technology ecosystem. *Electronic Commerce Research and Applications*, *14*(5), 372–391. DOI: 10.1016/j.elerap.2015.03.003

Liu, Y., Tantithamthavorn, C., Li, L., & Liu, Y. (2022). Deep learning for Android malware defenses: A systematic literature review. *ACM Computing Surveys*, *55*(8), 1–36. DOI: 10.1145/3544928

Liu, Y., Zhang, H., Wei, J., Yang, Y., Wang, J., & Zhao, L. (2025). Infrared small target detection based on prior guided dense nested network. *IEEE Transactions on Geoscience and Remote Sensing*, *63*, 1–15. DOI: 10.1109/TGRS.2025.3542232

Liu, Y., Zhang, X., Chen, W., Zou, D., & Jin, H. (2023). Deep learning for security analytics: A comprehensive survey. *IEEE Transactions on Information Forensics and Security*, *18*, 1632–1647. DOI: 10.1109/TIFS.2023.3234567

Liu, Z., Xue, Z., Blum, R. S., & Laganiere, R. (2006). Concealed weapon detection and visualization in a synthesized image. *Pattern Analysis & Applications*, *8*(4), 375–389. DOI: 10.1007/s10044-005-0020-8

Lopez-Martin, M., Carro, B., Sanchez-Esguevillas, A., & Lloret, J. (2017). Network traffic classifier with convolutional and recurrent neural networks for Internet of Things. *IEEE Access : Practical Innovations, Open Solutions*, *5*, 18042–18050. DOI: 10.1109/ACCESS.2017.2747560

Madhu, B., Chari, M. V. G., Vankdothu, R., Silivery, A. K., & Aerranagula, V. (2023). Intrusion detection models for IOT networks via deep learning approaches. *Measurement. Sensors*, *25*, 100641. DOI: 10.1016/j.measen.2022.100641

Madhushree, B., Sowmya, K. N., & Chennamma, H. R. (2021). Automatic weapon detection in video using deep learning. In Data Engineering and Intelligent Computing [Springer Singapore.]. *Proceedings of ICICC*, *2020*, 503–510.

Ma, N., Zhang, H., Hu, H., & Qin, Y. (2022). ESCVAD: An Energy-Saving Routing Protocol Based on Voronoi Adaptive Clustering for Wireless Sensor Networks. *IEEE Internet of Things Journal*, *9*(11), 9071–9085. DOI: 10.1109/JIOT.2021.3120744

Manikandakumar, M., & DK, S. S. (2019). A Detailed Study on Security Concerns of VANET and Cognitive Radio VANETs. In Cognitive Social Mining Applications in Data Analytics and Forensics (pp. 252-264). IGI Global.

Manikandakumar, M., & Ramanujam, E. (2018). Security and Privacy Challenges in Big Data Environment. In Handbook of Research on Network Forensics and Analysis Techniques (pp. 315-325). IGI Global. DOI: 10.4018/978-1-5225-4100-4.ch017

Manoharan, A., & Sarker, M. (2023). Revolutionizing Cybersecurity: Unleashing the Power of Artificial Intelligence and Machine Learning for Next-Generation Threat Detection. DOI: https://www. doi. org/10.56726/IRJMETS32644, 1.

Matthews, B. W. (1975). Comparison of the predicted and observed secondary structure of T Alicia phage lysozyme. *Biochimica et Biophysica Acta*, *405*(2), 442–451. DOI: 10.1016/0005-2795(75)90109-9 PMID: 1180967

Ma, X., Zhang, J., & Qi, C. (2010). Hallucinating face by position-patch. *Pattern Recognition*, *43*(6), 2224–2236. DOI: 10.1016/j.patcog.2009.12.019

Mazher, N., Basharat, A., & Nishat, A. (2024). AI-Driven Threat Detection: Revolutionizing Cyber Defense Mechanisms. *Eastern-European Journal of Engineering and Technology*, *3*(1), 70–82.

MDPI. (2025, April 5). *Dual-domain prior-driven deep network for infrared small-target detection.* https://www.mdpi.com/2072-4292/15/15/3827

MDPI. (2025, April 7). *Infrared small-target detection using multiscale local average gray difference measure.* https://www.mdpi.com/2079-9292/11/10/1547

MDPI. (2025, April 7). *Multi-scale hierarchical feature fusion for infrared small-target detection.* https://www.mdpi.com/2072-4292/17/3/428

Meena, G., & Choudhary, R. R. (2020). A review paper on IDS classification using KDD 99 and NSL-KDD dataset in Weka. In *International Conference on Computer, Communications and Electronics (Comptelix)* (pp. 553–558).

Melis, M., Maiorca, D., Biggio, B., Giacinto, G., & Roli, F. (2018). Explaining black-box Android malware detection. In *26th European Signal Processing Conference (EUSIPCO)* (pp. 524-528). IEEE. https://doi.org/DOI: 10.23919/EUSIPCO.2018.8553598

Microsoft. (2023). *Microsoft digital defense report 2023.* https://www.microsoft.com/en-us/security/business/security-intelligence-report

Misra, S., & Goswami, S. (2014). Routing in Wireless Sensor Networks. In Network Routing: Fundamentals, Applications, and Emerging Technologies (pp. 285–325). Wiley. DOI: 10.1002/9781119114864.ch11

MIT Technology Review. (2023). *The global state of AI in cybersecurity.* https://www.technologyreview.com/

Modi, C., Patel, D., Borisaniya, B., Patel, H., Patel, A., & Rajarajan, M. (2017). A survey of intrusion detection techniques in cloud. *Journal of Network and Computer Applications*, *36*(1), 42–57. DOI: 10.1016/j.jnca.2012.05.003

Mousa, M., Bahaa-Eldin, A. M., & Sobh, M. (2016, December). Software defined networking concepts and challenges. In 2016 11th International Conference on Computer Engineering & Systems (ICCES) (pp. 79-90). IEEE. DOI: 10.1109/ICCES.2016.7821979

Mousa, R. S., & Shehab, R. (2025). Applying risk analysis for determining threats and countermeasures in workstation domain. *Journal of Cyber Security and Risk Auditing*, *2025*(1), 12–21. DOI: 10.63180/jcsra.thestap.2025.1.2

Moustafa, N., & Slay, J. (2016). The UNSW-NB15 dataset. *Military Communications and Information Systems Conference*, 1-6.

Muda, Z., Yassin, W., Sulaiman, M. N., & Udzir, N. I. (2024). Intrusion detection based on k-means clustering and naïve Bayes classification. In *7th International Conference on Information Technology in Asia* (pp. 1–6).

Musleh, D., Alotaibi, M., Alhaidari, F., Rahman, A., & Mohammad, R. M. (2023). Intrusion detection system using feature extraction with machine learning algorithms in IoT. *Journal of Sensor and Actuator Networks*, *12*(2), 29. DOI: 10.3390/jsan12020029

Muthusamy, M., & Periasamy, K. (2019). A comprehensive study on Internet of Things security: Challenges and recommendations. In *Advancing Consumer-Centric Fog Computing Architectures* (pp. 72–86). IGI Global. DOI: 10.4018/978-1-5225-7149-0.ch004

Muzammal, S. M., Murugesan, R. K., & Jhanjhi, N. Z. (2021). A Comprehensive Review on Secure Routing in Internet of Things: Mitigation Methods and Trust-Based Approaches. *IEEE Internet ofThings Journal*, *8*(6), 4186–4210. DOI: 10.1109/JIOT.2020.3031162

Namala, K. K., AV, K. K. P., Math, A., Kumari, A., & Kulkarni, S. (2016, December). Smart irrigation with embedded system. In 2016 IEEE Bombay section symposium (IBSS) (pp. 1-5). IEEE.

Narejo, S., Pandey, B., Esenarro Vargas, D., Rodriguez, C., & Anjum, M. R. (2021). Weapon detection using YOLO V3 for smart surveillance system. *Mathematical Problems in Engineering*, *2021*(1), 9975700. DOI: 10.1155/2021/9975700

Narla, S. (2022). Big data privacy and security using continuous data protection and data obliviousness methodologies. *Journal of Science and Technology*, *7*(2), 423–436. DOI: 10.46243/jst.2022.v7.i02.pp423-436

National Institute of Standards and Technology. (2020). *Security and privacy controls for information systems and organizations* (NIST Special Publication 800-53, Rev. 5). U.S. Department of Commerce.

National Institute of Standards and Technology. (2023). *Computer security incident handling guide* (NIST Special Publication 800-61r2). https://nvlpubs.nist.gov/

National Institute of Standards and Technology. (2024). *Security and privacy controls for information systems and organizations* (NIST Special Publication 800-53, Rev. 5). U.S. Department of Commerce.

Nawshin, F., Unal, D., Hammoudeh, M., & Suganthan, P. N. (2024). AI-powered malware detection with differential privacy for zero trust security in Internet of Things networks. *Ad Hoc Networks*, *161*, 103523. DOI: 10.1016/j.adhoc.2024.103523

Neshenko, N., Bou-Harb, E., Crichigno, J., Kaddoum, G., & Ghani, N. (2019). Demystifying IoT security: An exhaustive survey on IoT vulnerabilities and a first empirical look on Internet-scale IoT exploitations. *IEEE Communications Surveys and Tutorials*, *21*(3), 2702–2733. DOI: 10.1109/COMST.2019.2910750

Nguyen, L., Simmons, A., Tran, H. A., & Tran, T. (2023). Security Testing of a Smart Home Management System using Formal Method and Gray-box Testing.

Nguyen, T. D., Khan, J. Y., & Ngo, D. T. (2018). A Distributed Energy-Harvesting-Aware Routing Algorithm for Heterogeneous IoT Networks. *IEEE Transactions on Green Communications and Networking*, *2*(4), 1115–1127. DOI: 10.1109/TGCN.2018.2839593

Oki, E., Ota, M., Nakanoko, T., Tanaka, Y., Toyota, S., Hu, Q., Nakaji, Y., Nakanishi, R., Ando, K., Kimura, Y., Hisamatsu, Y., Mimori, K., Takahashi, Y., Morohashi, H., Kanno, T., Tadano, K., Kawashima, K., Takano, H., Ebihara, Y., & Mori, M. (2023). Telesurgery and telesurgical support using a double-surgeon cockpit system allowing manipulation from two locations. *Surgical Endoscopy*, *37*(8), 6071–6078. DOI: 10.1007/s00464-023-10061-6 PMID: 37126192

Okoli, U. I., Obi, O. C., Adewusi, A. O., & Abrahams, T. O.Ugochukwu Ikechukwu OkoliOgugua Chimezie ObiAdebunmi Okechukwu AdewusiTemitayo Oluwaseun Abrahams. (2024). Machine learning in cybersecurity: A review of threat detection and defense mechanisms. *World Journal of Advanced Research and Reviews*, *21*(1), 2286–2295. DOI: 10.30574/wjarr.2024.21.1.0315

Olmos, R., Tabik, S., & Herrera, F. (2018). Automatic handgun detection alarm in videos using deep learning. *Neurocomputing*, *275*, 66–72. DOI: 10.1016/j.neucom.2017.05.012

Onih, V. A., Sevidzem, Y. S., & Adeniji, S. (2024). The Role of AI in Enhancing Threat Detection and Response in Cybersecurity Infrastructures. *International Journal of Scientific and Management Research*, *7*(4), 64–96. DOI: 10.37502/IJSMR.2024.7404

Open Source Security Foundation. (2023). *State of open source security report 2023*. https://openssf.org/research/security-report-2023

Otoom, S. (2025). Risk auditing for Digital Twins in cyber physical systems: A systematic review. *Journal of Cyber Security and Risk Auditing*, *2025*(1), 22–35. DOI: 10.63180/jcsra.thestap.2025.1.3

Palo Alto Networks. (2023). *State of cloud native security report 2023*. https://www.paloaltonetworks.com/state-of-cloud-native-security

Panneer, K. S. V., & Jaganathan, K. (2024). Adaptive Elite Ant Lion Optimizer tuned optimal controller for underactuated systems. *Franklin Open*, *6*, 100085. DOI: 10.1016/j.fraope.2024.100085

Parthasarathy, K. (2023). Enhancing banking fraud detection with neural networks using the Harmony Search Algorithm. *International Journal of Management Research and Business Strategy*, *13*(2), 34.

Patel, N. R., Kumar, S., & Singh, S. K. (2021). Energy and Collision Aware WSN Routing Protocol for Sustainable and Intelligent IoT Applications. *IEEE Sensors Journal*, *21*(22), 25282–25292. DOI: 10.1109/JSEN.2021.3076192

Patel, V., Saikali, S., Moschovas, M. C., Patel, E., Satava, R., Dasgupta, P., Dohler, M., Collins, J. W., Albala, D., & Marescaux, J. (2024). Technical and ethical considerations in telesurgery. *Journal of Robotic Surgery*, *18*(1), 40. DOI: 10.1007/s11701-023-01797-3 PMID: 38231309

Patil, D. (2024). Artificial Intelligence In Cybersecurity: Enhancing Threat Detection And Prevention Mechanisms Through Machine Learning And Data Analytics. Available at *SSRN* 5057410.

Picozzi, P., Nocco, U., Puleo, G., Labate, C., & Cimolin, V. (2023). Telemedicine and robotic surgery: A narrative review to analyze advantages, limitations and future developments. *Electronics (Basel)*, *13*(1), 124. DOI: 10.3390/electronics13010124

Piza, E. L., Welsh, B. C., Farrington, D. P., & Thomas, A. L. (2019). CCTV surveillance for crime prevention: A 40-year systematic review with meta-analysis. *Criminology & Public Policy*, *18*(1), 135–159. DOI: 10.1111/1745-9133.12419

Ponemon Institute. (2023). *2023 Cost of insider threats global report*. https://www.proofpoint.com/us/resources/threat-reports/cost-of-insider-threats

Proofpoint. (2022). *Behavioral analysis and AI/ML threat detection: Going behind the scenes*. https://www.proofpoint.com/us/blog/email-and-cloud-threats/behavioral-analysis-and-aiml-threat-detection-going-behind-scenes

Qaddos, A., Yaseen, M. U., Al-Shamayleh, A. S., Imran, M., Akhunzada, A., & Alharthi, S. Z. (2024). A novel intrusion detection framework for optimizing IoT security. *Scientific Reports*, *14*(1), 21789. DOI: 10.1038/s41598-024-72049-z PMID: 39294195

Ranaweera, P., Jurcut, A. D., & Liyanage, M. (2021). Survey on multi-access edge computing security and privacy. *IEEE Communications Surveys and Tutorials*, *23*(2), 1078–1124. DOI: 10.1109/COMST.2021.3062546

Red Hat. (2023). *The state of enterprise open source: A Red Hat report.* https://www.redhat.com/en/enterprise-open-source-report/2023

Reddy, S. K., Saikali, S., Gamal, A., Moschovas, M. C., Rogers, T., Dohler, M., Marescaux, J., & Patel, V. (2024). Telesurgery a Systematic Literature Review and Future Directions. *Annals of Surgery*, •••, 10–1097. DOI: 10.1097/SLA.0000000000006570 PMID: 39435556

ResearchGate. (2024, October). *Infrared small target detection based on robust principal component analysis joint directional derivative penalty.* https://www.researchgate.net/publication/350926236

Rohini, S., Ramesh, G., & Nair, A. R. (2024). MAGIC: Malware behaviour analysis and impact quantification through signature co-occurrence and regression. *Computers & Security*, *147*, 103735. DOI: 10.1016/j.cose.2024.103735

Sadeki, R. A., Solman, M. S., & Elisayed, H. S. (2020). Productive anomaly intrusion detection system (IDS) based on artificial neural network with indicator variables and rough sets of reduction, *13*.

Saikali, S., Covas Moschovas, M., Gamal, A., Reddy, S., Rogers, T., & Patel, V. (2024). Telesurgery: Humanitarian and surgical benefits while navigating technologic and administrative challenges. *Journal of Robotic Surgery*, *18*(1), 1–7. DOI: 10.1007/s11701-024-02156-6 PMID: 39499368

Salem, A. H., Azzam, S. M., Emam, O. E., & Abohany, A. A. (2024). Advancing cybersecurity: A comprehensive review of AI-driven detection techniques. *Journal of Big Data*, *11*(1), 105. DOI: 10.1186/s40537-024-00957-y

Santhanakrishnan, C., Annapurani, K., Pradeep, S., Senthilkumar, T., & Ramya, M. (2022). Physical features based authentication technique and key management for IoT networks. *Wireless Personal Communications*, *127*(2), 1809–1825. DOI: 10.1007/s11277-021-08724-5

Santhosh Kumar, S. V. N., Selvi, M., & Kannan, A. (2023). A Comprehensive Survey on Machine Learning-Based Intrusion Detection Systems for Secure Communication in Internet of Things. *Computational Intelligence and Neuroscience*, *2023*(1), 8981988. DOI: 10.1155/2023/8981988

Santos, T., Oliveira, H., & Cunha, A. (2024). Systematic review on weapon detection in surveillance footage through deep learning. *Computer Science Review*, *51*, 100612. DOI: 10.1016/j.cosrev.2023.100612

Sarker, I. H. (2024). Introduction to AI-Driven Cybersecurity and Threat Intelligence. In *AI-Driven Cybersecurity and Threat Intelligence: Cyber Automation, Intelligent Decision-Making and Explainability* (pp. 3–19). Springer Nature Switzerland. DOI: 10.1007/978-3-031-54497-2_1

Scott-Hayward, S., Natarajan, S., & Sezer, S. (2015). A survey of security in software defined networks. *IEEE Communications Surveys and Tutorials*, *18*(1), 623–654. DOI: 10.1109/COMST.2015.2453114

Security, I. B. M. (2023a). *X-Force threat intelligence index 2023*. https://www.ibm.com/reports/threat-intelligence

Security, I. B. M. (2023b). *Cost of a data breach report 2023*. https://www.ibm.com/security/data-breach

Selbst, A. D., Boyd, D., Friedler, S. A., Venkatasubramanian, S., & Vertesi, J. (2019). Algorithmic bias and fairness. *ACM Journal of Responsible Computing*, *1*(1), 1–20. DOI: 10.1145/3287560.3287598

Sezer, S., Scott-Hayward, S., Chouhan, P. K., Fraser, B., Lake, D., Finnegan, J., Viljoen, N., Miller, M., & Rao, N. (2013). Are we ready for SDN? Implementation challenges for software-defined networks. *IEEE Communications Magazine*, *51*(7), 36–43. DOI: 10.1109/MCOM.2013.6553676

Shagari, N. M., Idris, M. Y. I., Salleh, R. B., Ahmedy, I., Murtaza, G., & Shehadeh, H. A. (2020). Heterogeneous Energy and Traffic Aware Sleep-Awake Cluster-Based Routing Protocol for Wireless Sensor Network. *IEEE Access : Practical Innovations, Open Solutions*, *8*, 12232–12252. DOI: 10.1109/ACCESS.2020.2965206

Shaghaghi, A., Kaafar, M. A., Buyya, R., & Jha, S. (2020). Software-Defined Network (SDN) data plane security: issues, solutions, and future directions. Handbook of Computer Networks and Cyber Security: Principles and Paradigms, 341-387.

Shahana, A., Hasan, R., Farabi, S. F., Akter, J., Mahmud, M. A. A., Johora, F. T., & Suzer, G. (2024). AI-driven cybersecurity: Balancing advancements and safeguards. *Journal of Computer Science and Technology Studies*, *6*(2), 76–85. DOI: 10.32996/jcsts.2024.6.2.9

Shahin, M., Maghanaki, M., Hosseinzadeh, A., & Chen, F. F. (2024). Advancing Network Security in Industrial IoT: A Deep Dive into AI-Enabled Intrusion Detection Systems. *Advanced Engineering Informatics*, *62*, 102685. DOI: 10.1016/j.aei.2024.102685

Shalimov, A., Zuikov, D., Zimarina, D., Pashkov, V., & Smeliansky, R. (2013, October). Advanced study of SDN/OpenFlow controllers. In *Proceedings of the 9th Central & Eastern European Software Engineering Conference in Russia* (pp. 1-6).

Sharafaldin, I., Lashkari, A.H., & Ghorbani, A.A. (2018). Toward generating a new intrusion detection dataset and intrusion traffic characterization. *ICISSP*, 108-116.

Sharma, A., Anand, N., Mukherjee, S., Kumar, S., Kumar, S., & Mohapatra, H. (2024). Analyzing territorial variations in the implementation of IoT-based smart homes: A comprehensive review. In *Utilizing Technology to Manage Territories* (pp. 305–334). DOI: 10.4018/979-8-3693-6854-1.ch010

Sharma, R., Sharma, V., Vashishth, T. K., Kumar, B., Sharma, B. K., & Chaudhary, S. (2025, February). Implementation of adaptive cloud security framework for cloud computing monitoring system applications. In AIP Conference Proceedings (Vol. 3224, No. 1). AIP Publishing. DOI: 10.1063/5.0246104

Sharma, B., Sharma, L., Lal, C., & Roy, S. (2023). Anomaly based network intrusion detection for IoT attacks using deep learning technique. *Computers & Electrical Engineering*, *107*, 108626. DOI: 10.1016/j.compeleceng.2023.108626

Sharma, B., Sharma, L., Lal, C., & Roy, S. (2024). Explainable artificial intelligence for intrusion detection in IoT networks: A deep learning based approach. *Expert Systems with Applications*, *238*, 121751. DOI: 10.1016/j.eswa.2023.121751

Sharma, T., Rattan, D., Kaur, P., Gupta, A. K., & Gill, J. S. (2024). Enhancing Android Malware Detection: CFS Based Texture Feature Selection and Ensembled Classifier for Malware App Analysis. In Santosh, K. (Eds.), *Recent Trends in Image Processing and Pattern Recognition. RTIP2R 2023. Communications in Computer and Information Science* (Vol. 2027). Springer., DOI: 10.1007/978-3-031-53085-2_24

Shaukat, K., Luo, S., Chen, S., & Liu, D. (2020, October). Cyber threat detection using machine learning techniques: A performance evaluation perspective. In *2020 international conference on cyber warfare and security (ICCWS)* (pp. 1-6). IEEE. DOI: 10.1109/ICCWS48432.2020.9292388

Singh, M., & Gupta, A. K. (2016) "Physical Distance based Peer Organization in P2P network", *Proceedings of International Conference on Innovation and Challenges in Cyber Security*, ISBN: 978-93-84935-69-6.

Singh, R., Sharma, K. P., & Awasthi, L. K. (2024). A machine learning-based ensemble model for securing the IoT network. *Cluster Computing*, *27*(8), 10883–10897. DOI: 10.1007/s10586-024-04519-y

Sitaraman, S. R. (2023). *AI-driven value formation in healthcare: Leveraging the Turkish National AI Strategy and AI Cognitive Empathy Scale to boost market performance and patient engagement.* Intel Corporation.

Sommer, R., & Paxson, V. (2010). Outside the closed world: On using machine learning for network intrusion detection. In *2010 IEEE Symposium on Security and Privacy* (pp. 305-316). IEEE. https://doi.org/DOI: 10.1109/SP.2010.25

Sreelakshmi, S., Babu, A. A., Lakshmipriya, C., Gracious, L. A., Nalini, M., & Subramanian, R. S. (2024, October). Enhancing Intrusion Detection Systems with Machine Learning. In *2024 2nd International Conference on Self Sustainable Artificial Intelligence Systems (ICSSAS)* (pp. 557-564). IEEE. DOI: 10.1109/ICSSAS64001.2024.10760341

Srinivasan, V., Raj, V. H., Thirumalraj, A., & Nagarathinam, K. (2024). Original Research Article Detection of Data imbalance in MANET network based on ADSY-AEAMBi-LSTM with DBO Feature selection. *Journal of Autonomous Intelligence*, *7*(4), 1094. DOI: 10.32629/jai.v7i4.1094

Sudhakaran, P., & Baitalik, S. (2022). XGBoost optimized by adaptive tree Parzen estimators for credit risk analysis. In *IEEE 2nd Mysore Sub Section International Conference (MysuruCon)* (pp. 1–6). DOI: 10.1109/MysuruCon55714.2022.9972596

Sung, H., & Mukkamala, S. (2023). Identifying important features for intrusion detection using support vector machines and neural networks. In *Symposium on Applications and the Internet* (pp. 209–216).

Szymoniak, S. (2024). Key Distribution and Authentication Protocols in Wireless Sensor Networks: A Survey. *ACM Computing Surveys*, *56*(6), 1–31. DOI: 10.1145/3638043

Tang, T. A., McLernon, D., & Ghogho, M. (2020). Deep learning approaches to network intrusion detection: A review. *IEEE Access : Practical Innovations, Open Solutions*, *8*, 219398–219418.

Tekin, N., Acar, A., Aris, A., Uluagac, A. S., & Gungor, V. C. (2023). Energy consumption of on-device machine learning models for IoT intrusion detection. *Internet of Things : Engineering Cyber Physical Human Systems*, *21*, 100670. DOI: 10.1016/j.iot.2022.100670

Toet, A. (2003, September). Color image fusion for concealed weapon detection. In Sensors, and Command, Control, Communications, and Intelligence (C3I) Technologies for Homeland Defense and Law Enforcement II (Vol. 5071, pp. 372–379). SPIE. DOI: 10.1117/12.484845

Tong, X., Sun, B., Wei, J., Zuo, Z., & Su, S. (2021). EAAU-Net: Enhanced asymmetric attention U-Net for infrared small target detection. *Remote Sensing*, *13*(16), 3200. Advance online publication. DOI: 10.3390/rs13163200

Ubale, T., & Jain, A. K. (2020). Survey on DDoS attack techniques and solutions in software-defined network. Handbook of Computer Networks and Cyber Security: Principles and Paradigms, 389-419. DOI: 10.1007/978-3-030-22277-2_15

Vallabhaneni, S. (2023). Research and Implement Solutions to Tackle Security Threats in Surgical Robotics.

van Veen, A., Vranken, H. P. E., Koning, R., Schutijser, C. J. T. M., & Poll, E. (2024). Achieving Application-Level Requirement-Based Path Selection Within SCION.

Vashishth, T. K., Sharma, V., Samania, B., Sharma, R., Singh, S., & Jajoria, P. (2025). Ethical and Legal Implications of AI in Cybersecurity. In Machine Intelligence Applications in Cyber-Risk Management (pp. 387-414). IGI Global Scientific Publishing.

Vashishth, T. K., Sharma, V., Sharma, K. K., Kumar, B., Chaudhary, S., & Panwar, R. (2024). Enhancing Cloud Security: The Role of Artificial Intelligence and Machine Learning. In Improving Security, Privacy, and Trust in Cloud Computing (pp. 85-112). IGI Global.

Vashishth, T. K., Sharma, V., Sharma, K. K., Kumar, B., Chaudhary, S., & Panwar, R. (2024). Revolutionizing cloud computing security with the power of artificial intelligence: Advancements, challenges, and opportunities. Smart Electric and Hybrid Vehicles, 163-177.

Vashishth, T. K., Sharma, V., Sharma, K. K., Kumar, B., Chaudhary, S., & Panwar, R. (2024). Security and Privacy Challenges in Blockchain-Based Supply Chain Management: A Comprehensive Analysis. In Achieving Secure and Transparent Supply Chains with Blockchain Technology (pp. 70-91). IGI Global. DOI: 10.4018/979-8-3693-0482-2.ch005

Vashishth, T. K., Sharma, V., Sharma, K. K., & Kumar, B. (2025). Enhanced Security and Privacy from Industry 4.0 and 5.0 Vision. In *Building Embodied AI Systems: The Agents, the Architecture Principles, Challenges, and Application Domains* (pp. 133–158). Springer Nature Switzerland.

Vashishth, T. K., Sharma, V., Sharma, K. K., Kumar, B., Chaudhary, S., & Panwar, R. (2024). Security and Privacy Considerations in Cloud-Based Data Processing Solutions for Sensitive Data. In *Developments towards Next Generation Intelligent Systems for Sustainable Development* (pp. 35–61). IGI Global. DOI: 10.4018/979-8-3693-5643-2.ch002

Velasco-Mata, A., Ruiz-Santaquiteria, J., Vallez, N., & Deniz, O. (2021). Using human pose information for handgun detection. *Neural Computing & Applications*, *33*(24), 17273–17286. DOI: 10.1007/s00521-021-06317-8

Verizon. (2023). *2023 Data breach investigations report*. https://www.verizon.com/business/resources/reports/dbir/

Wahio, S. K., Pachelgare, V. K., & Kolhe, S. R. (2024). Surveying on intrusion detections networks using machine learning method. *International Journal of Computer Applications*, *78*(16), 30–37.

Wang, C., Zhang, Y., Wang, X., & Zhang, Z. (2018). Hybrid Multihop Partition-Based Clustering Routing Protocol for WSNs. *IEEE Sensors Letters*, *2*(1), 1–4. DOI: 10.1109/LSENS.2018.2803086

Wang, K., Yu, C. M., & Wang, L. C. (2021). DORA: A Destination-Oriented Routing Algorithm for Energy-Balanced Wireless Sensor Networks. *IEEE Internet of Things Journal*, *8*(3), 2080–2081. DOI: 10.1109/JIOT.2020.3025039

Wang, K., Zhang, T., Liu, M., Li, J., Xu, W., & Song, X. (2024). AFE-Net: Attention-guided feature enhancement network for infrared small target detection. *IEEE Journal of Selected Topics in Applied Earth Observations and Remote Sensing*, *17*, 4208–4221. DOI: 10.1109/JSTARS.2024.3354244

Wang, S., Balarezo, J. F., Kandeepan, S., Al-Hourani, A., Chavez, K. G., & Rubinstein, B. (2021). Machine learning in network anomaly detection: A survey. *IEEE Access : Practical Innovations, Open Solutions*, *9*, 152379–152396. DOI: 10.1109/ACCESS.2021.3126834

Wang, Z., Ding, H., Li, B., Bao, L., & Yang, Z. (2020). An Energy Efficient Routing Protocol Based on Improved Artificial Bee Colony Algorithm for Wireless Sensor Networks. *IEEE Access : Practical Innovations, Open Solutions*, *8*, 133577–133596. DOI: 10.1109/ACCESS.2020.3010313

Warnecke, A., Arp, D., Wressnegger, C., & Rieck, K. (2020). Evaluating explanation methods for deep learning in security. In *IEEE European Symposium on Security and Privacy (EuroS&P)* (pp. 158-174). IEEE. https://doi.org/DOI: 10.1109/EuroSP48549.2020.00018

Wei, Z., Lo, S. W., Liang, Y., Li, T., Shen, J., & Deng, R. H. (2015, October). Automatic accident detection and alarm system. In *Proceedings of the 23rd ACM International Conference on Multimedia* (pp. 781–784). DOI: 10.1145/2733373.2807402

Westerlund, M. (2019). The emergence of deepfake technology: A review. *Technology Innovation Management Review, 9*(11), 39–52. DOI: 10.22215/timreview/1282

Wheeler, D. A., & Schankin, S. (2023). Open source security tools in enterprise environments. *Journal of Cybersecurity, 9*(2), 45–62. DOI: 10.1093/cybsec/tyad006

Wikipedia. (2024, September 18). *Adaptive histogram equalization.* https://en.wikipedia.org/w/index.php?title=Adaptive_histogram_equalization&oldid=1246281583

Wikipedia. (2025, April 8). *Dilation (morphology).* https://en.wikipedia.org/wiki/Dilation_%28morphology%29?utm_source=chatgpt.com

Wikipedia. (2025, March 22). *Normalization (image processing).* https://en.wikipedia.org/w/index.php?title=Normalization_(image_processing)&oldid=1281843106

Wu, B., Chen, S., Gao, C., Fan, L., Liu, Y., Wen, W., & Lyu, M. R. (2021). Why an Android app is classified as malware: Toward malware classification interpretation. *ACM Transactions on Software Engineering and Methodology, 30*(2), 1–39. DOI: 10.1145/3423096

Xin, Y., Kong, L., Liu, Z., Chen, Y., Li, Y., Zhu, H., Gao, M., Hou, H., & Wang, C. (2018). Machine learning and deep learning methods for cybersecurity. *IEEE Access : Practical Innovations, Open Solutions, 6*, 35365–35381. DOI: 10.1109/ACCESS.2018.2836950

Xplore, I. E. E. E. (2025, April 5). *Infrared small target detection via low-rank tensor completion with top-hat regularization.* https://ieeexplore.ieee.org/document/8867952

Xu, B., Sun, L., Mao, X., Ding, R., & Liu, C. (2023). IoT Intrusion Detection System Based on Machine Learning. *Electronics (Basel), 12*(20), 4289. DOI: 10.3390/electronics12204289

Xu, C., Xiong, Z., Zhao, G., & Yu, S. (2019). An Energy-Efficient Region Source Routing Protocol for Lifetime Maximization in WSN. *IEEE Access : Practical Innovations, Open Solutions, 7*, 135277–135289. DOI: 10.1109/ACCESS.2019.2942321

Xu, H., Zhong, S., Zhang, T., & Zou, X. (2023). Multiscale multilevel residual feature fusion for real-time infrared small target detection. *IEEE Transactions on Geoscience and Remote Sensing, 61*, 1–16. DOI: 10.1109/TGRS.2023.3269092

Xu, Y., Jiao, W., & Tian, M. (2021). An Energy-Efficient Routing Protocol for 3D Wireless Sensor Networks. *IEEE Sensors Journal, 21*(17), 19550–19559. DOI: 10.1109/JSEN.2021.3086806

Yamini, B., Kaneti, V. R., Nalini, M., & Subramanian, S. (2023). Machine Learning-driven PCOS prediction for early detection and tailored interventions. *SSRG International Journal of Electrical and Electronics Engineering, 10*(9), 61–75. DOI: 10.14445/23488379/IJEEE-V10I9P106

Yao, Q., Huang, A., Shan, H., Quek, T. Q. S., & Wang, W. (2016). Delay-Aware Wireless Powered Communication Networks—Energy Balancing and Optimization. *IEEE Transactions on Wireless Communications, 15*(8), 5272–5286. DOI: 10.1109/TWC.2016.2555803

Yuan, F., Shang, Y., Liu, Y., Cao, Y., & Tan, J. (2020). Data augmentation for insider threat detection with GAN. In *2020 IEEE 32nd International Conference on Tools with Artificial Intelligence (ICTAI)* (pp. 632–638). IEEE. DOI: 10.1109/ICTAI50040.2020.00102

Yuan, S., & Wu, X. (2021). Deep learning for insider threat detection: Review, challenges and opportunities. *Computers & Security, 104*, 102221. Advance online publication. DOI: 10.1016/j.cose.2021.102221

Yun, W. K., & Yoo, S. J. (2021). Q-Learning-Based Data-Aggregation-Aware Energy-Efficient Routing Protocol for Wireless Sensor Networks. *IEEE Access : Practical Innovations, Open Solutions, 9*, 10737–10750. DOI: 10.1109/ACCESS.2021.3051360

Zahmatkesh, A., & Kunz, T. (2017). Software defined multihop wireless networks: Promises and challenges. *Journal of Communications and Networks (Seoul), 19*(6), 546–554. DOI: 10.1109/JCN.2017.000094

Zhang, K., Zuo, W., Chen, Y., Meng, D., & Zhang, L. (2017). Beyond a Gaussian denoiser: Residual learning of deep CNN for image denoising. *IEEE Transactions on Image Processing, 26*(7), 3142–3155. DOI: 10.1109/TIP.2017.2662206

Zhang, P., Zhao, L., Wu, Y., Wei, J., Yang, Y., & Liu, Y. (2024). Multiscale progressive fusion filter network for infrared small target detection. *IEEE Transactions on Geoscience and Remote Sensing, 62*, 1–14. DOI: 10.1109/TGRS.2023.3343496

Zhao, Y., Bi, S., Zhang, H., & Chen, Z. (2023). Dynamic weight and mapping mutation operation-based salp swarm algorithm for global optimization. *Applied Sciences (Basel, Switzerland), 13*(15), 8960. DOI: 10.3390/app13158960

Zhao, Z., Yin, H., Wang, Y., Yan, W., Wang, J., & Wang, H. (2019). Improving the detection accuracy of complex solution components based on multi-dimensional spectroscopy fusion method. *Infrared Physics & Technology*, *102*, 103062. DOI: 10.1016/j.infrared.2019.103062

About the Contributors

Abdalwali Lutfi is an assistant professor at the business school of King Faisal University. Dr Lutfi holds an undergraduate degree in accounting from Irbid University, a master's degree in accounting from Jadara University, and a PhD in accounting information systems from the Universiti Utara Malaysia. His teaching and research interests are in the areas of accounting and accounting information systems. His current research involves end-user computing, the usage of accounting information systems, and information technology. He has published many refereed articles in journals such as Technology in Society, Global Business Review, the EuroMed Journal of Business, and the Journal of Open Innovation: Technology, Market, and Complexity.

Mohammed Almaayah is an Associate Professor in the Department of Cybersecurity and Cloud Computing. He has published over 95 research papers in highly reputed journals such as the Engineering and Science Technology, an International Journal, Education and Information Technologies, IEEE Access and others. Most of his publications were indexed under the ISI Web of Science and Scopus. His current research interests include Cybersecurity and Cyber-risk assessment and mobile apps.

***

A. R. Deepti is a Professor in the Department of MCA at Acharya Institute of Graduate Studies, Bengaluru. She has published research articles in national and international journals and conferences and serves as a reviewer for IGI Global. Her areas of interest include Cryptography, network Security, Machine Learning, and Data Analytics.

Aswin Aanand is a pre-final year M.Tech student in Artificial Intelligence and Data Science at SASTRA University, India. He holds a B.E. degree in Electrical and Electronics Engineering from the SRM Group of Institutions. His research interests include machine learning, intelligent systems, and AI applications in energy systems. He has hands-on experience with AI/ML tools and has completed an industry internship in power plant automation and simulation.

Mohamed Uvaze Ahamed Ayoobkhan received his B.E and M.E degrees in Computer Science and Engineering from Anna University, Chennai, India. He has completed his PhD in Information Technology from Multimedia University, Malaysia. He worked as an Assistant Professor in the Department of Information Technology, Sri Ramakrishna Engineering College, Coimbatore India for the period of June 2012 to April 2014. He received a scholarship under Graduate Research Assistantship scheme from Multimedia University, Malaysia. Further he served as an Assistant Professor in Department of Computer Science and Engineering-Specialization, School of Engineering and Technology, Jain University, India from February 2018 to September 2018. Currently, he is working as an Assistant Professor, Cihan University-Erbil, Kurdistan region, Iraq. He has published 12 research papers in reputed international journals and conferences in the areas of Computer Vision and Machine Learning. Also, he is serving as a reviewer for international journals and conferences in the same field of research. His research mainly focused on Medical Imaging, Image compression/retrieval and Deep/Shallow Learning.

B. Manimekala is working as an Assistant Professor in the Department of Computer Science, Christ University, Bengaluru. She has 17 years of teaching experience. She has published research articles in National and International journals. She has also presented 18 papers in National and International conferences. She has authored in 1 book, 3 book chapters and she owned 2 patents. Her areas of interest are IoT, networking, machine learning and AI.

Farzeen Basith is an Assistant Professor in the Department of MCA with 17 years of experience. She has secured a design patent and has published research papers in national and international journals. Her research interests include IoT, AI, machine learning, and data analytics.

SanthanaKrishnan is an Associate Professor in the Department of Computing Technologies, S.R.M Institute of Science and Technology, Kattankulathur Campus, Chennai, India. He received the Ph.D. degree from the Department of Computer Science and Engineering, SRM Institute of Science and Technology, Kattankulathur. He has published more than 15 SCI/Scopus-indexed journals. His current research interests include the secure Internet of Things, deep learning, and machine learning. He is a member of ACM,ISTE,IEI

Uma E is currently working as an Associate Professor in Department of Information Science and Technology, Anna University, Chennai, Tamil Nadu, India. She possesses 20 years of experience in teaching and research. She completed her Ph.D. in Computer Science from Anna University in 2014, her M.E. in Computer Science from Annamalai University in 2005, and her B.E. in Computer Science from Bharathidasan University in 2002. She has been recognized with several awards, including the Best Presentation Award at the ECBA-2016 Conference in Singapore and the Young Teacher Award by the IET CLN Ambition and Achievement Awards in 2014. She has extensive expertise in various cutting-edge areas of computer science and information technology, including network security and forensics, blockchain, machine and deep learning, cloud computing, Internet of Things (IoT), service-oriented architecture, the semantic web, and .Net framework development.

Anuj Kumar Gupta is working as a professor in the CSE Dept. at Chandigarh Group of Colleges, Landran, Punjab. He has a Ph.D. in Computer Science & Engineering with a vast academic & administrative experience of 22+ years. He has guided 24 PG & 10 PhD research scholars. He has published more than 100 research papers in reputed journals and conferences. He has filed more than 15 patents and published 5 books. His area of research is Wireless Networks, Security & Image Processing. He is a life member of the Computer Society of India & ISTE.

Kamatchi K received BTech degree in IT from Jeppiaar SRR Engineering College, Chennai which was then affiliated to Anna University, Chennai, Tamil Nadu, India in 2018 and MTech degree in IT from Anna University, Chennai, Tamil Nadu, India in 2020. She is currently pursuing her Ph.D. in Cybersecurity at Anna University. Her research interests are in networking, artificial intelligence, cybersecurity, and web technology.

L. A. Anto Gracious is an accomplished academic professional in Information Technology and Computer Science, known for his dedication to education, technology, and research. He holds a B.Tech in IT from C.S.I Institute of Technology (2006), an MBA in Technology Management, and an M.Tech in IT from Francis Xavier Engineering College (2011). He began his career as a Programmer at Software Solutions Integrated Limited, later transitioning to academia in 2011 as an Assistant Professor at Marthandam College of Engineering and Technology. Over eight years, he excelled in teaching, led the Software Development Cell, and earned multiple awards for his contributions. He later served at St. Xavier's Catholic College of Engineering and currently holds a position at R.M.K. College of Engineering and Technology. A prolific researcher, Anto focuses on machine learning, wireless sensor networks, and healthcare technologies. His work is widely published, and he has received accolades such as the Best Paper Award and multiple Best Faculty Awards.

M. Janani received a Bachelor's degree in Information Technology from PSNA College of Engineering and Technology, affiliated with Anna University, in 2016. She obtained a Master's degree in Computer Science and Engineering from Karunya University, Coimbatore, in 2018. She completed her Ph.D. in Computer Science and Engineering at SRM Institute of Science and Technology, Chengalpattu, India. Currently, she works as an Assistant Professor in the department of Computing Technologies at SRM Institute of Science and Technology, Chengalpattu.

Manikandakumar Muthusamy was awarded the B.Tech., degree in Information Technology in 2009, and M.E., degree in Computer Science and Engineering in 2013 from Anna University, Chennai, India where he has completed Ph.D. He is currently a Assistant Professor in the Computer Science & Engineering Department, Christ University, Bangalore, India. His research interests include artificial intelligence, data science and networking.

N. Sasikaladevi received Ph. D. Degree in Computer Science in 2013. She has published more than 42 papers in reputed International journals and conferences including publications in SCI-Indexed Journals. She is a reviewer of more than a dozen of reputed journals including IEEE transactions on Services Computing and IEEE Journal of Internet of Things. s. Her research focus includes the design of machine learning strategies to solve Discrete Logarithm Problem. She published several books and chapters in reputed publisher including Prentice Hall of India, Lambert Academic Publisher, IGI Global, Springer and Science Direct. She has received fund from Department of Science and Technology, Government of India to carry out projects in the domain of Services computing and Security System. She has received young scientist award and women scientist award from DST, India. She is also involved in the security enriched payment system design as a part of Digital India Initiative. Her current research interests include information security, digital authentication, security of wireless sensor networks, computer vision, deep learning and security of vehicular ad-hoc networks.

Winner Pulakhandam is an experienced Systems Administrator with a strong academic background, holding Masters degrees in Computer and Information Science. With a focus on managing and optimizing secure IT infrastructures, Winner brings expertise in network security, cloud technologies, and system performance. His work ensures reliable, scalable, and efficient IT operations that support organizational goals.

R. Regan is an Assistant Professor and Head of the Department of Computer Science and Engineering at University College of Engineering Villupuram, Anna University. With over 16 years of experience in academia, he has contributed significantly to research and education. He has published 18 papers in national and international conferences and journals, authored four international books, and holds three patents. Additionally, he has actively participated in and organized Faculty Development Programs (FDPs). His research interests include Mobile Ad Hoc Networks, Wireless Sensor Networks, and Wireless Security.

Visrutatma Rao Vallu is an accomplished Clinical Data Management (CDM) professional with over 8 years of experience managing and leading complex clinical trials across therapeutic areas, including Oncology, Rare Diseases, Cardiovascular, Nephrology, and Renal Medicine. With advanced degrees in Information Technology and Business Administration, Vish combines technical expertise with strategic insights to deliver high-quality data management solutions.

S. Venkatasubramanian received a B.E. degree in Electronics and Communication from Bharathidasan University, M.E. degree in Computer science from Regional Engineering College, Trichy and Ph.D. from Annamalai University. He has 26 years of teaching experience. His areas of interest include mobile networks, Network Security and Software Engineering. He has published 60 papers in international journals and 25 papers in international conferences. He has also registered four patents. At present, he is working as an Associate Professor in the Department of Computer science and Business systems at Saranathan College of Engineering, Trichy, India. He is also AWS Certified Cloud Practitioner and Microsoft certified Azure fundamentals. He has also passed NPTEL certification exams. He has given many technical talks outside his institution and participated in many workshops and FDPs. He has also authored books on “Software Engineering” and “Fundamentals of Mobile and Pervasive Computing”, “Big data Analytics”, “Basic Electrical and Electronics Engineering”, “python programming” and “Industrial Data Communication”. He is the recipient of the Global teacher award from AKS academy, Dr.Sarvepalli Radhakrishnan lifetime achiever national award and Best Teacher award from Institution of Engineers in 2024.

Vibinchandar Selvaraj is an Associate Professor and Head of the Department of Master of Computer Applications (MCA) at Acharya Institute of Graduate Studies. He brings over 14 years of international academic and research experience, having served in esteemed institutions across India, Africa, and Malaysia. His global exposure has shaped his progressive teaching methodologies and research perspectives. He specializes in Data Mining, Bioinformatics, Software Testing, and

Software Engineering, and has made significant contributions to these fields through both teaching and research. He has published numerous research articles in reputed national and international journals, reflecting his active engagement in advancing knowledge. In addition to his publications, he is also a prolific innovator, holding multiple patents in emerging areas of computer science and applied technologies. His patented works demonstrate a practical orientation to research, aiming to solve real-world problems with impactful technological solutions. He is professionally certified in ISTQB Software Testing, Oracle, and is a Certified Robotic Process Automation (RPA) Professional, underlining his commitment to continuous learning and industry relevance

Kewal Krishan Sharma is a Professor in Computer Science and Application department, IIMT University, Meerut, U.P, India. He did his Ph.D. in computer network with this he has MCA, MBA and Law degree also. He did variously certification courses also. He has an overall experience of around 33 year in academic, business and industry. He wrote a number of research papers and books.

Rajeev Sharma is the Assistant professor and Head in Department of Computer Science and Engineering, IIMT Engineering College, Meerut. He has more than 15 years of teaching as well as administrative experience. He has a conference Proceeding on Modified CPU Scheduling Process to his Credit published by Springer Nature. He has published five research papers and reputed journals. He has attended many conferences, workshops, FDP's and symposium and presented research papers. His research area is fuzzy logic, Neural Networks and CPU scheduling.

Sangeeta Sharma is a dedicated professional and lifelong learner, currently pursuing her Master of Computer Applications (MCA) from Punjab Technical University, Punjab while serving as a Assistant Professor in Department of Computer Application, IAMR College, Baghpat Road, Meerut, U.P, India. With a strong academic foundation, she completed her Bachelor of Science (BSc) from Chaudhary Charan Singh University, Meerut.

Vikas Sharma completed his Graduation and Post Graduation from Chaudhary Charan Singh University, Meerut, U.P. Currently Pursuing his Ph.D. in Computer Science and Engineering from Govt. Recognized University. Presently, he is working as an Assistant Professor in the Department of Computer Science and Applications, IIMT University, Meerut, U.P. He has been awarded as Excellence in teaching award 2019. He is the reviewer member of some reputed journals. He has published several book chapters and research papers of national and international reputed journals.

Nithya V., M.Tech (Ph.D.) is a Teaching Fellow in the Department of Computer Science and Engineering at the University College of Engineering, Villupuram Campus, Anna University. She is currently pursuing a Ph.D. in Information and Communication Engineering at Anna University, Chennai. Her research interests include web application security, cryptography, and network security. She has published 6 international journal papers, 2 national conference papers, and 4 international conference papers. Additionally, she has authored 4 international books and 1 academic book. Nithya has actively participated in faculty development programs and workshops. She holds an M.Tech in Information Security from Pondicherry Engineering College and a B.E. in Computer Science from Mailam Engineering College.

Tarun Kumar Vashishth is an active academician and researcher in the field of computer science with 21 years of experience. He earned Ph.D. Mathematics degree specialized in Operations Research; served several academic positions such as HoD, Dy. Director, Academic Coordinator, Member Secretary of Department Research Committee, Assistant Center superintendent and Head Examiner in university examinations. He is involved in academic development and scholarly activities. He is member of International Association of Engineers, The Society of Digital Information and Wireless Communications, Global Professors Welfare Association, International Association of Academic plus Corporate (IAAC), Computer Science Teachers Association and Internet Society . His research interest includes Cloud Computing, Artificial Intelligence, Machine Learning and Operations Research; published more than 50 research articles with 2 book and 80 book chapters. He is contributing as member of editorial and reviewers boards in conferences and various computer journals published by CRC Press, Taylor and Francis, Springer, IGI global and other universities.

Index

M

N

O

P

R

S

T

U

V

W

Y

www.ingramcontent.com/pod-product-compliance
Lightning Source LLC
LaVergne TN
LVHW080342011026
849161LV00009B/2164
* 9 7 9 8 3 3 7 3 2 1 1 5 8 *